UNDERSTANDING ACCOUNTING and FINANCE

Theory and Practice

DR. CRYFORD MUMBA

Order this book online at www.trafford.com
or email orders@trafford.com

Most Trafford titles are also available at major online book retailers.

Printed in the United States of America.

ISBN: 978-1-4669-7459-3 (sc)
ISBN: 978-1-4669-7458-6 (e)

Trafford rev. 01/29/2013

 www.trafford.com

North America & international
toll-free: 1 888 232 4444 (USA & Canada)
phone: 250 383 6864 ♦ fax: 812 355 4082

CONTENTS

BOOK ONE
Financial Recording, Presentation, And Analysis

BOOK TWO
Financial Management

ABOUT THE AUTHOR

Dr. Cryford Mumba read Economics at The University of Zambia and graduated with a Bachelor of Arts Degree. He complemented his Economics degree with the Advanced Diploma in Project Management (Institute of Commercial Management, UK), Diploma in Banking and Financial Services(Zambia Institute of Banking and Financial services, Zambia), Diploma in Marketing(ICM, UK). He then expanded his knowledge of business through the accountancy program (ACCA, UK) for which he is a finalist. He holds an MBA(MANCOSA, South Africa) with a thesis "Limited Access to Credit Among Women Market Traders". Finally, he holds a PhD in Economics (Cambell State University, USA) with a thesis "Understanding Money Intelligence".

Dr. Mumba is the Proprietor and Chief Executive Officer of Premier college of Banking and Finance, a firm specializing in financial training and consulting. His specialist teaching areas include Financial Mathematics, Statistical Analysis, Corporate Finance, Financial Reporting and Economics. He has written extensively on banking and financial services course. He is the author of Understanding Money Intelligence, Understanding Statistical Analysis and a host of other Banking and Financial Services training manuals. He is also the Editor of The Student Banker Magazine and a columnist on financial matters for Business analysis Newspaper.

He resides in Lusaka, married and is a supporter of Arsenal Football Club. His hobbies include reading and writing.

PREFACE

If you have bought or are thinking of buying this book you will want to know what you can expect it to do for you and how you ought best to use it. The book has been developed from practical teaching of accounting and finance. It covers all the accounting principles required for first and intermediate examination and other courses requiring accounting and finance. The guiding principles for this book are that it is "user-friendly" with numerous worked examples and related to the current accounting and finance practice. To this end a variety of real life examples from economics and business have been used. One difficulty encountered in the production of this book is that some students have little or no practical experience of the subject. Therefore, a step-by-step explanation has been adopted which has made me guilty of one offence: "over simplification". The book can be used with confidence because it is designed to be user-friendly, interesting to read and to stimulate learning by the use of clear examples with detailed solutions. The book seeks to set the subject of accounting and finance as enjoyable as any other subject. The book is divided into two books: Financial Recording, Presentation and Analysis; and Financial Management.

At this juncture I should sound some caution. The book provides you with the knowledge and the skills in applying it which you need to pass. However, if you aspire to excel, perhaps even to win a place or a prize, you cannot expect to rely on one book alone! The highest marks are given to those candidates who display evidence of the widest reading absorbed by critical mind, a combination, that is, of extensive information and of a highly intellectual appraisal of it. No single book can provide either of these things. What it can do, however, is to provide an adequate amount of information and acceptable competence in handling it. No doubt the Accounting and Finance course will include matters which I have omitted, and some lecturers may not consider all the items I have covered as appropriate. I do hope, however, that a large proportion of the text will be helpful to students of Accounting and Finance.

It should be stressed that this book is written to teach you and not merely to tell you. The more work and effort you put into all your studies, the greater the chance of success. Be determined, have a positive attitude and all the very best in your future courses and exams.

Cryford Mumba

28th December 2012

ACKNOWLEDGEMENTS

I am emotionally attuned and profoundly indebted to our Great Company—PREMIER COLLEGE, for the opportunity of exposure and experience enabling me to venture into this humble project. This text grew out of the accounting and finance subjects I have been teaching at Premier College of Banking and Finance during the past few semesters. I was very fortunate to have had many excellent and dull students, who with their questions and comments contributed much to the clarity of exposition of this text.

I owe a great intellectual debt to my brilliant former teachers at all levels in my educational radar. Quite extra-ordinary for an educational book, no one reviewed the manuscript. It is fresh from the farm.

Finally, I would like to express my gratitude to myself for my efficiency and cheerful disposition in typing the manuscript.

I shall greatly appreciate guidance/suggestions for further enrichment of the compendium in course of time, both from the teachers and students of the subject.

DEDICATION

This book is dedicated to:

- My mother Janet Mumba and my late father Nelson Mumba for double gifts—life and life support (education) though themselves did not reach higher levels in education radar.

- My wife Nivea Mumba for ensuring that no paper is thrown away no matter how tattered it looks and providing an environment conducive to the writing of this book.

- Students and lecturers who will use it for it is theirs.

QUOTATIONS

"I am a beau in nothing but my books".   **Adam Smith (1723—1790)**

"A man who kills another man destroys a living creature, but a man who kills a good book kills reason itself".   **unknown**.

"If people do not believe that Mathematics is simple, it is only because they do not realize how complicated life is."   **John Louis von Neumann (1903-1957)**

BOOK ONE

Financial Recording, Presentation, And Analysis

CHAPTER 1

INTRODUCTION TO ACCOUNTING FRAMEWORK

This first chapter of the book introduces some of the principles underlying the preparation of financial statements. Financial statements are prepared for a variety of users with a variety of needs. In general though, all user groups need information that will be useful for making economic decisions.

Learning outcomes

- Define accounting and the information it provides
- Identify the users of financial accounting information
- Identify and explain the various accounting conventions

WHAT IS ACCOUNTING?

A definition of accounting issued by the American Accounting Association in 1966 suggested that accounting consists of identifying, measuring and communicating business information to facilitate judgement and decision making. This definition placed its emphasis firmly on the provision of data for users and played down the more traditional roles of the accountant in recording, classifying and summarizing financial data. It is of course, necessary to record and summarize transactions before financial information can be measured and used by decision-makers. Of great importance to accountants, however, is the need to communicate the information derived from their records, and if necessary to interpret that information to improve its comprehension by the users, who may after all have borne the cost of the information systems. Thus, accounting is seen not as an end in itself but as a costly activity with a purpose whose benefits must exceed the cost.

Accounting is, therefore, concerned with:

1. *Identification and recording of economic transactions*. A transaction is an economic event which will affect the financial situation of the entity, such as the sale of a product, payment of salaries, purchase of machinery, and so on. The system must be organized so that all transactions are recognized when they occur and are then recorded by being entered into the accounting system. This is part of the bookkeeping aspect of accounting and concerns the maintenance of accurate records of what has taken place.

2. *Classification and measurement of transactions* once they are recorded. Economic events may create assets (items which the business owns), or liabilities (what is owed), or revenues (income from sales), or expenses (amounts incurred to make products or operate the business), so classification is important. Once transactions are classified into appropriate headings, measurement must be undertaken to ensure that each classified transaction is processed in the accounting system at a proper value. It is at

this point that bookkeeping gives way to accounting, and judgement is required to measure each transaction properly, e.g. how much of the costs concerns this year's accounts, and how much should be carried forward to next year. Two accountants may exercise judgement in different ways over the same item such as the valuation of a doubtful debt, so what is considered to be correct may depend on estimate and opinion.

3. ***Summarizing of what has been recorded***, to assess the performance of the entity during a period (a month or a year) and its financial position at the beginning and end of the period. Financial statements such as the income statement and the balance sheet are summaries of economic events, and the cash flow statement gives yet another view of how transactions have affected the cash and liquid funds held by the entity.

4. ***Communicating, analysis and interpretation.*** Financial statements report to a wide range of users and must therefore be drafted with care to enable the recipient to understand the message which they contain. If necessary the accountant will analyze and interpret that message to enhance the value of the information provided.

Purpose of accounting

It is important for businesses to maintain accurate financial records for the following reasons:

1. **Stewardship.** A traditional purpose of accounting has been that of 'stewardship', which implies that a financial statement is made to report events, performance, and position. Thus when the board of directors of a company issue their 'corporate report', the annual accounts of the company, they are reporting on their stewardship of the business to the shareholders, who are the legal owners. Such a report gives a measure of control to owners, who can dismiss management if they do not approve of its activities. The right of shareholders to receive such information is enshrined in company law. The company law sets out in detail the statutory minimum of information which must be disclosed and the form which such disclosures must take. Stewardship also discloses the profit which has been made and the amount which can, therefore, be paid to the owners as a dividend. Further, it should be appreciated that there are, of course, many other stakeholders who have a claim to be informed of past performance and present position, so the stewardship relationship is not confined to directors and shareholders. It can extend to management committees, etc. in 'not for profit' organizations such as charities. Accountability is a term implying the duty to report to interested parties.

2. **Decision usefulness.** A further purpose of accounting concerns the decision usefulness function of financial statements. This idea holds that a purpose of accounting is to provide information which will enable those who use it to make decisions about their future interest in the entity. A shareholder wishes to know whether to sell shares, hold them or increase the investment; just as a donor needs information when deciding whether to give more to a charity or to donate elsewhere. The difficulty in achieving

this purpose is that, whilst stewardship reports on past transactions, decision making requires information about the future which the cautious accountant is loath to make public because of the uncertainty associated with forecasting future events.

3. **Management accounting**. The purpose explained above have dealt with reporting to interested parties outside the business, but management accounting concerns the ways in which accounting skills can be used to help managers within the business. The tasks of managers can be analyzed as planning, deciding, communicating, organizing, and controlling, so financial information will be of great assistance in successful management. The management accounting sees the functional relationship of accounting as covering;
    a) Financial accounting; the recording and classification of transactions;
    b) Cost accounting; the analysis and classification of costs to products and cost centres;
    c) Budgeting; the planning and co-ordination of future activities in financial terms, to fit them into the corporate plan or strategy of the organization;
    d) Control; comparison of actual performance with that set out in the budget or plan to formulate action to remedy and departures from the plan;
    e) Treasurership; the funding of the organizations and the provision of adequate finance to support managerial operations;
    f) Audit; the attest function to protect and prove the effectiveness of the recording / reporting system.

From the above, we can now see that the task of the accountant is to look back at the past, to record, analyze, and report as a steward, and also to look into the future and assist management with decision making and control. Both aspects of this task require figures to be assembled in statements that are easily assimilated, interpreted and used in the evaluation of performance by both accountant and non-accountants. Businesses need to determine easily how much profit or loss has been made, identify the assets and liabilities that the business has at any one time, determine which customers owe the business money, and how much and also to determine who the business owes money to, and how much. The information is also used by various third parties, such as government departments and investors, who rely on the figures shown in the financial statements. It cannot, therefore, be overemphasized that any successful business must prepare and maintain accurate financial records.

Users of Financial Accounts and their key needs

The purpose of accounting is to provide information to users of the financial statements. In this perspective accountants take a stakeholder view of the organization, i.e. an organization does not only exist for shareholders but for stakeholders who are rightfully interested in financial information, and accountants have a responsibility to provide meaningful information for such groups. If business uses resources of society, in terms of wealth, people and the environment, then appropriate reporting should ensue. A proper management of resources will benefit members of society and not only the legal owners of the business. Different users have different needs. The various users and their needs are noted below.

1. **Management**. Management is perhaps the most important users of accounting information. An analysis of past and expected future revenue and expenses will provide information which is useful when plans are formulated and decisions made. Once the budget for a business is complete, the accountant can produce figures for what actually happens, as the budget unfolds, so that they can be compared with the budget to measure achievement. Management will need to know, in great detail and soon after the event, the cost consequences of a particular course of action, so that steps can be taken to control the situation if things go wrong. Speed and ability to communicate and interpret are needed here. Managers have access to confidential information which the business may not wish to publicize, since it may prove useful to competitors. Managers are vitally interested in the progress of the company since their own career prospects may depend upon its success but they will rarely use published accounts to gain such information because internal management accounts are more frequent, more detailed and forward looking, and therefore show much useful information. Some managers may not have access to summarized financial information within the business, and will therefore use the published accounts for an overview.

2. **Shareholders and potential shareholders**. These are another important group of user of accounting information. This group includes the investing public at large and the shareholders, financial analysts and commentators who advise them. The shareholders should be informed of the manner in which management has used their funds which have been invested in the business. They are interested in the profitability and safety of their investment, which helps them to appraise the efficiency f management. This is simply a matter of reporting on past events. However, both shareholders and potential shareholders are also interested in the future performance of the business, and use past figures as a guide to the future if they have to vote on proposals or decide whether to disinvest. Financial analysts advising institutional investors such as insurance companies, pension fund, unit trusts and investment trusts are among the most sophisticated users of accounting information.

   A specialist group of potential shareholders are takeover bidders. This group comprises of the managers of other rival companies who plan to buy the shares of a company in order to control its operations and add it to their group. These users are more sophisticated in their appreciation of financial statements than the normal shareholder, and are interested in the detailed notes which accompany the financial statement. However, this class of users would also expect to obtain market information about the company which they propose to take over, from sources other than the published accounts.

   The accountant has an obligation to ell those in this category to provide information on which they can depend when making their economic decisions, but the fact that some members of the group are more financially sophisticated than others causes difficulties, since the volume of information required by the financial analyst may confuse the ordinary shareholder.

3. **Employees and their trade union representatives**. These also use accounting information to assess the potential of the business. This information is relevant to the employee, who wishes to discover whether the company can offer safe employment and promotion through growth over a period of years, and to the trade unionist, who uses past profits and potential profits in the calculation of claims for higher wages or better conditions. The viability of different divisions of a company are of interest to this group. Employees have invested in their careers and efforts in the business, and thus have a right to accounting information. Good industrial relations are fostered if there is disclosure of such information, so that employees can participate in decisions, and negotiate profit-sharing arrangements. This fact is recognized by many companies which produce an 'employee report' based on the accounts, but highlighting certain items such as training expenditure and statistics (sales per employee, profit per employee) of interest to employees.

4. **Lenders**. These users of published accounts comprise long term and short term lenders. The long term lenders will be investors in debentures or loan stock who have entered into a contract to allow the business to use their money for a long period of time, usually more than 5 years, in return for a fixed rate of interest. These lenders check that profits are sufficient to cover the interest which they are to receive. Some long term lenders have their investment secured either against certain fixed charge, or as a floating charge over the general assets of the business. Therefore they are also interested to use the published accounts to check that the value of the security is sufficient to cover them in the event of liquidation.

   Short term lender comprise trade creditors who may have lent money to the business for the matter of months or weeks; the bank which may have provided overdraft facilities renewable after a period of months; and perhaps the Zambia Revenue Authority who are awaiting payment of taxes due on a certain date. These users of the published accounts will be concerned to check via the balance sheet that there is ample working capital in the business, and that current assets to be turned into cash during the forthcoming months will be more than adequate to repay the current liabilities. This is a matter of future cash flow but published accounts do not provide this information. It is left to the users to draw their own conclusions as to future circumstances from the financial statements which report on past transactions.

5. **Business contact group**. Customers are interested users of the financial statements of a business in order to ensure that they are buying from a reputable business which is likely to have ample recourses to complete the contract. If a company purchases, say, a large piece of item like a step-up transformer, if would be wise to review the financial position of its supplier before placing an order, to ascertain that it is getting into a contractual relationship with a company whose financial position is such that it will be able to complete the contract. This is the reason why a buying company will always ask the suppliers to provide their financial statements along with other pieces of information like past customers when bidding to supply goods. It would be very costly for a buying company to enter into a contract with a supplier who fails to meet the contractual obligations.

Competitors are also interested in the published financial statements of a business to compare profitability and financial status of their rivals with themselves. Some industries organize inter-firm comparison schemes which compute accounting ratios as an average for all the companies participating in the scheme, and set ratios of each individual company against the averages in a report to the company. Competitors are particularly interested to discover an analysis of turnover from the company's published accounts to compute the market share of their rivals. For this reason directors may be unwilling to disclose too much information in the published accounts and are allowed by the Companies Act to treat certain disclosures as confidential if to make the information public would harm the company.

6. **Government agencies.** These are interested users of financial accounting information for two main reasons. First, the accounting profit forms the basis on which tax adjustments are made in order to determine the taxable profit of the business. Clearly, a tax computation which begins at the point of audited accounts is based on a firm foundation. Zambia Revenue Authority is also interested to check o capital expenditure and other items in the accounts which are adjusted on the tax computation. Central government is also interested in published financial accounts from the point of view of new statistics. The Ministry of Commerce, Trade and Industry gathers statistics concerning employment, capital expenditure, exports and other significant information which will assist in economic decisions.

7. **The public at large**. As explained earlier, a business is using community resources and may affect the physical and commercial environment within its locality. Thus the public may be interested to use the financial statements of the business.

8. Let me summarize the above discussion on users of financial statements and their respective information needs.

User	Information needs
1. Management	—Detailed information in order to control their business and plan for future —information about profitability of individual departments and products. —information must be up-to-date hence normally produced monthly.
2. Shareholders and	—This group include investors and their advisors potential shareholders —Performance of management in achieving profit growth while ensuring the continued solvency of the company. —The risk inherent in the company's operations revealed by the financial strength and solvency as shown in the balance sheet.

3. Employees and their	—Stability and survival of the company trade union
	—Ability of the company to provide renumeration, representatives employment opportunities and retirement benefits.
	—Salaries and benefits enjoyed by seniors
	—Divisional profitability will also be useful if a part of Business is threatened with closure.
4. Lenders	—Solvency of the company
	—profitability to ensure payment of interest when due.
	—Asset values as long-term loans may be backed by security given by the business over specific assets.
5. Government agencies	—How the economy is performing in order to plan their financial industrial policies
	—ZRA uses financial statements as a basis for assessing the amount of tax payable by a business.
6. Business contact group	—This group includes suppliers, customers and other creditors.
	—Information as to the solvency of the company and its ability to pay probably over a shorter period than lenders
	—information about the continuance of the company especially if they have a long-term involvement with it.
7. The Public	—There are many other user groups and interest groups e.g. members of the local community where the company operates, environmental pressure groups, area member of parliament, etc.

Note: Financial statements serve a wide variety of user groups, who have different interest and also different levels of financial sophistication. This makes it particularly difficult to produce financial statements that are simple enough for the layman to understand, but also comprehensive enough for the expert!

Desirable Qualities of useful Accounting Information

Having identified the users of financial information, the problem arises as to what information is useful to them. Much thought has been given to improving the statements which accountants prepare for users, and gradually a group of basic characteristics has emerged which should be present in a useful accounting statement. These are given as follows;

1. **Relevance**. This is an important characteristic, which disciplines the accountant to select and show data which are of interest to the user, say a manager, and to hold back information which may confuse or be of little use to the manager when that information is assimilated. For example, information about the cleaner resigning is

irrelevant to the users and must be left out. Relevance implies that the accountant must be ready to adapt the form of statements to the changing needs of the users.

2. **Reliability**. An accounting statement must be reliable if it is to be used with confidence. Verification by an independent auditor with a high reputation for skill and care enhances that confidence, but creates an impetus to exclude from accounting statements amounts which cannot be verified by such an objective test.

3. **Comparability**. This is held to be a useful characteristic in an accounting statement. It allows the accounts of one company to be compared with those of another, or comparison within the firm over time, or with a preconceived norm or average for the industry, which acts as a yardstick for success. Standard Accounting Practice, when applied, reduces the differences in technique experienced from one accounting statement to another, and this facilitates comparison of performance across an industry, and of the same company in the previous years. Without this characteristic, there will be no ratios in accounting.

4. **Understandability**. A useful statement must be understandable, and formulated in such a way as to highlight significant figures. This is the reason why standard formats are provided for financial statements. This characteristic faces the accountant with the dilemma of the need to disclose relevant items balanced against the danger of confusing users by presenting them with a complicated mass of data.

5. **Completeness**. Accounts should be complete, showing all aspects of a situation. It is not easy to comply with this characteristic in the statement. For example, full information about the performance of various divisions of a company may be of great interest to shareholders if published, but it may be of greater interest to competitors, who can put such information to uses which might be harmful to the company, apart from increasing resultant volume.

6. **Objectivity**. Accounting information must not be subjective but rather objective. It must not be biased towards one user group. Remember, financial statements are prepared by one user group—management. I must mention here that complete objectivity is not possible as accountants must always use their judgement on such matters as coming with a figure for provision for bad debts.

7. **Timeliness**. This is important for users, be they managers, shareholders or creditors, since they benefit from up-to-date information, which reveals the current situation, and serves as a mirror to reflect what is likely to happen in the future. Managers in particular need information at an early stage to check performance in the immediate past and to adjust their plans for future action. Investors and creditors receive little help from data which are six months old, because the situation of the business could have changed during the intervening months. This is the more reason why Company Act requires companies to prepare and publish their financial statements within three months after the financial year end.

8. **Cost-effectiveness**. Financial information is very expensive to produce; therefore, accounting statements should only be created if the benefits derived from them exceed their cost. This is the reason why small businesses are exempt from preparing financial statements which must thereafter be audited by independent auditors.

The above characteristics are summarized below.

Criteria	Comment
1. Relevant	—The information should be relevant to the needs of the users, so that it helps them to evaluate the financial performance of the business and to draw conclusions from it. —**Problem**. To identify these needs given the variety of users.
2. Reliability	—The information should be of a standard that can be relied upon by users, so that it is free from error and can depended upon by users in their decisions. —**Problem**. The complexities of modern business make reliability difficult to achieve in all areas.
3. Comparability	—Accounts should be comparable with those of other similar enterprises, and from one period to the next. —**Problem**. Use of different accounting policies by different enterprises. Accounting standards have reduced but not eliminated this problem
4. Understandability	—The information should be in form which is understandable to user groups. —**Problem**. Users have very different levels of financial sophisticated, also the complexities of business transactions make it difficult to provide adequate disclosure whilst maintaining simplicity.
5. Completeness	—Accounting statements should show all aspects of the business. —**Problem**. The resultant volume of the information
6. Objectivity	—Accounting statements should not be biased towards the Needs of one user, they should be objective. —**Problem**. Financial statements are prepared by one user group-management. An external audit should remove this bias, but some authorities question the effectiveness of the audit in this respect.

7. Timeliness	—Accounting statements should be published as soon as possible after the year-end .
	—**Problem**. There is a conflict between this criterion and that of reliability, in that quicker accounts mean more estimates, and hence reduce reliability.
8. Cost-effectiveness	—Benefit of accounting information must exceed it cost.

The accountancy profession has attempted to identify users of accounting information and the information which they require. As yet, however, insufficient consideration has been given to the problem of the whether a set of accounts produced by a business to report to shareholders (using the annual report) does provide all the required information, and whether other supplementary statements are needed to cover any deficiency.

Accounting Concepts/Conventions

Accounting concepts are simply rules that guide preparers of financial statements as how to make entries as well as users to check whether the financial statements have been properly prepared. Accounting concepts which are also called accounting conventions can be broadly classified into three categories namely: Basic principles which are assumed to underlie the production of all accounting statements, conventions which influence the measurement of assets or profits, and conventions which concern the presentation of information.

A. Basic Accounting Concepts

1. **Going concern concept**: This assumes that the business will continue in operation for the foreseeable future. The profit and loss account and the balance sheet are drawn upon the assumption that there is no intention to liquidate the business or curtail significantly its scale of operation. Thus unless there is evidence to the contrary, it is assumed when accounting statements are compiled that the firm which is the subject of those statements is going to continue in operation for an indefinite period. Without this postulate, year-end accounts would have to be worked out on a 'winding-up' basis, that is, on what the business is likely to be worth if sold piecemeal at the accounting date. This value is often different from its value if the present owners intend to carry on the business. The main reason is that goodwill which is an important asset usually has no market value when the firm is liquidated. Further, fixed assets are shown at cost less depreciation to date, rather than at their current value in the second-hand market, because they are held by the firm not for immediate resale, but to be used by the business until their working life is over. This is clearly an assumption on which the balance sheet is based, but some accountants feel that it is more a matter of common sense than something which needs to sanctified as a postulate.
Before accounts are certified as showing a true and fair view, which is the overriding objective of financial statements, the auditor must be satisfied that the company is a going concern and it will continue to function successfully in the future. The criteria

to be used in this appraisal will depend on the circumstances, but the following are general rules:

a) The market. Is there a steady demand for the firm's product which has a reasonable chance of being sustained in future?

b) Finance. Does the firm possess sufficient liquidity to meet all known liabilities in the future? A profitable business may be brought to a halt if creditors no longer give if financial support and it is unable to pay its way. This is because there is a big difference between liquidity and profitability.

c) Sound capital structure. Are there sufficient long term funds in the business to give enough strength to overcome inflation, high interest rates, a credit squeeze, increases in taxation or any other hazard of the business world?

d) What is the firm's competitive condition? Here one must consider the efficiency of the firm compared to that of its rivals, and its ability to acquire sufficient raw materials and labour and to replace worn-out plant and equipment.

To illustrate consider, a firm that produces and sales a simple product to mining firms. If as a result of a fall in metal prices the mining firms are closed down, this firm will no longer be a going concern as there will be no market for its only product. It must therefore be accounted at the price obtainable if it is sold piecemeal.

2. **Accruals or matching concept**: Revenues are accrued in the period in which they are received. Against these revenues are matched the costs of earning the revenues. Costs are dealt with as they are incurred rather than as they are paid for. The purpose of this concept in accounting is to match effort to accomplishment by setting the cost of resources used up by a certain activity against the revenue or benefits of that activity. When a profit statement is compiled, the cost of goods sold should be set against the revenue from the sale of those goods even if cash has not yet been received. Expenses and revenue must be matched up so that they concern the same goods and time period, if a true profit is to be computed. Costs concerning the future period must be carried forward as a prepayment of that period, and not charged in the current profit and loss account. Expenses of the current period not yet entered in the books must be estimated and inserted as accruals. There has been much argument among accountants about whether overheard expenses should be charged against the period in which they are incurred or carried forward to the period in which the goods made when these costs were incurred are eventually sold. Whenever the accruals concept and the prudence concept conflict, the prudence concept prevails. It may be wiser to write off the cost of certain stock rather than carry it forward to match with revenue which may not be received in the future.

Consider a retailer who bought stock worth K10 million on 1st January 2011. At 31st December 2011 his sales (revenue) is K650 000 and stock counting on the same day reveals that stock which cost him K800 000 is unsold. What is his profit for the year? If we simply say that profit is K650 000 less k10 million we would get a loss of K350 000. But is this the correct situation? Certainly not. We need to match the actual cost of the stock that generated K650 000 and that cost is K200 000. Therefore the correct calculation is K650 000 less K200 000 giving him a profit of K450 000! The cost of goods sold is only K200 000 while K800 000 is the closing stock which we record as a current asset in the balance sheet and in the income statement it is subtracted from the purchases figure. Without this concept profit calculations would be misleading to say the least.

3. **The consistency concept**: This concept states that there is consistency of accounting treatment of similar items, both within each accounting period to the next to facilitate comparison. With many accounting transactions there is more than one method which can be adopted to deal with the items in the accounts. It's like a question of how do you reach Lusaka Central Business District. You may use Great North Road or Great East Road, or Mumbwa Road or Kafue Road and many others using a car. But certainly, if you intend to measure the distance you have to use the same road next time around. Similarly accountants must use their judgement to select the most appropriate method, but once that choice is made the same method must be used with consistency in forthcoming periods. Such consistency enables users to make a useful comparison of results over time. Thus investors can see the extent of profit or loss, comparing this year with last year, and make their investment decisions accordingly. The methods used should only be changed if the new method selected improves the true and fair view given by the accounting statements. A note of the change of accounting policy must be appended to the statement concerned, since the calculation of profit may be radically affected during the period of change. Every set of accounts has a full note concerning the accounting policies which have been used, and details of the change, the reason for the change and the effect of the change must be disclosed in this note.

To illustrate, consider a firm that calculates depreciation charge at 20% per annum using straight line method for its premises. The cost of premises which were bought four years ago was K100 million. In the income statement a depreciation charge of K20 million per annum will be charged as an expense. Now, in the third year assume that depreciation charge is K50 million already provided and the company decides to use reducing balance method at 20% in the fourth year, depreciation charge will be K10 million, that is, 20% of (K100 million—K50 million). This will affect the profit figure which will increase by K10 million while fixed assets in the balance sheet will also increase by the same amount because less depreciation is charged due to a change in the method used to depreciate fixed assets!

It would be quite unfair to use a procedure which gave the best profit each year, since the accounts would then show the best possible position rather than the true and fair position, and comparison of one year with another would be impossible.

Consistency may give comparison over time for the same company, but it cannot offer a comparison between companies unless the same basis is consistently used in each of them. Unfortunately, the idea of consistency is used as a weapon to resist change, since any new method suffers from the disadvantage that it is inconsistent with what has gone before. The answer to this dilemma is to change as little as possible, but when a change is made, to inform users of accounts, by means of a note to the statement, of exactly what the change is, why it has been made, and the impact it has had on the profit and loss account and the balance sheet.

4. **The prudence concept**: This is also called the conservatism concept. It state that revenue and profits are only included in the profit and loss account when they are realized either in cash form or the asset close to cash. Provision should be made for all known liabilities. Business transactions are characterized by uncertainty which exists until the deal is complete. The accountant responds to this uncertainty by a prudent or conservative approach to the valuation of assets such as stocks; or by not accepting that a profit has been made until a situation is certain.

   The concept has resulted in accountants being thought of by businessmen as pessimists. Whenever there are alternative procedures or values, the accountant selects the one which results in a lower asset value or profit and a higher liability. The concept can be summarized by the phrase 'anticipate no profit and provide for all possible losses', and stems from the accountants' fear that if they approach the compilation of accounting statements with too much optimism they may overstate profits and cause dividends to be paid out of capital. If an unrealized profit is distributed to shareholders as dividend, the danger exists that the funds will be paid out, yet the profit may never be realized, and may even melt away. In the absence of certainty it is best to be prudent. It is considered preferable to understate where doubt arises, since mistakes in this direction can be corrected later when the situation is clarified.

   Prudence can be misused by accountants, for it is wrong to deliberately understate asset values and understate earnings. To understate is as bad as to overstate, and accountants must not lose sight of the need for correct, reliable figures.

   To illustrate, consider a farmer who has bought all the necessary agriculture inputs at the start of the season. He calculates total cost to be K100 million. He anticipates favorable rainfall and good price for his crop. Based on this he calculates that he will make a profit of K150 million. Should this profit be recognized now in the financial statements? The answer is a categorical no because it is not certain that weather will be favorable and a good price will be secured. Similarly, other catastrophic events may emerge, such as an outbreak of locusts which destroys the crop.

B. Concepts concerning the measurement process in accounting

1. **Money measurement concept**: This states that financial accounting can only deal with items capable of being expressed in money terms. This concept is relevant in deciding whether or not an asset can be recognized in the balance sheet. If an asset cannot be valued with reasonable accuracy, it cannot be dealt with in financial accounting. For example, the expertise of a company's research staff may be a significant factor in its success, but it is almost impossible to put a value on it and therefore cannot appear in the balance sheet.

   Accounting statements are expressed in monetary terms, since money acts as a common denominator to express the many different facets of an organization, e.g. costs, sales, the value of stocks, machinery, debts and investments. If all the items covered by an accounting statement are stated as an amount of money, then the relative cost or value of these items can be seen and their aggregate cost or value determined. The disadvantage of monetary measurements is, of course, that the value of money may not remain stable, especially in a period of inflation. Not only does this hinder comparison of statements computed at different times, but it also creates difficulties when the costs of assets bought at different times are added together in the same statement. For example, on 26th June 2012 I ordered 100 copies of Statistical Analysis Textbook from Trafford Publishing Inc. at $2 450 and on that day the exchange rate between the kwacha and US$ was K5 500 i.e. K13 750 000. A week later the exchange rate was now K5 050 per US$. I ordered the same quantity but at a total cost of K12 387 650. Now when preparing the accounting statements, would it be correct for me to add these two amounts together to express the two consignments in a position statement? Certainly, K26 137 650 has been invested in these assets, financed by funds entrusted to the business by the investors , who will expect to paid to be repaid K26 137 650 if the business is terminated. Liabilities are payable, according to the law, as an agreed amount of money, so it seems correct to record them in money terms. If the purpose of financial statements is to disclose the legal obligation of the business to repay lenders and shareholders, then monetary measurement is a useful convention, but for decision making purposes monetary measurement must be adjusted to reflect changing price levels.

Accountants are now beginning to realize, however, that some elements of a business, such as morale of the workforce and strength of competition, cannot be measured in money terms, even though they must be regarded as assets since profit derives from them. A good labour relations record in a company means that there will be little disruption of production through strikes, and thus profits will increase, but it is hard to work out exactly the profit that would have been made had labour relations in the business been less harmonious, and impossible to compute an accurate value for such an 'asset' which could be disclosed in a balance sheet. Other assets which are difficult to quantify are 'know-how', the possession of a good management team, and goodwill. This last intangible asset often appears in balance sheets of companies, though its existence and valuation may not be agreed upon by all accountants. Fixed assets can be quantified in money terms, but the figure shown makes no comment about their state of repair, or their suitability for the tasks which they undertake. The fact that a competitor has developed a new rival product and is poised to take a considerable share of a company's market does not appear on the balance sheet as a liability.

2. **Realization.** This concept states that revenue is created at the time when the sale is made, and not necessarily when cash is received. This postulate is significant in the calculation of sales revenue and profit, since it determines the point at which the accountant feels that a transaction is certain enough to be completed for the profit made on it to be calculated and taken to the income statement, and if necessary distributed to the shareholders as dividends. Realization is when a sale is made to a customer, and stock at cost becomes cash or a debt measured at a selling price. The basic rule is that revenue is created at the moment the sale is made, and not when the price is later paid in cash. Profit can be taken to the income statement on sales made, even though the money has not been collected. The firm has acquired a debt, and a provision

must be made in the income statement for debts not likely to be collected. The sale is deemed to be made when the goods are delivered, and thus profit cannot be taken to the income statement on orders received and not yet filled. Goods manufactured but not yet delivered are not deemed sold, so no element of profit can enter into the value of stocks of such goods at the accounting date. There are some exceptions to this basic rule, e.g. long term contracts, which involve payments on account before completion of the work.

Realization implies that no increase in the value of an asset can be recognized as a profit unless it is realized. Assets are recorded at the historical cost at which they were purchased (the objectively determined amount which was paid out for them) and it is often considered prudent to keep them in the books at this amount even if there is reliable information that they are worth more. It is a matter of certainty. The prudent accountant will prefer to use the lower figure until the profit is realized, in case the value increase is only temporary. An economist would not agree with this prudent approach, preferring to recognize a value increase as it takes place.

To illustrate, a college that enroll students on credit must recognize the sale immediately the student is enrolled and not when the student actually paid what he owes.

3. **Objectivity**. This concept states that accounting statements must be free from bias. It holds that an accounting statement should not be influenced by personal bias on the part of the accountant who compiles it. Of course, there are times when an accountant has to use judgement when drawing up a set of accounts, but he must use his own expertise to ensure a correct result. For example, a change in value of an asset should be recognized when it can be measured in objective terms. Estimates sometimes have to be made in accounting and are permissible if they are made with care and within reasonable tolerances and accuracy, e.g. provision for doubtful debts. Another example of an objective figure is the amount actually paid out by the company when it acquires an asset. This figure is real and can be proved by documentation recording the transaction. Unfortunately, such a figure for an asset purchased many years ago is not indicative of current value.

   Figures built into accounting statements should rely as little as possible on estimates or subjective decisions. Historical cost represent an amount actually paid out for an asset, which can be proved by means of a voucher and verified as the market cost of the asset at its date of purchase. This amount, it is argued, is to be preferred to a subjective valuation of an asset based on estimates of its future profitability.

4. **Cost.** Fixed assets are shown in the accounts at the price paid to acquire them, i.e. their historical cost less depreciation written off to date. They are acquired by a company to be used, and it is argued that their historical cost should be spread as an expense to the income statement over the years of their useful life. However, inflation or obsolescence may change the value of a long-lived asset. The concepts of consistency, objectivity, and conservatism are used to support the use of historical cost in accounting for such assets. The opponents of the historical cost principle use the concepts of disclosure and materiality to support their arguments that current cost amounts are more useful to readers of accounting statements.

Accountants distrust the idea of value, since a value is often a matter of personal bias and may change according to the method of valuation used. Under the going concern postulate we account for assets at their value in use, which we interpret as the historical cost of the asset net depreciation to date. If this amount is out of line with the true value, then the asset should be revalued by an expert.

To account for an asset at an amount in excess of its cost is to assume that a profit has been made by holding the asset. Such a profit is a matter of estimate and uncertainty which is only realized when the asset is sold for its current value. The convention of prudence argues against recognition of an unrealized profit because the value of the asset may subsequently fall before the asset is sold.

Conversely, users of financial statements should be informed of the current value of assets, if decisions or judgements are to be made in the light of the most recent information.

To illustrate, suppose a company bought premises in 1980 at K10 million and the current market value is K10 billion. At what amount should this asset be recorded in the financial accounts? The historical cost is K10 million as recorded in the books, but of course there is a great difference between what K10 million could buy at that time and what it could buy now. Thus historical cost does not show the real capital employed in an asset or any fluctuations in the values of the asset that has taken place since it was bought. If depreciation written off the premises during its working life amounts to K9 million, then the net book value would be K1 million, and this amount might not all be representative of the true value of the asset, as calculated on the basis of what it can earn if it can still be used for housing offices, including production plant, or what it would fetch if sold now. An accountant might argue that the use of historical cost is consistent and objective, since it is based on a transaction which actually took place rather than an estimate of the value, and conservative, since it does not overstate the value of the asset. The, shareholders, however, might scoff at an accounting statement which shows the premises at K1 million, since to them such a valuation would be unrealistic!

C. CONVENTIONS CONCERNED WITH THE PRESENTATION OF INFORMATION

1. **Substance over form**: It may be that the legal form of a business transaction differs from its real nature. For example, if a company's acquiring fixed assets under a hire purchase agreement, the legal position is that ownership does not pass until the last hire purchase payment is made. The substance over form convention is that the reality and commercial effect of the transaction are recognized-the asset is controlled by the company and is therefore included as such in the balance sheet, with a corresponding liability recognized for the unpaid amount.

   A new concept, which is not yet completely accepted, is that in order to show a true and fair view, it is sometimes necessary to account for the economic substance of a transaction instead of its strict legal form. Some transactions can be carefully staged so that by following the legal form of the deal, a misleading position will be disclosed in the accounting statements. The accounting profession is slowly coming to the opinion that it is preferable to ignore the legal interpretation of a transaction if accounting for the economic substance, or commercial effect, will lead to the disclosure of true and fair information. Another example of substance over form concerns the accounting treatment of leases.

Suppose a company does not own the premises it is using, but instead lease it from another company, in return for the payment of a rental each year. The premises belong to the leasing company legally and should appear as an asset on this company's balance sheet. The company, however, has a lease contract that gives it the right to the exclusive use of the asset for its economic life, and the liability to pay a series of rentals over that life. The commercial effect of the lease is that the company can use the asset which is no different from other assets which it owns, and it has a liability to pay a series of rentals which become due as the years go by. The economic substance is that the asset and the liability should appear on the company's balance sheet to disclose a true and fair view, but if strict legal form is followed neither asset nor liability would be disclosed. IAS 17: Leases discussed later in the book, for finance leases, the accounting policy should follow substance over form.

2. **Business entity concept**. In accounting, it is necessary to define the boundaries of the enterprise concerned. In the case of a limited liability company, only transaction of that company must be included. There must be no confusion between the transactions of the company and the transactions of its owners and managers. If the entity concept is not followed, the profit, financial position and cash flow may all be distorted to the point where they become useless.

This concept separates the individuals behind a business from the business itself, and records transactions in the accounting statements as they affect the business, and not its owners. In a large company this concept emphasizes the division between owners and managers. The accountant prepares reports to the shareholders on how the managers have used the funds entrusted to them by the owners. This aspect of accounting is sometimes called reporting on stewardship, as opposed to management accounting, where reports are prepared to assist management in their job of controlling the business and deciding on the future courses of action.

In a small business run by partners or a sole trader, this concept avoids confusion between business transactions and those of private life. The accountant is trying to measure the profit made by an individual in his business, and thus a loss made when the family car is scrapped and money is withdrawn from the bank account to replace it is not a business transaction. A man running a retail shop will want to know what profit hi is making, and that profit will be incorrect unless goods taken from the shop for his own consumption are accounted for as sales. Goods taken for the owner's use are part of the profit withdrawn by the man from his business. There must also be a reasonable apportionment of the costs incurred partly for the family and partly for business reasons, e.g. rent and rates of a shop or office with a flat for the proprietor above it.

The law does not recognize the distinction between owner and the business, since if a business cannot pay its debts the creditors can take the possessions of the owner or partners to satisfy their claims. In the case of a company, however, the shareholders are the owners, and their liability for the debts of the business is limited to the extent of their investment in the business. The business entity concept ensures that the amount invested by the owners in the business is defined (capital) and allows a return on capital employed to be computed to show whether the investment is worthwhile. Some owners may have investments in more than one business, and in any case will be interested in the results of their business activities unencumbered by the financial details of their private lives. The capital invested by a shareholder represents the original investment when the business commenced plus undistributed profits are accumulated since that time. This concept is sometimes confused with a less important idea, that of the accounting unit, which seeks to define the area of business activity to be encompassed by a set of accounts. Often the entire business is accounted for within one set of books, but more often nowadays business operations are fragmented, and the management accounting unit is found at the level of subsidiary companies, divisions, or factories, which have their own accounting systems.

3. **Materiality concept**: Information is material if its omission from, misstatements in, the financial statements could influence the economic decisions of the users. Materially cannot always be measured in monetary or percentage terms, but a commonly used measure is 15% of normal pre-tax profit. Above that level, for, example, an exceptional item would need to be disclosed by note or on the face of the profit and loss account statements.

Accounting statements should concern themselves with matters which are significant because of their size, and should not consider trivial matters. Analysis is expensive and the presentation of too much detail can be confusing, so insignificant items in financial statements are merged with others, and not reported separately, since they are considered immaterial. The difficulty lies in setting a dividing line between what is material and what is immaterial. Individual opinions differ on this point, but perhaps the cost of collecting accounting information can be used here as a decision criteria, together with the relative importance of the item in the picture revealed by the statement as a whole. What is material in a small business may prove to be immaterial in a large business. In a case concerning an international group, the collapse of a foreign subsidiary with losses in the region of $8 million to the group was not clearly shown in the consolidated accounts. There are some criticisms of the accounting treatment of these losses, and the answer made by those responsible for the accounts was that in their view the amount of $8 million was not material in such a large company when the position of the group income statement had to be considered.

If the materiality concept is not followed, financial statements could become confused by the inclusion of unnecessary detail of trivial matters, or could be rendered misleading by the exclusion of reference to important matters.

4. **Duality concept.** This concept states that transactions must be recorded twice in accounting books, i.e. in one book as a debit entry and in another as a credit entry. It is the basis of double-entry book-keeping and stems from the fact that every transaction has a double effect on the position of the business as recorded in the accounts. When an asset is acquired, either another asset (cash) is reduced or a liability (a promise to

pay) is acquired at the same time. When a sale is made, stock (an asset) is reduced, while either cash or debtors (assets) are increased. If the business borrows money, a liability to the lender is created and at the same time an asset (cash) is increased. It follows that the assets of the business are equaled by claims on the business, either by creditors or owners, for the funds they have invested in the business and which have been translated into assets for use by the business. The balance sheet which summarizes assets and claims (liabilities), must therefore balance and can be expressed by 'the accounting equation', which is that assets equal liabilities plus capital invested, i.e. assets= liabilities + capital.

To illustrate, when the business buys a car, it acquires an asset, by reducing it cash, another asset, and when it buys goods on credit, it acquires an asset (stock) and at the same time a liability to the trader. When the liability is discharged, cash, an asset, is reduced. Thus assets equal liabilities at all times. The double entry book-keeping system is explained in Chapter 3 of this book.

PROGRESS CLINIC 1

Question 1

Even in time of inflation, published financial statements continue to be prepared under the historical cost convention despite its added limitations.

Required

(a)   List and explain six (6) reasons why historical cost accounting has been critised.

(b)   List and explain four (4) advantages of historical cost accounting over the other methods of accounting.

Question 2

Your Finance Director is proposing that certain International Accounting Standards should not be applied on the published accounts. Some of the items are "material" and some are "immaterial".

Required:

Explain what is meant by the term "Immaterial item".

Question 3

The International Accounting Standard Boards (IASB's) framework states that the objective of financial statements is to provide information about the financial position, performance and financial adaptability of an enterprise that is useful to a wide range of users.

Required:

List seven (7) users of company financial statements and briefly explain for each type of user why they need information about the company.

Question 4

Accounting principles, concepts and conventions are a set of legislative information relating to the treatment of financial information.

You are required to explain briefly the following terms:

(a)   Accrual concept

(b)   Dual Aspect Concept

(c)   Business Entity Concept

(d)   Going Concern Concept

(e)   Money Measurement Concept

Question 5

For each of the following items, discuss the way each issue should be treated in a set of accounts with reference to accounting principles.

a) A company decides that its future would be enhanced by sending key individuals on finance training. This is estimated to cost K20 million in the current financial year.
b) A company has recently picked up a ten-year contract for managing the collection of TV license fees payable each year by television viewers. It is confident that it can make over K100 million a year from the deal.
c) A company decides that it will make 50 employees redundant during the next financial year at a total cost of K1.4 billion .
d) Tusole cars Ltd gives a three-year warranty on all cars sold. On average there are K5 million of warranty costs on each car.
e) A chemical company recruits a top chemist who is likely to be able to add an important new product to the company's portfolio, and an estimated K1 billion to annual profits. He cost K25 million to recruit and will be paid K300 million per annum.

Question 6

Qualitative characteristics are the attributes that make the information provided in the financial statements useful to users. There are four principal qualities described by the IASB Framework, namely a) Understandability, b) relevance, c) reliability d) comparability.

You are required to describe and analyze each of these four qualities.

Question 7

The following is an extract from a letter written to you by Mr. Mbewe, a retailer, whose final accounts you have recently prepared.

"I have examined the accounts you have sent me and am puzzled about the following:

a) During the year I used a business cheque to buy a new washing machine for my wife to use at home. Why is this not included in the balance sheet?

b) I cannot understand why the business bank overdraft has increased in spite of the fact that the business has made a profit. Can you give me three possible reasons why this may have happened?

c) My friend, Tyola says that I should keep an eye on my gross profit margins. What does this mean?

d) Why have you included my freehold shop at its original cost of K45 million, although its current market value is about K100 million?

e) I bought a van two years ago for K12 million, assuming it would be in use for 5 years and worth nothing. Why have you included this van in the balance sheet at a value of K7.2 million when the market value of the van, according to second-hand vehicles guide, is only K5 million".

Required
Comment on each of the five above, making reference, where appropriate, to the accounting concepts. Assume that Mr. Mbewe has very little accounting knowledge.

Question 8

TJ Plc sells a product with a five-year parts and labour warranty. In what ways could it treat expenses that it expects to incur as a result of the product warranty? Explain the fundamental accounting concepts involved.

Question 9

What is the convention of **'consistency'**? Does this convention help users in making a more valid comparison between businesses? Give reasons for your answer.

CHAPTER 2

REGULATORY AUTHORITY IN ACCOUNTING

Sources of authority in accounting

Each country has its own legislation governing accounting and the operation of companies. In Zambia, the regulatory authority in accounting includes the following:

1. **International Accounting Standards (IASs).** These are used as a basis of accounting in many countries Zambia inclusive. The main aim is to achieve global convergence of accounting standards.

2. **Company law legislation** especially the Companies Act 1985 governs accounting and the operation of companies. Though derived from English law, company law in many countries Zambia inclusive has similar provisions.(Refer CA 1994).

3. **Local Accounting Standards (LASs).** Each country has its own local accounting standards which are developed in line with International Accounting Standards. In Zambia we have the Zambia Accounting Standards (ZASs), in UK, they have SSAPs, FRSs while USA has FABS.

4. **The Stock Exchange.** The stock exchange has accounting rules that listed companies are obliged to comply with. One of the m common is the publishing of the company's interim financial statements semi-annually.

   The last three forms the Generally Accepted Accounting Practice (GAAP) applied in a given country.

STANDARD SETTING PROCESS AND THE STRUCTURE OF INTERNATIONAL ACCOUNTING STANDARD BOARD

The international Accounting Standards committee (IASC) was set up in 1973 but changed, its name to International Accounting Standards Board (IASB) in 2001. The old IASC published 'International Accounting Standard', whereas the new IASB publishes 'International Financial Reporting Standards'.

The major aim of the IASB is to achieve global convergence of accounting standards. The adoption of IASs among countries has been reinforced by two major events namely:

(a) The European Union requires all listed companies to use IASs effective 2005.

(b) The International Organization of Securities Commissions (1OSCO) requires all listed companies in member countries to use IASs in order to facilitate cross-borders listing.

OBJECTIVES OF THE IASB

The objectives of the IASB are:

- To develop, in public interest, a single set of high quality, understandable and enforceable global accounting standards that require high quality, transparent and: comparable information in financial statements and other financial reporting to help participants in the world's capital markets and other users to make economic decisions

- To promote the use and rigorous application of those standards.

- To bring about convergence of national accounting standards and international accounting standards to high quality solutions.

THE STRUCTURE OF THE IASB

The following diagram shows the structure of the IASB.

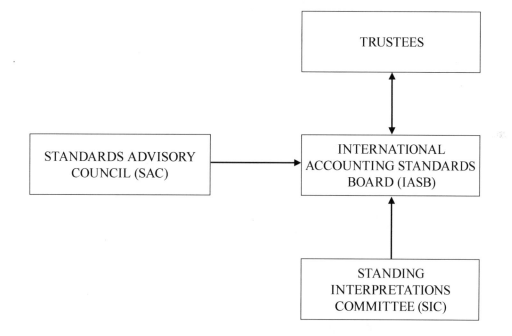

The roles of the above four components are explained below:

TRUSTEES

There are 19 trustees, appointed to ensure a wide geographical spread as follows:

- 6 from North America
- 6 from Europe
- 4 from Asia/Pacific region
- From any area

The main duties of the trustees are:

- Fundraising
- Appointing the members for the IASB, the SIC and the SAC
- Annually reviewing strategy.

The trustees have no involvement in technical matters relating to accounting standards.

THE BOARD (IASB)

The Board has 14 members, 12 of whom work-full-time. There is no geographical restriction on the appointment of the Board members, but to achieve a balance of perspectives and experience, the following stipulations are made:

- Five or more members: practicing auditing background.
- Three or more members: Concerned with preparation of financial statements
- Three or more members: Users of financial statements.
- At least one member: Academic background

The Board has complete responsibility for all technical matters.

The procedures in developing standards are normally:

- Form a steering committee to advice on major projects.
- Consult the Standards Advisory Council
- Publish a Draft Statement of \Principles or other discussion documents, inviting comment from interested parties.
- Publish an Exposure Draft, again inviting comment
- Publish the final International Financial Reporting Standards (IFRSs)

Exposure Drafts and IFRSs require the approval of 8 out of the 14 members of the Board. Other decisions of the Board, including the issuance of a Draft statement of principles or Discussion Paper, require a simple majority at a meeting attended by at least 60% of the members of the Board.

International financial reporting interpretations committee (IFRIC)

The IFRIC's main task is to interpret the application of IASs and IFRSs if difficulties arise. They may issue Draft Interpretations for public comment before finalizing an interpretation. They report to IASB and must obtain Board approval for their interpretations before issue

Standards advisory council (SAC)

The SAC exists to provide the IASB with the advice on major standard setting projects and other matters. It has about 30 members including representatives of national standard setters and other interested parties.

International accounting standards and international financial reporting standards.

The syllabus requires you to have working knowledge on the following IASs and IFRSs.

- IAS 1: Presentation of financial statements
- IAS 2: Inventories
- IAS 7: Statement of cash flows
- IAS 8: Accounting policies, changes in accounting estimates and errors
- IAS 10: Events after the reporting period
- IAS 11: Construction contracts
- IAS 12: Income taxes
- IAS 14: Segments Reporting
- IAS 16: Property, plant and Equipment
- IAS 17: Lease
- IAS 18: Revenue
- IAS 19: Employee Benefits.
- IAS 20: Government Grants
- IAS 23: Borrowing costs
- IAS 24: Related party disclosures
- IAS 27: Separate financial statements
- IAS 28: Investment in Associates and joint ventures
- IAS 32: Financial instruments: presentation
- IAS 33: Earnings Per Share
- IAS 34: Interim financial reporting
- IAS 36: Impairment of Assets
- IAS 37: Provisions, Contingent Liabilities and Contingent Assets
- IAS 38: Intangible Assets
- IAS 39: Financial instruments: recognition and measurement
- IAS 40: Investment Property
- IFRS 1: First-time adoption of IFRS
- IFRS 2: Share –based payments
- IFRS 3: Business combinations
- IFRS 5: Non-current assets held for sale and discontinued operations
- IFRS 7: Financial Instruments: disclosures
- IFRS 8: Operating Segments
- IFRS 9: Financial Instruments
- IFRS 10: Consolidated financial statements
- IFRS 11: Joint arrangements
- IFRS 12: Disclosure of interest in other entities
- IFRS 13: Fair value measurement

Standardization

The Companies Act 1994 states that the necessity to give a true and fair is of overriding importance, and the disclosure 'rules' required by legislation may be broken in order to present a true and fair view.

Accounting standards have the following advantages:

- They reduce or eliminate confusing variations in the methods used to prepare accounts.

- They provide a focal point for debate and discussions about accounting practice

- They oblige companies to disclose more accounting information than they would otherwise have done if standards did not exist.

- They are a less rigid alternative to enforcing conformity by means of legislation.

- They oblige companies to disclose accounting policies used in the preparation of accounts.

- It is easier to amend a standard than to change a Companies Act and as circumstances change it may be necessary to amend hitherto acceptable accounting treatments.

The disadvantages of accounting standards are:

- A set of rules which gives backing to one method of preparing accounts might be inappropriate in some circumstances. For example. IAS16 on depreciation was inappropriate for investment property (IAS 40) was eventually issued henceforth.
- Standards may be subject to lobbying or government pressure

- They are not based on a conceptual framework of accounting and so some place more emphasis on the balance sheet and others on the profit and loss account

- There may be a trend toward rigidly, and away from flexibility in applying the rules.

The annual report

Companies are required by Company Law to prepare and distribute an annual report to the shareholders. This report must be distributed to the shareholders 21 days before the company's Annual General Meeting(AGM). At law, 21 days is presumed to be enough time for shareholders to study the report and frame questions for clarification during the AGM. This report is composed of the following:

1. **Balance Sheet**—This is a financial snapshot at a moment in time. The financial position of a business is comparable to 'pressing' the 'pause' button on a video player. The video in play mode shows what is happening as time goes on. When you press 'pause' the video stops on a picture. However, this picture does not tell what has happened over the period of time up to the pause. The balance sheet reports the financial position of a business at a specified point in time. It is basically a summary of a business's assets, liabilities and equity at a point in time. A major purpose of the balance sheet is to provide financial information to the external users.

2. **The income statement** is the video in 'play' mode. Net profit is calculated from revenues earned throughout the period between two 'pauses', minus expenses incurred from earning those revenues. The income statement reports on the profit or loss made by the business over a certain period of time. It reflects the revenue generated through its operating activities such as sales and then deducting the expenses incurred in generating that revenue and operating the business. Losses and gains arising from non-operating activities are also reported.

3. **The cash flow statement** is the video again in 'play' mode. It summarizes the cash inflows and outflows and calculates the net change in the cash position throughout the period between two 'pauses'. It reflects the sources of cash and how the cash was used during the year. This is done by reporting on the changes in all the other balance sheet items. The changes in all these other balance sheet items will equal to the change in cash. The purpose of the cash flow statement is to provide information to investors, creditors and other users to assess the ability of the business to meet its cash requirements.

4. **The statement of changes in equity.** This reflects the changes to the components of the equity during the year. It provides a summary of all changes in equity arising from transactions with owners in their capacity as owners. This includes share capital, share premium, revaluation, retained earnings and dividends.

5. **Notes to accounts.** The financial statements are usually accompanied by notes on the accounting policies and detailed information about many of the amounts reflected in the financial statements. The notes are intended to assist the users of financial statements by providing additional information that is deemed necessary by the business and its auditors. These notes are indispensable because published financial statements are highly summarized. For the user to understand something explanatory notes are required by IAS1.

6. **Audit Report.** All limited liability companies have to be audited by an independent firm of accountants. An auditor is required essentially to review the accounts of a company and express an opinion as to whether or not they give a proper presentation of the financial affairs of the company. The object of this check is to give a reassurance to users of the financial reports that the figures may be relied upon.

This opinion is given by the auditors within the confines of a stylized format, which arguably needs interpretation itself. The auditors should express their view as to whether or not the financial statements presents a true and fair view of the position of the company. Usually an auditor's opinion will fall into four main categories:

● Unqualified (a 'clean' certificate).

●Qualified (the accounts show a true and fair view, subject to some reservations on the auditor).

●Adverse

●No opinion (insufficient information or some other major impediment).

I reproduce an example of an unqualified opinion, taken from the 2011 financial statements of Copperbelt Energy Corporation PLC(visit www.cec.co.zm). This is the kind of audit certificate which is most frequently given. But it is not uncommon for a company to receive a qualified opinion. Until relatively recently, it would have been considered a major criticism to receive a qualified report, but with the growth of accounting standards there has also appeared a technical type of qualification where auditors are obliged to point out that some matter has not been dealt with totally in accordance with the accounting standards, but that this does not affect the 'true and fair view' given in the accounts.

Other types of qualification are more serious, but are relatively rare, since most companies will amend their accounts in the face of a threatened serious qualification. Qualified report or unqualified report, the auditor's opinion has to be published along with the accounts on which the opinion is based.

Most companies wish to avoid a qualification of their audit report, but it is worth nothing that some companies will accept a qualification offer repeated year after year for the sake of implementing a policy or transaction with which the company agrees but the auditors do not. Analysts tend to be careful to qualifications as they are mainly concerned with the effects of it on company value.

In order to express an opinion the auditor must examine the accounts and record-keeping systems of a company in considerable detail, and this is a costly process for which companies are obliged to pay. However, you should not run away with the idea that auditors check every transaction recorded by the company. In fact they use sophisticated techniques to keep the amount of detailed checking down to a minimum. But there are still many staff-hours involved in performing an audit, and the fees are therefore considerable. For example, the 2011 audit fee paid by CEC PLC was $48,000 or K245,616,000. The techniques of auditing are a separate study of their own and is beyond what this book is intended to teach you.

The auditor's formal responsibility is to prepare an independent report on the company for the shareholders – and they are appointed by shareholders at their annual general meeting.

7. The chairman's report. Most large companies include a chairman's report in their published financial statements. This is purely voluntary as there is no statutory requirement to do so. It can be unduly optimistic and subjective. It is very opinionated statement of the company's past and 'bright' future prospects. It gives useful background information to the figures in the accounts.

●Assessment of the year's results
●Influencing factors – economic and political
●Major developments – takeovers, mergers, disposals, new products
●Capital expenditure plans
●Assessment of positive future prospects.

8. The directors' report. Attached to every balance sheet there must be a directors' report. The purpose of the report is to give users of accounts a more complete picture of the state of affairs of the company. Narrative descriptions help to put flesh on the skeleton of details provided by the figures of the accounts themselves.

However, in practice the directors report is often a rather dry and uninformative document, perhaps because it must be verified by the company's external auditors, whereas the chairman's report need not be. It provides information on the company and its subsidiary undertakings during that year and of their position at the end of it. No guidance is given on the form of neither the review, nor the amount of detail it should go into.

Other disclosure requirements are:

- Recommended dividend
- Principal activities of the company in the financial year.
- Policy for employment of disabled persons
- Policy on environmental protection
- Corporate social responsibility concerns
- Names of persons who were directors at any time during the financial year.
- Interests of the directors in shares and debentures
- Political and charitable contributions made.
- Likely future developments
- Activities of company in the field of R and D
- Particulars of purchases of its own shares by the company
- Particulars of other acquisitions of its own shares during the year
- A note on employee involvement (250 employees)
- Particulars of any important events affecting the company (post-balance sheets events)

9. Corporate Governance Report. Corporate governance is defined by the Organization for Economic C-operation and Development (OECD) as:
"The system by which business corporations are directed and controlled. The corporate governance structure specifies the distribution of rights and responsibilities among different participants in the corporation, such as the board, managers, shareholders and other stakeholders, and spells out the rules and procedures for making decisions on corporate affairs. By doing this, it also provides the structure through which the business objectives are set, and the means of attaining those objectives and monitoring performance."
From the above definition we can see that corporate governance ids multi-faced. It covers processes, systems and cultures amongst others, and from the viewpoint of many stakeholders.
The OECD sees corporate governance as a key element in improving economic efficiency and growth as well as enhancing investor confidence. Good corporate governance should ensure that directors and managers pursue objectives within the business that are in the interests of the business and its stakeholders, not just themselves. The aim of the corporate report is to allow the reader to make a judgement on whether the corporate governance of the business is

adequate to achieve this aim. Weak and non-transparent regimes can lead to unethical behavior in a business and ultimately loss of market integrity.

A Corporate Report will cover matters such as:

- Board composition and independence
- Board responsibilities
- Appointment to the board
- Determination of executive renumeration
- Audit committee
- Board performance evaluation
- Risk management and internal controls
- Relations with stakeholders
- Compliance with any codes

10. **Other Statements**. The subject of reporting to stakeholders and the concept of the annual reports is ongoing and within annual reports you may see examples of the following:

- Social and environmental reports
- Past trends in key financial figures
- Value added statements
- Employment reports
- Statement of future prospects
- Management commentaries
- Operating and financial review.

Finally, you will enhance your understanding of annual reports if you access several of them that are freely available on the internet.

Complete set of financial statement

A complete set of financial statements shows assets, liabilities, equity, capital gains or losses, income, expenses, cash flows and notes to accounts.

In most jurisdictions the structure and content of financial statements are defined by local law. In Zambia they are defined by Companies Act 1994 and the International Accounting Standards (IASs). According to the provisions of IAS1 Presentation of Financial Statements, a complete set of financial statements comprises:

- a statement of financial position(balance sheet)
- either a comprehensive income or an income statement plus a statement showing comprehensive income
- a statement of cash flows
- a statement of changes in equity
- accounting policies and explanatory notes

Elements of financial statements

The following are the elements of financial statements:

1. **Assets.** An asset is a resource controlled by the entity as a result of past events and from which future economic benefits are expected to flow to the entity. To explain further the parts of the definition of an asset:
● Controlled by the entity – control is the ability to obtain the economic benefits and restrict the access of others(e.g. by the company the sole user of its land, or by selling surplus land)
● Past events – the event must be 'past' before an asset can arise. For example, land will only become an asset when there is the right to demand delivery or access to the asset's potential.
● Future economic benefits – these are evidenced by the prospective receipt of cash. This could be cash itself, a debt receivable or any item which may be sold. For example, a factory may not be sold (on a going concern basis) if it houses the manufacture of goods. When these goods are sold the economic benefit resulting from the use of the factory is realized as cash.

2. **Liabilities**. Liabilities are an entity's obligations to transfer economic benefits as a result of its past transactions or events.
To explain further the parts of the definition of a liability:
● Obligations – these may be legal or constructive. A constructive obligation is an obligation which is the result of expected practice rather than required by law or a legal contract.
● Transfer of economic benefits – this could be a transfer of cash, or other property, the provision of a service, or the refraining from activities which could otherwise be profitable.
● Past transactions or events – similar points are made here to those under assets.

Equity interest. This is the residue amount after deducting all liabilities of the entity from all of the entity's assets.
The definition describes the residue nature of equity interest. Owners' wealth can be increased whether or not a distribution is made. The sharing may be in different proportions. Equity interest is usually analyzed in financial statements to distinguish interest arising from owners' contributions from that resulting from other events. The latter is split into different reserves which may have different applications or legal status.

4. **Income**. Income is:
● an increase in economic benefits during the accounting period in the form of inflows or enhancements of assets or decreases in liabilities
● transactions that result in increases in equity, other than those relating to contributions from equity participants.
● This definition follows a statement of financial position approach rather than the more traditional income statement approach to recognizing income.

5. **Expenses**. Expenses are:
• decreases in economic benefits during the accounting period in the form of outflows or depletions of assets or occurrences of liabilities
• transactions that result in decreases in equity, other than those relating to distributions to equity participants.

Recognition of elements of financial statements

Asset is recognized only if it gives right or other access to future economic benefits controlled by an entity as a result of past transactions or events, it can be measured with sufficient reliability and there is sufficient evidence of its existence. A liability will only be recognized if there is an obligation to transfer economic benefits as a result of past transactions or events, it can be measured with sufficient reliability and there is sufficient evidence of its existence.

Income is recognized in the income statement when an increase in future economic benefits arises from an increase in an asset (or a reduction in a liability), and the increase can be measured reliably. Similarly, expenses are recognized in the income statement when a decrease in future economic benefits arises from a decrease in an asset or increase in a liability, and can be measured reliably. As income and expenses are therefore recognized on the basis of changes in assets and liabilities, this is known as a financial position (balance sheet) approach to recognition.

CHAPTER 3

BOOKKEEPING PRINCIPLES

The purpose of this chapter is to explain the main elements of the bookkeeping system which provides this information.

In this chapter, ledger accounts will be introduced and the 'rules' of double entry bookkeeping examined. The process of balancing the ledger accounts and producing a list of account balances will be examined but the actual preparation of financial statements will be dealt with in a later chapter.

By the time you finished this chapter you should be able to:

- Understand the principles of double entry bookkeeping
- Write up simple transactions in the ledger accounts
- Balance off ledger accounts and prepare a trial balance (also called a list of account balances)
- Deal with opening balances in ledger accounts
- Understand the types of error that may occur in bookkeeping systems and whether they are detected by the Trial Balance
- Understand the recording of cash discounts.

The system of recording transactions

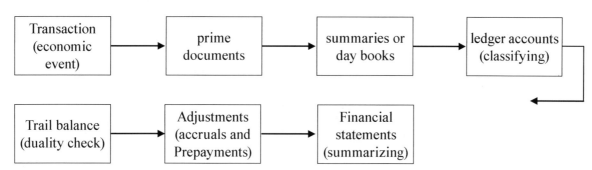

Sequence of events

1. to record the transaction on a prime document
2. to record the prime documents in a day book which is a summary
3. to classify the transactions by entering them into an appropriate ledger account
4. to balance the ledgers at the end of the accounting period – a trial balance
5. to adjust the ledger balances into financial statements. The profit and loss account and the balance sheet.

The main data sources and their function

Whenever a business transaction takes place there is a need to record the transaction on or in a document.

A source document is an individual record of a business transaction-for example, a sales invoice is a formal record of a sale having occurred.

Since financial statements only need to be prepared at set intervals, not every day, the sufficient first stage is to have a sensible system of source documents which can be used as the raw materials for our later entries.

In this section we will examine the type of source documents which exist. Most business transactions revolve around the purchase and sale of goods and services and thus most documents relate to either of these items.

Sales and purchase invoices

A purchase order is an agreement to purchase goods/services from a business. It is prepared by the purchaser.

A sales order is an agreement to sell goods/services to a business. It is prepared by the seller.

A sales or purchase order is normally the first occasion when an intended transaction is put in writing. It does however record an intended rather than an actual transaction and thus a more important document in terms of recording financial transactions is the invoice.

Sales and purchase invoices

When a business sells goods or services to a customer it sends a sales invoice to the customer.

A sales invoice is a formal record of the amount of money due from the customer as a result of the sale transaction.

To the customer, the invoice represents a purchase and thus he will refer to it as a purchase invoice.

The invoice may contain a lot of detailed information about the transactions, e.g.:

- name and address of seller and purchaser
- date of sale reference to order
- description of goods
- amount due
- terms of payment

It is an essential document which provides the information which will be entered into the accounting records of a business.

Credit and debit notes

A credit note records goods returned by a customer or the reduction of monies owed by a customer. The credit not is issued subsequent to a sales invoice and will refer to that invoice. There are many reasons why the original sale may have been incorrect. Faulty goods may have been supplied or the price charged on the invoice was incorrect.

A debit note is sometimes raised by a purchaser of goods and is a formal request for a credit note to be issued by the supplier.

Accounting Records

Summary of stages of accounting

Accounting records are any listing or book which records the transactions of a business in a logical manner. The source documents above are part of the accounting records of a business, but the information contained in them needs to be more clearly laid out. This is achieved by the use of books of prime entry.

The chart below shows the route by which transactions are recorded in the final output of the accounting system: the financial statements.

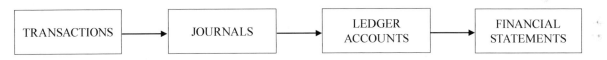

Journals record the similar transactions of each day. They are used as an initial 'store' of information of the business transactions prior to storing the information in the ledger accounts.

A **ledger account** or 'T' account is where all transactions of a similar type are recorded, e.g. all cash transactions or all purchases of non-current assets. Ledger accounts are pages in a book (the ledger) with a separate page reserved for transactions of the same type.

The form of journals will be considered in a later chapter. The important point to note about them for the moment is that their prime function is to list transactions of a common nature and these listing will be used to make further entries in the accounting system.

For example, a sales journal will list all the sales invoices raised by the business, and will contain sufficient information about each sale so that further entries can be made at a convenient later date without having to refer back to the sales invoices.

Initially we will assume journals do not exist as a better understanding of the double entry system used in operating ledger accounts will be obtained. Transactions will thus be entered direct into the ledger accounts.

Ledger accounts and double entry

In the previous chapter, an examination was made of the effect on the balance sheet, day by day of a series of transactions.

All transactions affect the accounting equation and all transactions could, if we wished, be recoded directly by drawing up a balance sheet.

The problem with this approach is that it becomes cumbersome in a practical situation involving a large number of transactions. In practice, therefore, it is necessary to summarize all categories of transactions so that the balance sheet need only be produced at intervals of, say, twelve months. The approach used is called the **double entry** system of bookkeeping. This involves the use of journals and ledger accounts.

Theory of Double Entry

As has been shown, every transaction affects two items in the balance sheet. To follow the rules of double entry, every time a transaction is recorded, both aspects must be taken into account.

Traditionally, one aspect is referred to as the debit side of the entry (abbreviated to Dr) and the other as the credit side of the entry (abbreviated to Cr).

Ledger accounts Format

Each aspect is recorded in the relevant ledger account. Any business of reasonable size will have a large number of accounts. Each account has two sides-the **debit side** and the **credit side**.

Ledger account

		K			K
Debit side (Dr)			Credit side (Cr)		
Date	Detail	Amount	Date	Detail	Amount

Note:

1. Remember that by tradition, debit is on the left-hand side, and credit is on the right-hand side.
2. Date refers to the period when the transaction took place

3. Detail refers to the other account where the same information is found. This is key when checking for errors.
4. Amount refers to the monetary value of the transaction
5. For each transaction there is need to identify which two accounts are involved and which one should be debited and which one should be credited.
6. To decide which account is to be debited and which one to be credited use the rule *'Debit the receiving account and credit the giving account'*.
7. Where cash is involved matters are simplified. If the business receives cash the cash account is debited and the other account—the paying account-is credited. Similarly, if the business pays out cash, the cash account is credited and the other account-the receiving account-is debited.
8. It is important know that certain accounts have entries on one side only always. For example, sales account always has entries on the credit side while purchases account has entries on the debit side only. Check for details under the heading preparing a trial balance without ledger accounts given later.

The ledger account is usually set out in practice in three columns thus:

	Debit	Credit	Balance
	K	K	K

However, for examination purposes the 'two-sided' ledger account or T—account illustrated above is more convenient and is what is recommended.

Debit and credit and the format of ledger accounts

In bookkeeping, the terms 'debit' and 'credit' have bookkeeping. Here is a table to explain them.

Entries on the DEBIT side	Entries on the CREDIT side
Assets	Liabilities
Expenses	Income
Losses	Profits

One fundamental ledger account in a bookkeeping system is the **cash account**, recording cash received and paid by the business. The balance of cash in hand, being an asset, is on the debit side of the cash account. If we spend some of this cash, this could be for three reasons:

- to buy an asset
- to pay an expense
- to repay a debt or liability

The bookkeeping entry to record a payment of cash is on the **credit** side of the cash account (reducing the cash balance) and on the debit side of the account recording the other aspect of the transaction:

To buy an asset	Debit the asset account to record the fact that we have more of the asset concerned.
To pay an expense	Debit the expense account to record the fact that we have paid the expense
To repay a debt or liability	Debit the liability account to record the fact that we owe less as a result of the payment

The example which follows shows the procedure in action. Note the format of the ledger account, with columns for the date and the details of the transaction.

Drawing up ledger accounts

In practicing the following examples, provide plenty of space between the ledger accounts so that the entries can be made. It is essential that the examples are practiced by opening ledger accounts and writing down the entries. In this way the practice and theory of double entry will be more quickly understood.

Also allow a full page width for each ledger account. This will enable narrative and figures to be clearly written and also emphasize the 'left-hand 'and right-hand' nature of the entries.

Example

The following information relates to the twelve days transaction for John Banda. You are required to prepare the relevant ledger accounts.

Day 1   John commences in business introducing K1, 000 cash.
Day 2   Buys a motor car for K400 cash
Day 3   buys goods for K200 cash
Day 4   Sells all the goods bought on Day 3 for K300 cash
Day 5   Buys goods for K400 on credit
Day 6   Sells half of the goods bought on Day 5 on credit for K250.
Day 7   Pays K200 to his supplier
Day 8   Receives K100 from a customer
Day 9   Proprietor draws K75 in cash
Day 10   Pays rent of K40 in cash

Day 11   Receives a loan of K600 repayable in two years
Day 12   Pays cash of K30 for insurance

Solution

Day 1

John introduced cash of K1, 000 into the business. What are the two aspects of this transaction? Quite clearly cash (an asset) is increased and so are the claims of the proprietor (his capital). As this is new business we must open up ledger accounts for cash and capital.

The cash account has the debit entry and the capital account has the credit entry.

Cash account

Date	Details	K	Date	Details	K
(1)	Capital	1,000			

Capital account

Date	Details	K	Date	Details	K
			(1)	Cash	1,000

Note that the items (1) refer to the date of the transaction. The details refer to the other account that is being debited or credited.

On the cash account, the receipt of K1, 000 is by convention entered on the left-hand side (the debit side) and its description 'capital' indicates where the other side of the double entry (the aspect of the transaction) may be found. In the capital account, K1, 000 appears on the right-hand side (the credit side) and the description 'cash' shows where the other side of the double entry may be found.

Whenever a business receives cash there is a debit entry made in the cash account.

Day 2

On this day the business purchases a motor car (which is a non-current asset) for cash. The payment of cash is a credit in the cash account and the other side of the double entry is a debit in the motor car account. Using the cash account already opened, the transaction appears as follows:

Cash account

Date	Details	K	Date	Details	K
(1)	Capital	1,000	(2)	Motor car	400

Motor car account

Date	Details	K	Date	Details	K
(2)	Cash	400			

Whenever a business pays out cash there is a credit entry made in the cash account.

An asset (or an increase in an asset) is always a debit entry.

Day 3

The purchase of goods on Day 3 is a cash purchase and so the cash account is credited.

So which is debited? The temptation may well be to answer 'inventory, of course', but this would be wrong. Inventory is refers to goods purchased for resale. For the moment the thing to remember is that it is the purchases account which is debited.

Cash account

Date	Details	K	Date	Details	K
(1)	Capital	1,000	(2)	Motorcar	400
			(3)	Purchases	200

Purchases account

Date	Details	K	Date	Details	K
(3)	Cash	200			

The purchases account contains items which are held for resale by the business or are raw materials which will be used to manufacture goods.

Day 4

The sale of goods for cash involves a receipt of cash and thus a debit to the cash account. What then is credited? Again the answer is not inventory but sales revenue account.

Cash account

Date	Details	K	Date	Details	K
(1)	Capital	1,000	(2)	Motor car	400
(4)	Sales revenue	300	(3)	Purchases	200

Sales revenue account

Date	Details	K	Date	Details	K
			(4)	Cash	300

The sales revenue account collects the sales that have been made by the business during the period.

Income to the business is always a credit entry

The effect of having a separate sales revenue and purchases accounts is that profit is not computed when each sale is made. As many sales are being made each day, it is not practical to compute profit on each transaction. Profit is instead calculated at the end of the period.

Day 5

This produces a minor problem: cash is not involved!

The transaction involves a purchase of goods (as did the Day 3 transaction), purchases accounts is therefore debited. But what is credited? The answer is a liability account for the supplier of the goods. The credit on his account represents a liability to him. We normally refer to amounts due to creditors as' accounts payable' or 'payable'

Purchases account

Date	Details	K	Date	Details	K
(3)	Cash	200			
(5)	Accounts payable	400			

Accounts payable

Date	Details	K	Date	Details	K
			(5)	Purchases	400

A liability (or an increase in a liability) is always a credit entry.

Day 6

A similar problem now arises. The transaction is a sale (like Day 4), so the sale revenue accounts, representing all the sales taking place in the period, is credited.

The debit side of the double entry goes to a debtors account. Debtors are assets-they represent amounts owing to the business, i.e. promises to pay cash at some future date. We normally refer to amounts due from debtors as 'accounts receivable' or 'receivables'.

Sales revenue account

Date	Details	K	Date	Details	K
			(4)	Cash	300
			(6)	Accounts receivable	250

Accounts receivable

Date	Details	K	Date	Details	K
(6)	Sales revenue	250			

The information about only half of the goods being sold does not concern us at this stage. At the end of the period when the financial statements are drawn up, account will be taken of any closing inventory (representing unsold goods).

Day 7

What about payment of K200 to the account payable? What effect does this have? The two aspects are, firstly, that the asset cash is reduced (a credit) and, secondly, that liabilities or amounts owing are reduced (debit to account payable).

Cash account

Date	Details	K	Date	Details	K
(1)	Capital	1,000	(2)	Motor car	400
(4)	Sales revenue	300	(3)	Purchases	200
			(7)	Accounts payable	200

Accounts payable

Date	Details	K	Date	Details	K
(7)	Cash	200	(5)	Purchases	400

Day 8

The receipt of K100 from a debtor increases the asset cash (debit cash) and reduces the asset accounts receivable (credit accounts receivable).

Cash account

Date	Details	K	Date	Details	K
(1)	Capital	1,000	(2)	Motor Car	400
(4)	Sales revenue	300	(3)	Purchases	200
(8)	Accounts receivable	100	(7)	Accounts payable	200

Accounts receivable

Date	Details	K	Date	Details	K
(6)	Sales revenue	250	(8)	Cash	100

Day 9

Drawings of cash must clearly be credited to cash. The debit side of the double entry should be taken to a drawings account.

Cash account

Date	Details	K	Date	Details	K
(1)	Capital	1,000	(2)	Motor car	400
(4)	Sales revenue	300	(3)	Purchases	200
(8)	Accounts receivable	100	(7)	Accounts payable	200
			(9)	Drawings	75

Drawings account

Date	Details	K	Date	Details	K
(9)	Cash	75			

Day 11

The loan represents a receipt of cash (debit cash). But the business now owes K600 to a third party (i.e. a liability). A loan account must be credited. Note that a separate account should be open for each liability (i.e. each third party).

Cash account

Date	Details	K	Date	Details	K
(1)	Capital	1,000	(2)	Motor car	400
(4)	Sales revenue	300	(3)	Purchases	200
(8)	Accounts receivable	100	(7)	Accounts payable	200
(11)	Loan	600	(9)	Drawings	75

Days 10 and 12

The payments of rent and insurance represents expenditure. Cash is credited and the respective expense accounts debited.

Cash account

Date	Details	K	Date	Details	K
(1)	Capital	1,000	(2)	Motor car	400
(4)	Sales revenue	300	(3)	Purchases	200
(8)	Accounts receivable	100	(7)	Accounts payable	200
(11)	Loan	600	(9)	Drawings	75
			(10)	Rent	40
			(12)	Insurance	30

Rent account

Date	Details	K	Date	Details	K
(10)	Cash	30			

DR. CRYFORD MUMBA

An expenses account collects the costs of the various expenses of running the business. These expenses eventually find their way to the income statement.

Expenses of the business are always a debit entry.

Final ledger accounts

The final ledger accounts would appear as follows:

(Note: the totals in brackets are there merely for convenience later in the chapter. They form no part of the double entry).

Capital account

Date	Details	K	Date	Details	K
			(1)	Cash	1,000

Cash account

Date	Details	K	Date	Details	K
(1)	Capital	1,000	(2)	Motor car	400
(4)	Sales revenue	300	(3)	Purchases	200
(8)	Accounts receivable	100	(7)	Accounts payable	200
(11)	Loan	600	(9)	Drawings	75
			(10)	Rent	40
			(12)	Insurance	30
		(Total K2, 000)			(Total K945)

Motor car account

Date	Details	K	Date	Details	K
(2)	Cash	200			

Purchases account

Date	Details	K	Date	Details	K
(3)	Cash	200			
(5)	Accounts payable	400			
	(Total K600)				

Sales revenue account

Date	Details	K	Date	Details	K
			(4)	Cash	300
			(6)	Accounts receivable	250
					(Total K550)

Accounts payable (for each supplier)

Date	Details	K	Date	Details	K
(7)	Cash	200	(5)	Purchases	400

Accounts receivable (for each customer)

Date	Details	K	Date	Details	K
(6)	Sales revenue	250	(8)	Cash	100

Drawings account

Date	Details	K	Date	Details	K
(9)	Cash	75			

Rent account

Date	Details	K	Date	Details	K
(9)	Cash	40			

Loan account

Date	Details	K	Date	Details	K
			(11)	Cash	600

Insurance account

Date	Details	K	Date	Details	K
(12)	Cash	30			

Summarize the debit and the credit entries for each of the transactions that John made.

Can you draw any general conclusions regarding the entries to be made for assets, liabilities, income and expenses?

Asset, liability, revenue and expense accounts

The above activity should provide some clues as to the distinction between asset, liability, revenue and expense accounts.

An **asset account** collects information about particular assets of a business. It mainly consists of debit entries.

A **liability account** collects information about particular liabilities of a business. It mainly consists of credit entries.

Asset and liability accounts appear on the balance sheet at the end of the accounting period.

An **expense account** collects information about particular costs of a business. It mainly consists of debit entries.

A **revenue account** collects information about particular income of a business. It mainly consists of credit entries.

Revenue and expense are transferred to the income statement in order to compute profit for a period. The only revenue account we have come across so far is the sales account.

We will see later that some revenue/expense accounts will also record assets and liabilities – known as accruals and prepayments.

Usefulness of cash

Only a combination of experience and bought will provide familiarity with double entry techniques. Even experienced accountants occasionally have to ask which account is credited!

It was clear in the previous illustration how useful cash was in establishing one side of the double entry. If cash was received, then cash account was debited and it was a question of deciding what had to be credited. Conversely, a payment of cash involved a credit to cash account and it was then a question of deciding in which ledger account the debit was to appear.

The Trial Balance

The nature and purpose of a trial balance

The large number of transactions recorded in ledger accounts means that there is the possibility of errors occurring. Periodically some assurance is required as to the accuracy of the procedures. This can be done by listing all the balances. In the case of a moderate-sized business, although final accounts will usually be prepared annually, a trial balance will be extracted at more frequent intervals (say, monthly).

A trial balance is simply a memorandum listing of all the ledger account balances. In an accounting context 'memorandum' means that the listing is not a part of the double entry.

If the double entry procedures have been carefully followed, then the trial balance should show that the total of the debit balances agrees with the total of the credit balances, because every transaction has been recorded by means of a debit entry and a credit entry. Thus, the purpose of a trial balance is to check the accuracy of double entry bookkeeping principles.

Format of the trial balance

Illustrated below is the format of a trial balance.

Account Name	Debit	Credit
	K	K
.Cash		X
.capital		X
.purchases	X	
.debtors	X	
.rent	X	
.Salaries	X	
.sales		X
.creditors		X
Total	X	X

Preparing a trial balance from ledger accounts

Before a trial balance can be drawn up, the ledger accounts must be balanced

Where there are several entries in a ledger account, the computation of the balance of the ledger account to go onto the list of account balances can be shown in the ledger account by **carrying down** and **bringing down** a balance.

The procedure is as follows:

Add up the total debits and credits in the account and make a (memorandum) note of the totals.

Insert the higher total at the bottom of both the debits and credits, leaving one line for the inclusion of a **balance c/d** (carried down).

The totals should be level with each other and underlined.

Insert on the side which has the lower arithmetical total, the narrative 'balance c/d' and an amount which brings the arithmetical total to the total that has been inserted under step 2 above.

The same figure is shown on the other side of the ledger account but underneath the totals. This is the **balance b/d** (brought down).

The opening balance c/d is known as the **closing balance**. The balance b/d is known as the **opening balance**.

Example

The cash account from the example John Banda is reproduced below:

Cash account

		K			K
(1)	Capital	1,000	(2)	Motor car	400
(4)	Sales revenue	300	(3)	Purchases	200
(8)	Accounts receivable	100	(7)	Accounts payable	200
(11)	Loan	600	(9)	Drawings	75
			(10)	Rent	40
			(12)	Insurance	30
	(Total K2, 000)			(Total K945)	

Step 1

The arithmetic totals have already been computed

Step 2

The higher total is inserted, K2, 000.

Cash account

		K			K
(1)	Capital	1,000	(2)	Motor car	400
(4)	Sales revenue	300	(3)	Purchases	200
(8)	Accounts receivable	100	(7)	Accounts payable	200
(11)	Loan	600	(10)	Drawings	75
			(10)	Rent	40
			(12)	Insurance	30
		2,000			2,000

Note that credits do not yet add up to K2, 000

Steps 3 and 4

Insert the balances b/d and c/d. The balance can be found from the arithmetical totals K2, 000 – K945 = K1, 055.

Cash account

		K			K
(1)	Capital	1,000	(2)	Motor car	400
(4)	Sales revenue	300	(3)	Purchases	200
(8)	Accounts receivable	100	(7)	Accounts payable	200
(11)	Loan	600	(9)	Drawings	75
			(10)	Rent	40
			(12)	Insurance	30
				Balance c/d	1,055
		2,000			2,000
	Balance b/d	1,055			

The K1, 055 is known as a debit balance because the b/d figure is on the debit side of the account, i.e. the debit entries in the account before it was totaled must have exceeded the credit entries by that amount. This balance means that there is K1, 055 cash left within the business at the end of the period and also at the beginning of the next period.

The carrying down of balances causes problems to some students. However, if the procedure is practiced it soon becomes second nature. It is helpful to have a clear mental picture of the form of a ledger account when practicing examples.

Balance off the remaining ledger accounts in the example of John.

(Note that where there is only one entry in an account, there is no necessity to carry out the balancing procedure as this one entry is the balance c/d and the balance b/d.)

Once the ledger accounts have all been balanced, a trial balance can be drawn up. This is done by listing each of the ledger account names in the business's books showing against each name the balance on that account and whether that balance is a debit or a credit balance brought down. Note that it is the balance brought down which determines whether the account is said to have a debit or credit balance. Naturally, if b/d is on the credit side of the respective account, then that account will have a credit entry in the trial balance. Similarly, if b/d is on debit side that account will have a debit entry in the trial balance.

Example

Continuing the example of John, prepare his trial balance at the end of Day 12.

Solution

John's Trial Balance at the end of Day 12

Account	Debit K	Credit K
Capital		1,000
Cash	1,055	
Motor car	400	
Purchases	600	
Sale revenue		550
Accounts payable		200
Accounts receivable	150	
Drawings by proprietor	75	
Rent	40	
Loan		600
Insurance	30	
	2,350	2,350

Preparing a trial balance without ledger accounts

There are times when you are asked to extract a trial balance from the list of account balances but without having to prepare and balance of the ledger accounts. In such a situation all that is required is to have a working knowledge regarding which side of a trial balance a given item is recorded. For example, sales are always recorded as a credit entry in the trial balance. The following guide can be helpful in this exercise.

1. All overheard expenses are debit entries in the trial balance. This makes logical sense because when an expense is paid the cash account is credited. Which account then must be debited? Certainly it has to be the respective expense account. The same applies whether an expense is paid by cheque or by cash.
2. Sales, depreciation, discount received, capital, provision for doubtful debts, bank, purchase returns are all credit entries in the trial balance.
3. Debtors, drawings, purchases, returns inwards, discount allowed, stock, bad debts are all debit entries.

Different accounting groups: RECAL

The five distinct accounting groups are identified by the acronym 'RECAL' which stand for:

1. Revenue—this represents income earned by a business when it sells its goods or services.
2. Expenses—these are the day to costs of running a business, e.g. wages, advertising postage etc.
3. Capital—this represents owner's investment in the business.
4. Assets—these are things of value owned by the business, e.g. premises, stock, equipment etc.
5. Liabilities—these are things of value that the business owes.

General recordings

Account Group	To increase the account	To decrease the account
Revenue	Credit	Debit
Expenses	Debit	Credit
Capital	Credit	Debit
Assets	Debit	Credit
Liabilities	Credit	Debit

Finally, I must mention that with practice you will have no problems whatsoever regarding the above. So check the following example and them practice.

Example

The following balances were extracted from the ledger of Stanford Simuuba who operates a hardware retail shop at Mtendere Market in Lusaka on 31st December, 2011

	K'000
Cash in hand	10 800
Cash at bank	38 790
Petty cash at hand	1 350
Stock (1st January 2011)	54 000
Motor vehicles	270 000
Sundry debtors	147 150
Sundry creditors	119 340
Purchases	351 900
Purchase returns	14 400
Sales	789 300

Sales returns	15 300
Carriage inwards	6 750
Carriage outwards	7 875
Discount received	15 750
Discount allowed	12 600
Rent and rates	36 000
Wages and salaries	162 000
Printing and stationery	33 300
Drawings	22 500
Telephone and telegraph	5 625
Office equipment	90 000
Furniture	67 000
Electricity	6 525
Water	1 575
Bank charges	540
Insurance	16 200
Motor expenses	25 200
General office expenses	19,350
Capital	?
Stock(31st December, 2011)	102 150

Required:

Using the above details extract a trial balance for Mr. Simuuba as at 31st December, 2011.
Solution
Note that closing stock i.e. stock at 31st December, 2011 must never appear in the trial balance.

STANFORD SIMUUBA
TRIAL BALANCE AS AT 31ST DECEMBER 2011

	Dr	Cr
	K'000	k'000
Cash in hand	10 800	
Cash at bank	38 790	
Petty cash in hand	1 350	
Stock(1st January 2011)	54 000	
Motor vehicles	90 000	
Furniture	270 000	
Office equipment	67 000	
Sundry debtors/creditors	147 150	119,340

Purchases	351 900	
Purchase returns		14,400
Sales		789,300
Sales returns	15 300	
Carriage inwards	6 750	
Carriage outwards	7 875	
Discount allowed	12 600	
Discount received		15 750
Rent and rates	36 000	
Wages and salaries	162 000	
Printing and stationery	33 300	
Drawings	22 500	
Telephone and telegraph	5 625	
Electricity	6 525	
Water	1 575	
Bank charges	540	
Insurance	16 200	
Motor expenses	25 200	
General office expenses	19 350	
Capital		464 040
	1 402 830	1 402 830

Note: Capital figure is found as a balancing figure so that total debit equal total credits. Further the closing stock figure i.e. stock at 31st December must never appear in the trial balance.

Errors not revealed by the trial balance

The fact that two totals agree may be reassuring but it is not final proof that the accounts are correct! It is possible for certain types of error to occur and yet the overall effect is that the list of balances still appears to balance.

To 'post' amounts to a ledger account means to write the amount up in the ledger accounts.

Such errors include:

1. **Errors of omission** where no entry of a transaction has been made at all.

2. **Errors of commission** where an amount has been correctly posted but to the wrong account, although it is the right type of account, e.g. John Banda, a customer, pays K50 by cheque which is debited to the cash book and then in error posted to the credit of the account of James Banda, another customer.

Although there will have been a debit and a credit, nevertheless the account of James Banda shows a credit balance of K50 higher than it should be, while the account of John Banda is also K50 out.

3. **Errors of principle** this occurs where an item is incorrectly classified by the bookkeeper and posted to the wrong type of account, e.g. the sale of surplus office equipment has been classified as sales of goods.

4. **Errors of entry** this occurs where an incorrect amount if posted to both the accounts in question, e.g. K2.00 is misread as K200 and so entered on both debit and credit sides of the correct accounts

Some accountants refer to this error as an error of original entry as it often arises due to the entry originally being recorded in a journal (see later) at the wrong amount.

5. **Compensating errors** these occur where two or more errors cancel out each other. They are difficult to locate and fortunately tend not to occur frequently.

6. **Reversal entry** where the debits and the credits of a posting have been reversed. For example, debiting the cash account and crediting the cash book following a sale of a product.

PROGRESS CLINIC 3

Question 1

In each of the following five (5) transactions, identify the Account to be debited and also the Account to be credited.

   a) Bought motor van for cash

   b) Bought office machinery on credit from James Gwaba & Sons.

   c) Introduced additional capital in cash

   d) A debtor, Mailesi Banda pays us by cheque

   e) Paid a creditor, Mr Aaron Muleya in cash.

CHAPTER 4

ADJUSTMENTS TO THE FINAL ACCOUNTS

Accruals, Prepayments and Drawings

Adjustment to the final accounts are required because any transaction which specifically belongs to an accounting period whether paid or incurred (due to be paid) part of what is called the accruals capital in accounting for example if a business owed wages at K2500 at the end of the year, this must be included in the accounts for the year. Similarly if an expense was paid in advance of the accounting period the sum prepaid would be deducted from the accounts at the end of the year. These adjustments are part of the matching concept in accounting which attempts to match as exactly as possible earned in one period with the expenses incurred in the same period in order to arrive at a true assessment of profit or loss

Types of adjustments

The major types that are usually indicated as note to the accounts after the trial balance are:

Types	Meaning
Closing stock	Values of stock
Accrued expenses	Expenses still owing
Prepaid expense	Expense paid in advance
Revenue accrued	Income owed to the business
Revenue prepaid	Income paid in advance
Owner's drawings	Value taken for personal

Each of these adjustments will have a two-fold effect on the final accounts namely.
●They are included in the Trading and Profit and Loss Account because they affect the profit or loss for the period.

●They are included in the Balance Sheet because they affect the value of assets, liabilities or capital.

How these adjustments affect the Profit and Loss Account and the Balance Sheet is shown below:

Types of adjustment	Profit and loss account	Balance sheet
Closing stock	Reduce cost of goods	Current asset
Accrued expenses	Increase expense	Current liabilities
Prepaid expense	Reduce expense	Current asset
Revenue prepaid	Reduce revenues	Current liability

| Revenue accrued | Increase revenues | Current asset |
| Owner's drawings | Reduce expenses | Reduce capital |

FURTHER ADJUSTMENTS

Bad debts and provision for bad debts

Any business that offers credit to its customers and therefore create account receivable (debtor) must make every effort to ensure that debts are paid. This, for businesses particularly means having an effective credit control section which has the responsibility of ensuring debtors pay their bills in reasonable time as guided by the invoice date.

Accounts must be monitored on a regular basis and customer chased up if they are late in making their payments. Inevitably a large number of businesses do have to write off some of their customers at one time or another. This is costly to a business because an account receivable (asset) has to be written off as an expense. The double entry to write off the debtor is:

Debit: bad debts account (expense)
Credit: The debtor's account (asset)

Types of adjustments

The following adjustments are made in relation to debtors' accounts.

(1) provision for bad debts
(2) recovery of bad debts
(3) provision for cash discounts

Each of these adjustments affects the Profits and Loss Account and the Balance Sheet as follows:

Types of adjustment	Profit and loss account	Balance sheet
Create provision for bad debts	Increase expense	Debtors – provision
Increased provision for bad debts	Increase in expenses	Debtors – provision
Reduce provision for bad debts	Reduce expenses	Debtors – provision
Recovery of bad debts	Reduce expense	Increase bank
Create provision for discounts	Increase expense	Debtors – provision
Increase provision for discounts	Increase expense	Debtors – provision
Reduce provision for discount	Reduce expense	Debtors – provision

Note that to create a provision refers to making a start and entering a provision account in the nominal ledge, there after these provision can be increased or decreased according to the level of debtors and amount to be provided. When a provision for bad debts or discount is reduced, the expense is reduced thereby reducing the firm to be deducted from debtors in the balance sheet.

Examples

Provisions

On 31 December it was decided to make a 10% provision for bad debts against Mr. Chimbwali's debtors figure of K850,000. This creates an expense against the Profit and Loss Account and a new account is opened in the nominal ledger. The double entry is

Dr: P & L account K85 000 (expenses increase)
Cr: Provision for bad debts account K85, 000 (asset decrease)

Profit and Loss Account Extract (year 1)

Expenses:	K	K
Provision for bad debts		85000

Balance sheet extract (year 1)

Current assets:	K	K
Debtors	850 000	
Less provision for bad debts	(85000)	765000

Nominal ledger

	Dr	Cr	Balance
Provision for bad debt			
Year 1			
31.12 P and L A/c account		85000	85 000 Cr
Year 2			
1/ 1 balance			85 000 Cr

Example 2

At the end of 31 December in year 2, Harrison had the following information

- Bad debts written off K135,000
- Debtors K1550,000
- 10% provision for debt is to be maintained

Profit and Loss Account Extract at the end of year 2

Expenses:	K	K
Bad debt	135,000	
Less provision for bad debts	70,000	205,000

Balance Sheet extract for (year 2)

Current assets:	K	K
Debtors	1550,000	
Less provision for bad debts	(155,000)	1395,000

Note: that 10% of debtors equal K155,000 but only K70,000 need to be charged to the Profit and Loss Account as K85,000 is already credited to that account, in this way the provision for bad debts account is adjusted each year and balances considered to be doubtful or unreliable.

Transfer of bad debts to provision for bad debts

Alternatively the bad debts account at the end of the period. After all the provision account is a firm set aside to cover any bad debts that might occur in the future so it would be logical to make this transfer.

The recovery of bad debts

If the event of the customer paying back a debt which had previously being written off either in part payment or in full, the debt must first be reinstated in the customer's sales ledger or account. It is important to do this because the record will then show that the customer did in fact honour the debt at some future point in time. Once the check have been recovered and balanced, the posting to the ledger account clear the debt. The procedure for this type of transaction is as follows.

Reinstate the debt

Dr: customer's accounts with amount received/recovered
Cr: bad debts account

Bank the amount received

Dr: Bank account
Cr: Customer's account (sale ledger account)

Provision for debtor's discounts

If it is the policy of the business to allow customer to have cash discount on their sales it may be seen as prudent to make an appropriate provision for it in the same way as providing for bad and doubtful debts. The amount of provision for discounts is therefore.

Dr: P and L account (an expense)
Cr: provision for discounts allowed accounts (negative assets)

It should be noted that the provision for discount must always be calculated on the net value of debtors, that is, after deducting the provision for bad debts. The balance sheet will then indicate the gross debtors figure less both provisions for discount and bad debts. The provision for discounts allowed to customer may then be adjusted each year in relation to the amount of discount allowed ant the provision for bad debts.

The following are the key points relating to adjustments for bad debts and provision for debtors.

(1) **Bad debts** –this is debtor which is written off as unable to pay

(2) **Provision for bad debts** – this is a charge against profits to cover any possible bad debts

(3) **Bad debts recovered** – this is a former bad debtor who pays either the full sum of part sum which meaning written off.

(4) **Provision for discounts** – this is the charge against profits to cover an cash discount assets to debtors always made asset the provision key bad debtors to have been deducted from debtors.

(5) **Credit control** – this is the internal control of debtors to ensure their bills are paid within target debt.

(6) **Aged debtors list** – this a list of debtors indicated the age of debts usually in month order.

(7) **Credit rating** – this indicate hoe reliable the customer is in relation to paying debtors.

ADJUSTMENTS TO ACCOUNTS: A DETAILED ANALYSIS

1. **Prepayments**. These are expenses that have been paid in advance. Where a proportion of an expense, such as rent has been paid in advance (prepaid), this must be allowed for when the final accounts are drawn up. For example, if he firm paid K12 million rent for six months from 1 October, and the final accounts are made out for the year

ended 31 December, it would obviously wrong to debit the income statement with the full amount of K12 million. Only three months' rent should be debited, i.e. k6 million and the other three months' rent, i.e. K6 million should be carried forward and shown in the balance sheet as an asset, "Rent paid in advance".

. In the income statement the prepaid amount is subtracted from the respective expense recorded in the trial balance. In the above illustration, we will subtract k3 million from the rent figure in the trail balance.

. In the balance sheet, all the prepayments for the period will be added together and recorded as a current asset under the title 'prepayments'. In the above illustration, K3 million will be added to any other prepaid expense for the period and recorded as a current asset.

The above remarks apply equally to any other sum paid in advance, such as insurance premiums, rates, salaries and so no. This is in line with the matching concept in accounting.

2. **Accruals**. These are expenses which have been incurred but not yet paid for. It is often the case that a firm, at the end of the trading period, has incurred expenses which have not yet been paid (i.e. have accrued). For example, where rent is not payable in advance, a proportion of the rent for the period may be owing when the final accounts are drawn up. How is this to be accounted for?

   Obviously, the income statement will be debited with rent already paid, and it must also be debited with that proportion of the rent which is due to be paid. Having debited the income statement with this latter proportion, we must credit the rent account with it. The rent account will the show a credit balance and this must appear as a liability on the balance sheet – it is a debt owing by the business. Then, when this proportion of rent owing is paid, cash will be credited and rent account debited.

   . In the income statement the accrued amount is added to the respective expense recorded in the trial balance.

   . In the balance sheet all the accrued expenses for the period are added together and recorded as a current liability under the title "accruals".

3. **Stock.** The stock shown under the trial balance is the closing stock. Naturally, businesses will always have unsold stock at the end of the financial period. How should this be accounted for in the final accounts?

   . In the income statement it is used to calculate the cost of goods sold. It is subtracted from the purchases figure.

   . In the balance sheet, it is recorded as a current asset under the title 'stock or inventory'.

4. **Depreciation**. Depreciation is defined as the loss of value of fixed assets over time due to tear and wear. Assets such as plant and machinery, delivery vehicles, factory buildings, are used directly in the manufacture of goods or in trading, and as a result of this, their value must decrease owing to wear and tear. This decrease in value must be allowed for when overheard charges are being debited to the income statement.

Each year the depreciation account will increase in value, until such time as the balance on that account equals the cost price in the asset account. At this point no further depreciation should be charged to the income statement.

Depreciation of such assets as furniture must also be allowed for in the income statement. Where there is a profit or loss on the disposal of a fixed asset, this is shown in the income statement immediately after the expense of depreciation.

There are two commonly used methods for calculating depreciation namely;

(a) **Straight line method**. Under this method depreciation is calculated as a fixed percentage of the cost price of the fixed asset. It charges the same amount from one year to the next.

(b) **Reducing balance method**. Under this method depreciation is calculated as a fixed percentage of the net book value of the fixed asset. Net Book Value (NBV) is the difference between the cot and the depreciation charge shown in the trial balance. The amount of depreciation varies from year to year because NBV is not constant.

How should depreciation be accounted for in the final accounts?

● In the income statement, it is the depreciation charge for the year which is recorded as an expense of the business. It is usually recorded as the last expense in the income statement.

● In the balance sheet, it is the cumulative depreciation which is recorded and subtracted from the cost of fixed assets to arrive at the net book value of the fixed asset. Note that cumulative depreciation is the sum of the depreciation charge for the year plus depreciation charge shown in the trial balance.

The accounting treatment of depreciation is very important when it comes to preparing financial statements. You have to make sure you understand the mechanics involved in its calculation.

5. **Provision for bad debts**. If all the trade receivables of a firm paid their accounts, no mention of this item would be made. Unfortunately, they do not, and many firms incur what is known as bad debts. For instance, where a debtor is declared a bankrupt, the whole of his debt will not be settled. Consequently, the unsettled amount of debt is of no value, and it must be written off as loss. Similarly, if debtors disappear, or if their debts are not worth the trouble of court action, the debts must be written off.

The debtor's account is credited with the amount of bad debt, thus closing the account. To complete the double entry, the bad debts account is debited. All bad debts incurred during the trading period are debited to the bad debts account.

At the end of the trading period the bad debts account is credited with the total bad debts, to close the account. The double entry is preserved by debiting the income statement with the same amount. Bad debts are an expense of the business.

In addition to writing off bad debts as they occur or when they are known to be bad, a business should also provide for any losses it may incur in future as a result of its present trade receivables being unable to meet their obligations. If a business has book debts totaling K100 million, it is not very likely that all those trade receivables will pay their accounts in full. Some of the debts may prove to be bad, but this may not be known for some considerable time.

The amount of the provision should be determined by a careful examination of the list of trade receivables at the balance sheet date. If any of these debts is bad, it should be estimated how much a debtor is likely to pay. The balance of his debt is potentially bad, and the provision should be the total of such potential bad debts. The debtor's account will not, however, be written off until it definitely known that it is bad.

The provision for bad debts is formed for the purpose of reducing the value of trade receivables on the balance sheet to an amount which is expected will be received from them. It is not an estimate of bad debts which will arise in the succeeding period. Bad debts arising in the next period will result from credit sales made within that period as well as debit bad debts outstanding at the beginning of the period. It is therefore quite incorrect to debit bad debts against the provision for bad debts. Once the latter account has been opened, the only alteration in it is that required to increase or decrease its balance—by debit or credit to the income statement. The alteration is included as a financial expense when a debit.

- In the income statement, it is the increase or decrease in the provision which is recorded as an expense of the business.
- In the balance sheet, it is the full provision which is subtracted from the debtors figure. Never show provision for bad debts with the liabilities on the balance sheet – it is always deducted from the amount of trade receivables under the current assets on the balance sheet.

6. **Provision for discounts.** There are usually two discount accounts, one for discounts received and the other for discounts allowed. The former is a credit balance and the latter a debit balance. At the end of the trading period, discount received is debited and the income statement credited, as items under this heading are benefits received by the firm. Discount received is, therefore, source of revenue for the firm.

   If a business allows discount to its customers for prompt payment, it is likely that some of the trade receivables at the balance sheet date will actually pay less than the full amount of their debt. To include trade receivables at the face value of such debts, without providing for discounts which may be claimed, is to overstate the financial position of the business. So, a provision for discounts allowable should be made by debit to the income statement. If made on a percentage basis, it should be reckoned in relation to potentially good debts, i.e. trade receivables less provision for bad debts, for if it is thought that a debt is sufficiently doubtful for a provision to be raised against it, it is hardly likely that that debtor will pay his account promptly and claim discount!

   - In the income statement, discount received is recorded under other income immediately after the gross profit. Discount allowed is an expense of the business.
   - In the balance sheet, the provision for discount allowed appears as a deduction from trade receivables after the provision for bad debts has been deducted. This is very important to take note of.

7. **Drawings**. Drawings are the withdrawals of cash or goods or services from the business by the partner or sole trader. Drawings are not expenses of the business and must not, therefore, be debited to the income statement.

   - In the income statement, drawings of stock is used to calculate the cost of goods sold. It is, therefore subtracted from the purchases figure just like closing stock.

- In the balance sheet, the stock drawings is added to cash drawings and the total is subtracted from the capital under the financed by section of the balance sheet.

8. **Accrued revenue**. Accrued revenue is income which has already been worked for by the business but has not yet been received by it. It is the opposite of the accrued expense defined in point 2 above.
   - In the income statement, accrued revenue is added to the respective revenue such as discount received, commission received, rent received, interest received, and so on which are recorded under the heading 'other revenue' immediately after gross profit.
   - In the balance sheet, the accrued revenue appears as a current asset.

9. **Prepaid revenue,** Prepaid revue is income that has been received by the business before doing the work for the customer. For example, a customer may pay for goods to be supplied later by the business. This is a common scenario, especially for those companies that have offices to lease where tenants pay in advance. Quite alright, this income still belongs to the tenant until service provision is done. Now how should this be accounted for?
   - In the income statement it reduces revenue expected from customers. For example, a customer who is required to pay say, K2 000 000 rent per annum but pays K15 000 000 in advance, the excess of K3 000 000 will be for a latter financial year.

PROGRESS CLINIC 4

Question 1

a) .What do you understand by the following terms:
i). Straight line depreciation ii). Reducing balance depreciation.
b). A lorry bought for a business cost K17, 000,000. It is expected to last for five years and then be sold for K2, 000,000.
Calculate the depreciation to be charged each year on the lorry using:
i). Straight line method
ii). Reducing balance method at a rate of 35%.
c). Vehicles are often said to depreciate more quickly over the earlier years of their life and this means that one of the above two methods is preferable to the other. Explain which of the above two methods would be more suitable for depreciating the lorry.

Question 2

a) The following details regarding plant and machinery have been extracted from the balance sheet of a company as at 1 June 2011.
Cost K842,370; Accumulated depreciation K247,350
You ascertain that during the year to 31 May 2011:
- The relevant accounting policy is to provide depreciation on a straight line basis at a rate of 10% p.a. on plant and machinery held at year end.

●Additions during the year comprised plant purchased on 30 November 2010 at a cost of K172,000.

●Disposals consisted of the sale on 31 August 2010 of plant originally costing K148,000 and on which accumulated depreciation at the beginning of the year amounted to K68,000. The proceeds of sale amounted to K78,000.

Required:

Prepare the following accounts:

●the plant and machinery account

● the plant and machinery accumulated depreciation account

● the plant and machinery disposal account,

for the year ended 31 may 2011.

b). The machinery sold (referred to above) was replaced by a new but otherwise identical machinery costing K254,000.

One of the directors has just made the following comment: 'I cannot see the relevance of the depreciation charge. The proceeds of the sale together with the depreciation we had accumulated up to the date of sale fell well short of the cost of replacement and as a result we had to borrow from the bank.'

Required:

Draft a reply to the above comment, giving reasons for your answer.

Question 3

On 1 January 2002 which was the first day of a financial year, T Yangwe bought net worked computer hardware for K9,500,000. It is to be depreciated by the straight line method at the rate of 20 per cent, ignoring salvage value. On 1 January 2005, the system was sold for K4,250,000.

Required:

Show the following for the complete period of ownership:

(a) The Computer Account

(b) The provision for Depreciation Account

(c) The Computer Disposal Account

(d) The Extracts from Profits and Loss Accounts for four (4) years

(e) Prepare Balance Sheet Extracts for the years 2002, 2003, and 2004

CHAPTER 5

THE BANK RECONCILIATION STATEMENT

The Cash Book

Introduction

The cash book is used to record all cash and banking transactions. It is an extension of the ledger itself, concentrating only on cash or bank entries. Therefore, instead of having a separate bank and cash account in the nominal ledger as we had before, a Cash book can be used to record these cash and bank entries, making it more convenient to keep them together.

Any money paid into the business bank account either in cheque or in cash, using the bank's paying-in-slip as documentary evidence, may be recorded in the bank column of the cash book. Entries that are merely cash are recorded in the cash column.

There are two types of cash books namely:
1. 2-column cash book. In which one column is used for cash and bank receipts in and the other for cash and bank payments out.
2. 3-column cash book. This has columns to record cash discounts as well as cash and bank columns. Discount allowed is entered on the left side of the cash book and is given to debtors for prompt payment of their accounts and is treated as an expense of the business. Discount received is entered on the right side of the cash book and is received from creditors for prompt payment of debts and is treated as revenue to the business.

Example: 2-column cash book

Debit								Credit
Receipts				Payments				
Date	Detail	Cash	Bank	Date	Detail	Cash	Bank
		K	K			K	K

Example:3 - column cash book

Debit					Credit			
Receipts					Payments			
Date	Detail	Discount allowed	Cash	Bank	Date	Detail	Discount rec'd	Cash	Bank
		K	K	K			K	K	K

Note: Recordings are debit cash or bank in and credit cash or bank out. In practice, cash books rarely look the same because they are adapted to suit the needs of the business. Some businesses may prefer a number of columns for receipts and payments because they may want to analyze various aspects of the business, such as different categories of sales, VAT, or different types of expenses. Further a cash book may be in the form of two separate book—a cash receipts and a cash payments book, particularly if there are a great number of transactions for both receipts and payments.

Bank Reconciliation

The cash book's bank balance needs to be confirmed with the bank statement at frequency intervals as check that its receipts and payments are in line with the banks recording of these.

Bank reconciliation is a method of bringing together the bank balance as shown on the bank statement with the balance as shown in the cash book. These balances may not agree at any specific time because:

- Items in the cash book may not yet have been paid at the bank in time for these to be entered in the bank statement, or
- Items in the bank's statement may not yet be in the cash book.
- Due to error

Some examples are:

Items in the cash book not yet recorded in the statement:

- cheque payments entered on the credit side of the cash book but not yet presented for payment at the bank – these are 'unpresented cheques';
- cheques, cash entered on the debit side of the cash book, but not yet deposited at the bank-these are 'undeposited cheques, cash'.
- These items will then be recorded in the bank reconciliation statement.

Items in the bank statement not yet recorded in the cash book:

(a) payments and charges made by the bank and charged against the business:

- Standing orders
- Direct debits
- Interest and bank charges
- Cheques R/D (referred to drawer, due to insufficient funds).

(b) Receipts by the bank on the business's behalf and not yet recorded in the cash book:

- Cheques from customers paid through the Bank Giro
- Interest received on deposits at the bank
- Dividends received from investments
  These items will be entered on the debit side of the cash book, the receipts side.

Procedure for bank reconciliation

Checking must be made in some systematic order. Have the appropriate cash book pages ready to be compared with the latest batch of bank statements.

1. **Tick** those items that appear on both sets of records-for example, the receipts side of the cash with the receipts side of the statement. Also check the payments side of both records. If entries do appear on both sets of records, then no further action is required. Only those items that are not ticked on both sets of records need to be actioned.

2. If there any **unticked items** on the bank statement, such as bank charges, standing orders, direct debits or interest received, these need to be first entered in the cash book the all will require will then have been updated. Once the cash book has been adjusted the profit it go for the reconciliation – that, is, preparation of simple bank reconciliation adjustment thus, is composed of those items left unticked in the cash book.

The Bank Reconciliation Statement is then prepared usually in this format:

- Balance per bank statement (end of month balance)   X
- Add any undeposited cheques/cash (from debit side cash book)   X
- Deduct any unpresented cheques (from credit side cash book)   (X)
- This should equal the balance as per cash book   X

Or

- Balance as per cash book   X
- Add any unpresented cheques   X
- Deduct undeposited cheques   (X)
- This must equal the balance as pre bank statement   X

Example 1.

THE BANK RECONCILIATION STATEMENT

National Bank Plc				
Kirsty McDonald Statement of Account				
Date	Details	Debits	Credits	Balance
		K	K	K
Oct 30	Balance			841 ✓
Oct 31	606218	23		818
Nov 5	Sundry Credit		46 ✓	864
Nov 7	606219	161 ✓		703
Nov 9	Direct Credit	18		685
Nov 12	606222	93 ✓		592

Nov 15	Sundry credit		207 ✓	799
Nov 19	606223	246 ✓		533
Nov 19	Bank Giro Credit		146	699
Nov 20	Bank Giro Credit		246 ✓	945
Nov 21	606221	43 ✓		902
Nov 21	Sundry Credit		63 ✓	965
Nov 22	Bank Giro Credit		79 ✓	1,044
Nov 23	Loan Interest	391		653
Nov 26	606220	87 ✓		566
Nov 26	Deposit A/C Interest		84	650
Nov 27	606226	74 ✓		576
Nov 28	Sundry Credit		88 ✓	664
Nov 30	606225	185 ✓		479

Her cash book showed the following details:

Date	Detail	K	Date Detail		Cheque No.	K
Nov 1	Balance b/d	818✓	Nov 2	Rent	219	161✓
Nov 5	B Mason	46✓	Nov 5	H Gibson	220	87✓
Nov 8	K Dean	146✓	Nov 7	G Wise	221	43✓
Nov 14	G Hunt	207✓	Nov 8	T Allen	222	93✓
Nov 16	C Charlton	79✓	Nov	12 Gas	223	246✓
Nov 19	D Banks	63✓	Nov 15	F Chauster	224	692✓
Nov 26	P Perry	88✓	Nov 19	M Lewis	225	185✓
Nov 28	A Palmer	29	Nov 23	G Bridges	226	74✓
Nov 30	J Dixon	17	Nov 29	L Wilson	227	27
Nov 30	Balance c/d	206	Nov 29	P Brown	228	91
		1,699				1,699

Required

a) Bring the Cash Book balance of K206 up to date as at 30 November.
b) Draw up a bank reconciliation statement as at 30 November

Solution

The cash book is brought up-to-date by entering the unticked item taken from the bank statement:

Cash Book

Dr					Cr
Dec 1	Deposit interest	84	Dec 1	Balance b/d	206 (o/d)
	Bank giro credit	246		Direct debit	18
	Balance c/d	285		Loan interest	319
		615			615
				Balance b/d	285

Bank reconciliation statement as at November 30

				K
1	Balance as per bank statement (30/11)			479 Credit
2	Add deposits not yet credited:			
	Palmer	29		
	Dixon	17		46
				525
3	Less unpresented cheques:			
	Chauster	692		
	Wilson	27		
	Brown	91		
				(810)
4	Balance as per cash book			285 (o/d)

Example 2

Using a previous bank reconciliation statement

On 1 August A Simmonds had an overdraft of K33.65 in his Cash Book. The previous bank reconciliation statement as on 31 July showed:

Bank reconciliation statement 31/7

		K
Balance as per bank statement		149.25
Add		
Deposits not yet credited:		440.00✓
		589.25
Less		
Unpresented cheques:		
05625	37.50	
05634	133.20✓	

05637	98.80 ✓	
05651	200.00 ✓	
05653	153.40 ✓	622.90
Balance as per cash book		33.65 (overdrawn)

Cash Book-A Simmonds

4/8	Sales	300	1/8	Balance b/d	33.65 (overdrawn)
15/8	Sales	500	7/8	Rent	77
16/8	D Adams	345	8/8	Purchases	123.5
			9/8	A Jones	48
			11/8	SEB	108.5
			12/8	Petty Cash	95
			16/8	Insurance (DDR)	35
			16/8	Balance c/d	624.35
		1,145			1,145

Bank Statement to 16 August – A Simmonds

			Dr	Cr	Balance
Aug	1	Balance			149.25
	2	Credit		440 ✓	
	3	05634	133.20 ✓		
	4	Credit		300 ✓	
	7	05637	98.80 ✓		
	10	05651	200 ✓		
	10	05653	153.40 ✓		
	11	05654	77 ✓		
	11	05659	123.50 ✓		
	13	05663	48 ✓		
	14	DDR (Insurance)	35 ✓		
	16	Credit		500 ✓	
	16	Closing balance			520.35

Have you checked the figures? The deposits of K440 and all cheques except 05625 from the previous bank reconciliation statement, can be ticked off against the same entries on the bank statement above. The figures for August in the cash book can then be cross-checked against the remainder of the bank statement for August in the usual way. The reconciliation up to dither 16 August is shown below:

Bank reconciliation as on 16 August:

	K
Balance as per statement	520.35
Add deposits not yet credited:	<u>345.00</u>
	865.35
Less unpresented cheques:	
37.50	
108.50	
<u>95.00</u>	<u>(241.00)</u>
Balance as per cash book	<u>624.35</u>

Cheques dishonored by the bank

The bank statement may include cheques received from customers that have been lodged as deposits then at a later date, refused to be paid by the debtor's bank usually because of insufficient funds in the debtor's account. The entry would be first made as a credit at the bank then, once the cheque had been refused payment, a debit entry would be made on the statement.

If This occurs, the customer's account would have to be re-debited with the amount of the cheque and the bank account credited with the same figure: for example, if Mr. Soames cheques for K141 had "R/D" (refer to drawer) and was therefore dishonoured:

Sales ledger

			Debit	Credit	Balance
Soames account					
May	1	Balance			141 Dr
	9	Bank		141	0
June	10	Bank (R/D)	141		141 Dr

Cash book (extract)

			Payments (Credit)
June	10	Soames (R/D cheque)	141

Overdrafts

Remember that a bank overdraft is shown as a debit balance in the bank statement and is a credit balance in the bank account or cash book.

When preparing the bank reconciliation statement therefore, the additions and subtractions work in the opposite way:

Bank reconciliation as on 31 August:

	K
Balance as per statement	450 Dr
Less deposits not yet credited:	210
	240
Add unpresented cheques:	425
Balance as per cash book	665 (overdrawn)

Cheques

If a customer sends a cheque, remember that it must be correct in all detail including signature, title, figures matching with words etc. A cheque that is over 6 months old is referred to as a "sale" cheque and will not be accepted by the bank.

Remember that there may also be arithmetic errors in the cash book and the bank itself is the immune to making errors. Therefore, there may be questions which include all types of questions and errors as well as the 'run of the mill' unpresented cheques and sums not yet credited.

PROGRESS CLINIC 5

Question 1

Your firm's cash books at 30 April 2012 showed a balance at the bank of K2,490,000. Comparison with the bank statement at the same date reveals the following differences:

	K
Unpresented cheques	840,000
Bank charges not in the cash book	50,000
Receipts not yet credited by the bank	470,000
Dishonored cheques not in the cash book	140,000

Required

From the above details, calculate the correct bank balance at 30 April 2012.

Question 2

The following are the details of the Cash Book and also the Bank Statement collected from the records of Jakalasi for the month of December 2012.

CASH BOOK

DR		K000		CR	K000
Dec 1:	Balance b/f	1,740	Dec 8: A Daka		349
Dec 7:	T Mooya	88	Dec 15: R Muka		33
Dec 22:	J Esau	73	Dec 28: G Saamu		115
Dec 31:	K Wole	249	Dec 31: balance c/d		1,831
Dec 31:	M Bunda	178			
		2,328			**2,328**

Jan 1: Balance b/d 1,831

BANK STATEMENT

DATE	DETAILS	DR	CR	BALANCE
		K000	K000	K000
1.12	Balance b/d			1,740
7.12	Cheque		88	1,828
11.12	A Daka	349		1,479
20.12	R Muka	33	73	1,446
22.12	Cheque		54	1,519
31.12	Credit transfer: J Wasa	22		1,573
31.12	Bank charges			1,551

REQUIRED

(a) Write a revised (updated) Cash Book to date and state the new balance as on 31 December 2012.

(b) Draw up a Bank Reconciliation Statement as on 31 December 2012.

Question 3

The following transactions were collected from the books of a sole trader, for the month of May 2012. You are employed as Accounts Clerk at this firm.

		K
May 1:	Balances brought down from April:	
	Cash balance	29,000
	Bank balance	654,000
Debtors Accounts:		
	B Kangwa	120,000
	N Choongo	280,000
	D Siwale	40,000

DR. CRYFORD MUMBA

Creditors Accounts:

U Banda	60,000
A Akimo	440,000
R Lungu	100,000

May 2:   B Kangwa pays us by a cheque, having deducted
         2½ per cent cash discount K3,000   117,000

May 8:   We pay R Lungu his account by cheque, deducting
         5 per cent cash discount K5,000   95,000

May 11: We withdrew K100,000 cash from the bank for business use   100,000

May 16: N Choongo pays us by cheque, deducting 2½ per cent
         discount K7,000   273,000

May 25: We paid wages in cash   92,000

May 28: D Siwale pays us in cash after having deducted 2½ per cent
         cash discount   38,000

May 29: We pay U Banda by cheque less 5 per cent cash discount
         K3,000   57,000

May 30: We pay A Akimo by cheque less 2½ per cent cash discount
         K11,000   429,000

Required:

You are required to draw up the following for the month of May 2012:

(a) Three – Column Cash Book (i.e. showing Discount, Cash and Bank Columns).

(b) The following Ledger Accounts:

    (i)   B Kangwa Account
    (ii)   N Choongo Account
    (iii)   D Siwale Account
    (iv)   U Banda Account
    (v)   R Lungu Account
    (vi)   A Akimo Account
    (vii) Wages Account
    (viii) Discount Received Account
    (ix) Discount Allowed Account

Question 4

Kachepa prepares a bank reconciliation at the end of each month. The bank statement for May 2012 is as follows:

BANK STATEMENT

Barclays bank Plc
Cairo Road   Sheet:1
Lusaka.   1 May—31 May 2012
Account No: 00000000123456   **Account Name**: Kachepa

Date	Payment type and details	Paid out	Paid in	Balance
1/5/12	balance b/f			2,500.60 Cr
5/5/12	Counter credit		850.00	3,350.60 Cr
5/5/12	bank charges	68.75		3,281.85 Cr
8/5/12	Cash deposit		675.50	3,957.35 Cr
10/5/12	Cheque No: 100221	985.00		972.35 Cr
16/5/12	cheque No: 100222	263.98		2,708.37 Cr
18/5/12	SO bank loan	457.00		2,251.37 Cr
22/5/12	Cheque No: 100223	335.50		1,915.87 Cr
24/5/12	Cash deposit		1,200.63	3,116.50 Cr
29/5/12	Cheque No: 100224	85.62		3,030.88 Cr
31/5/12	DD—Council tax	135.00		2,895.88 Cr
31/5/12	BACS – Rent received		500.00	3,395.88 Cr

Cr: Credit balance   SO: Standing Order
Dr: Overdrawn balance   BACS: Banks automated clearing service
<u>DD: Direct debit</u>

You are supplied with a partially complete cash book for Kachepa for May 2012

<u>KACHEPA: CASK BOOK MAY 2012</u>

Date	Details	K	Date	Details	Cheque No.	K
1/5/12	Balance b/d	2,500.60	6/5/12	Mwaba	100221	985.00
2/5/12	Sales	850.00	10/5/12	Mwewa	100222	236.98
5/5/12	Sales	675.50	18/5/12	Bank loan	SO	457.00
20/5/12	Sales	1,200.63	19/5/12	Mainza & Co.	100223	335.50
29/5/12	Sales	840.85	27/5/12	Joe Ltd	100224	85.62
			30/5/12	Phiri Bros.	100225	695.00
			30/5/12	Counciltax	DD	135.00
			31/5/12	Zesco	100226	<u>228.95</u>
		6,067.58				**6,067.58**

DR. CRYFORD MUMBA

Required:

a) What are the outstanding lodgements and unpresented chaeques
b) Calculate the adjusted cash book balance for Kachepa as at 31 May 2012.
c) Prepare a bank reconciliation statement for Kachepa as at 31 May 2o12.
d) Explain why it is important to perform regular bank reconciliations.

Question 5

The cash book shows a bank balance of K5,675,000 overdrawn at 31 August 2012. It is subsequently discovered that a standing order of K125,000 has been entered twice and that a dishonoured cheque for K450,000 has been debited in the cash book instead of being credited.

Required:

From the above details, calculate the correct bank balance after making the above corrections.

Question 6

When preparing a bank reconciliation statement, it is realized that:
i) Cheques with a value of K1,050,000 have been sent to suppliers and correctly entered in the cash book, but have not yet been presented for payment by the suppliers.
ii) A cheque for K75,000 sent to a supplier has been incorrectly recorded in the cash book as K57,000
iii) Before correction, the cash book has a balance of K10,500,000
iv) Bank charges amounting to K175,000 have been recorded in the cash book.

Required:

Calculate the closing balance in the Bank Statement by using the cash book balance.

Question 7

On 31 December 2012 the bank columns of Mumba's cash book showed a balance of K4,500,000. The Bank Statement as at 31 December 2012 showed a credit balance of K8,850,000 on the account. As Mumba's Accountant, you checked the bank Statement with the Cash book and found that the following items had been entered in the cash book:
i) A standing order to Balle insurance for K600,000 had been paid by the bank.
ii) Bank interest receivable amounting to K720,000 had not been entered in the account.
iii) Bank charges of K90,000
iv) A credit transfer of an amount of K780,000 from kello ltd had been paid directly into the account.

v) Mumba's deposit account balance of K4,200,000 had been transferred into his current account.

vi) A returned cheque of K210,000, dishonoured by C Hara, had been entered on the bank statement.

You also discovered that two cheques payable to L. Yeta totaling to K750,000 and K. Chama totaling to K870,000, had been entered in the cash book but had not been presented for payment. In addition to that, a cheque for K2,070,000 had been paid into the bank on 31 December 2012 but had not been credited on the Bank Statement until 2 January 2013.

Required:

a) Starting with the Cash Book debit balance of K4,500,000, write up the cash book up to date.

b) Draw up a bank Reconciliation Statement as on 31 December2012.

Question 8

At 30 September 2012, the balance in the cash book of John was K805,000 debit. A bank Statement on the same day shown John to be in credit by K1,112,000. On investigation of the difference between the two sums, it was discovered that;

i) The cash book had been undercast by K90,000 on the debit side.

ii) Cheques paid in not yet credited by the bank amounted to K208,000, called outstanding lodgements.

iii) Cheques drawn not yet presented to the bank amounted to K425,000, called Unpresented cheques.

Note: Casting is an accountant's term for adding up.

Required:

a) Show the correction to the cash book.

b) Prepare a statement reconciling the balance per bank statement to the balance per cash book.

Question 9

A business had a balance at the bank of K2,500,000 at the start of the month. During the following month, it paid for materials invoiced at K1,000,000 less trade discount of 20% and a cash discount of 10%. The business received a cheque from a debtor in respect of an invoice for K200,000, subject to a cash discount of 5%.

Required:

Calculate the balance at the bank at the end of the month.

CHAPTER 6

SUSPENCE ACCOUNTS

A suspense account is an account to which you put that aspect of a transaction with which, through lack of information, experience or guidance, you feel unable to deal satisfactorily. For example, you might credit to a suspense account the double entry for a postal order or cash received (the cash book would be debited), if the name of the sender were not known. When this information became known, you would use the journal to transfer the item out of the suspense account and into the account of the customer who had sent it.

Similarly, if a firm has a substantial bill for repairs and improvements, the double entry (corresponding to the payment in the cash book) might be made in a suspense account until the correct proportion of revenue and capital expenditure had been agreed, when transfers would be made from the suspense account to the repairs account and the appropriate asset accounts.

A further use of a suspense account is that of a temporary location for a trial balance difference. In order to prepare a set of final accounts from unbalanced trial balance, the trial balance is made to agree artificially b putting into the suspense account a balancing debit or credit entry.

The main features of suspense accounts are that:
- They are temporary
- They are a substitute for the missing balance or balance in the trial balance
- They are closed as soon as the problem has been resolved
- They fulfill the basic rules of double entry.

Example 1

Draft a trial balance from the figures below, using control accounts as a balancing figure.

	K'000
Purchases 7	00
Sales	1100
Rent paid	250
Cash in bank (Dr)	840
Travel expenditure	160
Debtors	320
Creditors	350
Capital	710

Solution

	Dr K'000	Cr K'000
Purchases	700	
Sales		1100
Rent paid	250	
Cash in bank	840	

Travel expenses	160	
Debtors	320	
Creditors		350
Capital		710
Suspense account		110
	2270	2270

Example 2

A trial balance fails to balance and a suspense account with a credit balance is opened for K330, 000. Later the following errors are revealed:
   a) A sale, for K220,000 was debited to Smith instead of Simon.
   b) A sale of K420,000 was correctly entered in the sales account but was not debited to Mwale's personal account.
   c) A purchase of K750,000 was correctly entered in the purchase account but was not credited to Chimbwali's personal account.

Prepare journal entries to show the necessary corrections for all these items.

Solution

   a) Debit Simon's account and credit Smiths account with K220,000 being an adjustment of misposting to Smith instead of Simon.
   b) Debit Mwale's account and credit the suspense account with K420,000 being debit to personal account omitted from the books.
   c) Credit the suspense account and debit Chimbwali's account with K750,000 being credit to personal account omitted from the books.

STOCK VALUATION

The costing of materials issued to production is used in calculating the cost of goods sold or sometimes called the cost of sales (COS). A high pricing of the stock issued will increase the cost of sales and therefore decrease the operating profit. A lower stock costing will lower the cost of sales and increase the operating profit. It is therefore important to use the most representative costing method is the correct operating profit is to be calculated. The method adopted must be used consistently in line with the consistency concept.
The following stock valuation methods are used:

1.First in, first out (FIFO). This method assumes that the oldest stock is issued to production first, so charging store issues at the oldest price first. Once all the goods purchased at that price have been used, the next oldest goods will be issued. This avoids keeping the stock in the store for very long, hence avoiding deterioration or obsolescence. Imagine a store keeper not using this method and the stored stock have short life span. They will certainly go bad if not issued on time and the cost may be substantial. However, FIFO does not work for materials which are mixed, for example, liquids, though the pricing policy of charging the oldest stock first can still be adopted. This method is logical, but not easy to use. It does mean that the closing stock value is closer to the current economic value. The disadvantage is that the cost of production tends to relate to out-of-date prices.

2.Last in, first out (LIFO). This is the reverse of FIFO, and issues the newest materials first to production, charging the newest price to production. If the stock is actually issued following this method, there is a risk of materials becoming obsolete through staying in the stores for too long. The benefits of using of using this as a costing system are that production costs are always based on the latest material costs and therefore closer to the current economic value. However, as time goes on pricing will become more out of date as the older stock is used. The closing stock values will be out of date, as this will always relate to the oldest stock.

3.Average cost (AVCO). Using average cost method, such as the continuous weighted average, takes the total cost of stock at a point in time and averages it over the quantity in stock at that time. Simply put, average cost is found by dividing quantity in stock into total cost. In this case the price of the goods is related to quantities purchased, and is constantly updated as new stock is purchased. However, the average price still lags behind the current economic prices and may not relate to any actual purchase price.

In comparison to the other methods, LIFO could give a higher cost of production in times of inflation, since the stock will always be issued at the highest rate, whilst the lowest priced stock will remain in store. However, assuming the opening and closing stock levels remain reasonably constant, the low closing stock value will not significantly reduce the cost of sales. Given the variability and turnover of stock, these differences in accounting method are not likely to be material.

Example 3

You have been provided with the following stock information for your company, Tisunge Ltd, for the year ending 31 December 2012:
- January – bought 10 units at K30 000 each
- March—bought 10 units at K34 000 each
- April—issued to production 8 units
- September – bought 20 units at K40 000 each
- December—issued to production 12 units.

Required

a) Calculate the value of the closing stock at 31 December 2012, for Tisunge Ltd, using the following three methods of stock valuation:
  i) First in, first out
  ii) Last in, first out
  iii) Average cost
b) Which method of stock valuation would result in the highest trading profit? Explain your answer.

Solution

a) i) FIFO

Date	Units	Value(k'000)
January	10 @ k30 000 each	300
March	10@ K34 000	340
		640
April	8 issued @ K30 000	(240)
		400
September	20 000@ K40 000	800
		1200
December	12 – 2 issued @K30 000	(60)
	10 issued @K34 000	(340)
	Value of closing stock	800

ii) LIFO

Date	Units	Value
January	10@ K30 000	300
March	10@ K34 000	340
		640
April	8 issued@ K34 000	272
		368
September	20@ K40 000	800
		1168
December	12 issued@ K40 000	480
Value of closing stock		688

iii) AVCO

Date	Units	Value(k'000)
January	10@K30 000	300
March	10@K34 000	340
		640
April	(640 000/20 =K32 000	(256)
		384
September	20@K40 000	800
		1184
December	12 issued@(118400/32=K37)	(444)
Value of closing stock		740

b) FIFO as it produces the highest valuation of closing stock.

CONTROL ACCOUNTS

For management purpose, it is essential to know how much is owed by debtors of the business as well as how much is owed to creditors. Once the two control accounts have verified the correctness of the sales and purchase ledgers account balances, the control accounts will represent the totals for debtors and creditors in the trial balance.

Advantages of Control Accounts
The advantages of control accounts are as follows:
1. **The localization of errors**. If the total balances of the debtors ledger does not agree with its control account balance, the extent of the difference is known, and the search for it can be concentrated on that section of the ledgers. This saves much time and effort.
2. **They avoid delay in producing the final accounts**. The trial balance will balance using the control account balance from the general ledger. If mistakes have been made in the personal ledgers, these can be corrected later, after accounts are produced.
3. **They provide a useful check against inaccuracy and fraud**. If the control account is written up as part of the general ledger, it will act as an independent check on the personal ledger account. Fraudulent activity by the clerk in charge of the personal ledger will be disclosed unless collusion has taken place between employees operating the personal and general ledgers.

Terms used with Control Accounts

1. **Cheque dishonoured** refers to customer's cheques that have been stopped by the bank, usually because the customer has insufficient funds to pay the debt. These are debited in the sales ledger control account as well as debited in the individual customer's account.
2. **Contra entries** are sums offset between debtors and creditors balances when a business both sells and buys goods from the same person or organization. The entry is to debit purchase ledger control and credit sales ledger control accounts as well as debiting the individual accounts in the purchase ledger and crediting them in the sales ledger.
3. **Bills receivable** are notes from customers promising to pay at a future date. They are treated like post-dated cheque and are credited to the sales ledger control account.
4. **Bills payable** are the reverse of the bills receivable in that the business promises to pay its suppliers at a future date. These are debited to the purchases ledger control account.

General Structure of Control Accounts

Sales Ledger control account			
Balance b/f	X	Discount allowed	X
Sales day book	X	Cash and cheques	X
		Bad debts	X

		Sales returns	X
		Balance c/d	X
	X		X
Balance b/d	X		

Purchases Ledger control Account

Bank	X	Balance b/f	X
Returns outwards	X	Purchase(bal. fig)	X
Discount received	X		
Balance c/d	X		
	X		X

Note: The sales ledger control account is also called the debtors control account while the purchases ledger control account is also called the creditor control account.

Example 4

The following were collected from the books of John Ltd at the end of March 2012:

		K'000
March 1:	Sales ledger balances	6,708
	Totals for March:	
	Discount allowed	300
	Cash and cheques received from debtors	8,970
	Sales day book	11,500
	Bad debts written off	115
	Sales returns day book	210
March 31:	Sales ledger balances	?

Required:
Prepare a sales ledger control account and deduce the closing figure for the sales ledger balance as at 31 March 2012.

Solution

Sales Ledger Control Account

		K'000			K'000
1.3.	Bal. b/f	6,708	31.3.	Discount allowed	300
31.3.	Sales day book	11,500	31.3	Cash and cheques	8,970
			31.3.	Bad debts	210
			31.3.	Bal. c/d	8,613
		18,208			18,208

Example 5

The following information was corrected from the records of John Ltd:

	K'000
Opening creditor balance	142,600
Cash paid to creditors	542,300
Discounts received	13,200
Goods returned	27,500
Closing credit balances	137,800

Required:

Calculate value of purchases during the period.

Solution

Purchases Ledger Control Account

	K'000		K'000
Bank(payments)	542,300	Balance b/f	142,600
Discount received	13,200	Purchases(bal. fig.)	578,200
Returns out	27,500		
Balance c/d	137,800		
	720,800		720,800

Purchases is therefore K578,200,000

PROGRESS CLINIC 6

Question 1

You are given the following information relating to purchases by an enterprise and its trade creditors:

	K'000
Creditors at 1 November 2011	76104
Creditors at 31 October 2012	80 643
Purchases	286 932
Cash paid to suppliers	271 845
Debit balances transferred to trade debtors ledger	107
Credit balances offset against trade debtors ledger	
Debit balances	866
Sundry minor credit balances written off	82
Discount received	5 698

Required:

Calculate the amount of purchases returned to suppliers (i.e. Purchases Returns) during the year ending 31 October 2012.

CHAPTER 7

PREPARING FINANCIAL STATEMENTS: SOLE TRADER

From the trial balance together with adjustments to accounts, financial statements are prepared. These financial statements are:

THE BALANCE SHEET

The balance sheet shows the financial position of the business hence it is now called the statement of financial position. This accounting statement shows the status of a firm at any given moment .It is always stated 'as at' a certain date, and is a statement of the financial position of the business on that date. The balance sheet shows the items owned by the business, which are termed assets, and sets against them a list of claims on those assets by those who have provided the funds with which the assets have been purchased; these are termed liabilities, or what the business owes. Thus when shareholders have put money into the business or when a lender makes funds available to a business, a claim to the return of the funds is acquired. The funds are then invested by the business in assets which it buys and uses in its chosen trade. Thus everything owned by a business must have financed, and the finance must have been provided by those who have claims on the business, so liabilities or claims must equal assets.

An American term which is now been used globally for the balance sheet is 'position statement', since it implies that the balance should correctly reflect the position of a business rather than merely summarize the balances in its books. The balance sheet must always balance because of the accounting equation.

The balance sheet is like a photograph in that it shows the position of a business at one point in time but does not show how that position was arrived at. It also suffers from the disadvantages of the monetary measurement postulate, in that assets which cannot be measured objectively in money terms are left out of the statement, and assets included at historical cost are shown at an unrepresentative amount after inflation.

Functions of the Balance Sheet

a) **Financial position of the business**. The balance sheet is drawn up in order to give a picture of the financial position of the business. It reveals whether is solvent or insolvent. It shows how much is invested in different forms of property, and how the business is funded.

b) **Arithmetical accuracy of accounts**. The agreement of the balance sheet also provides a check on the accuracy of the revenue accounts in much the same way as the trial balance provides evidence of the arithmetical accuracy of the books.

c) **Bridge between financial years**. The balance sheet is also a bridge between one financial year and the next. All accounts which remain open after the manufacturing,

Trading and profit and loss accounts have been prepared are summarized in the balance sheet.

Components of the Balance Sheet

Thus the balance sheet has three major components namely;

1. **Assets**. An item belonging to the business is considered to be an asset so long as it conforms to three conditions. These are that the asset has a value, that the value can be objectively measured, and that the ownership of the asset can be proved. An auditor will consider these conditions when verifying the situation of assets included on the balance sheet. The market value of an asset is the amount which a user is prepared to pay to control and use that asset at one point in time. Value is therefore derived from expectations of what an asset can earn. A modern definition of an asset is that it is an item from which future economic benefits will flow as a result of its past transactions, the right to which belongs to the business.(See IAS 16: Property, Plant and Equipment, in chapter 12 of this book).

   Assets are usually recorded in the books at historical cost (the amount paid out when the asset was acquired). Some assets, however are excluded from the balance sheet because it is too difficult to obtain a precise value for them, or because they could quickly lose value. For example, the possession of a skilled workforce will enable a business to earn extra profits, so that the workforce is considered to be an asset to the business; but employees can leave, so that this asset cannot be considered as an item completely under the control of the business. A company with an established trade connection will make extra sales, and extra profits, from repeat offers when satisfied customers return for more goods, but this advantage can rapidly disappear if a company loses its reputation. The original cost and current value of these two assets are difficult to determine.

   Traditionally, accountants record assets at their historical cost and not their estimated current market value, in order to conform to the principles of objectivity, realization and prudence. It is considered imprudent to rely on a valuation for an asset which cannot be tested by a cross-market transaction, and which may subsequently be reduced by market forces and thus not realized. In some cases, however, the historical cost of an asset gets out of line with the current value of the asset, and a professional valuer is asked to revalue the asset so that the balance sheet can reflect current conditions with greater accuracy. If a building accounted for at cost K500 million is subsequently revalued at K1 billion, and disclosed on the balance sheet at this value, the surplus of K500 million must be shown as a reserve not available for distribution. This means that it is an unrealized profit (sometimes called a holding gain) which has not passed through the income statement, and is not available for distribution to shareholders under the prudence concept.

   The value of some assets cannot be assessed with accuracy. For example, a patent or trademark owned by a business, or the funds invested by a business in developing a new product, will both earn extra profits for the business but the amount of those extra profits is difficult to determine. Accordingly, 'intangible' assets of this type are recognized as assets but carried in the balance sheet at cost rather than value. An economist might wish to value an asset by determining the current value of the future stream of income to be derived from the asset. Such a value is of great uncertainty and for this reason the prudent accountant prefers to use the idea of cost rather than value when stating assets in the balance sheet. Assets are classified into three as fixed assets, current assets and intangible assets.

a) **Non—current liabilities**. These are traditionally called fixed assets. These are assets that the business uses to generate income and are not for sale. Further, they have to be used by the business for a period of more than one year or twelve months. Examples include premises, plant and equipment or machinery, fixtures and fittings covering computers, shelves, chairs, tables, motor vehicles and the like. I must hasten to mention that motor vehicles for an Automobile company that sells cars such as Toyota, those specific vehicles for sale are not a fixed asset as they will be turned into cash within a year. Motor vehicles for such are part of stock hence treated as a current asset.

b) **Current assets**. These are assets which will be turned into cash within a year. These include cash, accounts receivables (debtors), prepayments, inventory (stock).

2. **Liabilities.** These represent items owed by the business to outsiders. A theoretical definition of a liability is that it is a present obligation of a business, which entails a probable future sacrifice when the business transfers assets or provides a service , to another business. The term 'present obligation' has a wider scope than a mere 'legal liability' which can be proved at law. Liabilities are classified into two namely:

a) **Current Liabilities.** These are liabilities which must be settled within a year. They include trade creditors who have supplied goods and services and are awaiting payment, short term loans from the bank, usually in the form of an overdraft, the Zambia revenue authority awaiting payment of tax on the due date, and the shareholders themselves awaiting payment of a dividend from previous year's profits(for companies only).

b) **Long –Term Liabilities**. These include loans made for period of more than one year, and often for such long period as to be viewed as part of the long term capital employed in the business. These loans are sometimes termed mortgages or debentures for companies, and are often secured on the assets of the business. This means that if the company fails to pay the annual interest on loan, or goes into liquidation before the period of the loan is ended, the lender may take possession of some assets of the business and sell them to recoup the funds lent to the business.

Note: Contingent liabilities are amounts which might become liabilities of the business, depending upon circumstances which may arise after the balance sheet date, e.g. damages in a court action where judgement is pending at the balance sheet date. These items are shown as a note under the balance sheet and do not form part of the liabilities which are added to equal the total of the assets.

3. **Capital.** This represents the original amount invested in the business by the owner. In a company, capital takes the form of shares owned by the various shareholders.

As they are the last to be repaid in the event of the business being discontinued, they are deemed to take the biggest risk. Share capital is sometimes for this reason called venture capital. Next come the reserves of the business. They also belong to the shareholders, but represent profits made by the business in the past and not distributed. When profit is made it is appropriated or divided up, some being paid to the tax authority as taxation, some being paid to the shareholders in the form of a dividend (or to the proprietor as the sole trader as drawings), and the remainder being retained in the business as a source of finance. Thus reserves or profits 'ploughed back' into the business represent a further investment by the shareholders made out of profits. When added together, share capital and reserves total the owner's interest in the business, being the funds provided initially and out of past profits by the legal owners of the business. Sometimes this amount is termed the equity interest, since all ordinary shareholders have an equal right to participate pro rata to their holding of shares, if these funds are repaid. Some reserves are not available for distribution as dividend for legal reasons. These are known as capital reserves and they are disclosed on the balance sheet below share capital but above general reserves.

The accounting or balance sheet equation

The Balance Sheet or Statement of Financial Position is prepared in compliance with the accounting equation which can be presented in either of the following ways:

a) **Assets = Liabilities + Capital**

b) **Capital = Assets – Liabilities**

c) **Liabilities = Assets – Capital**

Every financial transaction will cause a change in the accounting equation. However, the equation will remain in balance after every transaction. The equation can be stated in an expanded form as to include items in each of the three elements of the equation. For example under assets we would include equipment, inventory, receivable, cash at bank and prepayments. Capital included capital itself as well as income and expenses. Income and expenses appear under capital or equity as they are used to calculate the net profit or loss that in turn increase or decreases capital or equity.

Finally, under liabilities we have bank overdraft, payables, long term loans(debentures for companies), and accruals.

Criticism of the Balance Sheet

The balance sheet has been criticized for many reasons, not least the fact that f shows up the position of the company at one point in time, and this can be very different from the position of the same company only a few days earlier or later than the balance sheet date. Some accountants see the balance sheet as a type of photograph catching the image of the business for a fleeting moment only, and are aware that some photographs are not all representative of their subject matter. The term 'window dressing' is used to describe the action taken by the company to temporarily improve its balance sheet in the published accounts, although of course there are limits to what can be done to make a poor position appear as a much better one. IAS 10 ' Events after balance sheet date' requires that adequate notes should explain significant events which have taken place soon after the balance sheet date, but which affect a proper understanding of the accounts, or reverse significant transactions undertaken during the year.

The balance sheet:

i)   Gives no information about the past or the future

ii) Does not tell the reader how the business reached its present position

iii) Provides little information from which a trend can be deduced unless comparison is made with figures from previous years

iv) The fixed assets of the business may be recorded at historical cost less depreciation, leaving unexpired portion of the capital cost.

v)   Does not show all the assets of the business. Intangible assets which cannot be quantified, such as good labour relations, know-how, or a team of hard-working executives, are ignored, unless included in the figure for goodwill. Some liabilities are also excluded; for example, the rental due in future years on a contract made by the business will be excluded since they are not outstanding at the balance sheet date, but if the business were to cease, the other party to the rental contact would no doubt seek assurance that arrangements would be made for the amounts due under the contract to be paid at the proper time.

vi) The historical cost is not a statement of the current worth of the assets, but many investors confuse the book value of the assets with their real or market value. The balance sheet may be consistent and drawn up along conservative lines, but it is not a realistic guide to the value of the business or of individual assets. Some companies revalue their assets from time to time so that their balance sheets are updated to meet changes in the value of assets owned by the business, but such valuations are expensive and liable to personal bias on the part of the valuer, so they are rarely carried out annually and the asset values in the balance sheet soon become outdated.

THE INCOME STATEMENT

The income statement reports on the profit or loss by an organization over a certain period of time. It reflects the revenue generated through its operating activities (e.g. sales) and then deducting the expenses incurred in generating that revenue and operating the organization. Losses and gains arising from non-operating activities are also reported. Thus, the income statement is the video in "play" mode. Net profit is calculated from revenues earned throughout the period between two "pauses", minus expenses incurred from earning those revenues.

The income statement starts with sales. the sales figure is for both cash and credit sales. The various expenses are deducted to arrive at the net profit (or net income).

Components of the income Statement

The following are the components that appear in the income statement:

1. **Sales**. This is sometimes called revenue or turnover and reflects the amount earned through the sale of merchandise to customers less any sales returns. In is important to bear in mind that the reported sales figure is for both cash and credit sales; credit sales may not after all be fully recovered.
2. **Cost of sales**. This is also called the cost of goods sold and reflects the cost of merchandise sold to customers.
3. **Gross profit**. This is also called the gross margin and is the difference between sales and the cost of sales. It represents the maximum amount from which all other expenses must be met before a profit can be realized.
4. **Other income or revenue** represents revenue into the organization apart from sales of merchandise. This includes rent received, commissions received, interest received, dividends received, and so on. These are always added to gross profit before subtracting expenses, by convention.
5. **Selling, general and administrative expenses** are the operating expenses of the organization. In the income statement each expense is shown as a separate item instead of being grouped together.
6. **Operating profit** is often used to measure the performance of management .
7. **Interest expense** represents the cost of borrowing funds.
8. **Net profit** will only result id the income exceeds expenses. A net loss results if expenses exceed income.

Criticism of the income statement

The purpose of the income statement is to meet the needs of investors who require information about earnings (profit). In companies, this information about earnings is useful for evaluating management decisions that affect payments to shareholders and share prices.

However, the income statement is also often the subject of critical comment. Some authorities take the view that, while this statement shows the profit or loss that has been made, it makes no mention of the risks taken to make that profit or the potential of the business in terms of what profit could or should have been made during the period under review. The income statement summarizes the past year's trading but makes no comment about the maximization or optimization of profit. Nor does it give any forecast for the future to assist those who have to decide on future policies. The idea of the accounting year could also be considered as a limitation of the income statement, since a year is hardly a long enough period over which to make a worthwhile comment about a capital project with a life of perhaps 10 or 15 years.

The task of the income statement is one of profit measurement, not profit determination. The profit calculation is, however, affected by the accounting policies adopted and the estimates made in its computation, so accountants using different bases could produce different profit figures for the same period for the same business. Once again the rate and method of depreciation, the basis of stock valuation, the method of absorption of overheard (whether they should be carried forward or written off during the period) and the treatment of advertising or research and development expenditure are all where the judgement, outlook, or view developed by the accountant can have an impact on the profit figure. In the face of such criticism of accounting methods the alternative method of computing profit advanced by the economists, that of viewing the business at two points in time and considering any increase in value over a period as the profit made, seems attractive, until the practicalities of its operation are considered.

Capital and Revenue Expenditure

A business spends money on two types of expenditure. One concerns the purchase of fixed assets or non-current assets such as vehicles and equipment and the other concern money spent on running the business with expenses such as purchases of stock, wage and salaries, light and heat, stationery etc.

Capital Expenditure

This is money that is spent on non-current assets or money spent on improving their value. For example, if a second hand vehicle was purchased for K3.5 million and latter required the new engine costing K1 million which was seen as better than one before then value of the vehicle under non-current asset should be K4.5 million. This is capital expenditure.

Capital expenditure on non-current assets must also include an cost incurred in bringing their value into agent's fees, land registry fees and any other involved with the purchases. If new plant and machinery were installed in a factory, the capital cost should include the carriage of it to the premises and all cost in the installation.

Revenue Expenditure

All aspects of expenditure in running the vehicles for business including petrol, repairs and maintenance, car tax and insurance, depreciation of the vehicle, replacement of types would be treated as part of revenue expenditure, that is, would be seen as part of day to day running of the business.

Capital and Revenue Expenditure and Financial Statements

In the financial statements, all capital expenditure is entered in the balance sheet under non-current assets whereas as all revenue expenditure appears as expenses in the income statement. Any unsold stock is also entered under current asset.

It is extremely important, therefore, to make the distinction between these two expenditure types otherwise serious errors will arise when the financial statement are purchased. For example if machinery was purchased for K5000 million and it was wrongly treated as purchased under revenue expenditure, this would have the effect of **understating** the values of non-current assets and **overstating** the values of chargeable expenses. The end result is that profits are understating and non-current assets are under stated. The revenue authority would also be displeased and would require an adjustment to the account, because it would reduce the tax payable on profits. Alternatively when expenditure on stationery is treated as capital expenditure in error, this will overstate the non-current asset and understate the expenses, the end result will be that profits will be overstated and non-current asset value overstated as well. Thus the company's financial performance and position can only be projected truthfully if capital and revenue expenditure are properly treated.

Example 1

The treatment of revenue and capital expenditure can be summarized as shown below.

	Transaction	Revenue expenditure	Capital expenditure
		Income statement	Balance sheet
1	New computer K2500		K2500
2	Installation of computer K1000		K1000
3	Gas and electricity K450	K450	
4	Modernization of paper K8000		K8000
5	Office building paint every 5 years K6000		
6	Wages and salaries K1750	K1750	
7	New vehicle manager K9500		K9500
8	Stock for resale K3200	K3200	
9	Motor expenses K800	K800	
10	Purchase of land K20,000		K20,000
11	Solicitors fees for purchase K550		K550
12	Running cost of computer K600	K600	

Distinction Between Capital and Revenue Income

When non-current assets are find the sale value of them is referred to as capital income, the profit or loss from the disposal of them will depend on how much they are find for and this will be recorded in the income statement. If a profit on the sale of a non current asset is made:

Other revenues:
Profit on sale of non-current asset
If a loss is made on sale:

Expenses:

Loss on sale of non-current asset

Revenue income refers to normal trading activities of the business when it sales of goods or services including further income from rent, interest commission received, discount received.

Example 2

Harrison's trial balance as on 31 December

	DEBIT	CREDIT
	K'000	K'000
Capital for Harrison		10000
Drawings	2600	
Premises	2000	
Fixtures and fittings	2000	
Equipment	3000	
Motor van	1250	
Building society mortgage		8000
Bank loan		1000
Stock (January)	1000	
Bank cash	400	
Debtors	850	
Creditors		950
Sales		11000
Returns inwards	250	
Purchases	5000	
Salaries	850	
Light and heat	300	
Printing and stationery	100	
Telephone	155	
Delivery expense	125	
Advertising	300	
Packaging materials	340	
Discount allowed	65	
Rates and water	285	
Motor expenses	500	
Interest paid	140	
Rent received		125
Commission received		85
Returns outwards		350
Total	**31510**	**31510`**

The following information is available as at 31 December regarding Harrison's accounts.
1. His closing stock was valued at K1, 500,000
2. Accrued expenses were gas owing K45, salaries K34,000
3. Prepared expenses were rates and water K40,000, stationery unused K20, 000 packing material unusedK60, 000
4. Revenue accrued were commission due K120, rent received in advance K240,000
5. Revenue prepaid were commission paid in advance K25,000
6. Drawings were the owner took K500, 000 stock and K50, 000 for personal telephone class.

Required

Prepare Harrison's financial statements for the year ended 31 December.

Solution

Trading and profit and loss account for a Harrison for the year

	K'000	K'000	K'000
Sales		11000	
Less returns inwards		(250)	1075
Less Cost of sales:			
Opening stock	1000		
Purchases	5000		
Less return outwards	(350)		
Closing stock	(1500)		
Stock drawings	(500)		
			3650
Gross profit			**7100**
Rent received (125 + 240)			365
Commission received (85 + 120 – 25)			545
			8010
Less expenses			
Light and heat (300 + 54)	354		
Rates and water (285 – 40)	245		
Printing and stationery (100 – 20)	80		
Packing materials (340—060)	280		
Salaries (850 +34)	884		
Motor expenses	500		
Discount allowed	65		
Delivery expenses	125		

Advertising	300		
Telephone (155 + 50)	105		
Interest paid	140		
			<u>3078</u>
Net profit			**<u>4567</u>**

Balance sheet for a Harrison as at 31 December

	K'000	K'000	K'000
Non current assets			
Premises	12,000		
Equipment	3,000		
Fixtures and fitting	2,000		
Motor van	1,250		
Current assets			**18,250**
Stock	1,500		
Debtors	8,50		
Cash	4,00		
Revenue accrued	3,60		
Prepayments	1,20	3,230	
Current liabilities			
Prepaid revenue	25		
Accruals	88		
Creditors	9,50	**<u>1,063</u>**	
Working capital			**<u>2,167</u>**
Capital employed			**20,417**
Long term liabilities			
Mortgage		8,000	
Long term bank loan		1,000	<u>(9,000)</u>
Net assets			**11,417**
Financed by:			
Capital: Harrison	10,000		
+Net profit	<u>4,567</u>		
	14,567		
-Drawings			
Cash	(2,600)		
Stock	(500)		
Telephone	(50)		**<u>11,417</u>**

Note: If working capital was a negative figure, then the term used is 'net current liabilities'.

Example 3

John Hake's trial balance as on 31 October, 2011

	Dr K'000	Cr k'000
Cash at bank/in hand	6,500	
Purchases/sales	26,000	75,100
Motor vehicles	12,500	
Provision for depreciation (motor vehicles)		5,000
Rent and rates	1,400	
Light and heat	700	
Carriage inwards	500	
Carriage outwards	400	
Opening stock	18,300	
Commissions received		1,500
Drawings	9,000	
Returns	1,800	1,400
Office salaries	26,000	
Debtors/creditors	24,000	6,000
Provision for bad debts		2,000
Fixtures and fittings	8,000	
Provision for depreciation (fixtures and fittings)		2,400
Land and buildings	50,000	
Bank loan		10,000
Interest on loan (10%pa)	1,000	
Capital		82,700
	186,100	186,100

The following additional information is available as at 31 October, 2011

(a) Closing stock K21 000 000
(b) Revenue accrued: K420 000 still to be received on commission
(c) Rates had been paid K200 000 in advance
(d) K120 000 is owed for electricity (heating and lighting).
(e) Provision for bad debts is to be increased to 10% of the debtors
(f) Provision for depreciation of 10%pa on cost is to be made on fixtures and fittings.
(g) Provision for depreciation of 20% pa on book value is to be made on motor vehicles
(h) During the financial year, John Hake took goods for own use from the business which cost K800 000.

Required

Prepare the trading and profit and loss account of John Hake for the year ended 31 October 2011and a balance sheet as tat that date, 31 October 2011.

Solution

John Hake's

Trading and profit and loss account for the year ending 31 October

	K'000	K'000	K'000
Sales			75,100
Sales returns inwards			1,800
			73,300
Lass cost of sales			
Opening stock		18,300	
Purchases	26,000		
Add carriage inwards	500		
Less returns outwards	(1,400)		
Less stock for own use	(800)	24,300	
		42,600	
Closing stock		(21,000)	21,600
Gross profit			**51,700**
Other revenue:			
Commission received (1500 + 420)			1 920
			53 620
Rent and rates paid (1,400—200)		1,200	
Light and heat paid (700+120)		820	
Carriage outwards		400	
Office salaries paid		26,000	
Interest on loan		1,000	
Increase in provision for bad debts		400	
Provision for depreciation:			
Fixtures and fittings		800	
Vehicles		1,500	
			32,120
Net Profit			**21,500**

DR. CRYFORD MUMBA

John Hake's balance sheet as at 31 October 2011

	K'000 Cost	K'000 Cumulative Deprecation	K'000 Net book value
Fixed Assets			
Land and building	50,000	—	50,000
Fixtures and fittings	8,000	3,300	4,800
Motor vehicles	12,500	6,500	6,000
	70,500	9,700	60,800
Current assets			
Stock	21,000		
Debtors	24,000		
-provision for bad debts (2,400)	21,600		
Pre-payments	200		
Bank/cash	6,500		
Revenue accrued	420	49,720	
Current liabilities			
Trade creditors	6,000		
Accruals	120	6,120	
Net current assets			43,600
Capital employed			104,400
Long term liabilities			
Bank loan			10,000
			94,400
Financed by			
Capital	82,700		
Add net profit	21,500	104,200	
		9,800	94,400

Workings
   1. Depreciation

Fixtures and fittings: 10% of K8000 gives k800 which is recorded as an expense in the income statement. In the balance sheet it is k800+K2400 i.e. k3200 which is recorded under fixed assets.

Vehicles: 20% of (12500-k5000) i.e. k1500 which will be recorded in the income statement. In the balance sheet it is k1500 +k5000=k6500.

Land: No depreciation for land as a matter of convention. It usually appreciates in value as time passes.

2. Provision for doubtful debts.
   In the income statement it is the increase that is recorded i.e. 10% of k24000 =k2400. In the trial balance k2000 is already provided so the increase is k400 i.e. k2400-k2000 which is an expense. However, in the balance sheet the full amount of k2400 is recorded and is subtracted from debtors under current assets.

PROGRESS CLINIC 7

Question 1

Classify the following items as to whether they are capital or revenue expenditure?

(a) The purchase of a new IBM computer for the office
(b) Cost of software for use of the new computer
(c) Cost of computer pay
(d) A refit of a stock room with new showing
(e) The payment of gas and electricity bills
(f) The purchase of stock for resale
(g) Discount allowed on the sale of stocks
(h) The acquisition of a new motor vehicle for the use
(i) The road tax and insurance of a vehicle
(j) The repairs and maintenance of motor vehicle
(k) The cost of new floppy disc for the use of the computer
(l) The computer decorations of official to last a number of years

Question 2

a) Why is it important to make the distinction between capital and revenue costs as those stated in question one above.
b) If the cost of a computer, K2800 was recorded in the purchasing account, and the cost of vehicle insurances, K40 was recorded in the motor vehicles account. What effect would it have on the final accounts?

Question 3

The following details were collected from the records of T Muke, for the year ended 31 December 2006.

		K000
Returns Inwards		490
Returns Outwards		560
Purchases		31,000
Sales		52,790
Stocks of goods:	1 January 2006	5,690
	31 December 2006	4,230
Carriage Inwards		1,700
Salaries and wages		5,010
Rent		1,460
Motor Expenses		3,120
General Expenses		420
Carriage Outwards		790

Required:

From the above details, draw up a Trading and Profit and Loss Account for the year ended 31 December 2012.

Question 4

The following list of balances was extracted from the ledger of Mr. Yoram, a sole trader for the period to 31 May 2012.

	K000
Sales	138,078
Purchases	82,350
Carriage	5,144
Drawings	7,800
Rent, Rates and Insurance	6,622
Postage and stationery	3,001
Advertising	1,330
Salaries and wages	26,420
Bad debts	877
Provision for doubtful debts	130
Debtors	12,120
Creditors	6,471
Cash in hand	177
Cash at bank	1,002
Stock as at 1 June 2011	11,927

Equipment at cost	58,000
Accumulated Depreciation on Equipment	19,000
Capital	53,091

The following additional information as at 31 May 2012 is available:

(a) Rent is accrued by K210,000
(b) Rates have been prepared by K880,000
(c) K2,211,000 of carriage represents Inwards on purchases
(d) Equipment is to be depreciated at 15% per annum using the straight line method (i.e. on cost)
(e) The provision for Bad debts is to be increased by K40,000
(f) Stock at the close of business has been valued at K13,551,000

REQUIRED

Prepare a Trading and Profit and Loss Account for the year ended 31 May 2012 and a Balance Sheet as at that date.

Question 5

The following balances have been extracted from the General Ledger accounts of Juma at 31 March 2012:

	K'000
Capital at 1 April 2011	57,801
Creditors	24,650
Debtors	36,975
Telephone	2,645
Purchases	110,925
Heat and light	6,720
Rent	12,000
Advertising	3,475
Sales	221,850
Stock at 31 March 2011	20,250
Plant—NBV at 31 March 2012	64,500
Motor Vehicles—NBV at 31 March 2912	30,750
Administrative expenses	4,424
Plant—depreciation for the year	9,675
Motor Vehicles—depreciation charge for the year	7,690
Drawings	15,000
Bank	4,782
Bank loan	20,000
VAT (credit balance)	5,510

The value of closing stock at 31 March 2012 was K23,400,000.

Required:

a) Explain the purpose of both The Trading, Profit and Loss Account and the Balance Sheet.
b) Using the above information, prepare a Trading, Profit and Loss Account for Juma for the year ended 31 March 2012, and a Balance Sheet as at that date.
c) Using the figures from your Balance Sheet in part (b), identify the accounting equation.

CHAPTER 8

PREPARING FINANCIAL STATEMENTS:PARTNERSHIP ACCOUNTS

Partnerships are a popular form of exam questions. There is some new terminology to learn but more importantly there are a number of special accounting entries that have to be dealt with.

The emphasis of exam questions is on dealing with the computational aspects of partnerships but there are occasional questions, or parts of questions, requiring an explanation of terms or accounting entries.

Objectives

By the time you have finished this chapter you should be able to:

- Divide profit between partners
- Prepare partnership financial statements

Note that partnership questions in the examination no longer deal with changes requiring goodwill alignments, or dissolutions.

Partnerships – basic principles

Identification of partnership

A partnership is a natural progression from a sole trader, the sole proprietor taking in one or more partners (co-proprietors) in common with a view to profit. In many countries a partnership is not a corporate entity, but a collection of individuals jointly carrying on business.

Advantages and disadvantages of partnerships

Comparing a partnership to sole trading, the advantages of operating as a partnership are as follows:

Business risks are spread among more than one person.

- Individual partners can develop special skills upon which the other partners can rely, whereas in a sole business one person has responsibility for everything.

- Certain partners may be able to draw upon larger capital resources to set up the partnership or expand the partnership.

The disadvantages are:

- There may be disputes partners on such matters as the direction the business is taking or how much money individual partners are taking out of the business. Some partners may feel they are contributing more time and effort to the partnership than others and not being sufficiently financially rewarded as a result.

- In many countries a partner is 'jointly and severally liable' for his partners. This means that if one partner is being sued in relation to the business of the partnership, the other partners share in the responsibility.

A partnership has some advantages over a company as the arrangement is less formal than setting up a company, which requires the issue of shares and the appointment of directors. If the partners wish to dissolve the business, that is easier to achieve by a partnership than by a company.

The advantage of a company is that the owners of the business – the shareholders – may be protected from the creditors of the company as regards the payment of outstanding debts. This point is looked at more closely when we examine company financial statements in a later chapter.

Dividing profit and maintaining equity

A partnership agreement, which need not necessarily be in written form, will govern the relationships between the partners. Important matters to be covered include:

- Name of firm, the type of business, and duration.
- Capital to be introduced by partners
- Distribution of profits between partners
- Drawings by partners
- Arrangements for dissolution, or on the death or retirement of partners
- Settling of disputes
- Preparation and audit of accounts

The division of profit stated in the partnership agreement may be quite complex in order to reflect the expected differing efforts and contributions of the partners. For example, some or all of the partners may be entitled to a salary to reflect the differing management involvement in the business. Interest on capital may be provided to reflect the differing amounts of capital contributed. The profit shares may differ to reflect seniority or greater skills.

It is important to appreciate, however, that all of the above examples are means of dividing the profits of the partnership and are not expenses of the business. A partnership salary is merely a device for calculating the division of profit; it is not a salary in the normal meaning of the term.

Accounting distinctions between partnerships and sole traders

The accounting techniques develop for sole traders are generally applicable to partnerships, but there are certain important differences:

Item	Sole trader's books	Partnership's books
Capital introduced	Capital account	Partners' fixed capital accounts
Drawings and share of the profit	Capital account	Partners' current accounts
Division of profits	Inapplicable-one only	Income statement (see below)

Preparing partnership financial statements

Capital accounts

At the commencement of the partnership, an agreement will have to be reached as to the amount of capital to be introduced. This could be in the form of cash or other assets. Whatever the form of assets introduced and debited to asset accounts, it is normal to make the credit entry to fixed capital accounts. These are so called because they are not the used to record drawings or shares of profits but only major changes in the relations between partners. In particular, fixed capital accounts are used to deal with:

- Capital introduced or withdrawn by new or retiring partners
- Revaluation adjustments.

The balances on fixed capital accounts do not necessarily bear any relation to the division of profits. However, to compensate partners who provide a larger share of the capital, it is common for notional interest on capital accounts to be paid to partners. This is dealt within the calculations for the profit shares transferred from the income statement.

Current accounts

Current accounts are used to deal with the regular transactions between the partners and the firm. i.e. matters other than those sufficiently fundamental to be dealt with through the capital accounts. Most commonly these are:

- Share of profits, interest on capital and partners' salaries, usually computed annually.
- Monthly drawings against the annual share of profit.

Ledger accounts and balance sheet presentation

Nab and Crag commenced in partnership on 1 January 20X6, contributing as fixed capital K5, 000 and K10, 000 cash respectively. All profits and losses are shared equally. The profit for the year ended 31 December 20X6 amounted to K10, 000. Drawings for Nab and Crag amounted to K3, 000 and K4, 000 respectively.

You are required to prepare the capital and current accounts and balance sheet extracts.

Partners' capital accounts

		Nab K	Crag K				Nab K	Crag K
				20X6				
				1 Jan	Cash		5,000	10,000

Partners' current accounts

		Nab K	Crag K			Nab K	Crag K
20X6				20X6			
31 Dec	Drawings	3,000	4,000	31 Dec	Income statement		
	Balance c/d	2,000	1,000		-profit share	5,000	5,000
		5,000	5,000			5,000	5,000
				20X7			
				1 Jan	Balance b/d	2,000	1,000

The above accounts are presented in a columnar format. This is convenient for examination purposes and is quite common in a partnership set of books as each partner will have similar transactions during the year. A columnar format allows two (or more) separate accounts to be shown using the same narrative. It is important to remember through that each partner's account is separate from the other partners(s).

Balance sheet at 31 December 20X6 (extract)

	Capital K	Current accounts K	K
Partners' accounts:			
Nab	5,000	2,000	7,000
Crag	10,000	1,000	11,000
	15,000	3,000	18,000

Note that the current account balances of K2, 000 and K1, 000 will be credited in the following year with profit shares and debited with drawings.

One of the main differences between the capital section of the balance sheet of a sole trader and a partnership is that the partnership balance sheet will often only give the closing balances whereas the sole trader's movements in a capital are shown. The main reason for difference is simply one of space. Movements in the capital and current accounts for a few partners cannot be easily accommodated on the face of the balance sheet. In answering examination question, the partners' capital and current accounts are often required as well as a balance sheet. It is a waste of time to repeat in the balance sheet detail already given in the partners' accounts.

Example 2

The information is the same in Example 1, except that Nab's drawings are K5, 300. The current accounts now become:

Partners' current accounts

		Nab	Crag			Nab	Crag
		K	K			K	K
20X6				20X6	Income statement		
	Drawings	5,300	4,000		-profit share	5,000	5,000
31 Dec	Balance c/d		1,000	31 Dec	Balance c/d	300	
		5,300	5,000			5,300	5,000
20X7				20X7			
1 Jan	Balance b/d	300		1 Jan	balance b/d		1,000

Note that Nab's current account is overdrawn. How do we present this in the balance sheet?

It is convenient to show it thus"

Balance sheet at 31 December 20X6 (extract)

	Capital Accounts	Current Accounts	Total
	K	K	K
Partners' accounts"			
Nab	500	(300)	4,700
Crag	10,000	1,000	11,000
	15,000	700	15,7000

Division of profit

The division of the profit among the partners is shown in an addition to the income statement.

It is important to realize that all allocations to partners are part of the process of dividing the profit, not expenses of the business.

Example 3

Pike and Scar are in partnership and have the following profit-sharing arrangements:

1. interest on capital is to provided at a rate of 8% p.a.
2. Pike and Scar are to receive salaries of K6,000 and K8,000 p.a. respectively
3. the balance of profit or loss is to be divided between Pike and Scar in the ratio 3:2.

Net profit for the year amounts to K20, 000 and capital account balances are Pike K12, 000 and Scar K9, 000.

You are required to prepare:

(a) a statement showing the division of profit between the partners
(b) relevant entries in the income statement.

Solution

(a) Division of net profit of K20, 000

	Pike	Scar	Total
	K	K	K
Interest on capital	960	720	1,680
Salaries	6,000	8,000	14,000
Balance of profits (K20, 000 – K15, 680) in ratio 3:2	2,592	1,728	4,320
	(3/5)	(2/5)	
Total	9,552	10,448	20,000

Note that this is only a calculation of profit and not part of the double entry bookkeeping system, merely providing the figures for the closure of the income statement.

(b) Extract from income statement for the year ended . . . .

	K	K
Sales revenue		x
Cost of sales		x
Gross profit		x
Expenses		x
Net profit		20,000
Allocated to:		
Pike	9,552	
Scar	10,448	
		20,000

The allocations are dealt with by transferring them to the credit of the partners' current accounts. The double entry is therefore.

Debit	Credit	With
Income statement	Pike's current account	K 9, 552
Income statement	Scar's current account	K10, 448

For the purposes of examinations (and in practice), parts (a) and (b) above can be amalgamated as follows:

Extract from income statement for the year ended . . .

	K
Sales revenue	X
Cost of sales	X
Gross profit	X
Expenses	X
Net profit for year	20,000

Division of profit

	Pike		Scar		Total
	K		K		K
Interest on capital	960		720		1,680
Salaries	6,000		8,000		14,000
Balance of profits (K20, 000—					
K15, 680) in ratio 3:2	2,592	(3/5)	1,728	(2/5)	4,320
Totals	9,552		10,448		20,000

The debits actually being made are as before (K9, 552 and K10, 448).

Example 4

The facts are the same as for Example 3, except that net profit is now only K3, 680.

You are required to show the division of profit between the partners.

Division of net profit of K3, 680

	Pike	Scar	Total
	K	K	K
Interest on capital	960	720	1,680
Salaries	6,000	8,000	14,000

Balance of profits (K3, 680 –
K15, 680 = K12, 000) in ratio 3:2   (7,200)   (4,800)   (12,000)
Totals   (240)   3,920   3,680

Debit	Credit	With
Income statement	Scar's current account	K3, 920
Pike's current account	income statement	K240

The relevant part of the income statement would show:

	K	K
Net profit		3,680
Allocated to:	3,920	
	(240)	
		3,680

One point which regularly causes difficulties is the partners' salaries. The key is to remember at the outset that a partner's salary is part of the division of profit, whereas a salary paid to an employee is an expense.

According a salary to which a partner is entitled is included as part of the credit to his or her current account as part of the division of profit. Questions sometimes state that a partner has withdrawn his salary. In this case:

Include the salary in the division of profit as usual
quite separately treat the withdrawal of the salary as drawings

Debit	Credit	With
Partners' current account	Bank	Amount withdrawn

Guaranteed minimum profit share

In certain partnership agreements, a partner can be guaranteed a minimum share of profits. The division of profit would proceed in the normal way. If the result is that the partner has less than this minimum, the deficit will be made good by the other partners in profit-sharing ratio or in any other way they have agreed.

Example 5

Tessa, Laura and Jane are in partnership and have the following profit-sharing arrangements;

1. Tessa and Laura to receive salaries of K20,000 and K30,000 respectively
2. The balance of profit or loss is to be divided Tessa 1, Laura 2, and Jane 3.
3. Tessa is guaranteed a minimum profit share of K25, 000.

The net profit for the year is K68, 000.

You are required to show the division of profit for the year.

Division of Profit

	Tessa	Laura	Jane	Total
	K	K	K	K
Net profit				68,000
Salaries	20,000	30,000	-	(50,000)
				18,000
Balance of profits in ratio 1:2:3	3,000	6,000	9,000	(18,000)
	23,000	36,000	9,000	
Adjustment	2,000			
Laura 2/5 X 2,000		(800)		
Jane 3/5 X 2,000			(1,200)	
Totals	25,000	35,200	7,800	68,000

Interest on drawings

Occasionally there is a provision in a partnership agreement for a notional interest charge on the drawings by each partner. The interest charges are merely a negative profit share-they are a means by which total profits are allocated between the partners.

The reason for on drawings provision is that those partners who draw out more cash than their colleagues in the early part of an accounting period should suffer a cost.

Example Dick and Dark are in partnership. The capital and current accounts as at 1 January 2012 show:

	Capital	Current
	K	K
Dick	50,000	2,500
Dark	20,000	3,000

The partnership agreement provides for the following:

1. Profits and losses are shared between Dick and Dark in percentages 60 and 40.
2. Interest on capital at 10% per annum is allowed
3. Interest on drawings is charged at 12% per annum

Drawings for the year to 31 December 2012 are:

	Dick	Dark
	K	K
1 February 2012	5,000	2,000
30 September 2012	2,000	5,000

The profit for the year is K20, 000.

Required

You are required to prepare a statement showing the division of profits and the current accounts for the year ended 31 December 2012.

Solution

Division of profits for the year ended 31 December 20X7

	Dick	Dark	Total
	K	K	K
Profit for the year			20,000
Add: interest on drawings (see working)	(610)	(370)	980
			20,980
Less: interest on capital:			
50,000 X 10%	5,000		
20,000 X 10%		2,000	(7,000)
			13,980
Balance in profit-sharing ratio:			
13,980 X 60%	8,388		
13,980 X40%		5,592	(13,980)
Total allocation	12,778	7,222	20,000

Current accounts

	Dick	Dark		Dick	Dark
	K	K		K	K
2012:			2012:		
1 Feb Drawings	5,000	2,000	Balance b/d	2,500	3,000
30 Sep Drawings	2,000	5,000	31 Dec Share of		
Balance c/d	8,278	3,222	profits	12,778	7,222
	15,278	10,222		15,278	10,222

Working

		Dick K	Dastardly K
Interest on drawings:			
1 February 2012	5,000 X 12% X 11/12	550	
	2,000 X 12% X 11/12		220
30 September 2012	2,000 X 12% X 3/12	60	
	5,000 X 12% X 3/12		150
		610	370

Example 6

Pulling the topics together

You should now be in a position to follow through from the list of account balances stage a full example of partnership accounts

You are provided with the following information regarding the partnership of Daka Hume and Terry:

1. Trial balance at 31 December 2012 is as follows:

	Dr K	Cr K
Sales revenue	50,000	
Inventory at 1 January 20X6	6,000	
Purchases	29,250	
Carriage inwards	250	
Carriage outwards	400	
Payables		4,000
Cash at bank	3,900	
Current accounts:		
Daka		900
Hume		750
Terry		1,350
Capital accounts:		
Daka		4,000
Hume		5,000
Terry		6,000
Drawings:		
Daka	2,000	
Hume	3,000	
Terry	5,000	
Sundry expenses	2,800	
Receivables	13,000	

Shop fittings:

Cost	8,000	
Accumulated depreciation		1,600
	73,600	73,600

2. Closing inventory is valued for accounts purposes at K5, 500.

3. Depreciation of K800 is to be provided on the shop fittings.

4. The profit-sharing arrangements are as follows:

- Interest on capital to be provided at a rate of 10% per annum

- Daka and Terry are to receive salaries of K3,000 and K4,000 per annum respectively

- The balance of profit or loss to be divided between Daka, Hume and Terry in the ratio of 3:8:4.

You are required to prepare the partnership financial statements for 20X6 and the current accounts of the partners.

Daka, Hume and Terry

Income statement for the year ended 31 December 2012

	K	K
Sales revenue		50,000
Opening inventory	6,000	
Purchases	29,250	
Carriage inwards	35,500	
	5,000	
Less: Closing inventory		30,000
		20,000
Gross profit	2,800	
Sundry expenses	400	
Carriage outwards	800	
Depreciation		4,000
Net profit		16,000
Allocated to:		
Daka	4,900	
Hume	4,500	
Terry	6,600	
		16,000

Balance sheet as at 31 December 2012

	Cost K	Acc dep'n K	NBV K
Non-current assets:			
Shop fittings	8,000	2,400	5,600
Current assets:			
Inventory		5,500	
Receivables		13,000	
Cash		3,900	
			22,400
			28,000

Partners' accounts

	Capital accounts K	Current accounts K	Total K
Daka	4,000	3,800	7,800
Hume	5,000	2,250	7,250
Terry	6,000	2,950	8,950
	15,000	9,000	24,000

Current liabilities		
Payables		4,000
		28,000

Partners' current accounts

		Daka K	Hume K	Terry K			Daka K	Hume K	Terry K
2012:					2012:				
	Drawings				1 Jan	Balance			
		2,000	3,000	5,000		b/d	900	750	1,350
31 Dec	Balance					income			
	c/d	3,800	2,250	2,950		stmt	4,900	4,500	6,600
		5,800	5,250	7,950			5,800	5,250	7,950
					2013:				
					1 Jan	Balance			
						b/d	3,800	2,250	2,950

Working and commentary

The adjustments for inventory and depreciation should by now be familiar.

The new development is that, having calculated the profit for the period, it has to be divided between Daka, Hume and Terry. To calculate their respective shares a statement of the form shown below is convenient:

	Daka	Hume	Terry	Total
	K	K	K	K
Interest on capital	400	500	600	1,500
Salaries	3,000	-	4,000	7,000
Balance of profit (K16, 000 – K8, 500) in ratio 3:8:4	1,500	4,000	2,000	7,500
	4,900	4,500	6,600	16,000

This gives us the figures for the double entry:

Dr income statement
Cr partners 'current accounts

In the case of a sole trader, the net profit is transferred to the credit of his or her capital account. The procedure is exactly the same for a partnership, except that each partner's share must first be calculated as shown.

Example 7

The following balances are in the accounting records of a partnership as at 31 December 2012.

		K
Capital accounts:	Leo, as at 1 January 2012	400 000
	Mark, introduced 1 July 2012	200 000
Drawings:	Leo	160 000
	Mark	80 000

Notes:

1. Until 30 June 2012, Leo run the business as a sole trade, Mark joined him on 1 July 2012 introducing capital of K200 000.

2. The following profit-sharing arrangements were agreed upon from that date:

(a) Both partners to receive interest on their capital account balances at 5% per year.
(b) Mark to receive a salary of K20 000 per year.
(c) Balance of profit to be shared-Leo 60%: Mark 40%

3. The profit for the year ended 31 December 2012 was K250 000. It was agreed that this profit had accrued one third in the six months ended 30 June 2012, and two third in the six months ended 31 December 2012, except for an irreversible debt of K20 000 charged in arriving at profit which was to be regarded as occurring in the six months ended 30 June 2012.

Required:

Prepare a statement showing the division of profit and prepare the partners' current accounts for the year ended 31 December 2012.

Solution

Statement of division of profit for the year ended 31 December 2012.

Six months ended 30 June 2012

	K	K
Leo (90 000 – 20 000) (see working)		70 000

Six months ended 31 December 2012

	K	K
• Profit		180 000
• Interest on capital		
Leo 5% X 400 000 X 6/12	10 000	
Mark 5% X 200 000 X 6/12	5 000	(15 000)
		165 000
• Salary – Mark 20 000 X 6/12		(10 000)
		155 000
• Balance of profit:		
Leo 60 X 155 000	93 000	
Mark 40% X 155 000	62 000	155 000
		0

Workings

	K	K
• Profit for the year		250 000
• Add: irrecoverable debt		20 000
• Profit for division		270 000
• Six months ended 30 June 2006	90 000	
• Less: irrecoverable debt	(20 000)	70 000
• Six months ended 31 December 2006		180 000
		250 000

Current accounts

		Leo K	Mark K		Leo K	Mark K
•	Drawings	160 000	80 000	30 June profit	70 000	-
•	Balance	13 000	-	31 Dec interest		
				On capital	10 000	5 000
		173 000	80 000			
				Salary	-	10 000
				Share of balance		
				(60:40)	93 000	62 000
				Balance	-	3 000
					173 000	80 000

Alternative format:

Statement of division of profit for the year ended 31 December 2012

		Leo K	Mark K	Total K
•	Six months ended 30 June 2006		-	70 000
	Leo: (90 000 – 20 000)	70 000		
•	Six months ended 31 December 2006			
•	Interest on capital:			
Leo 5% X 400 000 X 6/12				
	Mark 5% X 200 X 6/12	10 000	-	
•	Salary	-	5 000	15 000
	Mark 20 000 X 6/12		10 000	10 000
	Balance of profit (60:40)		62 000	
		103 000	77 000	180 000

Current accounts

		Leo K	Mark K		Leo K	Mark K
•	Drawings	160 000	80 000	2006		
•	Balance	13 000	-	30 June profit	70 000	-
		173 000	80 000	31 Dec share		
				of profit	103 000	77 000
				Balance		3 000
					173 000	80 000

A final point

The majority of examination questions specify separate capital and current accounts. Occasionally you may be faced with a question specifying only one account for each partner. Such an account acts as a capital and current account combined.

Conclusion

Accounting for partnerships is similar to accounting for sole traders in many respects, except that profit needs to allocated between the partners, and the capital section of the balance sheet is more complex.

PROGRESS CLINIC 8

Lombe and Maale are in partnership sharing profits in the ratio: Lombe three fifths (3/5) and Maale two fifths (2/5).

The following Trial Balance was extracted as at 31 March 2012.

Trial Balance As At 31 March 2012

	DR K000	CR K000
Office Equipment at cost	6,500	
Motor vehicles at cost	9,200	
Provision for Depreciation at 31 March 2011:		
- Motor Vehicles		3,680
- Office equipment		1,950
Stock at 31 March 2011	24,970	
Debtors and creditors	20,960	16,275
Cash at Bank	615	
Cash in Hand	140	
Sales		90,370
Purchases	71,630	
Salaries	8,417	
Office Expenses	1,370	
Discount allowed	563	
Current Accounts at 31 March 2011:		
- Lombe		1,379
- Maale		1,211
Capital Accounts:		
- Lombe		27,000
- Maale		12,000

Drawings:
- Lombe   5,500
- Maale   4,000   _____
                                                         153,865   153,865

The following additional information is applicable at 31 March 2012:

(i) Stock at 31 March 2012 was valued at K27,340,000.
(ii) Office expenses owing amounted to K110,000.
(iii)Provision for depreciation: Motor vehicles 20 per cent on cost, office equipment 10 per cent on cost.
(iv)Charge interest on capital at 10 per cent
(v) Charge interest on drawings: Lombe K180,000, Maale K21,000.
(vi)Charge K500,000 for salary for Maale.

Required:

From the above partnership details draw up the following financial statements:

(a) Trading Profit and Loss Account for the year ended 31 March 2012.

(b) Partnership Appropriation Account for the year ended 31 March 2012.

(c) Balance sheet as at 31 March 2012

CHAPTER 9

PREPARING FINANCIAL STATEMENTS: COMPANY ACCOUNTS

Company formation and documentation

Company accounts are regulated by Companies Act. The formation of a limited company needs only a minimum of two founder members (promoters) who are willing to subscribe share capital. There is no maximum required. Basically, there are two distinct types of limited companies namely:

(a) **Public limited company (Plc)** – A plc must bear these letters after its name on all correspondence to distinguish it from a private company (for example Zambia Sugar Plc). The word "limited" means that shareholders' liabilities are limited to the nominal capital of their shares, in the same way a limited partner is limited to the amount of capital subscribed.

(b) **Private limited company** – The private company can only sell its shares privately. It cannot issue a prospectus inviting the public to buy its shares. The privilege is only permitted to the plc. A private company, therefore, is restricted in the amount of shares capital it can raise because it cannot, by statute; advertise to sell its shares. It is likely to sell its shares to family and friends interested in financing a business venture.

Unlike the private company, the plc has the potential to raise sums of capital by offering its shares for public sale. Plc shares may be listed on the stock exchange, while private company share cannot be listed.

Documentation

The procedure to form a limited company is a little more involved than forming other business units. The sole trade has virtually no legal constraint and partnerships are advised to prepare Deeds of Partnership before starting up in business. A limited company must prepare two important documents that are sent to the Registrar of companies to obtain approval before it can proceed. These documents are the '**Memorandum of Association** and the **Articles of Association**.

The memorandum gives the "external " view of the company to the public, including details of its name (which should end with 'Ltd', address, registered office, share capital, and most important, its objectives (that is, what it proposes to do).

The Articles' give the "internal" view of the company which relates to rules and regulations governing the internal organization of the company, such as voting rights, conduct at meetings, power of directors and so forth.

Once these documents are approved by the Registrar, a limited company is issued a **Certificate of Incorporation** which gives it the status of being a separate legal entity from the owners of the business (the shareholders). The company has then the right of its own identity and can proceed under its own name, acting under its own name in the course of its business. A board of Directors is elected by the shareholders to take control of the company on their behalf. The directors control while the shareholders own the company.

A private limited company, like PCBF Ltd, on receipt of its certificate of incorporation, can commence trading.

A PLC must issue its prospectus to sell its share before it can begin. The directors of the company must state, in the prospectus, the minimum amount of share capital it requires in order to start business and that the share issue has been underwritten (guaranteed) to ensure that the minimum capital is raised. Once this minimum capital is raised, the Registrar can issue the PLC its **Certificate of Trading**—its right to commence business operations.

The capital of limited companies

Unlike the capital of sole traders and partnerships, there are a number of terms relating to a limited company's capital and you need to be able to distinguish each of them. These terms are:

i) **Authorized capital** – This is the nominal capital of the company and is normally the maximum amount of capital it can issue. It is the company's registered capital and is the sum stated in the company's Memorandum of Association. A company may set up with share capital of K5000 000, some of which may be preference shares. However, it is far much more likely that it will be ordinary shares, the most common shares of limited companies.

ii) **Issued capital** – This is that nominal capital issued to shareholders and cannot be in excess of authorized capital. If all the authorized capital is issued, then authorized and issued capital will equal the same sum. For example, if the nominal capital was K5000 000 and K3000 000 issued, there would be a further K2000 000 unissued shares that the company could still sell at a later date.

iii) **Called-up capital** – this refers to shares which have been allotted to shareholders and have only called up part of the sum due on the shares. The balance due can be called up at a later point of time. For example, if a company allots K500 000 K1 share and only calls up 50n per share, it will receive K250 000 as paid up capital. This means that although it has issued K500 000 of share capital, it has only called up half of it. The balance of K250 000 is the uncalled capital.

iv) **Paid up capital** – This refers to the issued capital paid for by shareholders. If some shareholders have not yet paid for their shares, they would be debtors to the company until they have paid for them. For example, if only K245 000 had been received for the called up capital, then K5000 represents unpaid capital.

Ordinary shares, preference shares and debentures

The capital of a limited company is divided into shares. An investor becomes a part owner (shareholder) of the company by buying shares. There are two classes of share capital that may be issued to shareholders, ordinary shares and preference shares.

- **Ordinary shares** are the most common and represents the 'true' taking the greater risks. They represent permanent capital of the company. The rate of dividends depends on how much profit is made and how much is to be distributed (i.e. dividends not fixed). Ordinary shares are given voting rights – one share, one vote. These votes may be used at Annual General Meetings but rarely are they exercised in PLCs because very few shareholders actually attend. Further, ordinary shares are the last to be paid, after the company has paid all its other financial obligations.

- **Preference shares** are paid a fixed rate of dividend and shareholders are entitled to be paid first before ordinary shares. The shares do not hold voting rights and are suitable for the less adventurous type of shareholder who wants a more reliable and consistent rate of dividend. Preference shares that may not have received a dividend this, it is taken to next year where it will rank before ordinary shares (cumulative preference shares).

- **Debentures** represent borrowed capital and not share capital. Thus, debenture holders are the creditors of the company and not shareholders. They are paid at a fixed rate of interest over a specified period of the loan. The interest paid is an expense entered into the income statement, and not the appropriate account.

The differences between shareholders and debenture holders are summarized in the following table:

Debenture holder	Shareholder
· Debentures are not part of the capital of a company.	· Shares are part of the capital of a company
· Debentures rank first for capital and interest.	· Shares are postponed to the claims of Debentures holders and other creditors.
· Debenture interest must be paid whether there are profits or not and is a change to the income statement.	· Dividends are paid out of profits only (appropriations) but only if there is adequate profit
· Debentures are usually secured by a charge on the company's assets	· shares cannot carry a charge

| · Debenture holders are creditors, not members of the company, and usually have no control over it. | · shareholders are members of the company and have indirect control over its management |

Note: Debentures are not capital and so they should not be grouped with the shares in the balance sheet.

Preparation of limited company financial statements

The procedures and the format used in preparing limited company financial statements are the same as the used when preparing sole trader financial statements. However, there are new terms which need special attention. These are:

1. **Preliminary Expenses** (limited company only). These are expenses incurred at the time a limited company incorporated, and consist chiefly of legal charges connected with the incorporation of the company. Under the companies Act they should be written off immediately.

2. **Director's Remuneration** – These refers to the fees directors are paid. They are an expense of the company and appear in the income statement.

3. **Goodwill** – this is an item which often appears as an asset of a business. Goodwill may arise in the business because it may have earned itself a good name or reputation built up over a period of time through its business activities. The value of goodwill can be calculated on certain factors like average sales over a period of time, or profits earned over a number of accounting periods. For examples, where a company purchases another, it may pay K900 million for tangible assets which are worth K600 million K300 million is the value of goodwill.

4. **Debenture interest** – As debenture holders are paid whether the company is able to show profit or not. Therefore, it is an expense, and as such must be debited to the income statement. However, the debenture itself is treated as a long term liability in the balance sheet. Further, remember the deference between debenture interest and dividends paid. The former is interest on an outside loan whilst the latter is merely a distribution of profit.

5. **Dividends paid** – this item, which will appear as a debit balance in the trial balance, represents profits which have been distributed amongst the shareholders of the company and must **not** be debited to the income statement. This item must be debited to the appropriation account. If no profit has been made, no dividends will be paid to shareholders. Note, however, that a provision for dividends (proposed dividends) is a current liability of the company.

6. **Reserves** – this item represents additions to the company's capital over a period of time. Reserves a broadly dividend into two namely capital reserves and revenue reserves. Capital reserves include sums transferred to the share premium account which have come its nominal value (face value). For example, 1000 K1 shares sold for K1.50 each means that there will be K1000 share capital and K500 in the premium account. A further example of capital reserves includes **revaluation** of non-current assets. If premium were valued at a cost K100 million and this was revalued by the company to K150 million, the company would show an increase of K50 million in its 'revaluation reserves' account which is part of capital and reserves in the balance sheet. Fixed assets replacement reserves is another name for the revaluation of fixed assets.

- Revenue reserves are retained profits from normal trading activity and any profit retained in the appropriation account could be transferred to the reserves account. Note that this is not actual money but represents an increase in the shareholders' capital and the net assets of the company. Often retained profits are simply held in the profit and loss account balance.

- Bonus shares may be issued to a company's shareholders without payment. They are 'free shares' coming out of the revenue reserves. For example, if there was K100 000 share capital and K50 000 in reserves, and shareholders were offered 1 bonus share for every 2 they held, then share capital becomes K150 000 and the reserves would be zero.

  Finally, note that the common reserves are share premium account, revaluation reserves, general reserves, and profit and loss balance (i.e. retained profits).

Other items which are common to both financial statements of limited companies and sole traders are partnerships are:

7. **Discounts** – There are two types of discounts, one for discount received and one for discounts allowed. Discount allowed is a debit balance. At the end of the trading period discount received account is debited and the profit and loss account credited, as items under this heading are benefits received by the firm. Discounts allowed account is credited and the profit and loss account is debited, as these items are expenses of the firm. Thus, discounts received represent other sources of income for the firm.

8. **Bad debts** – If all the debtors of a firm paid their accounts, no mention of this item would be made unfortunately, however, they do not, and many firms incur what are known as bad debts. For example, were a debtor is declared a bankrupt, the whole of his debt will not be settled. Consequently, this debt has no value and it must be written off a s a loss hence an expense in the income statement. The same will result when debtors disappear or if debts are not worth court action. The debtor's account is credited with the amount of bad, thus closing the account. To complete the double entry, the bad debts account is debited.

9. **provision for bad debts** – In addition to writing off bad debts as they occur, or when the are known to be bad, a business should also provide for any of its present debtors being unable to meet their obligations. The provision is formed for the purpose of reducing the value of debtors on the balance sheet to an amount which it is expected will be received from them. It is not an estimate of the bad debts which will arise in the succeeding period. (Note: Never show provision for bad debts with the liabilities on the balance sheet – it is always deducted from the amount of debtors under assets on the balance sheet).

10. **Provisions for discounts allowable** – If a business allows discounts to its customers for prompt payment, it is likely that some of the debtors at the balance sheet rate will actually pay less than the full amount of their debt. To include debtors at the face value of such debits, without providing for discounts which may be claimed, is to overstate the financial position of the business. So, a provision for discounts allowable should be made by debit to profit deduction in the balance sheet from debtors after the provision for bad debts has been deducted. It is a financial expense.

11. **Depreciation** – Assets such as plant and machinery, warehouse or factory buildings, delivery vehicles, have their value decrease owing to tear and wear. Each year the depreciation account will increase in value, until such a time as the balance on that account equals the cost price as shown in the asset account. At this point no further depreciation should be charged to the income statement

    Depreciation charge per annum is an expense in the income statement while the balance sheet shows the cumulative depreciation at the balance sheet date. Where there is a profit or loss on the disposal of a non-current asset, this is shown in the income statement immediately after the expenses of depreciation. Note the correct depreciation amount must be calculated to avoid overstating or understating the non-current asset values in the balance sheet and the expenses figure in the income statement.

12. **Financial expenses** – These include bank charges interest on loans, hire purchase agreements, debentures, mortgages, bank overdrafts, etc. No capital expense items must be debited to income statement. This is extremely important.

13. **Expenses paid in Advance or Arrears**. These are prepayments and Accruals. Prepayments represent a current asset in the balance sheet and a reduction in expenses in the income statement. Accruals, on the other hand, refer to a current liability in the balance sheet and an increase in expenses in the income statement.

    [Note: Refresh on the above points, by going through the chapter on Adjustments to final Accounts].

Classification of overhead expenses

All the overheard expenses may be subdivided according to their type as follows:

1. **Administration expenses**. These include rent, rates, lighting, heating, repairs of office buildings, directors' renumeration and fees, salaries of managers and clerks, office expenses of various types. In general, all the expenses incurred in the control of the business and the direction and formulation of its policy are administrative expenses.

2. **Sales expenses**. These include sales commission, salaries of sales staff, warehouse rent, rates and expenses in respect of warehouse , advertising, and any other expenses connected with the selling of the goods dealt ,e.g bad debts, warrant expenses, etc.

3. **Distribution expenses**. Here we have cost of carriage outwards.(Remember carriage inwards, i.e. on purchases, is debited to the trading account; it is not really an overheard charge as it increases the cost of purchase). Under this heading, we have such items as freight(where goods are sold to customers abroad), expenses of motor vans and wages of drivers, wages of packers and any other expenses incurred by the distribution or delivery of goods dealt in.

4. **Financial expenses**. There include bank charges, interest on loans, hire purchase agreements, debentures, mortgages, bank overdrafts, and any other expense incurred in raising funds for the business.

   Work through the following examples to familiarize yourself with company financial statements. This will show you how all the above are tested in the preparation of financial statement of limited companies.

Presentation of company financial statements

Whenever a business draws up its own financial statements for internal use, it may use any format it likes since there are no rules to prevent such accounts being drafted in the manner most suitable for management. This is usually the format recommended for students in examinations.
However, the **published** accounts of a business must be in accordance with the rules laid down in the legal framework of the country the business is resident in. They will also have to comply with relevant international accounting standards (with which we will deal later). Check the following illustrations.

Presentation of trading and profit and loss account and appropriation account, year end 31/12 (accounts for internal use)

	K'000	K'000	K'000
Turnover (net sales)			100,000
Less			

DR. CRYFORD MUMBA

Cost of sales

Stock (1/1)	4,000		
+ purchases	66,000		
70,000			
-Stock (31/12)	10,000		60,000
Gross profit			40,000

Distribution costs

Salesmen's salaries	8,500		
Distribution expenses	1,500		
Advertising	2,500		
Motor expenses	1,500		
Depreciation of motors			
Depreciation of equipment	2,000	16,500	

Administration expenses

Office salaries	7,350		
General office expenses	,400		
Discount	250		
Bad debts provision	350		
Rates and Insurance	500		
Miscellaneous costs	1,200		
Light and heat	150		
Depreciation of equipment (office)	1,300	12,500	29,000
			11,000

Other income

Discount	450		
Bank interest	350		800
			11,800

Income from shares

Dividends from other companies		800
Operating profit		12,600
Interest payable		
Bank loan interest accrued		250
Net profit (before tax)		12,350
Corporation tax		1,350
Provision for dividends:		9,200
8%preference shares	1,600	
Ordinary shares	3,000	4,600
Retained profits		4,600
Transfer to reserves		4,000
	600	
Profit and loss balance (1/1) b/f		400
Profit and loss balance (31/12) c/f		1,000

Balance sheet as at year end 31/12

K'000	K'000 Cost	K'000 Depn	NBV
Fixed Assets			
Premises	50,000		50,000
Equipment	35,000	8,000	27,000
Motor vehicles	4,000	1,000	3,000
Investments	10,000		10,000
	99,000	9,000	90,000
Current assets			
Stock	10,000		
Debtors	17,500		
Bank	3,500		
Pre-payments	1,000	32,000	
Less			
Creditors falling within 12 months			
Creditors	16,000		
Accruals	250		
Provision for dividends	4,600		
Provision for taxation	3,150	24,000	
Net current Assets			8,000
Total Assets less current liabilities			98,000
Less			
Creditors falling after 12 months			
Bank loan (5 years)			6,000
Net assets			92,000
Financed by			
Capital and Reserves	*Authorized Capital*		*issued and Paid – up capital*
Ordinary shares @ K1	100,000		50,000
8% preference shares @ K1	20,000		20,000
			70,000
Share Premium Account			5,000
Reserves			16,000
Profit and loss balance			1,000
			92,000

Note:

(a) The share premium account is the amount received in excess of the nominal value of shares when issued. In the above case, they sold at K1.10 each (5,000,000 X 10n = K5, 000).

(b) Creditors falling within 12 months and after 12 months relate to current and long-term liabilities.

(c) Net assets or capital employed represents the long term capital invested in the business. This would usually consist of two major parts: shareholders' funds and lond/medium-term loans. The shareholders' funds consists of two further parts: share capital, funds invested by shareholders, and reserves, profits retained in the business. The distinction between the two major parts is important as loans normally require annual servicing in the form of interest payments whereas shareholders' funds do not require a fixed payment. Consequently, high levels of loans in a business which has volatile profits will be viewed by interested parties as a high risk form of financing.(Note: calculation to capital employed is indispensable to calculation of the primary profitability ratio – return on capital employed(ROCE)).

The above financial statements can be converted into those suitable for external publication as follows:

INCOME STATEMENT FOR THE YEAR ENDED 31 DECEMBER

	K'000
Turnover	100,000
Cost of sales	(60,000)
Gross profit	40,000
Distribution costs	(16,500)
Administration expenses	(12,500)
Other income	1,600
Operating profit	12,600
Interest paid	(250)
Profit before tax	12,350
Corporation tax	(1,350)
Profit after tax	9,200
Provision for dividends	(4,600)
Retained profits	4,600
Transfer to reserves	(4,000)
	600
Profit and Loss balance (1/1)	400
Profit and Loss balance (31/12)	1,000

BALANCE SHEET AS AT 31 DECEMBER

	Cost	Dep'n	NBV
Fixed assets	99,000	9,000	90,000
Current assets		32,000	
Current liabilities		24,000	
Net current assets			8,000
Capital employed			98,000
Long term liabilities			(6,000)
Net assets			92,000
Financed by:			
Ordinary shares		50,000	

8% Preference	2,000	
	70,000	
Share premium account	5,000	
Reserves	16,000	
Profit and Loss account	<u>1000</u>	
		<u>92,000</u>

From the above published income statement and the balance sheet, it clear that not much information is provided. This is the reason why notes to accounts are required to give flesh to the figure (bones). Without explanatory nothing much can be derived from them by the reader.

Example 1

J. P. Mathew plc are wholesalers. The following is their trial balance as at 31 December 2012.

	Dr	Cr
Ordinary Share Capital: K1 shares		150,000
Share Premium		10,000
General Reserves		8,000
Retained Profits as at 31/12/2011		27,300
Stock: 31/12/2011	33,235	
Sales		481,300
Purchases	250,270	
Returns Outwards		12,460
Returns Inwards	13,810	
Carriage Inwards	570	
Carriage Outwards	4,260	
Warehouse Wages	50,380	
Salesmen's Salaries	32,145	
Administrative Wages and Salaries	29,900	
Plant and Machinery	62,500	
Hire of Motor Vehicles	9,600	
Provision for depreciation-plant & Machinery 1/1/12		24,500
Goodwill	47,300	
General Distribution Expenses	2,840	
General Administration Expenses	4,890	
Directors' Remuneration	14,800	
Rents Receivable		3,600
Trade Debtors	164,150	
Cash at Bank	30,870	
Trade Creditors		<u>34,290</u>
	<u>751,520</u>	<u>751,520</u>

You are given the following information

(1) Closing stock has been valued at K45,890
(2) Plant & machinery is to be depreciated at 20% straight line. 60% relates to distribution expenses, 40% relates to administrative expenses.
(3) Motor vehicles hire is to be split K6,200 to distributive and K3,400 to administrative expenses.
(4) An Audit accrual is needed of K600.
(5) A corporation tax provision of K29,100 is needed
(6) A proposed dividend of 36P per share has not yet been accounted for.

Required:

A trading and Profit and Loss Account for the year ended 31 December 2012 and a Balance Sheet as at 31 December 2012. Show all your workings.

Solution

J. P. Mathew Plc Trading and Profit and Loss Account for the year ending 31st December 2012

	K	K	K
Sales			481,370
Less returns inwards			(13,810)
			467,500
Cost of Sales			
Opening Stock		33,235	
Add: Purchases		250,270	
Less: Purchases Returns		(12,460)	
Carriage Inwards		570	
		271,615	
Less: Closing Stock		(45,890)	
			225,725
Gross Profit			241,835
Other Income –Rent Received			3,600
			245,435
Distribution Expenses			
Carriage Outwards	4,260		
Warehouse Wages	50,380		
Salesman Salaries	32,145		
Plant & Machinery Depreciation	7,500		
Motor Vehicle Hire	6,200		
General Expenses	2,840		
		103,325	
Administrative Expenses			

Wages & Salaries	29,900		
Motor Vehicle Hire	3,400		
General Expenses	4,890		
Directors' Remuneration	14,800		
Plant & Machinery Depreciation	5,000		
Audit Fee	600		
		58,590	161,915
Less: Taxation			83,520
			29,100
Less: Ordinary Dividend			54,420
Retained Profit for the year			54,000
			420

J. P. Mathews Plc
Balance Sheet as at 31st December 2012

	K	K
Fixed Assets		25,500
Tangible		47,300
Intangible		72,800
Current Assets		
Stock	45,890	
Debtors	164,150	
Cash at Bank	30,870	
	240,910	
Creditors – due within 1 year	117,990	
		122,920
		195,720
Capital and Reserves		
Paid up share capital		150,000
Reserves		
Share Premium Account	10,000	
General Reserves	8,000	
Retained profits	27,720	
		45,720
		195,720

Example 2

You are provided with the following trial balance of Goodyear, a limited company, at 31 December 2012:

	Dr K	Cr K
Ordinary Share Capital (50n shares)		60 000
5% Preference Share Capital (K1 share)		20 000
Sales Revenue		80 000
Discount Allowed	400	
Discount Received		200
Carriage Inwards	1 000	
Carriage Outwards	800	
Receivables and Payables	10 000	2 000
Inventory at 1 January 2012	10 000	
10% Loan notes 2017		50 000
Loan Interest Paid	5 000	
Non current Assets, at Cost	230 000	
Non Current Assets, Aggregate Depreciation		100 000
Purchases	49 000	
Administrative Expenses	4 000	
Salaries (excluding Directors)	4 000	
Preference dividend Paid	1 000	
Ordinary Dividend for Year ended 31 Dec 2012:		
Paid during year	3 000	
Accumulated Profit 1 January 2012		11000
Cash at bank	5 000	
	323 200	323 200

Adjustments are required for:

- Inventory at 31 December 2012, at cost K15 000
- Director's salaries not yet paid K5000
- Tax for the year K5000
- Depreciation charge for the year K4 600
- Accrued audit fee K1000
- Creation of a plant replacement reserve of K100.

Required:

Prepare a balance sheet and income statement suitable for presentation to the directors.

Solution

GOODYEAR LTD
INCOME STATEMENT FOR THE YEAR ENDED 31 DECEMBER 2012

	K	K
Sales Revenue		80 000
Opening Inventory	10 000	
Purchases	49 000	
Carriage Inwards	1 000	
Less: Closing Inventory	60 000	
	15 000	
Cost of Sales		45 000
Gross Profit		35 000
Discount Received		200
		35 200
Discount allowed	400	
Carriage Outwards	800	
Administrative Expenses	4 000	
Staff Salaries	4 000	
Directors' Salaries (W1)	5 000	
Audit Fee (W4)	1 000	
Depreciation (W3)	4 600	
Loan Interest	5 000	
		24 800
Profit before tax		10 400
Tax (W2)		5 000
Net Profit for Year		5 400

GOOD YEAR

BALANCE SHEET AS AT 31 DECEMBER 2012

	K	K
Non current Assets:		
· Land and buildings (K230 000 – 104 600) (W3)		125 400
Current Assets:		
· Inventory	15 000	
· Receivables	10 000	
· Cash at Bank	5 000	
		30 000
Total Assets		155 400
Capital and Reserves:		
· Share Capital:		
Ordinary 50n Shares	60 000	

5% Preference Shares	20 000	
Plant Replacement Reserves (W5)	1 000	
Accumulated Profit	<u>11 400</u>	
Total Capital and Reserves		92 400
Non Current and Liabilities:		
· 10% Loan notes		50 000
Current Liabilities:		
·Trade Payables	2 000	
· Tax (W2)	5 000	
· Accruals [(K5000 (W1) + K1000 (W4)]	<u>6 000</u>	
		<u>13 000</u>
Total liabilities + Total Capital and Reserves		<u>155 400</u>

Workings:

Many of the workings which follow are not necessary as the adjustments are straightforward. The ledger accounts have been shown to emphasize the double entry involved in the adjustments.

(W1) Directors' Salaries

	K		K
Balance c/d	5000	Income Statement	5000

(W2) Current Taxation

	K		K
Balance c/d	5000	Income Statement	5000

(W3) Non-current Assets – Accumulated Depreciation

	K		K
Balance c/d	104 600	Balance b/d	100 000
		Income Statement	<u>4 600</u>
	<u>104 600</u>		<u>104 600</u>

W

(W4) Audit Fee

	K		K
Balance c/d	1000	Income Statement	1000

(W5) Plant Replacement Reserve

	K		K
Balance c/d	1000	Accumulated Profit	1000

The creation of the reserve is shown as a movement in the statement of changes in equity.

Example 3

The trial balance Jomboni Plc of 30 September 2012 included the following:

	Debit K000	Credit K000
· Sales		6 840
· Purchases	1 200	
· Distribution costs	3 670	
· Administrative Expenses	880	
· Interest Payable	590	
· cost of a fundamental Recognition of the Company's Operations	560	
· Profit on Sale of Head Office Building (the Company Plans to move it's a rented building)		1 200
· Allowance for Receivables 1 October 2012		150

In preparing the company's income statement, the following further information is to be taken into account:

1. Inventory was taken on 27 September 2012 (all valued at cost) and amounted to K950 000. Between that date and the close of business on 30 September 2012, goods costing K68 000 were sold and there were no further receipts of goods. These sales were included in the sales figure of K6840 000.

2. During the year a debt of K400 000 proved to be irrecoverable and is to be written off.

3. The income tax expense on the profit for the year was K300 000.

Required:

Prepare the company's income statement for the year ended 30 September 2012 for publication and complying, so far as the information permits with the requirements of IAS 1.

Solution

JOMBONI PLC
INCOME STATEMENT FOR THE YEAR ENDED 30 SEPTEMBER 2012.

	K000
Sales Revenue	6840
Cost of Sales (1200 + 3670 – 950 + 68)	(3988)

Gross Profit	2852
Distribution Costs	880
Administration Expenses (590 + 400 + 50)	1040
Profit on sale of Property	1200
Cost of Re-organisation	(560)
Finance Costs	(300)
Profit Before Tax	1272
Income Tax Expense	(300)
Profit for the Period	972

Note:

1. Profit is stated after charging the write off of an exceptionally large bad debt of K400 000.

2. The above income statement is one prepared for publication (for external users). It is not as detailed as one required by the internal users (for management and directors).

Example 4

Hardly and Cena PLC had the following accounts at its year ended 31 December 2007.

	K
Net Profit (before tax)	80 000
Issued and Paid up Capital:	
8% K1 Preference Shares	200 000
K1 Ordinary Shares	800 000
Profit and Loss Account b/f (1/1)	18 000
8% Preference Dividend Paid (30/6)	8 000

The Board of Directors recommended on 31 December, the following:

- Provide K20 000 for corporation tax
- Provide for the remaining dividend balance to be paid to preference shareholders
- To provide 5% dividend to ordinary shareholders:

Required:

Prepare the company's appropriation account for the period ended 31 December 2007. Show an extract of the company's balance sheet indicating appropriate figures to be included for current liabilities and the 'financed by' section.

Solution

HARDY AND CENA PLC APPROPRIATION ACCOUNT YEAR ENDED 31 DECEMBER

	K	K
Net Profit (before tax)		80 000
Provision for Taxation		(20 000)
Net profit (after taxation)		60 000
·Provision for Dividend:		
8% Preference Paid	8 000	
8% Preference due	8 000	
Ordinary Shares Due	40 000	56 000
		4 000
Profit and Loss Balance b/f (1/1)		18 000
Profit and Loss Balance c/f (31/12)		22 000

Hardy and Cena Plc

Balance Sheet as at 31 December 2007 (Extract Only)

	K	K
Current Liabilities:		
· Provision for tax	20 000	
· Provision for Dividends	48 000	68 000
Capital and Reserves:		
8% K1 Preference Shares	200 000	
K1 Ordinary Shares	800 000	
Profit and less Account	22 000	1022 000

Note:

1. Half of preference dividend K8000 was paid during the year, 30 June. This is an interim dividend. The final provision of K8000 makes a total of K16 000 (i.e. 8% of K200 000 shares)

2. The 5% of K800 000 shares.

3. The profit and loss account balance (1 January) is the retained profit brought forward from the previous accounting period.

4. The profit and loss account balance (31 December) is the profit carried forward to the next accounting period. It is also entered in the balance sheet under capital and reserves section.

5. The provision for dividends and tax are current liabilities because they are due to be paid in the following financial period.

6. The appropriation account shows the division of profits before tax. Basically profits are distributed by:

    - Provision for taxation
    - Dividends to shareholders on the basis of the number of shares issued and paid up on the value of nominal capital
    - Transfer of profit to the company reserves (profits retained in the company helping it to expand and grow).

Thus, the appropriation account commences at profit before tax in the income statement.

PROGRESS CLINIC 9

Question1

The following Trial balance was extracted from the books of Dennis Ltd as on 31 December 2012:

DENNIS LTD
TRIAL BALANCE AS AT 31 DECEMBER 2012

	DR K'000	CR K'000
8% Preference share capital		35 000
Ordinary share capital		125 000
10% Debentures (repayable 2020)		20 000
General reserve		21 000
Profit & Loss A/C 31.12.11		13 874
Equipment at cost	122 500	
Motor vehicle at cost	99 750	
Provision for depreciation: Equipment 1. 1. 12		29 400
Provision for depreciation: vehicles 1.1.12		36 225
Stock at 1.1.12	136 132	
Sales		418 250
Purchases	232 225	
Returns Inwards	4 025	
General Expenses	1 240	
Salaries and wages	46 260	

Directors' remuneration	18 750	
Rent, rates and insurance	18 095	
Motor vehicle expenses	4 361	
Debenture interest	1 000	
Bank 1	2 751	
Cash	630	
Debtors	94 115	
Creditors		93 085
	791 834	**791 834**

The following adjustments need to be taken into account:

(i)   Stock at 31 December 2012 was K122 000 000
(ii)   Accrue rent K2 000 000
(iii). Accrue debenture interest K1 000 000
(iv)   Depreciate the equipment at 10% on cost and motor vehicles at 20% on cost
(v)   Transfer to general reserve K5 000 000
(vi)   It is proposed to pay the 8% preference dividend and a 10% dividend on the ordinary shares
(vii) Authorised share capital is K35 000 000 in preference shares and K200 000 000 in K1.00 ordinary shares.

Required

From the above details, you are required to prepare the following:

(a)   Trading and Profit and Loss and Appropriate Account for the year ended 31 December 2012.

(b)   Balance sheet as at 31 December 2012.

Question 2

The following information was extracted from the books of Nyama Ltd as at 30 September 2012:

	K'000
Creditors	18,900
Sales	240,000
Land at cost	54,000
Buildings at cost	114,000
Furniture and fittings at cost	66,000
Bank(credit balance)	18,000
Depreciation: Buildings	18,000
Furniture and fittings	30,000
Discount received	5,292

Un appropriated Profit at 1 October 2011	6,000
Provision for doubtful debts	2,448
Goodwill(intangible fixed asset)	49,200
Cash in hand	696
Stock at 1 October 2011	42,744
Interim dividend on preference shares	1,800
Rates	6,372
Wages and salaries	24,000
Insurance	5,688
Returns inwards	1,116
General expenses	1,308
Debtors	37,920
Purchases	131,568
Debenture interest	1,200
Bad debts	2,028
5% Debentures	48,000
6% K1 preference shares	60,000
K1Ordinary shares	60,000
General Reserve	30,000
Share Premium Account	3,000

Additional information:

i) Stock on hand at 30 September 2012 was K46,638,000
ii) Insurance paid in advance was valued at K300,000
iii) Wages owing totaled K840,000
iv) Depreciation is to be provided at 10% on cost of buildings and at 20% on the written down value of furniture and fittings
v) Provision for doubtful debts is to be reduced to 5% of debtors
vi) Debenture interest outstanding is valued at K1,200,000
vii) The directors propose to pay a 5% ordinary dividend and the final preference dividend and transfer K24,000,000 to General Reserves
viii) The corporation tax charge for the is K20,000,000

Required:

a) Prepare the Trading and Profit and Loss (Income Statement) and Appropriation Account for the year ended 30 September 2012
b) Prepare a balance Sheet (Statement of Financial Position) as at 30 September 2012.

Question 3

The following Trial balance was collected from the records of Asoza Ltd at 31 December 2012

TRIAL BALANCE AS AT 31 DECEMBER 2012

	DR	CR
	K'000	K'000
Ordinary share capital (K0.5 each)		60,000
5% Preference share capital (K1 each)		20,000
Sales		80,000
Discount allowed	400	
Discount received		200
Carriage inwards	1,000	
Carriage outwards	800	
Debtors and Creditors	10,000	2,000
Stock at 1 January 2012	10,000	
10% debentures		50,000
Debenture interest paid	5,000	
Fixed assets at cost	230,000	
Fixed assets: Aggregate Depreciation		100,000
Purchases	49,000	
Administrative expenses	4,000	
Salaries(excluding Directors')	4,000	
Preference dividend paid	1,000	
Profit and loss Account balance		8,000
Cash at bank	5,000	
	320,200	320,200

Adjustments are required relating to the following items:
i) Stock at 31 December 2012 , at cost K15,000,000
ii) Directors' salaries not yet paid K5,000,000
iii) Corporation tax for the year K5,000,000 still due
iv) Proposed ordinary dividend K0.025per unpaid
v) Depreciation charge for the year K4,600,000
vi) Accrued audit fee K1,000,000
vii) Creation of a plant replacement reserve of K1,000,000

Required:

From the above details:

Prepare the income statement for Asoza Ltd for the year ended 31 December 2012 and the balance sheet as at the same date.

CHAPTER 10

INTERPRETATION OF FINANCIAL STATEMENTS: CASHFLOW STATEMENTS

Introduction

The balance sheet and the income statement of a business give a good indication of how healthy the business is financially and how successfully it is performing. But neither statement gives direct information about a crucial aspect in the stability and success of any business: namely, its ability to generate cash.

Financial accounting is primarily concerned with external financial reporting. IAS7 requires all companies to publish a cash flow statement showing how cash inflows have been generated and how the cash has been spent. The preparation of cash flow statements will be illustrated by a number of examples. Thus, the best way to acquire knowledge of IAS7 is to work through the examples in this chapter.

Purposes of cash flow statement

The objective of IAS 7 is to ensure that all companies provide information about the historical changes in cash and cash equivalents by means of a cash flow statement which classifies cash flow during the period between those arising from operating, investing and financing activities.

Users of financial statements need information the liquidity, viability and financial adaptability of entities. During this information involves the user making assessments of the future cash flows of the entity.

Future cash flows are regarded in financial management theory as the prime determinant of the worth of a business. Thus, a cash flow statement is needed as a consequence of the differences between profits and cash.

The purpose of a cash flow statement is to help achieve the following:

- Provide additional information on business activities
- Help to assess the current liquidity of the business
- Allow the user to see the major types of cash flows into and out of the business
- Help the user to estimate future cash flows
- Determine cash flows generated from trading transactions rather than other cash lows.

Format of cash flow statement

IAS 7 requires the cash flow to be presented using standard headings. The objectives of the standard headings is to ensure that cash flow are reported in a form that highlights the significant components of cash flow and facilitates comparison of the cash flow performance of different businesses.

The standard headings shown in the statement are:

Operating activities
Investing activities
Financing activities

The above heading is discussed in detail below:

1. **Cash flows from operating activities**

   Cash flows from operating activities are in general the cash effects of transactions and other events relating to operating or trading activities. Net cash flow from operating activities represents the net increase or decrease in cash resulting from the operations shown in the income statement in arriving at profit from operations

   IAS 7 permits a choice between two possible methods for reporting net cash flow from operating activities namely:

   (a) The **direct method** shows operating cash receipts and payments, (including in particular, cash and cash payments to and on behalf of employees), aggregating to the net cash flow from operating activities. The information for the direct method could be found in the accounting records or derived from other financial statements. This method is encouraged because of the value of the extra information given but not required because of the recognize extra costs involved in extracting the operating cash flows.

   Under the direct method the operating element of the cash flow statement should be shown as follows:

   Operating activities

		K'000
•	Cash received from customers	X
•	Cash payments to suppliers	(X)
•	Cash paid to and on behalf of employees	(X)
•	Other cash payments	(X)
•	Net cash flow from operating activities	X

Note:

1. Cash received from customers represent cash flows received during the accounting period in respect of goods and services.

2. Cash payments to suppliers represent cash flows made during the accounting period in respect of goods and services.

3. Cash payments to and on behalf of employees represent amount paid to employees' including the associated tax and national insurance. It will, therefore, comprises gross salaries, gross wages, insurance, employers' NAPSA contributions (pensions), gratuity and any other benefits.

The direct method is, in effect, an analysis of the cash book. This information has never appeared directly in the financial statements before and so many companies might find it difficult to collect the information

(b) **Indirect method** – this starts with profit before tax and adjusts it for non-cash charges and credits to reconcile it to the net cash flow form operating activities. Some income statements do not provide the operating profit figure (profit before tax) hence the need to calculate it. Essentially operating profit = Gross profit – Expenses before interest and tax.

The information for the indirect method is found in other financial statements. Generally, two balanced sheets for last and current accounting periods will be given together with the income statement of the current accounting period.

Reconciliation of operating profit to net cash flow from operating activities should be shown as follows:

Operating activities

	K'000
• Operating profit	X
• Depreciation charge	X
• Loss on sale of tangible non-current assets	X
• Profit on sale of non-current investments	(X)
• (increase)/decrease in inventory	(X) or X
• (increase)/decrease in receivables	(X) or X
• increase/(decrease) in payables	X or (X)
• (increase)/decrease in prepayments	(X) or X
• Increase.(decrease) in accruals	X or (X)
• Net cash flow from operating activities	X

Note:

The following items are treated in a way that might seem confusing, but the treatment is logical if you think in terms of cash. Cash outflow is negative (subtracted) while cash inflow is positive (added).

1. Increase in inventory is treated as negative (in bracket). This is because it represents a cash outflow: cash is being spent on inventory. For the decrease, the opposite is time.

2. An increase in receivables would be treated as negative for the same reasons: More receivables means less cash.

3. By contrast, an increase in payables is positive because cash is being retained and not used to pay off trade creditors. There is therefore more of it.

4. Depreciation charges are positive since they are a non-cash charge.

5. Loss on sales of tangible non-current asset is positive because it does not come from normal trading activities.

6. Profit on disposal of non-current investment is negative because it does not come from normal trading activities.

7. Increase in prepayments is negative as there is less cash

8. Increase in accruals is positive as cash is retained

9. Interest expense is positive because it is not part of cash generated from operations (the interest actually paid is deducted later).

10. Interest paid, dividends paid and income taxes paid represent the amounts actually paid in the year and are thus negative.

11. The opening cash and cash equivalent balance is found by subtracting bank overdraft from cash for the previous year i.e. cash (at beginning) – overdraft (at beginning).

12. The closing cash and cash equivalent balance is found by subtracting bank overdraft from cash for the current year i.e. cash (now) – overdraft (now). In fact we use this figure to check the correctness of the cash flow statement we have prepared. If the last figure agrees with the closing balance then we are 99% sure that the cash flow statement is correctly prepared.

The above points are critical to reconciliation of operating profit to net cash flows from operating activities.

Finally, it should be noted that the direct and the indirect methods differ only as regards the derivation of the item 'net cash inflow from operating activities.' Subsequent inflows and outflows for investing and financing are the same.

Cash flows from investing activities

The items here are cash spent on non-current assets, proceeds for sale of non-current assets and income from investments. Cash flows here generally include:

- Cash received on the sale of property, plant and equipment and other non-current assets.

- Cash received on the sale of property, plant and equipment and other non-current assets.

- Cash paid for investments in or loans to other companies

- Cash received for the sale of investments or the repayments of loans to other companies
- Interest received on investments or loans

- dividends received on investments

Cash flows from financing activities

Under this heading go the proceeds of issue of shares and long-term borrowings made or repaid. Financing cash inflow includes:

- Receipts from issuing shares or other equity instruments

- Receipts from issuing debentures, loans, notes and bonds and from other long-term and short-term borrowings (other than overdrafts, which are normally included in cash and cash equivalents)

Financing cash outflows include:

- Repayments of amounts borrowed (other than overdrafts)
- The capital element of finance lease rental payments.
- Payments to re-acquire or redeem the entity's shares.

Net increase/decrease in cash and cash equivalents

This is the overall increase (or decrease) in cash and cash equivalents during the year. After adding the cash and cash equivalents at the beginning of the year, the final balance of cash and cash equivalents at the end of the year emerges.

'Cash' means cash on hand and deposits available on demand.

'Cash equivalents' means short-term highly liquid investments that are readily convertible to known amounts of cash and which are subject to an insignificant risk of changes in value. Note that investments are not cash equivalents unless they have these two attributes of being readily convertible and with little or no risk of change in value.

Bank overdrafts may be counted as a negative element in cash and cash equivalents, though longer-term bank loans (borrowing) are generally considered to be financing activities.

The components of cash and cash equivalents should be disclosed in a note to the cash flow statement, with reconciliation to the equivalent items in the balance sheet as follows:

Cash and cash equivalents:

	At end of year K'000	At beginning of year K'000
• Cash on hand and balance at banks	X	X
• Short-term investments	X	X
Total	X	X

Short term investments represent investment in current assets.

Finally, a reconciliation of net cash flow to movement in net debt may be required which is generally presented as follows:

	K'000
• Increase/decrease in cash (closing cash figure)	X
• Cash received from issue of loan	X
• Cash used to invest in treasury bills	(X)
• Change in net debt	X or (X)
• Net debt at beginning of year	X or (X)
• Net debt at end of year	X or (X)

SPECIMEN FORMAT FOR CASH FLOW STATEMENT

The specimen format for a cash flow statement from IAS7 is given:

DR. CRYFORD MUMBA

Cash flow statement for the year ended

	K'000	K'000
Cash flows from opening activities:		
• Net profit before taxation	2850	
Adjustments for:		
• Depreciation	490	
• Interest expense	400	
• Operating profit before capital charges	3740	
• Increase in trade receivables	(500)	
• Decrease in inventories	1050	
• Decrease in trade payables	(1740)	
• Cash generated from operations	2550	
Interest paid	(270)	
Dividends paid	(300)	
Income taxes paid	(420)	
Net cash inflow from operating activities		1560
Cash flow from investing activities:		
Purchase of plant and equipment, property	(900)	
Proceeds of sale of equipment	20	
Interest received	200	
Dividends received	200	
Net cash used in investing activities		(480)
Cash flows from financing activities:		
Proceeds of issue of shares	1210	
Repayment of loans	(2000)	
Net cash used in financing activities		(790)
Net increase in cash and cash equivalents		290
Cash and cash equivalents at the beginning of period		120
Cash and cash equivalents at the end of period		410

Preparing a cash flow statement

In essence, preparing a cash flow statement is very straightforward. Simply make sure that you understand the format and make entries as appropriate General Steps applicable are the following:

Step 1: Set out the pro forma leaving plenty of space.
Step 2: Complete the reconciliation of operating profit to net cash flows, as far as possible.

Step 3: Calculate the following where appropriate.

- Tax paid
- Dividends paid
- Purchase and sale of non current assets
- Issues of shares
- Repayments of loans
- Debentures issued

Step 4: Work out the profit if not already giving using opening and closing balances, tax charge and dividend.

Step 5: Complete the note of gross cash flows. Alternatively, the information may go straight into the statement.

Step 6: Slot the figures into the statement

Step 7: Complete the note of the analysis of changes in net debt (cash and cash equivalent statement)

Step 8: Complete the reconciliation of net cash flow to movement in net debt
Note that above steps is simply a guide!

Example 1

PCBF Limited commenced trading on 1st January 2012 with a medium term of K21 000 000 and a share issue which raised K35 000 000. The company purchased fixed assets for K21 000 000 cash and during the year to 31st December 2012, entered into the following transactions.

(a) Purchases from suppliers were K19500 000 of which K2 550 000 was unpaid at the end of year.

(b) Wages and salaries amounted to K10 500 000 of which K750 000 was unpaid at the year end.

(c) Interest at 10% on the loan of K21 000 000 was fully paid in the year and a repayment of K5 250 000 was made

(d) Sales turnover was K29 400 000 including K900 000 receivables at year end

(e) Interest on cash deposits at the bank amounted to K75 000

(f) A dividend of K4000 000 was proposed as at 31 December 2012.

Required:

Prepare a historical cash flow statement for the year ended 31 December 2012.

SOLUTION

PCBF Ltd

CASH FLOW STATEMENT FOR THE YEAR ENDED 31 DECEMBER 2012

	K'000	K'000
• Cash flow from operating activities:		
• Cash from customers (29400 – 900)	28 500	
• Cash paid to suppliers (19500 – 2550)	(16 950)	
• Cash paid to employees (16500 – 750)	(9 750)	
• Interest paid	(2 100)	
• Interest received	75	
Net cash flows from operating activities		(225)
Investing activities		
• Purchase of fixed assets		
Financing activities		(21 000)
• Issue of shares		
• Proceeds from medium term loan	35 000	
• Repayment of loan	21 000	
Net cash flow from financing activities		50750
Net increase in cash and cash equivalents		29525
Cash and cash equivalents at 1 Jan 2012		-
Cash and cash equivalents at 31 December 2012		29525

Note:

1. Information provided in the question strictly specifies that only the direct method has to be used.

2. The dividend is only proposed and so there is no related cash flow in 2012.

Example 2

The summarized financial statements of ABC for the 2011 and 2012 are below.

Reference to notes	Balance sheets are as at			
	31 Dec 2012		31 Dec 2011	
	K'000	K'000	K'000	K'000
Non-current assets cost	3400		2100	
Less accumulated depreciation	(720)	2680	(550)	1550
Current assets:				
• Inventory	600		400	
• Receivables	1500		1700	
• Cash	80	2180	50	2150
		4860		3700
Equity and liabilities				
Ordinary share capital		900		600
Share premium account	500		320	
Retained earnings 2	920	1420	500	820
		2320		1420
Non-Current liabilities				
10% loan notes		1200		1000
Current liabilities				
• Bank overdraft	140		280	
• Trade payables	900		800	
• Current tax payable	300	1340	200	1280
		4860		3700

Notes:

1. Non-current assets that had cost K200 000 with a written down value of K60 000 were sold for K80 000 during the year.

2. The increase in retained earnings is made up as follows:

	K'000	K'000
• Opening balance		500
• Operating profit	1090	
• Less: finance cost paid	(120)	
• Profit before taxation	970	
• Income tax expense	(300)	
• Dividends paid	(252)	
• Retained profit for year		420
• Closing balance		920

Required:

Prepare a cash flow statement for ABC for the year ended 31 December 2012, using the format in IAS 7 cash flow statements.

Solution

The information provided in the question requires us to use the indirect method for calculating the net cash flow from operating activities.

ABC
CASH FLOW STATEMENT FOR THE YEAR ENDED 31DECEMBER 2012

	K'000	K'000
Cash flow from operating activities.		
• Profit before taxation	970	
• Adjustment for:		
• Depreciation (W2)	310	
• Profit on sale of non-current asset (W3)	(20)	
• Interest expense	120	
• Cash flow before working capital changes	1380	
• Increase in inventory (600 – 400)	(200)	
• Decrease in receivables (1500 – 1700)	200	
• Increase in payables (900 – 800)	100	
	1480	
Cash generated from operations		
• Interest paid	(120)	
• Income tax paid	(200)	
Net cash flow from opening activities		1160
Cash flows from investing activities:		
Purchase of non-current assets (W1)	(1500)	
Proceeds of sale of non-current assets (W3)	80	
Net cash used in inventory activities		(1420)
Cash flows from financing activities:		
• Proceeds from issue of share capital (300 + 180)	480	
• Proceeds from issue of loan notes	200	
Dividends paid	(250)	
Net cash flow financing activity		430
Net increase in cash and cash equipment		170
Cash at beginning of period		(230)
Cash at end of period		(60)

Workings

(1)

Non-current assets – cost

	K'000		K'000
Opening balance	2100	Transfer to disposal	200
Purchases (balancing figure)	1500	Closing balance	3400
	3600		3600

(2)

Non-current assets – accumulated depreciation

	K'000		K'000
Transfer to disposal	140	opening balance	550
		Income statement – depreciation	
Closing balance	720	(balancing figure)	310
	860		860

(3)

Non-current assets – disposal

	K'000		K'000
Transfer – cost	200	Transfer – depreciation	140
Income statement	20	cash	80
	220		2

PROGRESS CLINIC 10

Question 1

Chiko Ltd provides the following information relating to Fixed Assets in the company's Balance Sheet,

Plant and machinery

	Cost	Depreciation	Net Book Value
	K000	K000	K000
Opening balance	453	143	310
Additions/charge	102	11	91
Disposals	(79)	(64)	(15)
Closing balance	**476**	**90**	**386**

The additional machinery was purchased for cash. The disposals were made at a loss of K6 000.

Required

Compute the net cash outflow figure on plant and machinery during the period.

Question 2

The Balance Sheets of Kanyelele Ltd as at 31 March 2012 and 2012 were as follows:

	2011	2012
	K	K
Fixed Assets	2 140 000	3 060 000
Accumulated depreciation	580 000	840 000
	1 560 000	2 220 000
Net Current Assets	1 520 000	1 570 000
	3 080 000	3 790 000
Ordinary share capital	1 000 000	1 100 000
Share premium	800 000	900 000
Retained Earnings	480 000	590 000
	2 280 000	2 590 000
6% Loan	800 000	1 200 000
	3 080 000	3 790 000

Notes

i)   The Net cash generated from operating activities for the year is K746 000.
ii)   During the year the company sold fixed assets which had cost K480 000 for K280 000.
iii) The Net Current Assets figures include cash at bank:

    31 March 2005   K14 000
    31 March 2006   K18 000

iv)   All other movements in Net Current assets have already been allowed for computing the Net Cash flow from operating activities given above. Dividends paid, when computed should be included in operating activities.
v)   The loan issued during the year took place on 1 April 2011 and all interest for the year ended 31 March 2012 was paid in the year.
vi)   The profit for the year ended 31 March 2012 before allowing for dividends paid was K260 000.
vii) Ignore taxation.

Required

Prepare the company's Cash Flow Statement for the year ended 31 March 2012, beginning with the Net Cash generated from operating activities in note (1) above.

Question 3

The following information relates to PCBF Ltd for the year ended 31 December 2012

	K'000
Operating profit before tax	146
Depreciation charge for the year	81
Proceeds for the sale of fixed assets	63
Dividends paid	47
Tax paid	189
Cash received from new loans	142
Increase in stock	38
Increase in creditors	74
Share issue	30
Decrease in debtors	78
Interest paid	106
Purchase of fixed assets	264
Interest received in cash	22

REQUIRED:

a) Prepare a cash flow statement for the year to 31 December 2012
b) What are the main uses of a cash flow statement?

Question 4

Kamuzatu Tiles ltd is preparing its accounts for the year ended 31 March 2012

You are the company's new financial accountant, and you have been given the following information:

Kamuzatu Tiles Ltd
Profit and loss Account for the year ended 31 March 2012

K'000	
Revenue	78,210
Cost of sales	(42,193)
Gross profit	36,017
Distribution costs	(12,076)
Administrative expenses	(8,463)
Interest received	111
Interest payable	(1,556)

Profit before tax	14,033
Tax expense	(3,771)
Profit for the period	10,262

Statement of changes in retained earnings for year ended 31 March 2012

Retained earnings brought forward at 1/4/2011	37,564
Profit for the period	10,262
Dividends	(4,601)
Retained profit carried forward at 31/3/2012	43,225

Balance sheets as at:

	31/3/2012	31/3/1211
	K'000	K'000
ASSETS		
Non-current assets:		
Property, plant and equipment	115,911	81,814
CURRENT ASSETS:		
Inventories	22,614	21,225
Trade receivables	10,532	13,869
Cash on hand and bank balances	2,548	1,569
	35,694	36,663
TOTAL ASSETS	151,606	118,477
EQUITY AND LIABILITIES		
Equity:		
Share capital	25,061	22,761
Share premium account	12,036	10,018
Revaluation reserve	16,242	5,251
Retained earnings	43,225	37,564
	96,564	75,594
Non—current liabilities:		
6% debentures	26,170	20,901
Current liabilities:		
Bank overdraft	6,144	77
Trade and other payables	16,335	16,239
Current tax payable	3,082	2,826
Proposed dividends	3,310	2,840
	28,871	21,982
TOTAL EQUITY AND LIABLITIES	151,605	118,477

Notes:
i)   There were no creditors or debtors in respect of interest payable or receivable as at either year end.
ii) "Profit before tax" is stated after charging depreciation of K6,991,000.
iii) During the year, the company sold a piece of equipment for K4,900,000,reaizing a profit of K1,436,000. This equipment had never been revalued, and there were no other disposals of tangible non-current assets during the year.
iv) A piece of freehold land was valued at K490,000 during the year, and this adjustment has been incorporated in the above accounts. The valuations of other non-current assets did not materially differ from their carrying amounts.
v)   The issued share capital of Kamuzatu Ltd comprises of ordinary shares only.
vi) The proposed dividends shown under current account in the balance sheets were declared before the respective year end dates.

Required:

a)   Prepare a cash flow statement for the company in respect of the year ended 31 March 2012
b)   Discuss the importance of the cash flow statement and briefly explain why cash and profit are not the same.

Question 5

A company, Choombe Ltd, made a profit for the year of K18,750,000 after accounting for depreciation of K1,250,000. During the year, fixed assets were purchased for K8,000,000, debtors increased by K1,000,000, stock decreased by K1,800,000 and creditors increased by K350,000.

Required:

From the above details, calculate the increase in cash and bank balances during the year.

Question 6

The Balance Sheets of Jonah Co Ltd at 31 December 2011 and 2012 were as follows:

	Year Ended 31 December	
	2011	2012
	K000	K000
Fixed Assets		
Property, plant and equipment	730	1,100
Investments at cost	100	50
	830	1,150
Current Assets		
Inventory	80	110
Receivables	110	180
Cash at bank	20	30
	210	320
	1,040	**1,470**
Equity		
Called-up share capital	300	380
Share premium	200	300
Revaluation reserve	100	200
Retained earnings	200	190
	800	1,070
Non Current Liabilities		
10% Loan notes	100	150
	900	1,220
Current Liabilities		
Trade payables	70	80
Bank overdraft	40	130
Final dividend	30	40
	140	250
	1,040	**1,470**

©

Notes:

1. Property, plant and equipment
   During the year tangible assets with a net book value of K80,000 were sold for K60,000. The depreciation charge for the year on all property, plant and equipment held at the end of the year was K100,000.

2. Investments
   Investments which cost K50,000 were sold during the year for K40,000.

3. Final Dividend

   The final dividends are on the company's ordinary share capital. No interim dividends were paid. Final dividends were declared before the year end.

4. 10% Loan notes

   K50,000 of 10% loan notes were issued on 1 January 2012. All interest to 31 December has been paid.

5. Called up share Capital

   The company's called up share capital at 31 December 2011 consists of 300,000 ordinary shares of K1 each. Another 80,000 shares were issued during the year at a price of K2.25 per share.

6. Revaluation reserve

   The freehold land and buildings were revalued upwards by K100,000 during the year.

REQUIRED

Prepare the company's Cash flow statement for the year ended 31 December 2012 complying with IAS 7: Cash Flow Statements. Ignore taxation.

CHAPTER 11

INTERPRETATION OF FINANCIAL STATEMENTS: RATIO ANALYSIS

Introduction

As well as preparing financial statements, candidates need to be able to interpret them and draw conclusions which can be expressed in the form of a report to non-financial managers. Such a task often involves, as a first step, the calculation of relevant accounting ratios.

In addition to asking candidates to evaluate the financial performance of an undertaking (which could be a not-for-profit undertaking) a typical question might ask candidates to reflect on the non-financial criteria which should be borne in mind to make a more rounded evaluation of the undertaking's performance. It cannot be over-emphasized that it is not sufficient for you to demonstrate that you can calculate ratios. You must also be able to comment on the ratios and give suggested reasons for trends and differences.

The Basic Questions

There is a set of basic questions to which an interpreter will seek answers. The answer to each question will lead to further questions, so that gradually a picture of what is happening in the company will emerge.

1. The first question usually concerns **profitability**. It is not enough to discover whether a profit or a loss is being made, since a measure of the adequacy of profit is needed. The return on capital employed (ROCE) should show whether profits are sufficient to warrant the amount of funds invested in a business, the risk taken by investing those funds, and whether a better return for the class of risk could be earned by an alternative employment of the funds. This approach leads on to questions to determine whether the assets are employed in the right way or in the best combination, and whether the company is on the threshold of a profit breakthrough after some lean years when reorganization has taken place.

2. The second question investigates **solvency**, or ability of the firm to pay its way. Some argue that this should be the first question asked as sometimes a profitable business is brought to a halt through insufficient liquid funds. The interpretation of the solvency position revolves around the availability of cash to repay creditors and the adequacy of working capital resources to finance the level of activity required by management. The liquidity of current assets, the rate of expansion of stocks and debtors to an 'overtrading' position, and the ability of the business to borrow are all significant in this part of the pattern.

3. The third major question concerns **ownership** of the business. One individual or a group may control a firm through significant shareholdings, and thus may be in a position to influence management policy. The voting rights of various classes of capital are important in this case. Rights to dividend and repayment of capital if the business is wound up are important matters to a potential shareholder. Often the ownership of shares is obscured through the use of nominee holdings. Ownership, however, has a deeper significance, since it can be used to comment on the relative importance of the various groups who have supplied funds utilized

to finance the business. In this sense all those who have provided the funds for use in the business, shareholders, long-term lenders, and current liabilities, are seen as owners of the assets which their finance has helped to buy, especially since, if the firm ceased trading, they would expect to be paid out of the proceeds of those assets. If, for example, trade creditors become a significant provider of finance, they may begin to have more power over the destiny of the firm than its legal owners, the shareholders. When assets are charged as security for the loans the actions of the management may be inhibited, since they cannot dispose of certain assets without permission of the lender.

4. The forth major question deals with **financial strength**. A weak firm is one which has used up all its credit facilities and thus can borrow no more, or one which is over-dependent on sources of finance outside the business. If a firm has unused overdraft facilities or uncharged assets which can act as security for borrowings it can use extra finance to extricate itself from financial difficulties, or mount an expansion scheme. A different view of financial strength measures the amount of assets which the firm controls year by year, so that growth in assets, financed by increasing reserves from profits retained in the business, is seen as a healthy sign.

5. A fifth avenue of approach is to investigate **trends**. If the accounting statements for several years are expressed in a columnar form and placed side by side, changes in the relative importance of certain items can be identified. For example, when all costs are expressed as a percentage of sales, the fact that one cost is becoming a larger proportion of the total as year succeeds year can be seen, or when all sources of finance are expressed as a percentage of total capital employed, the changing relative importance of the various classes of capital providers can be noted. When variations from a settled pattern are observed, an attempt should be made to discover the cause. If, for example, the proportion of debtors or stock to total assets has increased, further investigation to establish the reason for such a change should be initiated. It is also possible to extrapolate figures to forecast what is likely to happen if the present rate of change is maintained.

6. The last basic question concerns **cover**, to reveal the adequacy of the margin of profits over a required rate of dividend, or the value of a secured asset over the principal of the loan. A loan of K1 million secured against a building worth K2 million is said to be twice covered by its security. Further questions concerning gearing are raised from this point to find the effect of a fluctuation in profit on the ability of the company to pay a dividend or to meet its liability for loan interest.

Once the answers to these six basic questions and their associated queries have been found, the accountant knows a great deal about the position of the business. Three techniques are used to answer these questions and to help form an opinion on a set of accounts. They are ratio analysis, cash flow statement and balance sheet criticism. These techniques are not used in isolation, but together, each provides evidence to support the conclusions drawn from another. In this chapter we cover ratio analysis while the previous chapter covered cash flow statement.

RATIO ANALYSIS

A ratio shows the relationship of one figure to another and can be used in accounting to demonstrate the interplay between balance sheet items, or between the income statement and the balance sheet. Ratios are used in that they summarize a position and simplify an explanation of a complicated statement by its expression in one figure. However, a major disadvantage of their use is that they are sometimes over-simplify a situation, and thus without a proper understanding of the definition of the constituent parts, false conclusions may be drawn, e.g. the definition of net profit (before or after tax), of capital employed, can seriously affect the return on capital employed.

USES OF RATIOS

Accountants often use ratios to focus attention on important items in accounting statements or to illustrate points made in reports, but these techniques must be treated with caution. Ratios should be used as a guide, not as a basis for definitive conclusions. Too much reliance should not be placed on the impression gained from one ratio alone. The findings should be checked against other ratio, and perhaps against a cash flow statement until gradually a clearer picture emerges. Sometimes compensating changes in the constituent parts of a ratio can obscure the extent of the change that has taken place; for example, although profit and capital employed may double, this important change does not show up in the ratio of net profit to capital employed. A change in both constituent parts at the same time will alter the ratio, but can cause confusion when the reason for the change is investigated,; for example, if ROCE falls is it because net profit has fallen or because capital employed has increased?

Another use for ratios is as comparators. Absolute figures in an accounting statement are made more meaningful when they are put into perspective by comparison. Although the profit made by a company is always interesting, its significance is properly demonstrated only when it is measured against the capital employed in making that profit. An increase in profit may be considered as a good result until the extent of the extra capital employed to earn it is shown. The comparison of ratios of one company with those of another, or with the average ratios of a group of similar companies, is helpful. Comparison of the ratios of the same company at different time periods will reveal important changes from the established pattern for the company, which should prompt an investigation. Some companies treat ratios as guidelines or targets to be reached during the planning and budgeting operation. Because ratios reflect a relationship, they can transcend national barriers. The ROCE, compiled from figures expressed in dollars, pounds, yen or kwacha, enables international comparison to take place.

Ratios can be expressed:

    a) As percentages, mainly profitability ratios, such as 18%

    b) As a relationship or proportion e.g. liquidity ratios, such as 1.6:1

    c) As one figure times another, e.g. interest cover, such as 4 times

    d) In terms of time , e.g. debtors and creditors period , such as 45 days or 3.2 months
        Note: It is very important to express ratios in the required form.

The broad categories of ratios

- Ratio analysis involves comparing one figure against another to produce a ratio, and assessing whether the ratio indicates a weakness or strength in the company's affairs.

- Broadly speaking, basic ratios can be grouped into five (5) categories.

1. Profitability and return
2. Short term solvency and liquidity
3. Long term solvency and stability
4. Efficiency (turnover ratios)
5. Shareholder's investment ratios.

- Ratio analysis on its own is not sufficient for interpreting company accounts, and that there are other items or information which should be looked at, for example:

a) Comments in the chairman's report, the directors' report and the operating and financial review

b) The age and nature of the company's assets.

c) Current and future developments in the company's markets, at home and abroad, recent acquisitions or disposals of a subsidiary by the company.

Any other noticeable features of the reports and accounts, such as post balance sheet events, contingent liabilities, a qualified auditors' report, the company's taxation position, and so on.

Exam focus points

It cannot be emphasized enough that a deeper level of analysis is required for financial ratios. You must answer the question from the view point of the person needing the ratios – bankers, perspective investors/predator.

A. Profitability and return on capital

1) One profit figure that should be calculated and compared over time is PBIT, profit before interest and tax, the amount of profit which the company earned before having to pay interest to providers of loan capital. By providing of loan capital, we usually mean longer – term loan capital, such as debentures and medium term bank loans, which will be shown in the balance sheet as 'creditors: amounts of falling due after more than one year'. Also, tax is affected by usual variations which have a distortion effect.

Profit before interest and tax is therefore the profit before the profit on ordinary activities before taxation plus interest charges on long-term loan capital.

2) Return On Capital Employed (ROCE)

$$ROCE = \frac{PBIT}{\text{Capital employed}} \times 100 = \frac{PBIT}{\text{total assets less current liabilities}}$$

When interpreting ROCE look for the following.

- How risk is the business?
- How capital intensive is it?
- What ROCE do similar business have?

Problems: which items to consider to achieve comparability?

- Revaluation reserves
- Policies, e.g. good will, R and D
- Bank overdraft: short/long term liability
- Investments and related income exclude

The following considerations are important:

- Change year to year
- Comparison to similar companies
- Comparison with current market borrowing rates.

3. Return on Equity (ROE)

ROE = Net profit x 100
Ordinary share capital + reserves

ROE gives a more restricted view of capital than ROCE, but the same principles apply.

4. Gross Profit Percentage (Margin)

Gross profit margin = gross profit x 100
Turnover

= Sales – cost of sales x 100
             Sales

- It is useful to compare profit margin to investigate movements which do not match. Take into account:
- Sales prices, sales volume and sales mix

- Purchase prices and related costs (discounts, carriage, etc)
- Production costs, both direct (materials, labour) and indirect (overheads both fixed and variable)

5. Operating Profit Margin

OPM = $\underline{PBIT}$ X 100
       Sales

6. Net Profit Margin

NPM = $\underline{Net\ profit}$ X 100
        Sales

For net profit margin, compare trends in:

- Sales expenses in relation to sales levels
- Administrative expenses, including salary levels
- Distribution expenses in relation to sales levels
- Depreciation should be considered separately for each expense category.

B. Liquidity ratios

Profitability is of course an important aspect of a company's performance and debt or gearing is another. Neither, however, addresses the key issue of liquidity in the short term.
Liquidity is the amount of cash a company can put its hands on quickly to settle its debts (and possibly to meet other unforeseen demands for cash payments too)
Liquid funds consist of:

a) Cash

b) Short-term investments for which there is a ready market.

c) Fixed term deposits with a bank, for example, a six-month high – interest deposit.

d) Trade debtors (because they will pay what they owe within a reasonably short period of time.

e) Bills of exchange receivable (because like ordinary trade debtors, these represent amounts of cash due to be received within a relatively short period of time.

A company can obtain liquid assets from sources other than sales, such as issue of shares for cash, a new loan or the sale of fixed assets. But a company cannot rely on these at all times, and in general obtaining liquid funds depends on making sales and profits. Even so profits do not always lead to increases in liquidity. This is mainly because funds generated from trading may be immediately invested in fixed assets or paid out as dividends liquidity position can be determined by calculating the following ratios.

1) Current ratio = <u>Current Assets</u>
Current Liabilities

Assuming assets are realizable at book level. Therefore, theoretically 2: 1 is acceptable. It depends on the type of industry.

2) Quick ratio = <u>Current Assets—Stock</u>
Current Liabilities

Eliminates illiquid and subjectively valued stock. Care is needed. It could be high if overtrading with debtors, but no cash.

Is 1:1 ok? Many supermarkets operate on 0.3: 1!

C. Efficiency Ratios Or Resource utilization Ratios

Efficiency ratios indicate how well a business is controlling aspects of its working capital.

Efficiency ratios include the following:

a) Collection period

Average collection period = <u>trade debtors</u> X 365 days
credit sales

Is it consistent with quick / current ratios? If not investigate.

b) Creditor's payment period = <u>trade creditors</u> X 365 days
Purchases

Use cost of sales if purchases are not disclosed.

c) Stock turnover = <u>cost of sales</u>
average stock

d) Stock days = <u>stock</u> X 365 days
cost of sales

- Higher the better? But remember
- Lead times
- Seasonal fluctuation in orders
- Alternative uses of warehouse space

- Bulk buying discounts
- Likelihood of stock perishing or becoming obsolete.

e) Asset turnover = $\dfrac{\text{turnover (sales)}}{\text{Total assets less current liabilities}}$

- This measures the efficiency of the use of assets. Amend to just fixed assets for capital intensive business.

- A high asset turnover means that the company is generating a lot of sales, but to do this it might have to keep its prices down and accept a low profit margin per K1 of sales.

- A high profit margin means a high profit per K1 of sales, but this also means that sales prices are high, there is a strong possibility that sales turnover will be depressed, and so asset turnover lower.

f) Cash cycle

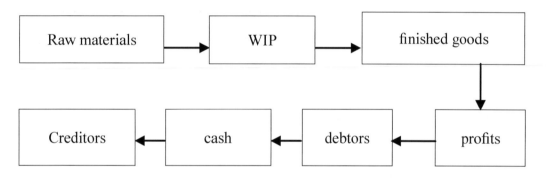

- Holding stock delays the time between payments for goods and sales receipts.
- Reasons for changes in liquidity
- Credit control efficiency altered
- Altering payment period of creditors as a source of funding
- Reduce stock holding to maintain liquidity.

D. Long-term Solvency: Debt and Gearing

Debt and gearing ratios are concerned with a company's long-term stability, how much the company owes in relation to its size, whether it is getting into heavier debt or improving its situation, and whether its debt burden seems heavy or light.

- When a company is heavily in debt, banks and other potential lenders may be unwilling to advance further funds.

- When a company is earning only a mount profit before tax and interest, and has a heavy burden of debt, there will be very little profit (if any) left over for shareholders after the interest charges have been paid.

- And so if interest rates were to go up (on bank overdrafts and so on) or the company were to borrow even more, it might soon be incurring interest charge in excess of PBIT. This might eventually lead to the liquidation of the company.

- Gearing is, amongst other things, an attempt to quantity the degree of risk involved in holding equity shares in a company, both in terms of the company's ability to remain in business and in terms of expected ordinary dividends from the company. The problem with a highly geared company is that, by definition, there is a lot of debt. Debt generally carries a fixed rate of interest (or fixed rate of dividend if in form of preference shares), hence there is a given (and large) amount to be paid out from profits to holders of debt before arriving at a residence available for distribution to holders of equity.

Debt and gearing can be measured using the following ratios, among others

a) Debt / equity ratio = $\dfrac{\text{interest bearing net debts}}{\text{Shareholders' funds}} \times 100$

There is no definitive answer, elements included are subjective. The following could have an impact.

- Convertible loan stock
- Preference shares
- Deferred tax
- Goodwill and development expenditure capitalization
- Revaluation reserve.

b) Debt / total assets ratio = $\dfrac{\text{total debt}}{\text{Total assets}} \times 100$

c) Gearing ratio = $\dfrac{\text{prior change capital}}{\text{Total capital}}$

d) Interest cover = $\dfrac{\text{PBIT}}{\text{Interest payable}}$

Is it better way to measure gearing? Company must generate enough profit to cover interest. Is a figure of 3 + safe?

E. Shareholders' Investment Ratios

There are ratios which help equity shareholders and other investors to assess the value and quality of an investment in the ordinary shares of a company.

The value of an investment in ordinary shares in a listed company is its market value, and so investment ratios must have regard not only to information in the company's published accounts, but also to the current price.

Earnings per share (EPS) is a valuable indicator of an ordinary share's performance

a) EPS = $\dfrac{\text{Net profit} - \text{Preference dividends}}{\text{Number of ordinary shares}}$

b) Dividend yield = $\dfrac{\text{Dividend per share}}{\text{Current market price}} \times 100$

- Low yield: the company retains a large proportion of profits to reinvest
- High yield: this is a risky company or slow – growing.

c) Dividend cover = $\dfrac{\text{EPS}}{\text{Dividend per share}}$

   or $\dfrac{\text{Profit after tax and preference dividend}}{\text{Dividend on ordinary shares}}$

This shows how safe the dividend is or the extent of profit retention. Variations are due to maintaining dividend when profits are declining.

d) Price / Earnings ratio = $\dfrac{\text{Current market price}}{\text{EPS}}$

The higher the better here: it reflects the confidence of the market. A rise in EPS will cause an increase in P/E ratio, but may be not to same extent, look at the context of the market and industry norms.

e) Earnings yield = $\dfrac{\text{EPS}}{\text{Current market price}}$

This shows the dividend yield if there is no retention of profit. It allows you to compare companies with different dividend policies, showing growth rather than earnings.

Uses and Limitations of Ratio Analysis

As noted earlier, ratio analysis is used by three main groups:

- Manager, who employs ratios to help analyze, control, and thus improve their firms' operations.

●Credit analysts, such as bank loan officers or bond rating analysts, who analyze ratios to help ascertain a company's ability to pay its debts; and

●Stock analysts, who are interested in a company's efficiency, risk, and growth prospects.

In later chapters we will look more closely at the basic factors which underlie each ratio, and at that point you will understand better how to interpret and use ratios. Note, though, that while ratios analysis can provide useful information concerning a company's operations and financial condition, it does have limitations that necessitate careful judgement. Some potential problems are listed below:

a) Many large firms operate different divisions in different industries, and for such companies it is difficult to develop a meaningful set of industry averages for comparative purposes. Therefore, ratio analysis is more useful for small, narrowly focused firms than for large, multidivisional ones

b) Most firms want to be better than average, so merely attaining average performances is not necessarily good. As a target for high-level performance, it is best to focus on the industry leader's ratios. Benchmarking helps in this regard.

c) Inflation may distort firms' balance sheet, causing reported values to be substantially different from "true" values. Further, since inflation affects both depreciation charges and inventory costs, profits are also affected. Thus, a ratio analysis for one firm over time, or a comparative analysis of firms of different ages, must be interpreted with judgement.

d) Seasonal factors can also distort a ratio analysis. For example, the inventory turnover ratio for a food processor will be radically different if the balance sheet figure used for inventory is the one just before versus just after the close of the canning seasonal. This problem can be minimized by using monthly averages for inventory (and receivable) when calculating turnover ratios.

e) Firms sometimes employ "**window dressing" techniques t**o make their financial statements look stronger. To illustrate, a Chicago builder borrowed on a two-year basis on December 29, 1998, held the proceeds of the loan as cash for a few days and then paid off the loan ahead of time on January 2, 1999. This improved his current and quick ratios, and made his year-end 1998 balance sheet look good. However, the improvement was strictly window dressing, because a few days later the balance sheet was back at the old level.

f) Different accounting practices can distort comparisons. As noted earlier, inventory valuation and depreciation methods can affect financial statements and thus distort comparisons among firms. Also, if one firm leases a substantial amount of its productive equipment, then its assets may appear low relatives to sales because leased assets often do not appear on the balance sheet. At the same time, the liability associated with the lease obligation may not be shown as a debt. Therefore, leasing can artificially improve both the turnover and the debt ratios. However, the accounting profession has taken steps to reduce this problem.

g) It is difficult to generalize about whether a particular ratio is "good" or "bad" for example, a high current ratio may indicate a strong liquidity position, which is good, or excessive cash, which is bad (because excess cash in the bank is a non-earning assets). Similarly, a high fixed assets turnover ratio may denote either a firm that uses its assets efficiently or one that is undercapitalized and cannot afford to buy enough assets.

h) A firm may have some ratios that look "good" and others that look "bad" making it difficult to tell whether the company is, on balance, strong or weak. However, statistical procedures can be used to analyze the net effects of a set of ratios. Many banks and other lending organizations use discriminate analysis, a statistical technique, to analyze potential borrowers' financial ratios, and on the basis of this analysis, classify companies according to their probability of getting into financial trouble.

Ratio analysis is useful, but analysts should be aware of these problems and make adjustments as necessary. Ratio analysis conducted in a mechanical, unthinking manner is dangerous, but used intelligently and with good judgement, it can provide useful insights into a firm's operations. Your judgement in interpreting a set of ratios is bound to be weak at this point, but it will improves as you go through the remainder of the book.

Looking Beyond the Numbers

Hopefully, working through this chapter has given you a better understanding of how to analyze financial statements and interpret accounting numbers. These are important skills when making business decisions, when evaluating performance, and when forecasting likely future developments.

While it is important to understand and interpret financial statements, sound financial analysis involves more than just calculating and interpreting numbers. Good analysts recognize that certain qualitative factors must also be considered. These factors are as follows:

1. **Are the company's revenues tied to one key customer?** If so, the company's performance may dramatically decline if the customer goes elsewhere. On the other hand, if the relationship is firmly entrenched, this might actually stabilize sales.

2. **To what extent are the company's revenues tied to one key product?** Companies that rely on a single product may be more efficient and more focused, but a lack of diversification increase risk. If revenues come from several different products, the overall bottom line will be less affected by a drop in the demand for any one product.

3. **To what extent does the company rely on a single supplier**? Depending on a single supplier may lead to unanticipated shortages, which is something that investors and potential creditors need to assess.

4. **What percentage of the company's business is generated overseas?** Companies with a large percentage of overseas business are often able to realize higher growth and larger profit margins. However, firms with overseas operations find that earnings from these operations are strongly affected by changes in the value of the local currency. Thus, fluctuations in currency markets create additional risks for firms with large overseas operations.

5. **Competition**. Generally, increased competition lowers prices and profit margins. In forecasting future performance, it is important to assess both the likely actions of the current competition and the likelihood of new competitors in the future.

6. **Future prospects.** Does the company invest heavily in research and development? If so, its future prospects may depend critically on the success of new products in the pipeline. For example, the market's assessment of a computer company depends on what next year's products look like. Likewise, investors in pharmaceutical companies are interested in knowing whether the company has developed any "break through" drugs that may be marketable in the years ahead.

7. **Legal and regulatory environment**. Changes in laws and regulations have important implications for many industries. For example, when forecasting the future of tobacco companies, it is crucial that an analyst factor in the effects of proposed regulations and pending or likely lawsuits, when assessing banks, telecommunications firms, and electric utilities, analysts need to forecast both the way in which these industries will be regulated in the years ahead and the ability of individual firms to respond to changes in regulation.

Now try the following problems

Example 1

The following information has been extracted from the recently published accounts of PCBF Ltd

EXTRACT FROM THE PROFIT AND LOSS ACCOUNT

	K'000	K'000
Sales	11,200	9,750
Cost of sales	8,460	6,825
Net profit before tax	465	320

This is after charging:

Depreciation	360	280
Debenture interest	80	60
Interest on bank overdraft	15	9
Audit fees	12	10

BALANCE SHEET AS AT 30ᵀᴴ APRIL

	2005	2004
	K'000	K'000
Fixed assets	1,850	1,430
Current assets		
Stock	640	490
Debtors	1,230	1,080
Cash	80	120
	1,950	1,690
Current liabilities		
Bank overdraft	110	80
Creditors	750	690
Taxation	30	2
Dividends	65	55
	955	845
Total assets less current liabilities (capital employed)	2,845	2,275
Long-term capital and reserves		
Ordinary share capital	800	800
Reserves	1,245	875
	2,045	1,675
10% debentures	800	600
	2,845	2,275

The following ratios are those calculated for PCBF Ltd, based on its published accounts for the previous year, and also the latest industry average ratio

PCBF Ltd	30 April 2004	industry average
ROCE (capital employed = equity and debentures)	16.70%	18.50%
Profit / sales	3.90%	4.73%
Asset turnover	4.29	3.91
Current ratio	2.00	1.90
Quick ratio	1.42	1.27
Gross profit margin	30.00%	35.23%

Creditors control	40 days	52 days
Stock turnover	13.90	18.30
Gearing	26.37%	32.71%

Required:

a) Calculate comparable ratios (to two decimal places where appropriate) for PCBF Ltd for the year ended 30 April 2005. All calculations must be clearly shown.

b) Write a report to your board of directors analyzing the performance of PCBF Ltd, comparing the results against the previous year and against the industry average.

SOLUTION

a)

	2004	2005	Industry average
ROCE	$\frac{320+60}{2,275}$ X 100 = 16.70%	$\frac{465+80}{2,845}$ X 100 = 19.16%	18.50%
Profit. /sales	$\frac{320+60}{9,750}$ X 100 = 3.90%	$\frac{465+80}{11,200}$ X 100 = 4.87%	4.73%
Asset turnover	$\frac{9,750}{2,275}$ = 4.29x	$\frac{11,200}{2,845}$ = 3.94x	3.91x
Current ratio	$\frac{1,690}{846}$ = 2.00	$\frac{1,950}{955}$ = 2.04	1.90
Quick ratio	$\frac{1080+120}{845}$ = 1.42	$\frac{1,230+80}{955}$ = 1.37	1.27
Gross profit margin	$\frac{9,750-6,825}{9,750}$ = 30.00%	$\frac{11,200-8,460}{11,200}$ = 24.46%	35.23%
Debtors turnover	$\frac{1,080 \times 365}{9,750}$ = 40 days	$\frac{1,230 \times 365}{11,200}$ = 40 days	52 days
Creditors turnover	$\frac{650 \times 365}{6,825}$ = 37 days	$\frac{750 \times 365}{8,460}$ = 32 days	49 days
Stock turnover	$\frac{6,825}{490}$ = 13.9x	$\frac{8,460}{640}$ = 13.2x	18.30x
Gearing	$\frac{600}{2275}$ = 26.37%	$\frac{800}{2845}$ = 28.12%	32.71%

B) REPORT

To: Board of Director Date! Xx/xx/xx
From: Management Accountant
SUBJECT: ANALYSIS OF PERFORMANCE OF PCBF LTD

This report should be read in conjunction with the appendix attached which shows the relevant ratios (from part (a)

-   Return on capital has improved considerably between 2004 and 2005 and is now higher than the industry average.

Net income as a proportion of sales has also improved noticeably between the years and is also now marginally ahead of the industry average. Gross margin, however, is considerably lower than in the previous year and is only some 70% of the industry average. This suggests either there has been a change in the cost structure of PCBF Ltd or that there has been a change in the method of cost allocation between the periods. Either way this is a marked change that requires investigation. The company may be in a period of transition as sales have increased by nearly 15% over the year and it would appear that new fixed assets have been purchased.

-   Asset turnover has declined between the periods although the 2005 figure is in line with the industry average. This reduction might indicate that the efficiency with which assets are used acquired in 2005 have not yet fully contributed to the business. A longer-term trend would clarify the picture.

Liquidity and working capital management

-   The current ratio has improved slightly over the year and is marginally higher than the industry average. It is also in line with what is generally regarded as satisfactory (2:1).

-   The quick ratio has declined marginally but is still better than the industry average. This suggests that PCBF Ltd has no short term liquidity problems and should have no difficulty in paying its debts as they become due.

-   Debtors as a proportion of sales is unchanged from 2004 and are considerably lower than the industry average. Consequently, there is probably little opportunity to reduce this further and there may be pressure in the future from customers to increase the period of credit given. The period of credit taken from suppliers has taken from 37 days to 32 days' purchases and is much lower than the industry average. Thus, it may be possible to finance any additional debtors by negotiating better credit terms from suppliers.

-   Stock turnover has fallen slightly and is much lower than the industry average and this may partly reflect stocking up ahead of a significant in sales. Alternatively, there is some danger that the stock could contain certain obsolete items that may require writing off. The relative increase in the level of stock has been financed by an increased overdraft which may reduce if the stock levels can be brought down.

- The high levels of stock, overdraft and debtors compared to that to creditors suggests a labour intensive company to that of creditors suggests a labour intensive company or one where considerable value is added to bought-in-goods.

Gearing

- The level of gearing has increase over the year and is below the industry average. Since the ROCE is nearly twice the rate of interest on debenture, profitability is likely to be increased by a modest increase in the level of gearing.

Signed: Accountant

EXAMPLE 2

Among the financial ratios sometimes encountered in schemes of ratio analysis are the following:

- i) Working capital: total assets
- ii) Retained earnings: total assets
- iii) Earnings before interest and tax: interest charges plus annual repayment of loans.

Required:

a) 1) Explain the purpose and meaning of each of these ratios

1. Use the data from the table below relating to Khosa Ltd and illustrate how each ratio might be calculated for each of the four years.
2. Discuss briefly trends apparent from this ratio analysis.

b) Appraise the way in which Khosa Ltd has financed its operations over the four year period on a comparison of years 1 and 4.

EXTRATACT FROM ACCOUNTS OF KHOSA LTD

Fixed assets	2004	2003	2002	2001
Intangible	K	K	K	K
Tangible	123,000	100,000	80,000	30,000
Investments	1,179,500	1,036,000	1,03,000	1,027,000

	10,000	10,000		
	1,312,500	1,146,000	1,110,000	1,057,000
Current assets	479,000	454,000	432,000	375,500
Stocks	1,774,500	1,585,000	1,329,000	1,263,000
Debtors	5,000	20,000	40,000	241,200
Cash & short term investments	2,258,500	2,059,000	1,801,000	1,879,700
Current liabilities				
Trade creditors	956,500	767,000	714,000	679,000
Bank overdraft	504,000	274,500	24,700	
Others	152,500	150,000	100,000	70,000
	1,613,000	1,191,500	838,700	749,000
Total assets less				
Current liabilities	1,958,000	2,013,500	2,072,300	2,187,700
Less: short term loans	124,000	248,000	372,000	496,000
Other liabilities	33,000	15,000	5,000	2,000
Net assets	1,801,000	1,750,500	1,695,300	1,689,700
Called up share capital	300,000	300,000	300,000	300,000
Profit & loss account				
Brought forward	1,450,500	1,395,300	1,389,700	1,324,400
Retained	50,000	55,200	5,600	65,300
	1,801,000	1,750,500	1,695,300	1,689,700
Turnover	6,660,000	6,343,000	6,041,000	5,492,000
Operating expenses				
Excluding depreciation	17,644	16,534	15,852	14,338
Earnings before				
Interest and tax	205,500	285,500	284,000	274,500
Interest charges	111,000	186,000	260,000	149,000

c) Briefly explain the relevance of three measures which may be used to assess performance in public sector services which provide education.

NOTE: It is assumed that loan repayments in year 1 were the same as in year 2 to 4.

DR. CRYFORD MUMBA

Solution

(a) (1) Working Capital: Total Assets Ratio

This ratio shoes the investment in working capital (current assets less current liabilities) as a proportion of a business' total assets. A high ratio would suggest an excessive investment in working capital, perhaps because of poor credit control, whereas a very low ratio would suggest over trading, which can lead to insolvency.

Retained Earnings: Total Asset Ratio

This shows the required earnings as a proportion of total assets. One would not expect this ratio to be very low. A company with substantial new finance to ensure their continued maintenance, effective use and eventual replacement. Retained earnings are a major source of new finance for most businesses.

Earnings before interest tax: interest charges plus annual repayment of loans ratios

This indicates a company's ability to meet its obligations to the providers of debt finance. Earnings should be much higher than those obligations, perhaps two or more times higher, so as to ensure that company can survive temporary fall in earnings.

(11) Relevant data on Khosa ltd

	20X1	20X2	20X3	20X4
	K'000	K'000	K'000	K'000
Working capital	1,130.7	962.3	867.5	645.5
Total assets	2936.7	2911	3205	3571
Retained earnings (BF plus current)	1389.7	1395.3	1450.5	1501
Earnings before interest tax	274.5	284	285.5	205.5
Interest charges plus annual repayment				2
Loans	273	384	310	35

Ratios expressed as percentages, are therefore as follows:

	20X1 %	20X2 %	20X3 %	20X4 %
Working capital: Total assets	38.5	33.1	27.1	18.1
Retained earnings: total assets	47.3	47.9	45.3	42
EBIT: interest charges	100.5	74.0	92.1	87.4

Trends in ratios
Working capital

Working capital steadily declining, both in amount and as a percentage of total assets. This is mainly due to a growth in current liabilities, mostly the bank overdraft.

Change in retained earnings

The fall in retained earnings as a proportion of total assets over the last two years, despite the rise on the amount of retained earnings, suggests that the dividend policy is too generous for a company with rapidly growing assets.

Earnings and interest charges

Earnings have not covered interest charges and loan repayments in any of the last three years. This may explain the company's increasing reliance on short term credit.

b) Financing of growth

Between year 1 and year 4, both fixed and current assets grew significantly. This growth had to be financed. The company had been committed to regular repayments of its long term loan, and has not obtained replacement long-term loans, so that the burden has fallen on current liabilities and on shareholders equity.

1. There was no bank overdraft in year 1, and an overdraft of 504,000 in year 4.

2. In addition, trade credit has increased from 12.4% of turnover in year 1 to 14.4% of turnover in year 4, and other current liabilities (possibly including taxation and proposed dividends) have more than doubled over the same period.

Implications of financing policy

This policy of finding increases in total assets, particularly fixed assets, almost entirely by increases in current liabilities is unwise. Bank overdrafts are often renewed indefinitely, but they are still repayable on demand and the bank could require re-payment if ever it thought that the company was getting into difficulties.

Similarly, further trade credit could be denied at any time. If all debtors realized their book values, the current liabilities could be met, avoiding immediate insolvency, but the company might then find it very hard to continue trading. A fresh injection of equity or long-term debt is called for.

c) Maximization of resources

The common problem facing all public sector organizations that are providing a service is that of maximizing the use of scarce resources. Thus in education as in other public services, the crucial measures are those which address the concept of value for money.
Performance measures that may be used include the following:

1) Amount of money spent on each student

The implication of this is that the services provided are similar and that the best providers are those which do so at the lowest cost.

2) Amount of money spent on special services

A similar measure can be applied to departments that are providing specialist services of educational institutions. For example, the cost per head of providing the school library service or specialist language teaching in primary schools.

3) Quality measures

In addition to cost measures, the government has tried to introduce measures of quality performance through services such as the league tables of school performance, etc.

PROGRESS CLINIC 11

Question 1

The following are the final accounts from two similar types of retail stores namely, J Pvt Co and K Pvt Co.

TRADING AND PROFIT AND LOSS ACCOUNTS FOR THE YEAR ENDED 31 DECEMBER 2012

	J Pvt Co	K Pvt Co
	K	K
Sales	80 000	120 000
Cost of goods sold		
Opening stock	25 000	22 500
Purchases	50 000	91 000
	75 000	113 500
Closing stock	15 000	17 500
	60 000	96 000
Gross profit	20 000	24 000
Expenses		
Depreciation	1 000	3 000
Other expenses	9 000	6 000
Net profit	**10 000**	**15 000**

BALANCE SHEETS AS AT 31 DECEMBER 2012

	J Pvt Co K	K Pvt Co K
Fixed Assets		
Equipment	10 000	20 000
Accumulated depreciation	8 000	6 000
	2 000	14 000
Current Assets		
Stock	15 000	17 500
Debtors	25 000	20 000
Bank	5 000	2 500
	45 000	40 000
Current Liabilities		
Creditors	(5 000)	(10 000)
	42 000	**44 000**
Financed by:		
Capital	38 000	36 000
Net profit	10 000	15 000
	48 000	51 000
Less: Drawings	6 000	7 000
	42 000	**44 000**

REQUIRED

a) From the above details you are required to calculate the following:

   i)   Gross profit ratio

   ii)   Net profit ratio

   iii) Expenses ratio

   iv)   Stock turnover ratio

   v)   Return On Capital Employed (ROCE)

   vi)   Current ratio

   vii) Quick ratio

   viii) Debtors Payment Period (in months)

   ix)   Creditors Payment Period (in months)

b) Comment on the comparative performance of the two businesses.

Question 2

Akimo Ltd has the following financial results for the last two years of trading.

AKIMO LTD
INCOME AND EXPENDITURE STATEMENT FOR THE YEAR

	31 Dec 2011	31 Dec 2012
	K000	K000
Sales	14,400	17,000
Less: Cost of sales	11,800	12,600
Gross Profit	2,600	4,400
Less: Expenses	1,200	2,000
Net Profit for the period	1,400	2,400

Balance Sheet as at

	31 Dec 2011	31 Dec 2012
	K000	K000
Assets		
Fixed Assets	2,500	4,000
Current Assts		
Stock	1,300	2,000
Receivables	2,000	1,600
Bank Balances	2,400	820
	8,200	**8,420**
Equity		
2.4 million ordinary shares of K1 each	2,400	2,400
Revaluation reserve	500	500
Retained earnings	1,200	2,820
	4,100	5,720
10% Loan	2,600	-
Current Liabilities		
Payables	1,500	2,700
	8,200	**8,420**

Note:

Dividends were K520,000 in the year 2011 and K780,000 in the year 2012.

REQUIRED

(a) From the above details, calculate for each of the two years, the following:

i) Gross profit ratio

ii) Net profit ratio

iii) Return on capital employed (ROCE)

iv) Current Ratio

v) Quick Ratio

(b) Comment on the comparison on the performance of the company over the period of two years.

Question 3

The following are extracts from the financial accounts of ABC Ltd for the year ended 30 November 2012:

ABC LIMITED
BALANCE SHEET AS AT 30 NOVEMBER 2012

	K'000 Cost	K'000 Dep'n	K'000 NBV
Fixed assets:			
Land and buildings	110,000	25,000	85,000
Plant and equipment	65,500	24,700	40,800
Fixtures and fittings	15,250	8,600	6,650
	190,750	58,300	132,450
Current assets:			
Stock	15,000		
Debtors	24,000		
Bank	2,300	41,300	
Current liabilities:			
Creditors	16,800		
Accruals	1,350	18,150	
Working capital			23,150
Capital employed			155,600
Capital Account:			
Capital at 1 April			165,000
Profit for the year			28,600
			193,600
Less: drawings			38,000
			155,600

Extract from the Trading, profit and loss Account for the year ended 30 November 2012

	K'000
Sales	288,000
Purchases	212,500
Cost of goods sold	216,000
Expenses	187,400
Net profit	28,600

Required:

a) Ratios are often divided into categories such as profitability, liquidity and resource utilization. Explain what is shown by ratios in each of these categories.

b) Calculate the following ratios for ABC Ltd for the year ended 30 November 2012(calculations to be taken to 1 decimal place):
   i) Gross profit margin
   ii) Net profit margin
   iii) Debtors days
   iv) Creditors days
   v) Current ratio
   vi) Acid test ratio(Quick ratio)

Question 4

In relation to the interpretation of financial statements, answer the following questions:

a) Some businesses operate on a lower net profit margin than other types of business(for example, a Supermarket chain). Does this mean that the return on capital employed from the business will also be lower? Give reasons for your answer.

b) What potential problems arise for the external analyst from the use of the balance sheet figures in the calculation of financial ratios

c) Two businesses operate in the same industry. One has a stock turnover period that is higher than the industry average. The other has a stock turnover period that is lower than the industry average. Give three possible explanations for each business's stock period.

d) Identify and discuss three reasons why the P/E ratio of two businesses operating within the same industry may differ.

CHAPTER 12

RELEVANT INTERNATIONAL ACCOUNTING STANDARDS (IASs)

IAS 10 EVENTS AFTER THE BALANCE SHEET DATE

Suppose the year end of a company is 31 December 2011 and the directors approve the financial statements at a Board meeting held on 22 March 2012. Certain events occurring during the intervening period will provide information which will help in preparing the financial statements:

- Events after the balance sheet date are those events, both favourable and unfavourable, that occur between the balance sheet date and the date on which the financial statements are authorized for issue.

- The date on which the financial statements are authorized for issue is the date the board of directors formerly approves a set of documents as the financial statements. In respect of unincorporated enterprises, the date of approval is the corresponding date in respect of consolidated accounts, the date of approval is the date when the consolidated accounts are formerly approved by the board of directors of the parent company.

There are two types of events after the balance sheet date:

1. Those that provide further evidence of conditions that existed at the balance sheet date (Adjusting events after the balance sheet date).

2. Those that are indicative of conditions that arose after the balance sheet date (non-adjusting events after the balance sheet).

- Adjusting events call for adjustment of amounts recognized in the financial statements.

- Non-adjusting events should be disclosed by note if they are of such importance that non—disclosure would affect the ability of the users of the financial statements to make proper evaluations and decisions.

- The note should disclose the nature of the event and an estimate of the financial effect or a statement that an estimate cannot be made.

- If an event after the balance sheet date indicates that the going concern assumptions is inappropriate for the enterprise, then the balance sheet should be adjusted onto a break up basis.

Proposed dividends

- A major change in IAS 10 is that equity dividends proposed or declared after the balance sheet date may no longer be included as liabilities at the balance sheet date. They are non-adjusting events after the balance sheet date and must be disclosed by note as required by IAS 1.

Examples of adjusting events

- These events provide additional evidence of conditions existing at the balance sheet date. For example, bad debts arising one or two months after the balance sheet date may help to quantify the bad debts allowance as at the balance sheet date. Such events may, therefore, affect the amount at which items are stated in the balance sheet. Examples include:
- Allowances for inventories and bad debts
- Amounts received or receivable in respect of insurance claims which were being negotiated at the balance sheet date.
- The discovery of fraud or errors.

Examples of non-adjusting events

- These are events arising after the balance sheet date but which, unlike those events above, do not involve conditions existing at the balance sheet date. Such events will not, therefore, have any effects on items in the balance sheet or income statements being prepared.

- However, where non-adjusting events after the balance sheet date are of such importance that non-disclosure would affect the ability of the users of the financial statements to make proper evaluations and decisions an enterprise should disclose the following information for each non-adjusting event after the balance sheet date.

- The nature of the event

- An estimate of its financial effect or a statement that such an estimate cannot be made.

The following are the examples of non-adjusting events after the balance sheet date may be of such importance that non-disclosure would affect the ability of the users of the financial statements to make proper evaluations and decisions:

- A major business combination after the balance sheet date

- The destruction of a major production plant by a fire after the balance sheet date.

- Abnormally large changes after the balance sheet date in asset prices or foreign exchange rates.

IAS 37 PROVISIONS, CONTINGENT LIABILITIES AND CONTINGENT ASSETS

- The objective of IAS 37 provisions, contingent liabilities and contingent assets is to ensure that appropriate recognition criteria and measurements bases are applied to provisions, contingent liabilities and contingent assets and that sufficient information is disclosed in the notes to the financial statements to make users understand their nature, timing and amount.

- It supersedes the parts of the old IAS 10 contingencies and events occurring after the balance sheet date which are dealt with contingencies.

Definitions

IAS 37 opens with a series of definitions:

Provision – A provision is a liability of uncertain timing or amount

- **Liability** – A liability is a present obligation of the enterprise arising from past events, the settlement of which is expected to result in an outflow from the enterprise of resources embodying economic benefits

- **Obligation event** – An obligation event is an event that creates a legal or constructive obligation that result in an enterprise having no realistic alternative to settling that obligation.

- **Legal obligation** – A legal obligation is an obligation that derives from:

  - A contract (though its explicit or implicit terms)
  - Legislation or
  - Other operation of law

- **Constructive obligation** – This is an obligation that derives from an enterprise's action where:

  - By an established pattern of past practice, published policies or a sufficiently specific current statement, the enterprise has indicated to other parties that it will accept certain responsibilities; and

  - As a result, the enterprise has created a valid expectation on the part of those other parties that it will discharge those responsibilities.

  - Contingent liability – A contingent liability is:

191

- A possible obligation that arises form past events and whose existence will be confirmed only by the occurrence or non-occurrence of one or more uncertain future events not wholly within the control of the enterprise: or

- A present obligation that arises from past events but is not recognized because:

- It is not probable that an outflow of resources embodying economic benefits will be required to settle the obligation : or

- The amount of the obligation cannot be measured with sufficient reliability

Contingent asset – a contingent asset is a possible asset that arises from past events and whose existence will be confirmed only by the occurrence or non-occurrence of one or more uncertain future events not wholly within the control of the enterprise.

Contingent liabilities and assets

- The requirements of IAS 37 as regards contingent liabilities and assets are very similar to those of the previous IAS 10.

- The requirements are summarized in the following table:

Degree of Probability	Contingent Liability	Contingent Assets
Virtually certain (therefore Not contingent)	provide	Recognize
• Probable	provide	Disclosure by note
• Possible	Disclosure by note	No disclosure
• Remote	No disclosure	No disclosure

Note that when there is a possibility of the recovery from a third party of all or part of a contingent liability, this must be treated as a separate matter, and a contingent asset only recognized if its receipts is virtually criteria as shown in the table above.

IAS 38 INTANGIBLE ASSETS

The objective of IAS 38 intangible assets is to provide the required accounting treatment for almost all intangible assets, including research and development.

- An intangible asset is an identifiable non-monetary asset without physical substance.

- An intangible asset is recognized if and only if:

(a) It is probable that the future economic benefits that are attributable to the asset will flow to the enterprise.

(b) The cost of the asset can be measured reliably.

Recognition is initially at cost, which could be in cash or the fair value of equity shares given in exchange.

Research and development expenditure

- Research is original and planned investigation undertaken with the prospect of gaining new scientific knowledge and understanding.

- No intangible asset arising from research should be recognized. (This does not, of course, debar the recognition of tangible assets used in research).

- Development is the application of research findings or other knowledge to a plan or design for the production of new or substantially improved materials, devices, products, process or systems before the start of commercial production or use.

- An intangible asset arising from development should be recognized if and only if, an enterprise can all of the following:

a) The technical feasibility of completing the intangible asset so that it will be available for use or sale.

b) Its intention to complete the intangible asset and use or sell it.

c) Its ability to use or sell the intangible asset.

d) How the intangible asset will generate probable future economic benefits. Among other things, the enterprise should demonstrate the existence of a market for the output of the intangible asset or the intangible asset itself, or if it is to be used internally, the usefulness of the intangible asset.

e) The availability of adequate technical, financial and other resources to complete the development and to use or sell the intangible asset.

f) Its ability to measure the expenditure attribute to the intangible asset during its development reliably.

- The amount to be included is the cost of the development. Note development expenditure once treated as an expense cannot be reinstated as an asset.

- Thus, development expenditure should only be deferred to future periods when the following conditions are met:

  S   Separately defined project
  E   Expenditure separately identifiable
  C   Commercially viable
  T   Technically feasible
  O   Overall profit expected
  R   Resources exist to complete the project

IAS 17 ACCOUNTING FOR LEASES

Leasing is very important means by which businesses acquire the use of non-current assets without having to pay the full cost at the outlet

- Accounting for leases is regulated by IAS 17 which requires many leased assets to be recognized as assets even though they may never actually be owned by the entity using them—the lessee. There is also an accounting problem for the lessor—the enterprise providing the asset.

- IAS 17 defines a lease as an agreement whereby the lessor conveys to the lessee, in return for a payment or series of payments, the right to use an asset for an agreed period of time.

- IAS 17 leases recognizes two types of lease:

(a) A **finance lease** – This transfers substantially all the risks and rewards incident to ownership of an asset. The title may or may not eventually be transferred.

(b) An **operating lease** – this is a lease other than a finance lease.

Accounting treatment

- Hire charges due under an operating lease is debited to an expense account as they are incurred and appear in the income statement as an expense.

- IAS 17 argues that an asset leased under a finance lease must be recorded as an asset and a corresponding liability in the lessee's accounting records

IAS 33 EARNINGS PER SHARE

- Earnings per share are an important figure to users of the financial statements of enterprises whose ordinary shares are publicity traded. Its calculation is stipulated in detail by IAS 33.

- The figure 'earnings per share' (EPS) is used to assess the ongoing financial performance of a company from one year to another, and to compute the major stock market indicator of performance. The price earnings ratio (P/E) ratio. The calculation for the PE is :

PE ratio = $\dfrac{\text{Market Value of Share}}{\text{EPS}}$

- Rightly or wrongly, the stock market places great emphasis on a company's PE ratio and therefore, a standard form of measurement of EPS is required.

- Examining the trend of EPS gives a more accurate indication of profitability than just comparing reported profits.

- IAS 33 makes a distinction between an ordinary share and a potential ordinary share. An ordinary share is an equity instrument that is subordinate to all other classes of equity instruments. A potential ordinary share is a financial instrument or other contract that may entitle its holder to ordinary shares. Examples of potential ordinary shares are:

  - Debt or equity instruments, including preference shares that are convertible into ordinary shares.

  - Share warrants and options – these are financial instruments that give the holder the right to purchase ordinary shares.

  - Employee plans that allow employees to receive ordinary shares as part of their remuneration and other share purchase plans.

  - Shares which could be issued upon the satisfaction arrangements, such as the purchase of a business or other assets.

Computational requirements of IAS 33: Basic EPS

The normal figure of EPS, as calculated below in accordance with IAS 33, is called **basic EPS**. The definition of both the numerator and the denominator can present difficulties of calculations in certain circumstances.

Earnings per share = $\dfrac{\text{Net profit for the year after preference dividend but before ordinary div.}}{\text{Number of ordinary shares in issue.}}$

- For the purpose of calculating basic EPS, the net profit or loss for the period attributable to ordinary shareholders should be the net profit or loss for the period after deducting preference dividends. In other, words, the earnings figure to be taken is the profit after:

- Minority interests
- Tax
- Preference dividends and any other appropriations in respect of preference shares.

- Where several classes of shares are in issue, the earnings should be apportioned according to dividend rights.

- Earnings should be apportioned over the weighted average equity share capital (i.e. taking into account of when shares are issued during the year).

Example

A company issued 200 000 shares at full market price (K3.00) on 1 July 2006.

Relevant Information

Ordinary profit attributable to ordinary shareholders	2006	2005
For the year ended 31 Dec	K550 000	K460 000
Number of ordinary share in issue at 31 Dec	1 000 000	800,000

Compute the EPS

Solution

$$2005 = \frac{K460\ 000}{800\ 000} = K57.50$$

$$2006 = \frac{K550\ 000}{800\ 000 + \frac{1}{2} \times 200\ 000)} = K61.11$$

Since the 200 000 shares have only contributed finance for half a year, the number of shares is adjusted accordingly. Note that the solution is to use the earnings figure for the period without adjustment, but divide by the average number of shares weighted on a time basis.

- Note that when a company makes a bonds issue or rights issue earnings should be apportioned over the shares in issue after the bonus or rights issue.

Diluted EPS

- If an enterprise has issued bonds convertible at a later date into ordinary shares, on conversion the number of ordinary shares will rise, but no fresh capital enters the enterprise. This effect is referred to as **dilution**.
- IAS 33 requires an enterprise to disclose, as well as the basic EPS, the diluted EPS, calculated using current earnings but assuming that the future dilution has already happened.

IAS 16 PROPERTY, PLANT AND EQUIPMENT

Key definitions of IAS 16 are:

1. Depreciable amount is the cost of an asset, or other amount substituted for cost in the financial statements less its residue value.

2. Depreciation is the systematic allocation of the depreciable amount of an asset over its useful life.

3. Property, plant and equipment are tangible assets held by an enterprise for more than one accounting period for use in the production or supply of goods or services for rental to others or for administrative purposes.

Recognition

An item of property, plant and equipment should be recognized as an asset when:

1. it is probable that future economic benefits associated with an asset will flow to the enterprise

2. The cost of the asset can be measured reliably

Initial measurement

An item of plant, property and equipment which qualifies as an asset should initially be measured at its cost subsequent expenditures should only be capitalized if it improves the asset beyond its originally assessed standard performance. All other subsequent expenditure should be written off.

Revision of lives

The useful life's of assets should be reviewed at least each financial year end and when necessary revised.

Disclosure requirements

The following should be disclosed in the financial statement for each major class of depreciable asset:

1. the measurement bases used e.g. cost or revaluation
2. the depreciation methods used
3. the useful lives or the depreciation rates used
4. total depreciation charged for the period
5. the gross amount of depreciable assets and the related accumulated depreciation.

IAS 20 ACCOUNTING FOR GOVERNMENT GRANTS AND DISCLOSURE REQUIREMENTS OF GOVERNMENT ASSISTANCE

- In many countries assistance from government is provided for enterprises and as standard procedure is necessary to define how to account for this assistance

- IAS 20 establishes that standard procedures, albeit with alternatives, and also requires disclosure of assistance provided by government in other forms.

General principles

- Grants should not be recognized in the income statement until conditions for receipt have been complied with and there is reasonable assurance that the grant will be received. (This is prudent).

- Subject to this condition, grants should be recognized in the income statement so as to match them with the expenditure towards which they are intended to contribute. (Application of the accruals concept). Grants for machines of non-current assets should be recognized over the expected useful life's of the related assets.

- IAS 20 permits two treatments. Both are equally acceptable and capable of giving a true and fair view.

Method 1 – Write off the grant against the cost of the non-current asset and depreciate the reduce cost. This method is obviously simple to operate.

Method 2 – Treat the grant as deferred income and transfer a portion to revenue each year, so offsetting the higher depreciation change on the original cost.

This method has the advantage of ensuring that assets acquired at different times and in different locations are recorded on uniform basis, regardless of changes in government policy.

Example

An enterprise opens a new factory and receives a government grant of K15 000 in respect of capital equipment costing K100 000. It depreciates all plant and equipment at 20% per annum straight-line show the balance sheet extracts to record the grant in the first year and methods 1 and 2 above.

Solution

1. Write off against asset

    Balance sheet extract

	K
Non –current assets:	
• Plant and machinery at cost (100 – 15)	85 000
• Less: Depreciation (20% of 85)	17 000
	68 000

2. Deferred income

    Government grant deferred income statement

	K		K
• Income statement transfer for year: 20% X 15 000	3 000	Cash receipt	15 000
Balance c/d	12 000		___
	15 000		15 000
		Balance b/d	12 000

    Balance sheet extract

	K
Non-current assets:	
• Plant and machinery at cost	100 000
• Less: Depreciation	20 000
Deferred income	80 000
Government grant	12 000

Other grants

Purpose of grant	recognize in income statement
1. To give immediate financial support	-when receivable
2. To reimburse previously incurred cost	-when receivable
3. To finance general activities over a period	-in relevant period
4. To compensate for loss of income	-in relevant period

Disclosure

The disclosure requirements of IAS 20 are:

1. The accounting policy adopted for government grants including the methods of presentation adopted in the financial statements.

2. The nature and extent of government grants recognized in the financial statements and an indication of other forms of government assistance from which the enterprise has directly benefited.

3. Unfulfilled conditions and other contingencies attacking to government assistance that has been recognized.

IFRS 3 BUSINESS COMBINATIONS: GOODWILL

IFRS 3 requires goodwill arising on an acquisition to be capitalized as an intangible non-current asset and then tested annually for possible impairment. No routine amortization of good will is required.

Definitions

1. Goodwill is the difference between the value of a business as a whole and the aggregate of the fair value of its separable net assets.

2. Separable net assets are those assets (and liabilities) which can be identified and sold of separately without necessarily disposing of the business as a whole. They include identifiable intangibles such as patents, licenses and trade-marks.

3. **Fair value** is the amount at which an asset or liability could be exchanged in an arm's length transaction between informed and willing parties, other than in a forced or liquidation sale.

Purchased and non-purchased (inherent) goodwill

- **Purchased goodwill** arises when one business acquires another as a going concern. The term therefore includes good will arising on conclusion of a subsidiary or associated company in the consolidated financial statements.

- Purchased goodwill is recognized within the financial statements because at a specific point in time the fact of purchase has established a figure of value for the business as a whole which can be compared with the fair value of the individual net assets acquired. The difference is incorporated in the financial statements of the acquiring company as the cost of the acquisition.

- **Inherent goodwill** – Goodwill exists in any successful business. However, if the business has never changed hands, this goodwill will not be recognized in the financial statements because no event has occurred to identify its value. It can only be subjectively estimated. This is inherent goodwill or non-purchased goodwill and its not recognized in the financial statements

Accounting for goodwill

- Non-purchased goodwill should not be recognized in the financial statements as an asset. It certainly exists but fails to satisfy the recognition criteria since it is not capable of being measured reliably.

- Purchased goodwill is dealt with in two accounting standards, according to how it arose. Goodwill arising on the purchase of a subsidiary is covered by IFRS 3, while all other goodwill is covered by IAS 38.

- IFRS 3 requires that goodwill acquired on the purchase of a subsidiary should be recognized as an asset but should not be amortized. Instead it must be tested for impairment annually or more frequently if events or circumstances indicate that it might be impaired, following the rules of IAS 36.

Example

- Z Ltd pays K100 000 cash to acquire 100% of X Ltd, whose net assets at the date of acquisition have an aggregate fair value of K80 000. Describe how the goodwill arising should be accounted for

  ### Solution

- Z's own accounts, the investment in X Ltd is recorded at its cost of K100 000.

	K	K
Dr investment in X Ltd	100 000	
Cr cash		100 000

- No goodwill arises in Z Ltd's own individual accounts

- In the consolidated accounts, goodwill arises to be accounted for in accordance with IFRS 3. The goodwill is initially recognized at its cost, being the excess of the price paid for the business over the aggregate fair value of the net assets acquired.

- Cost of goodwill = price paid – fair value of net assets acquired.

  = K100 000 – K80 000

  = K20 000

- The goodwill will be presented as an intangible non-current asset of K20 000 on the consolidated balance sheet, and subjected to annual impairment tests in accordance with IAS 36.

Negative goodwill

- There will be cases (e.g. to compensate for expected future losses) where the fair value of the separable net assets exceeds the value of the business as a whole. This difference is called negative goodwill. Thus, negative goodwill arises where the fair values of the separable net assets exceeds the value of the business as a whole

- IFRS 3 requires the following accounting treatment of negative goodwill.

- First check that the measurements of the fair values of the net assets acquired, and of the price paid, have been carried out accurately.

- After this reassessment has been carried out, any negative goodwill still remaining should be credited direct to the income statement.

IAS 40 INVESTMENT PROPERTY

- Investment property is defined by IAS 40 as and or a building held to earn rentals or for capital appreciation or both, rather than for use in the enterprise or for sale in the ordinary course of business

- An accounting treatment for investment properties different from that of other types of land and buildings is called for because the objectives or holding investment properties make them more in the nature of investments rather than usual properties which are consumed in the operations of the business.

Recognition

- IAS 40 requires recognition of investment properties as assets when they meet the normal requirements for the recognition of assets – future economic benefits will flow to the enterprise and the cost of the property can be measured reliably.

Initial measurement

- An investment property should initially be measured at cost, including transaction costs.

Measurement subsequent to initial recognition

IAS 40 gives an enterprise the choice of adoption a cost based policy (the cost model) or a fair value based policy (the fair value model) for its investment properties. The chosen policy must be applied to all the investment properties belonging to the enterprise

- **The cost based policy** – Under the cost-based approach, investment properties are treated like other properties using the cost model treatment in IAS 16 property, plant and equipment – that is, cost less accumulated depreciation and any accumulated impairment loss IAS 40 contains particular disclosure requirements when cost-based approach is used.

- **The fair value policy** – The fair value policy requires the enterprise to revalue its investment properties each year, any gain or loss being included in the net profit or loss for the period.

  Fair value is defined as the amount for which the property could be exchanged between knowledgeable properties in the same location and condition as the property under review. In the absence of such an active market, information from a variety of sources may have to be considered, including:

- Current prices on an active market for properties of a different nature, condition or location, adjusted to reflect those differences.

- Recent prices on less active market

- Discounted cash flow projections based on reliable estimates of future cash flows

Transfers

- Transfers to or form investment property may be made only when there is a change of use. There are four possibilities:

1. Transfer from investment property (at fair value) to owner-occupied property – use the fair value at the date of the change for subsequent accounting under IAS 16.
2. Transfer from investment property (at fair value) to inventory – use the fair value at the date of the change for subsequent accounting under IAS 2 inventories

3. Transfer from owner-occupied property to investment property to be carried at fair value-IAS 16 (cost less depreciation) will have been applied up to the date of the change. On adopting fair value, the normal treatment will be to recognize a decrease in the income statement or to credit any gain to equity under the heading of revaluation surplus.

4. Transfer from inventories to investment property to be carried at fair value – any difference between fair value at the date of the transfer and its previous carrying amount should be recognized in the income statement.

Disposals

- Gains as losses on the investment properties should be determined as the difference between net disposal proceeds and the carrying amount of the asset. They will be recognized in the income statement unless IAS 17 leases requires otherwise on a sale and leaseback.

Disclosure

- IAS 40 contains a number of disclosure requirements some of these are: cost model used, method of determining fair value, transfers, disposal, etc

PROGRESS CLINIC 12

QUESTION 1

IAS 38 Accounting for Research and Development defines certain categories of Research and Development Expenditure. The standard also lays down rules which must be applied for the captalisation of research and development expenditure.

REQUIRED

(a) List and explain the three (3) categories of research expenditure.

(b) List the four (4) criteria applied to research and development expenditure, according to IAS 38, to determine whether the cost should be capitalized or not.

QUESTION 2

Describe how the government grant –related aspects of the following event should be accounted for with respect to a limited company:

Where a grant towards revenue expenditure in one year, on the condition that if certain requirements were not met in the next five years, all or part of the grant might be repayable.

Question 3

a) Define a 'non-adjusting event'.
b) Identify and briefly describe three examples of non-adjusting events

CHAPTER 13

CONSOLIDATED FINANCIAL STATEMENTS

If one company owns <u>more than</u> 50% of the ordinary shares of another company;
- This will usually give the first company 'control' of the second company.
- The first company (the parent company, P) has enough voting power to appoint all the directors of the second company (the subsidiary, S)
- P is, in effect, able to manage S as if it were merely a department of P, rather than a separate legal entity.
- In strict legal terms P and S remain distinct, but in economic substance they can be regarded as a single unit (a 'group').

GROUP ACCOUNTS

The key principle underlying group accounts is the need to reflect the economic substance of the relationship

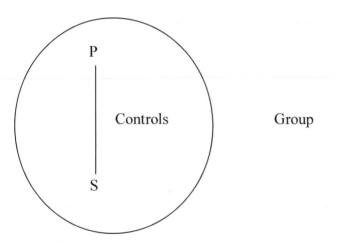

Group

- P is an individual legal entity.
- S is an individual legal entity.
- P controls S and therefore they form a single economic entity-the group.
- Subsidiary is an entity that is controlled by another entity (parent)
- Control is the power to govern the financial and operating policies of an entity so as to obtain benefits from its activities.

Purpose of consolidated accounts
- Present financial information about a parent undertaking and its subsidiary undertakings as a single economic unit.
- Show the economic controlled by the group.
- Show the obligations of the group.
- Show the results the group achieves with its resource.

Principles of the consolidated balance sheet

The basic principle of a consolidated statement of financial position (balance sheet) is that it shows all assets and liabilities of the parent and subsidiary.

- Intra-group items are included, e.g., receivables and payables shown in the consolidated balance sheet only include amounts owed from/to third parties.

Method of preparing a consolidated balance sheet is:

- The investment in the subsidiary (s) shown in the parents (P's) balance sheet is replaced by the net assets of S.
- The cost of the investment in S is effectively cancelled with the ordinary share capital and reserves of the subsidiary.

This leaves a consolidated balance sheet showing:
- The rest assets of the whole group (P+S)
- The share capital of the group, which always equals the share capital of P only.
- The retained profits, comprising profits made by the group (i.e. all of P's Historical profits +profits made by S post acquisition)

Note: Under no circumstances will any share capital of any subsidiary company ever be included in the figure of share capital in the consolidated balance sheet.

The mechanics of consolidation

A standard group accounting question will provide to accounts of P and the accounts of S and will require the preparation of consolidated accounts.

The best approach is to use a set of standard workings:

(W1) establish the group structure

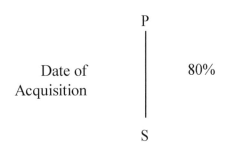

This indicates that P owns 80% of the ordinary shares of S and when they were acquired.

(W2) Net assets of the subsidiary

	At date of acquisition	At the reporting date
	K	K
Share capital	X	X
Reserves:		
Share premium	X	X
Retained earnings	X	X
	X	X

(W3) **Goodwill: proportion of net assets method**

Cost of investment (= value of subsidiary)	X
For: parent's % of subsidiary's net assets at acquisition	(X)
Goodwill on acquisition	X
Less: Impairments to date	(X)
Carrying Goodwill	X

Or

(W3) **Goodwill: fair value method**

Cost of investment (= value of subsidiary)	X
For: parent's % of subsidiary's net assets at acquisition	(X)
Goodwill on acquisition-parent's share	X
Fair value of non controlling interest (NCI) at acquisition	
(NCI shares X subsidiary share price at acquisition	X
Less: NCI% of subsidiary's net assets at acquisition	(X)
Goodwill—NNCI share	X
Total goodwill	X
Less: impairment to date	(X)
Carrying goodwill	X

(W4) non controlling interest (NCI)-proportion of net assets method NNCI % of subsidiary's

net assets at reporting date (W2)	X
W4) NCI-fair value method	
NCI % of subsidiary net assets at reporting date (W2)	X
NCI share of goodwill (W3)	X
NCI share of impairment (W3)	(X)
	X

(W5) Group retained earnings

P's retained earnings (100%)	X
P's % of subsidiary's post acquisition retained earnings	X
LESS: goodwill impairments to date (W3)	(X)
Group earnings	X

Example 1

The balance sheets of P and S at 31 December 2009 are:

	P	S
	K000	K000
Net current assets	60	50
Investment in S at cost	50	
Current assets	40	40
Total assets	150	90
Ordinary share capital (K1 shares)	100	40
Retained earnings	30	10
Current liabilities	20	40
Total equity +liabilities	150	90

Note: P acquired all the shares in S on 31 December 2009 for a cost of K50,000.
Required:

Prepare the consolidated balance sheet at 31 December 2009

Solution

CONSOLIDATED BALANCE SHEET AT 31 DECEMBER 2009

	K000
Non current assets (60 000 +50 000)	110
Current assets (40 000+40 000)	80
	190
Share capital (k1 ordinary shares)	100
Retained earnings	30
Current liabilities (20 000+40 0000	60
	190

NOTE: Share capital of the group, equals share capital of parent.
        Retained profits for the group only include k30 000 of the parent as S was purchased on the reporting date, therefore no post acquisition earnings to include in group accounts.

Example 2

Peter Ltd acquired 80% of the ordinary share capital of seller Ltd on 31 December 2009 for k 78 000. At this date the net assets of seller Ltd were k 85 000.
What goodwill arises on the acquisition if:

(a) The NCI is valued using the proportion of net assets method

(b) The NCI is valued using the fair value method and the fair value of the NCI on acquisition date is k19 000.

Solution
Using proportion of net assets method

	K
Cost of investments (= value of seller)	78 000
For: 80% of NA at acquisition	
(80% x k85 000 (w2)	(68 000)
Goodwill –parent's share	10 000

	K
(b) Using fair value method	
Cost of investment	78 000
For: 80% of NA at acquisition	
(80% of k 85 000 (w2)	68 000
Goodwill-parent's share	10 000

Fair value of NCI at acquisition	19 000	
NCI in NA at acquisition		
(20%x k 85 000)	(17 000)	
Goodwill-NCI		2000
Total goodwill		12 000

Example 3:

Draft balance sheets of John and Jack are as follows
On 31 March 2008:

	John	Jack
K'000 K'000		
Property, plant and equipment	100	140
Investment in S at cost	180	
Current assets:		
Inventory	30	35
Trade receivables	20	10
Cash	10	5
	340	190
Capital and reserves:		
Share capital: ordinary k 1 shares	200	100
Share premium	10	30
Retained earnings	40	20
	250	150
Non-current liability		
10% laon notes	65	-

current liabilities	<u>25</u>	<u>40</u>
	<u>340</u>	<u>190</u>

Notes:

- John bought 80 000 share in James in 2008 when James reserves included a share premium of k 30 000 and retained profit of k 5000
- John accounts show k 6000 owing to James' accounts show k 8000 owed by john. The difference is explained as cash in transit.
- No impairment of goodwill has occurred to date.
- John uses the proportion of net assets method to value NCI.

Prepare a consolidate balance sheet as at 31 march 2008.

Solution

JOHN CONSOLIDATED BALANCE SHEET AS AT 31 MARCH 2008

	K 000	K000
Non—current assets:		
Intangible assets-goodwill (w3)		72
Property, plant and equipment (100 +140)		<u>240</u>
		312
Current assets:		
Inventory (30+35)	65	
Trade receivables (20+8-6)	22	
Cash (10+7)	<u>17</u>	
		<u>104</u>
		<u>416</u>
Equity		
Share capital		200
Share premium		10
Retained earnings (w5)		52
Non controlling interest (w4)		<u>30</u>
		<u>292</u>
Non-current liabilities;		
10% loan notes		65
Current liabilities:		
Payables (25+40-6)		<u>59</u>
		<u>416</u>

Workings

Note: cash in transit

The K2000 cash in transit should be adjusted for in James' accounts prior to consolidation.

PROGRESS CLINIC 13

Question 1

On 1January2008 Jose Plc paid K153,000,000 for the purchase of 12,000,0000 K1 ordinary shares of Mau Ltd. Mau Ltd' reserves on that day were K140,000,000. Any goodwill arising is to be amortized over a period of eight(8) years.
The Statements of Financial Positions of these two companies five years later on 31 December 2012 are given below:

COMPANY STATEMENTS OF FINANCIAL POSITIONS AS AT 31 DECEMBER 2012

	Jose Plc K'million	Mau Ltd K'million
Tangible fixed assets	45	106
Investment in Mau Ltd at cost	153	-
Net current assets	71	179
Net assets	269	285
Ordinary share capital (K1 shares)	50	20
Share premium	25	15
Revenue reserves	194	250
	269	285

Required:
  a) Calculate the ownership interest(investment) that Jose Plc has in Mau Ltd
  b) Calculate the cost of the goodwill arising on the acquisition of Mau Ltd as on 1 January 2018
  c) Calculate the cumulative amortization and net book value of the goodwill as at 31 December 2012
  d) Calculate the Minority Interest (NCI) in Mau Ltd as at 31 December 2012
  e) Calculate the Group's Revenue Reserves as at 31 December 2012
  f) Prepare the consolidated Balance Sheet for the Jose Group as at 31 December 2012.

Question 2

The following Statements of financial position(Balance Sheets) were collected from the records of two companies Peter Ltd and Seta Ltd:

STATEMENTS OF FINANCIAL POSITION AS AT 31 DECEMBER 2010

	Peter Ltd K	Seta Ltd K
Investment in seta Ltd (at cost)	75,000	-
Stock	12,000	5,000
Other net assets	83,000	95,000
	170,000	100,000
Share capital (K1 Ordinary shares)	50,000	40,000
Profit and Loss account	120,000	60,000
	170,000	100,000

Peter ltd acquired 32,000 shares of Seta ltd on 1 January 2010 when the balance on the profit and loss account of Seta ltd was K50,000. During the year Seta sold goods to Peter ltd for k80,000 making a standard mark-up of 255. At 31 December 2010, Peter Ltd included in its stock value of K5,000 being the price paid for goods purchased from Seat Ltd. Goodwill is written off after 3 years.

Required:

a) Calculate the amount of goodwill on consolidation
b) Calculate the figure relating to Minority interest
c) Calculate the amount of Consolidated profit and loss Account
d) Prepare a Consolidated Statement of Financial position(Consolidated Balance Sheet) as at 31 December 2010

Question 3

The balance sheets of Hara Ltd and of its subsidiary Saka Ltd have been made up to 30 June. Hara Ltd has owned all the ordinary shares and 40% of the loan stock of Saka Ltd since its incorporation.
The following Statements of financial position as at 30 June 2010 were collected from each of the two companies:

HARA LIMITED
STATEMENT OF FINANCIAL POSITION (BALANCE SHEET) AS AT 30 JUNE 2010

	K'000	K'000
Non-current Assets:		
Property, plant and Equipment		120,000
Invstment in Saka Ltd, at cost:		
80,000 Ordinary shares of k1 each		80,000
K20,000 of 12% Loan stock in Saka Ltd		20,000
		220,000
Current Assets:		
Inventories	56,000	
Debtors	40,000	
Current account with Saka Ltd	12,000	
Cash	4,000	112,000
		332,000
Equity:		
Ordinary shares of K1 each, fully paid		100,000
Retained earnings		95,000
Non—current liabilities:		
10% Loan stock		75,000
Current Liabilities:		
Payables	47,000	
Taxation	15,000	62,000
		332,000

SAKA LIMITED'S STATEMENT OF FINANCIAL POSITION AS AT 30 JUNE 2010

	K'000	K'000
Non-current Assets:		
Property, plant and Equipment		100,000
Current Assets:		
Inventory	60,000	
Debtors	30,000	
Cash	6,000	96,000
		196,000
Equity:		
80,000 Ordinary shares of K1 each , fully paid		80,000
Retained Earnings		28,000
		108,000
Non-current Liabilities:		
12% Loan stock		50,000
Current liabilities:		
Creditors	16,000	
Taxation	10,000	
Current Account with Hara Ltd	12,000	38,000
		196,000

Required:

Prepare the Consolidated balance Sheet (Statement of Financial Position) of Hara Ltd and its subsidiary Saka Ltd as at 30 June 2010.

Question 4

H Ltd acquired 70% of the share capital of S Ltd 5 years ago for K60 million. At that time, the balance on S Ltd reserves was K10 million.
The summarized Balance Sheet s of H Ltd and S Ltd are given below:

	H Ltd K'000	S Ltd K'000
Assets:		
Non-current assets:		
Property, Plant and Equipment	50,000	20,000
Investment in S Ltd	60,000	-
Current Assets:		
Inventories	25,000	20,000
Trade receivables	20,000	15,000
Bank	5,000	15,000
	50,000	50,000
Total Assets	160,000	70,000

Equity and Liabilities:
Capital and Reserves:

Ordinary Share Capital	80,000	30,000
Retained Earnings	50,000	25,000
	130,000	55,000
Current liabilities:		
Trade Payables	30,000	15,000
Total equity and liabilities	160,000	70,000

Goodwill has suffered an impairment of 50%.

Required:

Prepare the Consolidated Balance Sheet of H Ltd.

Question 5

On 1 October 2005, Hero Ltd acquired 2 million of Chan Enterprises's ordinary shares paying K4.50 per share. At the date of acquisition, the retained earnings of Chan were K4,200,000. The draft balance sheets of the two businesses as at 30 September 2007 were as follows:

	Hero K'000	Chan K'000
Assets		
Non-current assets:		
Land	11,000	6,000
Plant and equipment	10,225	5,110
Investment in Chan	9,000	-
	30,225	11,110
Current assets:		
Inventory	4,925	3,295
Trade receivables	5,710	1,915
Cash	495	-
	11,130	5,210
Total assets	41,355	16,320
Equity and Liabilities		
Equity:		
Ordinary shares K1	5,000	2,500
Retained earnings	25,920	8,290
	30,920	10,790
Non-current liabilities:		
10% loans	6,000	2,000

Current liabilities:		
Trade payables	3,200	2,255
Bank overdraft	-	285
Tax	1,235	990
	4,435	3,530
Total equity and liabilities	41,355	16,320

Extracts from the income statement of Chan Enterprises before inter-group adjustments for the year ended 30 September 2007 are:

	K'000
Profit before tax	2,700
Taxation	800
Profit after tax	1,900

The following information is also relevant:

●During the year, Chan sold goods to hero for K0.9 million. Chan adds a 20% mark-up on cost to all its sales. Goods with a transfer price of K240,000 were included in Hero's inventory as at 30 September 2007.

● The fair value of Chan's land and plant and equipment at the date of acquisition was K1 million and K2 million respectively in excess of the carrying values. Chan's balance sheet has not taken account of these fair values. Group depreciation policy is land not depreciated, plant and equipment depreciated 10% per annum on fair value.

● An impairment review has been carried out on the consolidated goodwill as at 30 September 2007 and it has been found that goodwill has been impaired by K400,000 during the year.

Required:

Prepare the Consolidated balance Sheet of the Hero group as at 30 September 2007.

Question 6

High Ltd acquired all the share capital of Small Ltd 5 years ago when Small Ltd's reserves wereK15,000. Goodwill has suffered an impairment of K4,500.

BALANCE SHEETS AS AT 30 SEPTEMBER 2012

	High Ltd	Small Ltd
K'000 K'000		
Fixed Assets:		
Property, Plant and Equipment	37,000	25,000
Investment in Small Ltd	63,000	

Current Assets:		
Stock	40,000	23,000
Trade debtors	25,000	8,000
Bank	15,000	4,000
	80,000	35,000
Total Assets	180,000	60,000
Capital and Reserves:		
Ordinary Share capital	100,000	30,000
Retained earnings	63,000	20,000
	163,000	50,000
Current Liabilities:		
Trade creditors	17,000	10,000
Total Equity and Liabilities	180,000	60,000

Required:

Prepare the Consolidated Balance Sheet of High Ltd as at 30 September 2012.

CHAPTER 14

MANAGEMENT CONTROL: SHORT-TERM DECISION MAKING

BREAKEVEN ANALYSIS

This is the first chapter covering management control. This chapter is about decision-making in the short run. The next two chapters will cover investment appraisal and budgeting respectively. Specifically, this chapter covers the following topics:

- Cost behaviour
- Patterns of cost behaviour
- Break even analysis

Cost behaviour

Cost behaviour is the variability of input costs with activity undertaken. A number of cost behaviour patterns are possible, ranging from variable costs whose cost level varies directly with the level of activity, to fixed costs where changes in output have no effect upon the cost level.

Other factors do influence costs but the major factor is the level or volume of activity. The level of activity or output or volume refers to the amount of work done, or the number of events that have occurred. Depending on circumstances, the level of activity may refer to any of the following:

- Volume of production in a period
- Number of items sold
- Value of items sold
- Number of invoices issued
- Number of invoices received
- Number of units of electricity consumed
- Labour turnover and so on.

The basic principle of cost behaviour is that as the level of activity rises, costs will usually rise. For example, it will cost more to produce 2000 units of output than it will cost to produce 5000 units. This principle is common sense. The problem for the accountant, however, is to determine, for each item of cost, the way in which costs rise and by how much as the level of activity increases. For our purposes here, the level of activity for measuring cost will generally be taken to be the volume of production.

Cost behaviour patterns

The following are the most common cost behaviour patterns and belated examples.

1. **Fixed Costs** – A fixed cost is a cost which tends to be unaffected by increase or decrease in the volume of output. Fixed costs are a period charge in that they relate to a span of time: As time span increases, so too will the fixed costs (which are sometimes referred to as period costs for this reason).

Examples of fixed costs are:

*   The salary of the managing director per month or per annum
*   The rent of a single factory building per month or per annum
*   Straight-line depreciation of a single machine per month or per annum
*   Road tax per quarter or per year
*   Insurance premiums per month or per year

Note that fixed costs are only constant at all levels of activity within the relevant range of activity. The relevant range is the range of activity at which a firm expects to be operating in the future. So it is dangerous to predict costs at activity levels which are outside the relevant range.

A sketch graph of a fixed cost is like this.

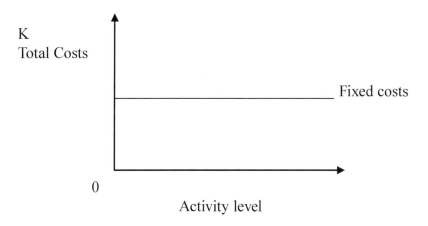

2. **Variable Costs** – A variable cost is a cost which tends to vary directly with the volume of output. The variable cost per unit is the same amount for each unit produced. A constant variable cost per unit implies that the price per unit of material usage/labour productivity is also constant.

Examples of variable costs are:

*   Cost of raw materials where there is no discount for bulk purchasing sine bulk purchasing discounts reduce the cost of purchases.

*   Direct labour costs are classed as variable costs for very important reasons even though basis wages are usually fixed.

- Sales commission is variable in relation to the volume or value of sales rather than the level of production

- Bonds payments for productivity to employees might be variable one a certain level of output is achieved.

The sketch of a variable cost is as follows:

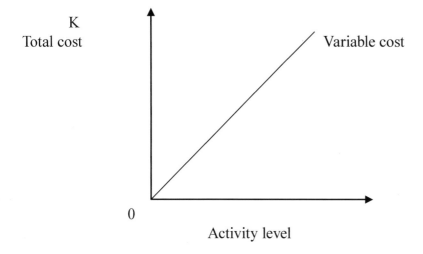

3. Semi variable costs/semi fixed costs/mixed costs

    A semi variable semi fixed/semi /mixed cost is a cost containing both fixed and variable components and which is thus partly affected by a change in the activity level.

Examples of these costs are:

- **Electricity and gas bills** – There is a standing charge plus charge per unit of consumption.

- **Salesman's salary** – The salesman may earn a monthly basic amount of say, K500 000 and then commission of 10%of the value of sales made.

- **Cost of running a car** – The cost is made up of a fixed cost (which includes road tax and insurance) and variable costs (of petrol, oil, repairs and so on) which depend on the number of miles traveled.

- **Step Costs** – Many items of cost are a fixed cost in nature within certain levels of activity.

Examples of step costs are:

- Depreciation of a machine may be fixed if production remains below 1000 units per month, but if production exceeds 1000 units, a second machine may be required, and the cost of depreciation (on two machines) would go up a step.

- Rent is a step cost in situations where accommodation requirements increase as output levels get higher.

- Basic pay of employees is nowadays usually fixed, but as output increases, more employees (workers, supervisors) are required.

A sketch graph of a step cost would look like this

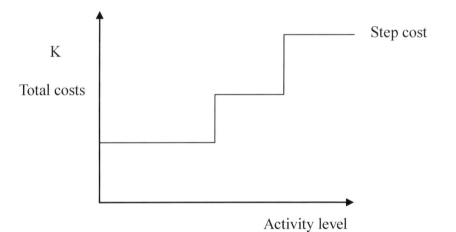

- **Curvilinear Costs** – These are costs where the relationship between cost and activity level is non-linear but a curve. It indicates lacks of direct proportionality between cost and the activity level.

Importance of cost behaviour

An understanding of cost behaviour is vital in all areas of cost and management accounting but particularly in the following:

1. **Decision making** – An understanding of cost behaviour is vital to facilitate an evaluation of different courses of action open to a firm. Examples of decision that require information on how costs and revenues vary at different activity levels include the following:

- What should the planned activity level be for the next period?
- Should the selling price be reduced in order to sell more units? Straight-line commission or a combination of the two?
- Should additional plant be purchased so that an expansion of output is possible?
- Should a particular component be manufactured internally or bought in?
- Should a contract be undertaken?

For each of the above decisions, management requires estimates of costs at different levels of activity for alternative courses of action. Without knowledge of the cost of making a component and the costs saved by buying a component, management is unable to make in-house or buy in. Thus, management needs to understand, for example, that fixed costs do not, in general, change as a result of a decision.

2. **Cost Control** – If the accountant does not know the level of costs which should have been incurred as a result of a firm's activities, how can he hope to control costs, there being no benchmark to which the actual costs incurred can be compared? Thus cost behavior knowledge is important for cost control purposes?

3. **Budgeting** – It is unlikely than an accountant could draw up a realistic budget without being aware of cost behaviour. Having established the number of units that can be sold, he will be unable to determine the associated costs, if he is unaware that the material costs per unit when 10 000 units are produced are less than the material costs per unit when only 5000 units are due to bulk purchase discounts.

BREAKEVEN ANALYSIS

Breakeven analysis is an application of variable costing techniques and is sometimes called cost-volume-profit (CVP) analysis. By using variable costing techniques, it is possible to ascertain contribution per unit. The total contribution from all sales during a period is compared with the fixed costs for that period: Any excess or deficiency of contribution over fixed costs represents the profit or loss respectively for the period.

Breakeven arithmetic

Breakeven arithmetic centers around the following concepts and formulae:

1. **Breakeven Point** – This is the level of activity at which there is neither profit nor loss. It is a point where total revenue is equal to total costs. Breakeven point can be expressed in units as well as in revenues. It can be calculated using any of the following:

(a) Breakeven point in units = $\dfrac{\text{Total Fixed Costs}}{\text{Contribution per Unit}}$

$$\text{Or} = \frac{\text{Fixed Costs}}{\text{Selling Price per Unit} - \text{Variable Cost per Unit}}$$

$$\text{Or} = \frac{\text{Contribution Required To Breakeven}}{\text{Contribution per Unit}}$$

Since contribution required to breakeven = Fixed Costs

(b) Breakeven point in revenue = $\dfrac{\text{Total Fixed Costs X Selling Price}}{\text{Contribution per Unit}}$

$$\text{Or} = \dfrac{\text{Total fixed costs}}{\text{Contribution/sales ratio}}$$

2. **Contribution Per Unit** – This is the difference between selling price per unit and variable cost per unit. It contribution towards profit for every unit sold.

    Thus, contribution per unit = Selling Price per Unit – Variable Cost per Unit

    Total contribution = Contribution per unit X Units sold.

3. **Contribution/Sales Ratio** – This is a measure of how much contribution is earned from each K1 of sales. For example, the C/S ratio of 37% means that for every K1 of sales, a contribution of 37n is earned.

    Contribution /sales ratio = $\dfrac{\text{contribution per unit X 100}}{\text{Selling price per unit}}$

    Note that C/S ratio is also called contribution margin ratio or profit volume ratio

4. **Margin of Safety** – In budgeting, the margin of safety (MS) is a measure by which the budgeted volume of sales compared with the volume of sales required to breakeven. It is the difference in units between the budgeted sales volume and the breakeven sales volume and it is sometimes expressed a percentage of the budgeted sales volume.

    Thus, MS = budgeted Sales Volume – Breakeven Sales Volume

    Alternatively: MS = $\dfrac{\text{Budgeted Sales Volume} - \text{Breakeven Sales volume X 100}}{\text{Budgeted Sales Volume}}$

5. **Target Profit** = this is the profit that a firm wishes to achieve during a period. To achieve this profit, Sales must cover all costs and leave the required profit.

    Sales required = $\dfrac{\text{Fixed Costs} + \text{Target Profit}}{\text{Contribution Per Unit}}$

    $$\text{Or} = \dfrac{\text{Required Contribution}}{\text{Contribution per Unit}}$$

    Since Required Contribution = Fixed costs + Target Profit.

6. Total Revenue = Selling Price X Units Sold

7. Total Cost = Fixed Costs + Total Variable Costs

   Where Total Variable Costs = Variable Cost Per Unit X Units produced

8. Total Profit = Total Revenue – Total Costs

Using marginal costing principles to calculate profit

Under the marginal costing principles, fixed costs are taken to be period costs which are subtracted from contribution to determine profit. Marginal costing statement for calculating profit is a follows:

	.K
Sales	X
Less variable costs	(X)
Contribution	X
Less fixed costs	(X)
Profit	X

From above, estimated Profit = Output X Contribution – Fixed Costs.

Example 1

The following information is available for a company that produces a sells a single product.

- Expected sales 10 000 units
- Selling price K8
- Variable cost K5
- Fixed costs K21 000

Required :

Calculate:

(a) Breakeven point in both units and revenue

(b) Contribution per unit

(c) Contribution margin ratio and use this result to confirm your breakeven point in revenue found in (a) above

(d) Margin of safety and interpret the result

(e) Total profit at full capacity using total revenue and total costs, and marginal costing principles.

Solution

(a) Breakeven point in units = $\dfrac{\text{Fixed cost}}{\text{Selling price} - \text{variable cost}}$

$$= \frac{\text{K21 000}}{\text{K}(8-5)}$$

$$= \underline{7000} \text{ units}$$

Breakeven point in revenue = Breakeven Point in Units X Selling Price

$$= 7000 \text{ units X K8}$$

$$= \underline{\text{K56 000}}$$

(b) Contribution Per Unit = Selling Price – Variable Cost Per Unit

$$= \text{K8} - \text{K5} = \text{K3}$$

(c) Contribution Margin Ratio = $\dfrac{\text{Contribution Per Unit X 100}}{\text{Selling Price}}$

$$= \frac{\text{K3 X 100}}{\text{K8}}$$

$$= \underline{37.5\%}$$

BEP in revenue = $\dfrac{\text{Fixed Costs}}{\text{Cost/sales ratio}}$

$$= \frac{\text{K21 000}}{37.5\%}$$

$$= \text{K56 000 confirming the answer}$$

(d) Margin of Safety = Budget Sales Volume – Breakeven Sales Volume

$$= 10\ 000 \text{ units} - 7000 \text{ units} = 300 \text{ units}$$

Alternatively, MS = Budgeted Sales Volume – <u>Breakeven Sales Volume X 100</u>
Budgeted Sales Volume

$$= \frac{10\ 000 - 7000}{10\ 000} \text{ X } 100$$

$$= 30\%$$

Interpretation: Current sales volume must fall by 3000 units or 30% before all the Profits are wiped out. It is really a very stable margin stable

(e) Total Profits = Total Revenue – Total Cost

Total Revenue = Selling Price X Units Sold

= K8 X 10 000 units

= K80 000

Total Costs = Fixed Costs X Total Variable Costs

= K21 000 + K5 (10 000)

= <u>K71 000</u>

Total Profit = K80 000 – K71 000

= K9000

Using marginal costing principles:

		K
• Sales (K8 X 10 000)		80 000
• Less variable costs (K5 X 10 000)		(50 000)
• Contribution		30 000
• Less Fixed costs		(21 000)
• Profit		K9 000 as calculated above

Example 2

ABC Limited makes a single product a vest which it sells for K70 per unit. The company currently manufactures 90 000 units of the product which represents 40% of its manufacturing capacity. At this level of output the total costs are K6 800 000 of which K2 750 000 are fixed.

Required :

      (a) Calculate the breakeven point in units

      (b) Express the breakeven point as a percentage of the total capacity.

      (c) Calculate the profit that would be earned if the company would operate at maximum capacity.

      (d) A new customer offers to buy 50 000 units of the product at a selling price of K50 per unit. Should the company accept this order? Give reasons for your answer.

      (e) The Financial Director sees this order in (d) as the chance for the company to breakeven for the year. Calculate the selling price for the 50 000 units that would achieve this.

Solution

    (a) To find the breakeven point we need to find the variable cost per unit first.

Total cost	K6 800 000
Fixed cost	2 750 000
Total variable cost	K4 050 000

Variable cost per unit = $\dfrac{4\ 050\ 000}{90\ 000\ units}$ = K45

$$BEP = \dfrac{Fixed\ Costs}{Contribution\ per\ Unit}$$

$$= \dfrac{K2\ 750\ 000}{K\ (70-45)}$$

$$= \underline{110\ 000}\ units\ or\ \underline{K7\ 700\ 000}$$

  (b) Total Capacity $\dfrac{100}{40}$ X 90 000 = 225 000 units

Breakeven point as a percentage of full capacity:

$\dfrac{110\ 000}{225\ 000}$ X 100 = 48.89%

(c) Using estimated profit = Out put X Contribution – Fixed Costs

- Contribution (225 000 XK25)   K5 625 000
- Fixed Costs   (2 750 000)
- Profit   k 2 875 000

Confirm above result using total revenue and total costs.

(d) Here we need to find the contribution per unit first contribution per unit

$$= \text{Selling Price} - \text{Variable Cost}$$

$$= K50 - K45 = K5$$

Total contribution from new order: 50 000 X K5 = 250 000

Thus, the company should accept the order as there is spare capacity, assuming there is no better offer.

(e) Here we need to determine the current loss first:

- Contribution (90 000 X K25)   K2 250 000
- Less Fixed costs   (2 750 000)
- Loss   (500 000)

The loss of K500 000 needs to be covered by the new order.

Required contribution per unit = $\dfrac{K500\ 000}{50\ 000\ \text{units}}$ = K10 per unit

New Selling Price = Contribution per Unit X Variable Cost

$$= K10 + K45$$

$$= K5$$

Example 3

A B C Limited makes pipes of one type only. The budget for the year 2007 is as follows:

	Units	K
Sales	27 500	550 000
Costs		
	Variable (K)	Fixed (K)

• Direct Materials	110 000	-
• Overheard: Production	82 500	140 000
• Administration	-	102 000
	247 500	242 000

Required:

Calculate:

a) Contribution per unit
b) Contribution margin ratio
c) Breakeven point in both units and sales
d) The margin of safety ratio

A B C Limited is considering the acquiring of a new machine. This will add K48 000 to fixed production overheard but will half variable labour costs. All other factors remain the same.

Required:

e) Calculate

(i) New breakeven point in both units and sales
(ii) Level of sales required to make the acquisition of the machine worthwhile.

Solution

	K
a) Sales	550 000
Less: Variable costs	247 500
Contribution	302 500

Thus contribution per unit = $\dfrac{\text{Total contribution}}{\text{Number of units}}$

$$= \frac{K302\ 500}{27\ 500} = \underline{K11\ per\ unit}$$

b) Contribution Margin Ratio = $\dfrac{\text{Total contribution}}{\text{Total sales}} \times 100$

$$= \frac{K302\ 500 \times 100}{K550\ 000}$$

$$= \underline{55\%}$$

Note that we could have used contribution per unit and selling price per unit to arrive at the same result.

c) Breakeven point in units = $\dfrac{\text{Fixed Costs}}{\text{Contribution per unit}}$

$$= \frac{\text{K242 000}}{\text{K11}}$$

$$= \underline{22\ 000}\ \text{units}$$

Breakeven point in sales = Breakeven point in units X selling price

$$= 22\ 000\ \text{units X K20}$$

$$= \text{K440 000}$$

d) Margin of safety ratio = $\dfrac{\text{Budget Sales} - \text{Breakeven Sales}}{\text{Budget Sales}}$ X 100

$$= \frac{\text{K550 000} - \text{K440 000}}{\text{K550 000}}\ \text{X}\ 100$$

$$= \underline{20\%}$$

e) i) New fixed costs = K (242 000 + 48 000) = K290 000

• New variable cost per unit = $\dfrac{\text{K110 000} + \text{K41 250} + \text{K55 000}}{27\ 500}$

$$= \text{K7.50}$$

• Contribution per unit = K20 – K7.50 = K12.50

• Breakeven point in units = $\dfrac{\text{K290 000}}{\text{K12.50}} = \underline{23\ 200}\ \text{units}$

• Breakeven point in sales = 23 200 X K20 = K464 000

ii) The extra fixed costs of K48 000 have to be recovered by the extra contribution of K12.50 – K11 = K1.50 per unit. This will be achieved at a level of sales of

: $\dfrac{\text{Required Contribution}}{\text{Contribution per Unit}} = \dfrac{\text{K48 000}}{\text{K1.50}}$

$$= 3200\ \text{units}$$

Example 4

XYZ limited makes and sells a single product for which variable costs are as follows:

		K
•	Direct materials	10
•	Direct labour	8
•	Variable production Overheard	6
		K24

The sales price is K30 per unit and fixed costs are K68 000. The company wishes to make a profit of K16 000 per annum.

Required:

Determine the sales required to achieve this profit.

Solution

Required Contribution = Fixed Costs + Target Profit

$$= K68\ 000 + K16\ 000$$

$$= \underline{K84\ 000}$$

Required sales can be calculated in two ways:

(a) $\dfrac{\text{Required Contribution}}{\text{Contribution per unit}} = \dfrac{\underline{K84\ 000}}{K\ (30-24)} = \underline{14000}$ units

   Or   K420 000

(b) $\dfrac{\underline{\text{Required Contribution}}}{\text{P/V ratio}} = \dfrac{\underline{K84\ 000}}{20\%} = \underline{K420\ 000}$ or $\underline{14000}$ units

   Note P/V ratio = $\dfrac{\text{Contribution per unit}}{\text{Selling price}} \times 100$

Example 5

XYZ Plc has the following data for its product y

Product Y	K/unit
• Selling price	10 000
• Variable product cost	6 000
• Variable selling cost	1 000
• Contribution per unit	3 000
• Fixed production cost based on annual sales of 20 000 units of y	1 000
• Fixed selling cost based on annual sales of 20 000 units of y	200
• Profit per unit	1 800

Required:

(a) Calculate the level of production needed for XYZ Plc to breakeven.

(b) XYZ Plc is planning of doubling its production. To do this, it will have to occupy additional premises at an annual rent of K42 million. Calculate the new breakeven point and the margin of safety.

Solution

	K'000
(a) Fixed costs: production (20 000 X K1000)	20 000
: Selling (20 000 X K200)	4 000
Total fixed costs	24 000

Contribution per product = K3000 (given).

$$\text{Breakeven point} = \frac{\text{Fixed costs}}{\text{Contribution per product}} = \frac{K24\ 000\ 000}{3000} = \underline{8000}\ \text{units}$$

	K'000
(b) Fixed costs as per (a) above	24 000
Additional premises	42 000
Total fixed costs	66 000

$$\text{Breakeven point} = \frac{\text{Fixed cost}}{\text{Contribution per unit}} = \frac{K66\ 000\ 000}{K3000} = \underline{22\ 000}\ \text{units}$$

Margin of safety = K (20 000 + 20 000) – 22 000 = $\underline{18\ 000}$ units

Note we have used 20 000 + 20 00 because the company wished to double its production from 20 000 units to 40 000 units.

Breakeven charts

A breakeven chart is a chart which indicates approximate profit or loss at different levels of sales volume within a limit range. Put simply a breakeven chart is a diagrammatic representation of the breakeven analysis.
To draw a breakeven chart the following lines are drawn

a. The vertical axis represents money (costs and revenue) and the horizontal axis represents the level of activity (volume of production or volume of sales).

b. Note that the vertical axis should be extended to the level of total revenue which the horizontal axis to the level of full capacity.

c. The fixed costs are represented by a straight-line parallel to the horizontal axis.

d. The variable costs are added on top of fixed costs, to give total costs. It is assumed that fixed costs are the same in total and variable costs are the same per unit at all levels of output hence both are straight-lines.

e. the sales lines is also drawn by plotting two points and joining them

f. The breakeven point is where the sales line intersects the total cost line. If we extend A line from this point vertically to the x-axis we read off breakeven point in units. Similarly, extending a straight-line from this point horizontally to the y-axis, we read off breakeven point in revenue.

g. The margin of safety as well as the profit and loss areas can be shown on the chart clearly as well.

Example

The budgeted annual output of a factory is 120,000 units. The fixed overheard amount to K40 000 and the variable costs are even 50n per unit. The selling price is K1 unit.

Required:

Construct a breakeven chart showing the current breakeven point and profit earned up to the present maximum capacity.

Solution

We begin by calculating the profit at the budgeted annual output using marginal costing principles.

	K
Sales (120 000 X K1)	120 000
Less: Variable costs (120 000 X K0.50)	60 000
Contribution	60 000
Less: Fixed costs	40 000
Profit	20 000

Note that to draw the breakeven chart; all we need are two points for each line. These points at zero output, total costs are equal to fixed costs of K40 000 giving us (0.40 000) as our first point for total cost line. When output is 120 000 units total costs will be K60 000, K40 000, K100 000 giving us (120 000, 100 000) as the second point. Similarly, when nothing is sold, sales revenue is zero giving us (0.0) as our first point. Further when 120 000 units are sold sales revenue is K120 000 giving us (120 000, 120 000) as our second point. The breakeven chart can now be drawn as follows.

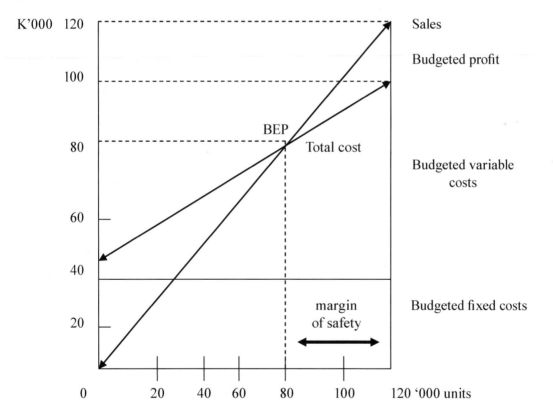

The multi-product breakeven chart

Since most companies sell more than one product, a multi-product chart of some type is required. A serious limitation of breakeven charts is that safety for a single product only, or

233

for a single "sales mix" of products. Thus, a multi-product breakeven chart cannot be drawn unless we know the proportions of the product in the sales mix.

Example

XYZ Limited sells three products A, B and C and the following information is available:

Product budget sales selling price variable:

Product	Budget sales	Selling price	Variable cost
A	2000 units	K8	K3
B	4000 units	K6	K4
C	3000 units	K6	K5

Fixed costs per annum are K10 000.

Required:

Draw a multi-product breakeven chart using the above information.

Solution

To draw a multi-product break even chart we make the assumption that output and sales of A, B and C are in the proportions 2000: 4000: 3000 at all levels of activity. In other words, we assume that the sales mix is fixed' in these proportions

Budgeted costs Costs Budgeted revenue Revenue

	K	K	
• Variable cost of A (2000 X 3)	6000	A (2000 X 8)	16 000
• Variable costs of B (4000 X 4)	16000	B (4000 X 6)	24000
• Variable costs of (3000 X 5)	15000	C (3000 X 6)	1 8000
• Total variable casts	37 000		____
• Total costs	10 000		58 000
• Total budgeted costs	47 000		

The breakeven chart can now be drawn as follows:

K'000

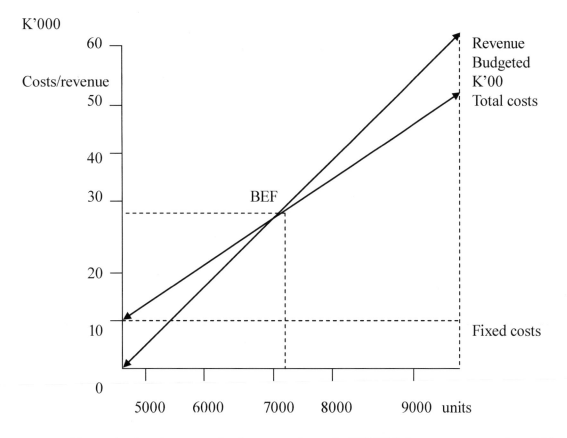

Thus, the breakeven point is approximately K27500 in revenue or sales. This may either be read from the breakeven chart or computed mathematically.

Sensitivity analysis and breakeven analysis

Sensitivity analysis is a term used to describe any technique whereby decision options are tested for their vulnerability to changes in any 'variable' such as expected sales volume, selling price per unit, material costs, labour costs or fixed costs.

Thus, sensitivity analysis can be applied to many areas of management accounting including breakeven analysis. Breakeven charts can be used in a form of sensitivity analysis to show variations in the possible selling price, variable costs or fixed costs and the resulting effects on the breakeven point and the margin of safety.

Example

A company sells a single product which has a variable cost of K2000 per unit and a fixed costs of K15 000 000. It has been estimated that if the selling price is set at K4400 per unit, the expected sales volume would be 7500 units: whereas if the selling price is lower at K4000 per unit, the expected sales volume would be 10 000 units.

Required:

Draw a breakeven chart to show the budgeted profit, the breakeven and the margin of safety at each of the possible selling prices

Solution

	Selling price K440 Per unit		Selling price K4000 per unit	
• Budgeted revenue	(7500 X K4400)	33 000 000	(10 000 X 4000)	40 000 000
• Variable costs	(7500 X K2000)	15 000 000	(10 000 X K2000)	20 000 000
• Contribution		18 000 000		20 000 000
• Fixed costs		15 000 000		15 000 000
• Profit		3 000 000		5 000 000

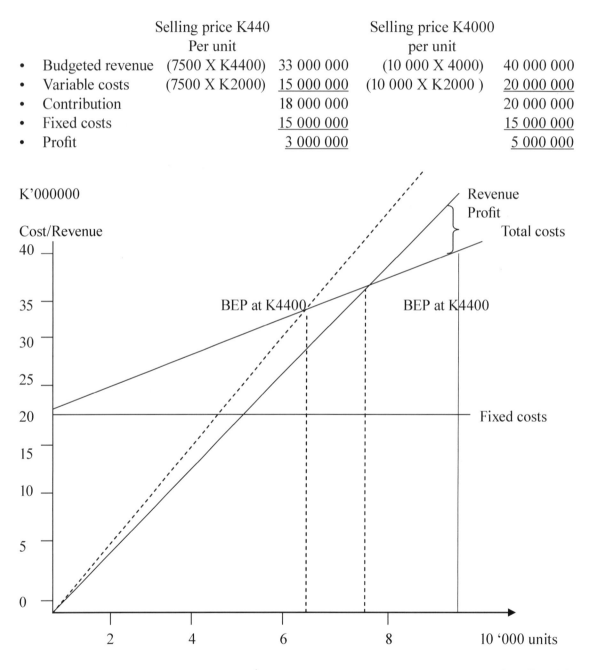

Thus, breakeven point at selling price of K4400 per unit is 6250 units or K27 500 000 while at selling price K4000 the breakeven point is 7500 units or K30 000 000. Therefore, the

appropriate price which will maximize profits for the company is at K4000 per unit so as to sell 10 000 units.

Limiting factor analysis

- A limiting factor also called a key factor is anything which limits the activity of an entity. An entity seeks to optimize the benefit it obtains from the limiting factor.

- Examples of limiting factors are as follows:

  a) Sales – There may be a limit to sales demand

  b) Labour – the limit may be either in terms of total quantity or of particular skills. Either way, there will be insufficient labour to produce enough to satisfy demand.

  c) Materials—there may be insufficient available to produce enough units to satisfy sales demand.

  d) Manufacturing capacity. There may not be enough sufficient machine capacity for the production required to meet sales demand.

  e) Financial resources. There may not be enough cash to pay for the necessary production.

It is worth noting that a limiting factor, if there is one, ought to be identified when the annual budget is being prepared since the budget will have to be based on what is achievable given the available resources. A company may be faced with just one limiting factor but there may also be several scarce resources, with two or more of them putting an effective limit on the level of activity that can be achieved.

It is also important to note that the limiting factor may change from time to time for the same entity or product. The limiting factor may be one criteria process in a chain of processes.

For example, if sales demand is the factor which restricts greater production output, profit will be maximized by making exactly the amount required for sales and no more provided that each product sold earns a positive contribution.

Contribution will be maximized by earnings the biggest possible contribution per unit of the limiting factor. The limiting factor decision therefore involves the determination of the contribution earned by each different product per unit of scarce resource.
Finally in limiting factor decisions, we generally assume that fixed costs are the same whatever production mix is selected, so that the only relevant costs are variable costs.

Assumptions in limiting factor analysis

- Fixed costs will be the same regardless of the decision that is taken.
- The unit variable cost is constant
- The estimates of sales demand for each product, and the resources required to make each product are known with certainty.
- Units of output are divisible.

Example

Maximum profit Limited makes two products, A and B, for which there is unlimited sales demand at the budgeted selling price of each. One unit of product A takes 3 hours to make, and has a variable cost of K18000 and a selling price of K30 000. One unit of product B takes 2 hours to make and has a variable cost of K10 000 and a selling price of K20 000. Both products use the same type of labour which is in restricted supply.

Required:

Determine which product should be produced (made) in order to maximize profits.

Solution

There is no limitation on sales demand, but labour is in restricted supply, and so to determine the profit –maximizing production mix, we must rank the products in order of contribution-earning capability per labour hour.

	Product A	Product B
	K	K
• Selling price	30 000	20 000
• Variable costs	18 000	10 000
• Contribution	12 000	10 000
• Hours per unit	3 hours	2 hours
• Contribution per labour hour	K4 000	K5000

The ranking is 1st product B
                2nd product A

Although product A has the higher unit contribution, product b is more profitable because it makes a greater contribution in each scarce hour of labour time worked. Three units of product B (providing a contribution of 3 X K10 000 = K30 000) can be made in the same time as two units of product A (providing a contribution of 2 X K12 000 = K24 000 only).

Sunk costs

The costs which should be used for decision making are referred to as **relevant costs**. Relevant costs are defined as costs appropriate to a specific management. Relevant costs future, incremental, cash flows.

- Incremental costs or differential costs are relevant costs which are simply additional costs incurred as a consequence of a decision.

- Avoidable costs are the specific costs of an activity or sector of a business which would be avoided if that activity or sector did not exist. They are mainly associated with shutdown or disinvestment decisions.

- Relevant costs may also be expressed as **opportunity costs** which are defined as the benefit foregone by choosing one opportunity instead of the next best alternative. Put in other words, opportunity cost is the value of the benefit sacrificed when one course of action is chosen, in preference to an alternative. It applies when there are mutually exclusive options.

Apart from relevant costs, there are also irrelevant costs for decision making which are either not future cash flows or they are costs which will be incurred anyway, regardless of the decision that is taken.

The following are some of the irrelevant costs:

- Sunk costs – these are costs that have been irreversibly incurred or committed prior to a decision point and which cannot therefore be considered relevant to subsequent decisions. They are also called **irrecoverable costs**.

  Sunk costs are used to describe the cost of an asset which has already been acquired and which can continue to serve its present purpose, but which has no significant realizable value and no income value from any other alternative purpose.

  Examples of sunk costs include the following:

  a) Dedicated fixed assets e.g. purchase of a machine two years ago for K200 000 000.

  b) Development costs already incurred e.g. bank expenditure of K200 000 000 in developing a new service for customers for which current marketing data reveals that there will be no customer acceptance.

Committed costs

A committed cost is a future cash outflow that will be incurred anyway, whatever decision is taken now about alternative opportunities.

Notional costs

A notational cost or imputed cost is a hypothetical accounting cost to reflect the use of a benefit for which no actual cash expense is incurred. Examples include notional rent e.g. that charged to a subsidiary: and notional interest charges on capital employed sometimes made against a profit centre or cost centre.

Assumptions of breakeven analysis

The following are the key assumptions of breakeven analysis

- Costs are either fixed or variable: no account is taken of semi-fixed costs.
- Fixed costs remain constant at all levels of output
- There are no opening or closing stocks
- A constant product mix is assumed
- It is assumed that production and sales are the same
- Variable costs behave in a linear fashion

Limitations of the breakeven analysis

- Breakeven analysis should be used carefully. The major limitations of breakeven analysis are as follows:

- A breakeven chart only applies to a single product or a single mix (fixed proportions) of a group of products. This restricts its usefulness.

- It is assumed that fixed costs are the same in total and variable costs are the same per unit at all levels of output. This assumption is a great simplification.

- It is assumed that selling price will be constant at all levels of activity. This may not be true, especially at higher volumes of output, where the price may have to be reduced to win the extra sales.

- Production and sales are assumed to be the same, therefore the consequences of any increase in stock levels (when production volumes exceed sales) or 'de-stocking' (when sales volume exceeds production levels are ignored).

- Uncertainty in the estimates of fixed costs and unit variable costs is often ignored in breakeven analysis, and some costs (for example mixed costs and step costs) are not always easily categorized or divided into fixed and variable.

Inspite of limitations, however, breakeven analysis is a useful technique for managers in planning selling prices, the desired sales mix, and profitability. (Breakeven charts are 'decorative' in the sense that they merely provide a graphical representation of the breakeven arithmetic).

Breakeven arithmetic should be used with a full awareness of its limitations, but can usually be applied to provide simple and quick estimates of breakeven volumes or profitability given variations in selling price, sales mix, variable and fixed costs and sales volumes, within a 'relevant range' of output/sales volumes.

PROGRESS CLINIC 14

The following information was collected from the books of Raso Ltd during the month of February 2006.

Plant capacity	1 600 units for the month
Fixed cost	K80 000 per month
Variable cost	K60 per unit
Sales price	K150

Required:

From the above details, calculate:

a) Breakeven point (in Kwacha)

b) Breakeven point (in units)

c) Contribution/ sales ratio

d) Margin of safety in units, revenue and percentage

e) Total profit at full capacity

f) Units that must be produced and sold if the company intends to make a profit of K1000 000.Comment on your answer.

CHAPTER 15

MANAGEMENT CONTROL: LONG TERM DICISION MAKING

CAPITAL INVESTMENT APPRAISAL

The key areas of capital investment appraisal covered by this syllabus are follows:

- Steps in project appraisal
- Accounting rate of return
- Payback period
- Time value of money
- Discounted cash flow
- Relevant costs

IMPORTANCE OF CAPITAL INVESTMENT APPRAISAL

A famous English saying is that you must speculate to accumulate. The saying means that one needs to invest money into something before one can expect a return. This is true not only when starting a business, but also during the whole life of that business. If the business is to flourish and reach its full potential, money must continue to be ploughed back it year after year. It is very tempting to extract the profits in the form of drawings or dividends, but failing to re-invest will cost the promoters or shareholders dearly in the future.

Since capital investment is therefore so important to the success of a business, it is important in the context of managing finances and organizations. Poor management leads to poor investment decisions which eventually lead to organizational failure.

From the above, then capital investment appraisal is important because:

- It involves large sums of money
- It ties the organization to that line of operation for a long term period e.g. if a bank decides to invest in ATM, once procured and installed it is difficult to reverse that decision.
- It is an indicator of good management. Successful firms have been said to be very good at capital investment decisions.

Steps in project appraisal

Different reference books may set out the steps in project appraisal differently, but the broad content is the same. You need to know what the steps are and be able to say a little bit about each. Broadly speaking they are as follows:

- **Initial Investigation of the Proposal**

Firstly, a decision must be made as to whether the project is technically feasible and commercially viable. This involves assessing the risks and deciding, whether the project is in line with the company's long term strategic objectives.

• Detailed Evaluation

A detailed investigation will take place in order to examine the projected cash flows of the projects. Sensitivity analysis is performed and sources of finance will be considered.

• Authorisation

For significant projects, authorization must be sought from the company's senior management and board of directors. This will only take place only once such person are satisfied that a detailed evaluation has been carried out, that a detailed evaluation has been carried out, that the project will contribute to profitability and that the project is consistent with the company strategy.

• Implementation

At this stage, responsibility for the project is assigned to a project manager or other responsible person. The resources will be made available for implementation and specific targets will be set.

• Project Monitoring

Now the project has started, progress must be monitored and senior management must e kept informed of progress. Costs and benefits may have to be re-assessed if unforeseen events occur.

• Post – Completion Audit

At the end of the project, an audit will be carried out so that lessons can be learned to help future projects planning.

Relevant and non-relevant costs

You need to understand the concept of relevant cash flows for decision-making. You may be required to either discuss relevant costing or apply the principles in a net present value (NPV) calculation.

• Relevant Costs Are Future Costs

A relevant cost is a future cost arising as a direct consequence of a decision. A cost which has been incurred in the past is therefore totally irrelevant to any decision that is being made now. Such past costs are called 'sunk costs'

● Relevant Costs Are Cash Flows

Only those future costs that are in form of cash should be included. This is because relevant costing works on the assumption that profits earn cash. Therefore, costs which do not reflect cash spending should be ignored for the purpose of decision-making. This means that depreciation charges should be ignored.

● Relevant Costs Are Incremental Costs

A relevant cost is the increase in costs that results from making a particular decision. Any costs or benefits arising as a result of a past decision should be ignored.

● Opportunity Costs

An opportunity cost is the value of a benefit foregone as a result of choosing a particular course of action. Such a cost will always be a relevant cost.

● Other-Non-Relevant Costs

Certain other costs committed costs! A committed cost is future cash out flow that will be incurred anyway, regardless of what decision will be taken. Interest costs are also ignored. This is not because they do not meet the above criteria, but because there are taken into account in the discounting process. If these costs were included as relevant costs they would be double counted.

Techniques of Investment Appraisal

The company must have as part of capital investment decision a working policy defining which projects will be acceptable and which ones will be rejected. There are many methods or techniques of investment appraisal available to a finance manager.

In this section, we discuss the following:

● Accounting rate of return (ARR) method
● Pay back period method
● Net present value (NPV) method
● Internal rate of return (IRR) method.
● Profitability index method i.e. benefit/cost ratio with 1 as a neutral

 Each of the above methods has got its own weaknesses and strengths as will be shown shortly.

1) Accounting Rate of Return(ARR)

You need to be able to calculate the accounting rate of return (ARR) of a project. Since ARR is based on profits rather than cash flows, the calculations may involve reconciling cash flow to profit.

There are several ways of writing the ARR formula. Whichever you choose, be sure to use the same one throughout the calculation. It may be that the question specifically tells you to use a certain ARR formula. If this is the case, be sure to use the formula given or you will fail to gain maximum marks for that question.

The most common formula is:

$$ARR = \frac{\text{estimated average}}{\text{Estimated average investment}} \times 100\%$$

To calculate the value of the average investment you must first add the initial investment cost to the residue or scrap value. This gives the total amount of money tied up and it should be divided by two to find the average as follows:

$$\text{Average investment} = \frac{\text{initial investment} + \text{scrap value}}{2}$$

What about the numerator i.e. estimated average annual profits? These are calculated by adding all the annual profits figures and subtracting annual loss figures, if any, to find total profits for the period which are then divided by the number of years as follows:

$$\text{Average accounting profits} = \frac{\text{Total profits} \times 100\%}{\text{number of years}}$$

Decision criteria

- If the ARR is greater than the required rate of return (cost of capital) the project is accepted.
- If two or more projects are being appraised the one with the highest ARR above the cost of capital will be accepted otherwise all will be rejected.
- Sometimes the acceptable ARR is fixed by senior management of a company arbitrarily.

Advantages of Accounting Rate of Return

The advantages of ARR as a method of project appraisal are:
- It is easy to understand
- It is widely used
- It is based on accounting profit whose data is readily available to calculate it.

Disadvantages of Accounting Rate of return

- It does not take into account the time value of money
- It is based on accounting profits and these are subjective.

2) Payback period (PBP)

You may be required to calculate a project's simple or discounted payback period or to discuss the usefulness of this method of project appraisal.

The simple payback period is calculated by identifying the point at which calculative net cash inflows equal the cost of the initial investment. To calculate the discounted payback period, all cash flows must first be discounted to take into account the time value of money. Then, as with simple payback, the payback period is calculated by identifying the point at which accumulative (discounted) net cash inflows equal the cost of the initial investment (also discounted if not occurring immediately).

Finally, note that payback period is calculated from cash flows rather than from profits.

Decisions criteria

- If two or more projects are being assessed, the one with shorter payback period is preferred.
- Management may also fix arbitrarily the payback period for all its projects.

Advantages of payback period

The advantages of the payback period method of project appraisal are set out below.

- It is easy to understand.
- It is widely used
- It helps to minimize risk by giving greater weight to earlier cash flows

Disadvantages of payback period

The disadvantages of this method are:

- Simple payback does not take into account the time value of money
- It ignores cash flows received after the end of the payback period
- It does not take into account the overall profitability of the project
- The payback period is also arbitrarily chosen by senior management.
- It fails to distinguish projects with similar payback periods

Depreciation and capital investment appraisal

Depreciation is defined as the loss of value of fixed assets due to fear and wear. This may arise because of usage, obsolescence, effluxion of time and / or depletion as is the case with mineral deposits.

For the sake of investment appraisal, depreciation is calculated by straight line method only in which the same amount is allocated through out the life of the fixed asset.

The formula is:

Depreciable amount = $\dfrac{\text{Cost} - \text{scrap value}}{\text{Useful life of the asset in year}}$

In investment appraisal depreciation is added back to profits to determine the cash flows for appraisal purposes. This is critical when appraising projects using the payback period and the net present value method as well as the internal rate of return method. Depreciation treatment has been a source of worry among most students but don't fall into this trap yourself.

Discounted cash flow methods

The methods take into account time value of money. Time value of money is a concept which says that a kwacha receivable 'now' is worth more than the same kwacha receivable in future. This is because of the following reasons:

• Inflation rates may rise which will reduce the purchasing power of that Kwacha in future.

• Interest is foregone which this kwacha could earn if earned now and invested.

• There is uncertainty to its receipt as the payer might have gone bankrupt or died.

Thus discounted cash flow technique of investment appraisal involve calculating the sum of the present values of all cash flows associated with a projects

By taking into account the time value of money and discounting cash flows according to when monies are paid out or received, projects can appraised before

The investment decision is made. It is important to note that it is the 'cash flows' of the project that are discounted, not the profits.

The common DCF methods are:

• Net present value (NPV)
• Internal rate of return (IRR

3.Net Present Value (NPV)

In the exam, you may be asked to calculate the NPV of a project and interpret the result. Alternatively, you may need to explain this method of project appraisal. NPV is the different between the present value cash outflows of a project.
Formerly, NPV = PV of cash inflows – PV of cash put flows.

When performing NPV calculations, the following approach should be taken:

• Identify the relevant cash inflows and out flows of the project, not forgetting the initial investment.

• Set up a table and discount each of the cash flows to its present value, using the company's required rate of return – discount factors may be provided or may have to be calculated from a calculator or read from the discount tables.

• Calculate the net present value of the project by taking the out flows away from the inflows.

• Decide whether or not the project should be accepted or rejected.

Note the following points carefully;

• It is normal to include a 'discounted factor' column, whether or not the value have been obtained using a calculator, given in an exam or read from tables.

• The figures in the 'year' are normally understood as 'end of year' in particular the first value, o, being interpreted as 'now' (i.e. ' end of year 0').

• Bracketed figures indicate negative amounts

Decision criteria

NPV can be interpreted loosely in the following way:
NPV > 0 – project is in profit (i.e. worthwhile)
NPV = 0 – project breaks even
NPV < 0 – project makes a loss (i.e. not worthwhile)

Thus, if the NPV of any project is negative, his means that the project does not earn as much as the discount rate (used in the calculation). Conversely, if the NPV is positive, this means that the project earns more than the discount rate. If the NPV is zero, then the project breaks even which means that the return from the project is not better than a safe investment of the original capital.

In sum,

NPV > 0 means project earns more than the discount rate
NPV = 0 means project earns the same as the discount rate
NPV <0 means project earns less than the discount rate

Note that the discount rate is that rate which is used to discount the cash flows. Also taxation and inflation are ignored in the above interpretation.

Advantages of NPV

• Shareholder wealth is maximized
• It takes into account the time value of money

• It is based on cash flows, which are less subjective than profits

• It uses all values hence does consider the overall profitability of the project

Disadvantages of NPV

• It can be difficult to identify an appropriate discount rate
• Some managers are unfamiliar with the concept of NPV
• Cash flows are usually assumed to occur at the end of the year, but in practice this is over simplistic
• Cash inflows in the future are simply estimates which may undermine the usefulness of NPV

Internal rate of return (IRR)

You may be asked to calculate the internal rate of return and interpret the results, or discuss its uses as a method of investment appraisal. The IRR tells us the rate at which the NPV of a project is neither positive nor negative (i.e. a rate at which NPV = 0)

There are four steps to an IRR calculation:

• Calculate the project's NPV at any reasonable discount rate (this may be given to you in exam).

• If the above NPV is positive, choose a higher discount rate (again this may be given in the exam) and calculate the NPV again. If the above NPV was negative, choose a lower discount rate

• Either way, you must end up with one positive and one negative NPV. You must now calculate the IRR by using the following interpolation formula:

DR. CRYFORD MUMBA

IRR = A% + [a X (B-A)%]
             a-b

Where A = lower discount rate

B=higher discount rate

a= NPV at the lower rate

b = NPV at the higher rate

The IRR must then be compared to the company's required rate of return

Note: the above steps of calculating IRR need the NPV calculated using two different discount rates.

Graphical estimation of IRR

In order to estimate IRR of the project graphically;

• Scale the vertical axis to include both NPVs
• Scale the horizontal axis to include both discount rates
• Plot the two points on the graph and join them with a straight line
• Identify the estimate of the IRR where the line crosses the horizontal (discount rate) axis.

Decision criteria

• If the IRR is higher than the required rate of return, the project should be accepted

• If the IRR is lower than the require rate of return, the project is rejected

• If two or more projects are being appraised the one with the higher IRR is preferred.

Advantages of IRR

• It takes into account the time value of money, which is a good basis for decision – making.

• The results are expressed as a simple percentage, and are more easily understood than other methods.

• It indicates how sensitive decisions are to a change in interest rates

Disadvantages of IRR

- Projects with unconventional cash flows can either have negative or multiple IRRs – this can be confusing to the user.

- IRR can be confused with ARR or return on capital employed (ROCE) since all methods give answers in percentage terms – hence, a cash-based method can be confused with a profit –based method.

- It may give conflicting recommendation to NPV

- Some managers are unfamiliar with IRR method

- IRR cannot accommodate changes in interest rates over the life of a project

- It assumes funds are reinvested at a rate equivalent to the IRR itself, which may be unrealistically high

Risk and capital investment decision

Risk is always part and parcel of any investment.

It becomes more important in capital projects because such projects involve long periods of time and huge capital outlay.

There are a number of ways in which risk can be taken into account when making capital investment decision. These include the following:

- **Set a short payback period**. If risk is deemed to increase with the length of time a company waits for its return, then selecting only those projects with a short payback period will tend to reduce the risk.

- **Use a higher discount rate.** This is referred to as adding a risk premium to the discount rate. If a project is considered to be fairly risky then say 3% could be added to the basic cost of capital. If it is considered to be very risky then say 7% could be added.

Note that changing the discount rate may make the project once accepted to be rejected. No wonder there is separation between those charged with the responsibility of appraising and implementing the project to avoid manipulation!

- **Use probabilities to assess the range of possible outcomes**. Managers could be asked to forecast a number of different values for sales, costs and so on together with their associated probabilities. This is where the topic on expected values becomes important in capital investment decisions.

- **Undertake a sensitivity analysis.** This involves asking a series of "what if" questions and re-evaluating the project with different sets of assumptions. For example, managers might ask what if sales volume is 5% lower than expected. The project would be re-evaluated to see how sensitive the final result is to this particular change. By carrying out a number of such sensitivity tests it is possible to highlight which particular forecasts are most important to the outcome of the project.

Forecasting errors in investment appraisal

All aspects of project forecasts are subject to errors hence the need to be aware of the effects of such errors. Errors may take the following forms:

- Investment required in fixed assets may be over or underestimated

- Investment required in working capital may be over or underestimated

- Date of acquisition of assets or commencement of revenue inflows and outflows may be earlier or later than forecast

- Life or residual value of assets may be misjudged

- Sales volume or sales price or costs may be greater or lower than expected

- Project life may be shorter or longer than forecast

- Government intervention in Zambia or in overseas export markets may result in a change in tax rates, import controls, foreign exchange controls, thus affecting expected cash flows.

Examples on capital investment appraisals

The following examples are designed to illustrate how the various methods used to appraise capital projects are calculated and interpreted. However, questions requiring your understanding of the methods may be asked without any calculations need.

Example 1
The following information relates to two possible capital projects to be understand by PCBF Ltd. Both projects have an initial capital cost of K400 million and only one can be undertaken.

Expected profits	project X	project Y
Year	K'000	(K'000)
1	160 000	60 000
2	160 000	100 000
3	80 000	180 000
4	40 000	240 000
Estimated resale value at end of year	4 80 000	80 000

Additional information

1. Profit is calculated after deducting straight line depreciation.
2. The cost of capital is 16%
3. The relevant discount factors are as follows:

End of year 1	0.863
2	0.743
3	0.641
4	0.552
5	0.476

Required: For both projects:

a) Calculate

   1) Payback period
   2) The accounting rate of return using average investment
   3) The net present value

b) Advise the company which project in opinion should be undertaken giving reasons for your decision

c) Explain what is meant by the cost of investment decision?

d) State three ways in which risk can be taken into account when making a capital investment decision.

Solution

Annual depreciation = $\dfrac{\text{Cost} - \text{scrap value}}{\text{Number of years}}$

$$= \dfrac{400\ 000 - 80\ 000}{4\ \text{years}}$$

$$= \text{K80 000 p.a.}$$

NB. Depreciation must be added back to the profits for each year to determine the cash flow for appraisal purposes.

DR. CRYFORD MUMBA

Project x: cumulative cash flows

Year	Profits K'000	Depreciation K'000	Cash flows K'000	Cumulative cash flows K'000
1	160 000	80 000	240 000	240 000
2	160 000	80 000	240 000	480 000
3	80 000	80 000	160 000	640 000
4	40 000	80 000	120 000	760 000

Payback period = year before full recovery + $\frac{\text{un-recovered amount}}{\text{Cash flow during year}}$

$1 + \frac{160\ 000}{240\ 000} = 1.67$ years

Project y: cumulative cash flows

Year	Profits K'000	Depreciation K'000	Cash flows K'000	Cumulative cash flows K'000
1	60 000	80 000	140 000	140 000
2	100 000	80 000	180 000	320 000
3	180 000	80 000	260 000	580 000
4	240 000	80 000	320 000	900 000

Payback period = $2 + \frac{80\ 000}{260\ 000} = 2.3$ years

2. Accounting rate of return

Project x

Average investment = $\frac{\text{initial investment + residue value}}{2}$

$= \frac{400\ 000 + 80\ 000}{2} = 240\ 000$

Average profits = $\frac{\text{Total profits}}{\text{Number of years}}$

$= \frac{160\ 000 + 160\ 000 + 80\ 000 + 40\ 000}{4 \text{ years}}$

$= 110\ 000$

Accounting rate of return = $\frac{\text{Average profits} \times 100}{\text{Average investment}}$

$$= \underline{110\ 000} \times 100 = 45.83\%$$
$$240\ 000$$

Project y

Average investment $= \underline{\text{K400 000} + 80\ 000} = 240\ 000$
$$2$$

Average profits $= \underline{\text{K60 000} + 100\ 000 + 80\ 000 + 240\ 000}$
$$2$$

$$= \text{K145 000}$$

ARR $= \underline{\text{K145 000}} \times 100 = \underline{60.42\%}$
$$240\ 000$$

3. Net present value for project x and project y

		Project x		Project y	
Year	DF 16%	Cash flows	Present Value	Cash flows	Present Value
		K'000	K'000	K'000	K'000
0	1.000	(400 000)	(400 000)	(400 000)	(400 000)
1	0.862	240 000	206 808	140 000	120 680
2	0.743	240 000	178 320	180 000	133 740
3	0.641	160 000	102 560	260 000	166 660
4	0.552	80 000	44 160	80 000	44 160
4	0.552	120 000	66 240	320 000	176 640
Net present value			198,160		241 880

b) Project Y should be undertaken because it gives the highest net present value. This is a more important measure than the accounting rate of return because it takes into account the timing of cash flows and the time value of money. However, the directors should bear in mind that project Y has a longer payback period which can lead to increased risk and reduced liquidity.

c) The cost of capital is the cost to the company of raising finance for capital expenditure projects; that is cost of shareholders capital and the cost of any loans raised.

It is important in an investment decision because it is the minimum return that a project should earn. If a project does not earn a return which is at least equal to the cost of funds invested in it is then not worthwhile.

d) There are a number of ways in which risk can be taken into account when making a capital investment decision.

- Set a short payback period
- Use a higher discount rate
- Use probabilities to assess the range of possible outcomes
- Undertake a sensitivity analysis.

Note in the above calculation, payback period has been calculated by cumulating the cash flows arrived at after adding depreciation to annual profits. This is because the payback period uses the cash flow and not profits. When calculating the ARR actual profits figures were used because ARR used profits. Finally, cash flows were employed to calculate the NPV. This recognition is key to capital investment appraisal. ***Cash flow = Profit + Depreciation per annum***

Example 2

Modern electric company is considering a new stove which will contribute to the conservation of forests. This product line will involve initial cash investment of K21.0 million in 2007 and K30.0 million in 2008. After tax cash receipts are K7.5 million in 2009, K9.0 million in 2010, K10.5 million in 2011 and K12.0 million each year thereafter up to 2017. While the stove may be viable after 2017, the directors prefer to be prudent and limit calculations to that time.

Required:

a) If the required rate of return is 15%, what is the net present value of the project? Comment on its acceptability?

b) What is the project's

    i) Internal rate of return (IRR)?
    ii) Payback period?

Solution

a) To start, we need to calculate NPV at, say, 15% as follows:

Year	Cash flow K'000	DF 15%	Present value (PV) K'000
2007	(21 000)	1.000	(21 000)
2008	(30 000)	0.870	(26 000)
2009	7 500	0.756	56 70
2010	9 000	0.658	59 22
2011	10 500	0.572	60 06
2012-17	12 000	2.164	25 968
	Net present value		(35 34)

Next, we need to calculate another NPV.

This can be calculated by selecting a lower discount rate which will give positive NPV and then using the interpolation formula. This entails recalculating the NPV at lower rate. Lets use 10%.

Year	cash flow K'000	DF 10%	PV
2007	(21 000)	1.000	(21 000)
2008	(30 000)	0.909	(27 270)
2009	7 500	0.826	6 195
2010	9 000	0.751	6 759
2011	10 500	0.683	7 172
2012-17	12 000	2.975	35 700
		NPV	7 556

IRR =A% + [a x (B-A)]%
      a-b

$$= 10\% + \frac{7556}{7557-(-3534)} (15-10)\% = \underline{13.4\%}$$

b) Payback period

Year	Cash flow K'000	Cumulative cash flow K'000
2008	(30 000)	(30 000)
2009	7 500	(22 500)
2010	9 000	13 500
2011	10 500	3 000
2012-17	12 000	69 000

Payback period is approximately 6 years.

Note: to calculate the discount factor for years 2012—17, we use annuities i.e. K12 000 has to be received each year from 2012 to 2017. Do you know the life of this project? It has 10 years. Discount factor at 15% of 2.164 has been found by subtracting the discount factor for year 4, i.e. 2.855 from the discount factor for year 10 i.e. 5.019. These factors could be found either using annuity tables or indeed the calculator. Use the same principle to find the discount factors for years 2012 – 17 at 10% discount rate.

Example 3

Poor Start ltd plans to undertake an investment project to cost K84 000 000 and the company's cost of capital is 20%. The annual net cash inflows, assumed to arise at the year end, are as follows:

Year	cash flows
	K'000
1	18 000
2	36 000
3	36 000
4	36 000
5	14 292

Table of factor for the NPV of K1 are:

Years	20%
0	1.000
1	0.870
2	0.756
3	0.658
4	0.572
5	0.497

Required:

Calculate:

a) The net present value (NPV)
b) The payback period for the project.

Solution

a) NPV

Year	cash flow	DF 20%	PV
	K'000		K'000
0	(84 000)	1.000	(84 000)
1	18 000	0.870	15 660
2	36 000	0.756	27 216
3	36 000	0.658	23 688
4	36 000	0.572	20 592
5	14 494	0.497	7 204
		NPV	K 10 360

b) Payback period

Year	cash flow	cumulative cash flow
	K'000	K'000
1	18 000	18 000
2	36 000	54 000
3	36 000	90 000
4	36 000	126 000
5	14 494	14 494

PBP = 2 + 30 000 X 12 months
        36 000
= 2 years 10 months

Example 4

PCBF Ltd is looking to automate one of its production process in order to produce cash savings and has spent K125 million on a management consultancy exercise. The exercise has identified two alternative projects that, if installed, would have the following profile of cost and cash savings over a project life of 5 years.

	Project	
	X	Y
	K'000	K'000
Cost	650 000	750 000
Cash savings year 1	150 000	50 000
2	225 000	100 000
3	275 000	150 000
4	75 000	450 000
5	50 000	300 000

Additional information:

1) Project x would have a residual value of K100 million and project y a residual value of K200 million at the end of year 5.

2) All cash flows will arise at the end of the relevant year.

3) The company's cost of capital is 12% and the relevant discount factors are

Year 1	0.893
2	0.797
3	0.712
4	0.636
5	0.567

Required:

a) Calculate the following for each of two projects

   i) The payback period
   ii) The accounting rate of return
   iii) The present value

b) Advice PCBF Ltd which project to invest in, clearly stating your reasons

c) Explain how the expenditure of k125 million on the management consultancy exercise should be treated when appraising the two projects.

Solution

a) i) payback period

Year	Project x cash savings	cumulative cash savings	Project y cash savings	cumulative cash savings
	K'000	K'000	K'000	K'000
1	150 000	150 000	50 000	50 000
2	225 000	375 000	100 000	150 000
3	275 000	650 000	150 000	300 000
4	75 000	725 000	450 000	750 000
5	50 000	775 000	300 000	1050 000

Payback period
   Project x = 3 years
   Project y = 4 years

ii) Accounting rate of return (ARR). To find ARR we need to take into account depreciation. ARR uses profits and not cash flows (cash savings). This means that we need to SUBTRACT depreciation charge for each year to determine the profits for the year for appraisal purposes.

Depreciation charge = $\dfrac{\text{cost} - \text{scrap value}}{\text{Useful life}}$

Project x = $\dfrac{650\ 000 - 100\ 000}{5}$ = 110 000

Project y = $\dfrac{750\ 000 - 200\ 000}{5}$ = 110 000

Thus we need to subtract K110 00 from the cash savings for each year to determine the profit for the year as shown below.

Year	dep	Project x		project y	
		cash savings	profits	cash savings	profits
	K'000	K'000	K'000	K'000	K'000
1	110 000	150 000	40 000	50 000	(60 000)
2	110 000	225 000	115 000	100 000	(10 000)
3	110 000	275 000	165 000	150 000	40 000
4	110 000	75 000	(35 000)	450 000	340 000
5	110 000	50 000	(60 000)	300 000	190 000
Total			**225 000**		**500 000**

ARR = $\dfrac{\text{average profits}}{\text{Average investment}}$ X 100%

Average profits = $\dfrac{\text{total profits}}{\text{Number of years}}$ thus project x = $\dfrac{225\ 000}{5}$

= K45 000

Project y = $\dfrac{500\ 000}{5}$

= K100 000

Average investment = $\dfrac{\text{cost} + \text{scrap value}}{2}$

For project x = $\dfrac{650\ 000 + 400\ 000}{2}$ =K375 000

DR. CRYFORD MUMBA

For project y = $\frac{750\ 000 + 200\ 00}{2}$ =K 475 000

ARR for project x = $\frac{k45\ 000}{K375\ 000}$ X 100 = 12%

iii) NPV. Here we use the cash savings earlier used in the calculation of payback period. Standard table must always be presented.

Year	DF (12%)	Project x cash flow	PV	project y cash flow	PV
0	1.000	(650 000)	(650 000)	(750 000)	(750 000)
1	0.893	150 000	133950	50 000	44 650
2	0.797	225 000	179325	100 000	79 700
3	0.712	275 000	195800	150 000 1	06 800
4	0.636	75 000	47 700	450 000	286 200
5	0.567	50 000	28 350	300 000	170 100
5	0.567	100 000	57 600	200 000	113 400
		NPV =	(7275)	NPV	50850

b) Technically, PCBF should invest in project y as it has a higher NPV and a higher ARR though longer payback period than project x.

c) I n investment appraisal only relevant costs are taken into account. These are costs which are directly attributed to the project such that if the project is not undertaken, these costs will be nil. Expenditure of k125 million is not a relevant cost. It is a sunk cost which will have been incurred whether or not the project is undertaken. It should, therefore, be ignored when appraising above projects.

Note: in the calculation of NPV above, each project has a scrap value which should not be ignored. This scrap value is an example of a cash inflow and is therefore discounted at 12% in the fifth year. Take note of this as it is a common exam trap.

PROGRESS CLINIC 15

Question 1
Lemba Ltd manufactures product X which it sells for K5 per unit. Variable costs of production are currently at K3 per unit and fixed costs are at 50 Ngwee per unit.

A new machine is available which would cost only K90,000 but which could be used to make product X for a variable cost of K2.50 per unit. Fixed costs, however, would increase by K7 500 a year as a direct result of purchasing the machine.

262

The machine would have an expected life of four (4) years and a resale value after that time of K10 000.

Sales of product X are estimated to be 75 000 units per annum. The company's cost of capital is 12% per year.

Required:

On the basis of the above information and using the Net Present Value method. Determine whether this investment should be undertaken.

Note

The Present Value Discount factors at 12% are as follows:

Year PV	Factor 12%
0	1.000
1	0.893
2	0.797
3	0.712
4	0.636

CHAPTER 16

MANAGEMENT CONTROL: BUDGETING

Introduction

A budget is a quantitative statement, for a defined period of time, which may include planned revenues, expenses, assets, liabilities and cash flows. It provides a focus for the organization, aids coordination of activities and facilitates control. Thus, budgets are not prepared and then filed away but are a concrete components of what is known as the budgetary planning and control system. A budgetary planning and control system is essentially a system for ensuring communication, co-ordination and control within the business.

Objective of Budgeting

Coordination, communication and control are general objectives: more information is provided by an inspection of the specific objectives of a budgetary planning and control system. These include:

●**To ensure the achievement of the organization's objectives**. Objectives for the organization as a whole, and for individual departments and operations within the organization, are set. Quantified expressions of these objectives are then drawn up as targets to be achieved within the timescale of the budget plan.

●**To compel planning**. This is probably the most important feature of a budgetary planning and control system. Planning forces management to look ahead, to set out detailed plans for achieving the targets for each department, operation and ideally each manger and to anticipate problems. It thus prevents management from relying on ad hoc or uncoordinated planning which may be detrimental to the performance of the organization.

●**To communicate ideas**. A formal system is necessary to ensure that each person affected by the plans is aware of what he or she is supposed to be doing. Communication might be one-way, with managers giving orders to subordinates, or there might be a to-way dialogue and exchange of ideas.

●**To coordinate activities**. The activities of different departments or sub-units of the organization need to be coordinated t ensure maximum integration of efforts towards common goals. This concept of coordination implies, for example, that the human resource department should base its budget on production requirements and that the production budget should in turn be based on sales expectations. Although straightforward in concept, coordination is remarkably difficult to achieve, and there is often 'sub-optimality' and conflict between departmental plans in the budget so that the efforts of each department are not fully integrated into a combined plan to achieve the company's set target.

•To provide a framework for responsibility accounting. Budgetary planning and control systems require managers of budget centers are made responsible for the achievement of budget targets for the operations under their personal control.

•To establish a system of control. A budget is a yardstick against which actual performance is measured and assessed. Control over actual performance is provided by the comparisons of actual results against the budget plan. Departures from the budget can then be investigated and the reasons for the departures can be divided into controllable and uncontrollable factors.

•To motivate employees to improve their performance. The interests and commitment of employees can be retained via a system of feedback of actual results, which lets them know how well or badly they are performing. The identification of controllable reasons for departures from budgets with managers responsible provides an incentive for improving future performance. Two levels of attainment can be set namely a minimum expectations budget and a desired standards budget which provides some sort of challenge to employees.

Approaches to Budgeting

The starting point of most budgets is the actual results for the present period. After examining the recent costs and revenue, these amounts are adjusted for changes that are expected in the following period. The problem with this incremental approach is that inefficiencies in the ways things done currently are carried into the future. Another budgeting technique is called zero-based budgeting. With zero-based budgeting cost estimates are built up from zero level and it rests on the philosophy that all spending must be justified. It is not automatically accepted that if some activity was financed this year it will be financed again in the future. A good case must be made for the allocation of scarce resources for the activity.

Budgeting Process

Budgets are often prepared for a budget period of one year and this is called a single-period budget. However, the budget period can extend over a shorter or sometimes longer period. Another, related type of budgeting is known as the rolling budget. The budget is initially prepared for an appropriate budget period , for example, one year. With each month that elapses, another month is added to the end of the budget, so that there will always be a full 12 month budget.

The first step in budgeting is to develop a set of broad assumptions about the economy, the industry, and the entity's strategy for the budget period. The operating budget or master budget is a collection of related budgets that includes the sales, purchases, production, material purchases, direct labour, manufacturing overheard, operating expense, income statement, cash and balance sheet budgets.

A sales budget is prepared first. All other budgets depend on the sales forecast. The quantity to be purchased or produced depends on expected sales and inventory levels. The material purchases, direct labour and manufacturing overhead budgets are prepared after the production budget is drawn up. Selling expenses depend on sales while other operating expenses depend on sales and purchases. A forecast income statement can now be prepared. The cash budget can next be prepared followed, finally, by the forecast balance sheet.

1. **Sales budget.** This may be described as a forecast of the number of units the business expects to sell for a predetermined period. The reliability of the sales budget is important as all other budgets are based on it. After the number of units that may be sold is estimated, the number of units that an be produce may be determined. Whilst the sales budget depends a lot on previous sales figures, consideration is also given to sales trends, future predictions and competitors.
2. **Purchases/production budget.** This must be compatible with the sales budget . However, other factors such as inventory level held by the entity are important. The purchases/production budget states the quantity of a product must be purchased or produced to meet an entity's sales and inventory requirements.
3. **Cost of sales budgets.** These are drawn up by both merchandising and manufacturing entities. For a merchandising entity, the cost of goods available for sale is first calculated by adding the opening merchandise inventory to the budgeted purchases. Closing inventory requirements are then deducted from this amount to determine the budgeted cost of sales. The process is identical for a manufacturing entity except that the cost of goods manufactured replaces expected purchases.
4. **Materials purchases budget**. This is prepared once the production budget has been drawn up. Many entities keep materials on hand at all times to accommodate unforeseen changes in demand.
5. **Direct labour budget.** This also depends on the production budget. It is prepared by multiplying the number of direct labour hours needed to produce each unit by the number of units to be produced.
6. **Manufacturing overheard budget**. Here overheard costs are estimated. These costs may be determined in a number of ways including department predetermined overheard rates and activity-based costing.
7. **Operating expense budget.** This includes the selling , general, administrative and other operating expenses. Some of these expenses are variable e.g. commissions, delivery expenses while others are fixed e.g. rent expense, insurance.
8. **Budgeted income statement**. This is drawn up from the sales budget, cost of sales budget and operating expense budget. It is a summary of the various component projections of income and expenses for the budget period.
9. **Cash budget.** Once all other budgets including the sales budget are prepared, the cash budget can be drawn up. The cash budget shows the expected receipts and expected payments for a certain period of time. It usually depicts the monthly cash position of the business. The cash budget is prepared for the purpose of each cash planning and control. It helps in avoiding to keep cash lying idle for long periods and identifying possible cash shortages.

Most cash budgets have the following feature:
●The budget period is broken down onto sub-periods usually months
●Receipts of cash are identified and totaled
●Payments of cash are identified and totaled

●the surplus or shortfall in cash for each month is calculated i.e. receipts minus payments

●the closing cash balance is calculated by taking into account the cash surplus or shortfall and opening cash balance.

10. **Budgeted balance sheet**. This is prepared by starting with the balance sheet for the period just ended and adjusting it using all the activities which are expected to take place during the budgeted period. A budgeted balance sheet can help management to calculate a variety of ratios. It also highlights future resources, obligations and possible unfavourable conditions. The budgeted balance sheet is affected by all the other budgets. Purchases and production budgets will indicate inventory estimates. Depreciation reflected in the operating expenses budget will affect the carrying value of non-current assets in the balance sheet. The expected net profit or loss reflected in the budgeted income statement will affect retained earnings. The cash budget is a source of many balance sheet amounts e.g. purchase of equipment, payment of dividends, etc.

CASH BUDGET

The usefulness of cash budgets

1. The cash budget is **one of the most important planning tools** that an organization can use. It shows the cash effect of all plans made within the budgetary process and hence its preparation can lead to a modification of budgets if it shows that there are insufficient cash resources to finance the planned operations. It is defined in the CIMA *Official Terminology* as 'A detailed budget of cash inflows and outflows incorporating both revenue and capital items.

2. It can also give management an indication of potential problems that could arise and allows them the opportunity to take action to avoid such problems. A cash budget can show four positions. Management will need to take appropriate action depending on the potential position.

Cash position		Appropriate management action
Short-term surplus	-	Pay creditors early to obtain discount
	-	Attempt to increase sales by increasing debtors and stocks
	-	Make short-term investments
Short-term deficit	-	Increase creditors
	-	Reduce debtors
	-	Arrange an overdraft
Long-term surplus	-	Make long-term investments

Long-term deficit	-	Expand
	-	Diversify
	-	Replace/update fixed assets
	-	Raise long-term finance (such as via issue of share capital)
	-	Consider shutdown/disinvestment opportunities

3. An examination question could ask you to recommend appropriate action for management to take based on the results of a cash budget. Ensure your advice takes account both of whether there is a surplus or deficit and whether the position is long or short term

What to include in a cash budget

4. A cash budget is prepared to show the expected receipts of cash and payments of cash during a budget period.

5. **Receipts** of cash may come from one or more of the following.

(a) Cash sales
(b) Payments by debtors (credit sales)
(c) Sale of fixed assets
(d) The issue of new shares or loan stock and less formalized loans
(e) The receipt of interest and dividends from investments outside the business

6. Although all of these receipts would affect cash budget they would **not all appear in the profit and loss account**.

(a) The issue of new shares or loan stock is a balance sheet item.

(b) The cash received from an asset affects the balance sheet, and the profit or loss on the sale of an asset, which appears in the profit and loss account, is not the cash received but the difference between cash received and the written down value of the asset at the time of sale.

7. **Payments** of cash may be for one or more of the following

- Purchase of stocks
- Payroll costs or other expenses
- Purchase of capital items
- Payment of interest, dividends or taxation

Not all payments are profit: and loss account items. The purchase of capital equipment and the payment of VAT affect the balance sheet.

8. To ensure that there is sufficient cash in hand to cope adequately with budgeted activities; management should therefore prepare and pay close attention to a cash budget rather than a profit and loss account. Cash budgets are most effective if they are treated as **rolling budgets**. Rolling budgets involve a process of continuous budgeting whereby **regularly each period** (week month, quarter) **a new future period is added to the budget whilst the earliest period is deleted**. In this way the budget is constantly revised to reflect the most up to date position.

The steps in preparing a cash budget

9. A guideline to the steps required to prepare a cash budget is shown below. If you are unfamiliar with cash budgets, check them carefully.

Step 1. Set out pro-forma cash budget month by month

CASH BUDGET

	Month 1	Month 2	Month 3
Cash receipts	K	K	K
Receipts from debtors			
Sales of capital items			
Loans received			
Proceeds from share issues			
Any other cash receipts			
Cash payments			
Payments to creditors			
Cash purchases			
Wages and salaries			
Loan repayments			
Capital expenditure			
Dividends			
Taxation			
Any other cash expenditure			
Receipts less payments			
Opening cash balance b/f	W	X	Y
Closing cash balance c/f	X	Y	Z

The closing cash balanced in one month becomes the opening cash balance in the next month.

Step 2. Sort out cash receipts from debtors

(a) Establish budgeted sales month by month
(b) Establish the length of credit period taken by debtors
(c) From (a) and (b), calculate when the budgeted sales revenue will be received as cash. Deduct any discount allowed for early payment.
(d) Establish when the opening debtors at the start of the periods will pay in cash. (Check for any discount that may be allowed).
(e) Put these cash receipts ingot the correct period of the budget.

Step 3. Other income

Establish whether any other cash income, such as cash from sale of fixed Assets will be received, and when.

Put these sundry items of cash receipts into the budget.

Step 4. Sort out cash payments to suppliers

(a) Establish production qualities and materials usage quantities each month.

(b) Establish materials stock changes and so the quantity and cost of materials purchased each month.

(c) Establish the length of credit period taken from suppliers.

(d) From (b) and (c), calculate when the cash payments to suppliers will be included in the budget.

Step 5. Establish other cash payments in the month

These will include the following.

(a) payments of wages and salaries

(b) Payments for sundry expenses. Be careful to exclude non-cash items of cost (such as depreciation) and to attribute payments to the month when they will actually occur. (Rental costs of K120, 000 per annum might be charged to the P&L account at K10, 000 per month. The cash budget should identify in which month or months the K120, 000 will actually be paid).

(c) Other one-off expenditures, such as fixed asset purchases, tax payments and so on.

10. You should now work carefully through the two illustrations which follow, ensuring that you understand where all of the figures in the cash budget are derived from

Example 1

Tiyeseko Ltd operates a retail business. Purchases are sold at cost plus 33⅓%

(a)

	Budgeted sales in month K	Labour cost in month K	Expenses incurred in month K
January	40,000	3,000	4,000
February	60,000	3,000	6,000
March	160,000	5,000	7,000
April	120,000	4,000	7,000

(b) It is management policy to have sufficient stock in hand at the end of each month to meet half of next month's sales demand.

(c) Creditors for materials and expenses are paid in the month after the purchases are made/expenses incurred. Labour is paid in full by the end of each month. Labour costs and expenses are treated as period costs in the P& L account.

(d) Expenses include a monthly depreciation charge of K2, 000.

(e) (75% of sales are for cash

(f) 25% of sales are on one month's credit

The company will pay equipment costing K18, 000 for cash in February and will pay a dividend of K20, 000 in March. The opening cash balance at 1 February is
   K1, 000.

Required:

(a) Prepare a cash budget for February and March

(b) Prepare a profit and loss account for February and March

Solution

(a) CASH BUDGET

	February K	March K
Receipts		
Receipts from sales	55,000 (W1)	135,000 (W2)

Payments

Trade creditors	37,500 (W3)	82,500 (W3)
Expense Creditors	2,000 (W4)	4,000 (W4)
Labour	3,000	5,000
Equipment purchase 1	8,000	-
Dividend	-	20,000
Total payments	60,500	111,500
Receipts less payments	(5,500)	23,500
Opening cash balance b/f	1,000	(4,500)*
Closing cash balance c/f	(4,500)*	19,000

Workings

			K
1. Receipts in February	75% of Feb sales (75% X K60, 000)		45,000
	25% of Jan sales (25% X K40, 000)		10,000
			55,000
			K
2. Receipts in March	75% of Mar sales (75% X K160, 000)		120,000
	25% of Feb sales (25% X K60, 000)		15,000
			135,000

3. Purchases January February

		K		K
For Jan sales	(50% of K30, 000)	15,000		
For Feb sales	(50% of K45, 000)	22,000	(50% of K45, 000)	22,500
For Mar sales		-	(50% of K120, 000)	60,000
		37,500		82,500

These purchases are paid for in February and March.

4. Expenses

Cash expenses in January (K4, 000—K2, 000) and February (K6, 000—K2, 000) are paid in February and March respectively. Depreciation is not a cash item.

(b) Profit and loss account

February March

	K	K	K	K
Sales		60,000		160,000
Cost of purchases (75%)		40,000		120,000
Gross profit		15,000		40,000
Less: Labour	3,000		5,000	
Expenses	6,000		7,000	
		9,000		12,000
Net Profit		6,000		28,000

Note the following.

●The asterisks show that the cash balance at the end of February is carried forward as the opening cash balance for March.

● The fact that profits are made in February and March disguises the fact that there is a cash shortfall at the end of February.

● Steps should be taken to ensure that an overdraft facility is available for the cash shortage at the end of February, or to defer certain payments so that the overdraft is avoided.

● Some payments must be made on due dates (payroll, taxation and so on) but it is possible that other payments can be delayed, depending on the requirements of the business and/or the goodwill of suppliers.

A comparison of profit and cash flows

You might notice in the example above that the total profit of K34, 000 differs from the total of receipts less payments (K18, 000). Profit and cash flows during a period need not be the same amount and, indeed, will not usually be the same.

●Sales and costs of sales are recognized in a profit and loss account as soon as they are incurred; the **cash budget** does not show a figure for sales or cost of sales. It is concerned with **cash actually received from customers or paid to suppliers.**

●A profit and loss account may include accrued amounts for rates, insurance and other expenses. In the **cash budget** such amounts will **appear in full in the months in which they are paid**. There is no attempt to apportion the payments to the period to which they relate.

●Similarly a profit and loss account may show a charge for **depreciation**. This is **not a cash expense** and will **never appear in a cash budget**. The cash budget will show **purchase of fixed assets as payments in the month when the assets are paid for,**

and may also show the **proceeds on disposal of a fixed asset as a receipt of cash**. No attempt is made to allocate purchase cost over the life of the asset.

Example: 2

From the following information which relates to George and Zola Ltd you are required to prepare a month by month cash budget for the second half of 2013 and to append such brief comments as you consider might be helpful to management.

(a) The company's only product, a vest, sells at K40 and has a variable cost of K26 made up as follows.

      Material K20   Labour K4   Overhead K2

(b) Fixed costs of K6, 000 per month are paid on the 28th of each month.

(c) Quantities sold/to be sold on credit.

May	June	July	Aug	Sept	Oct	Nov	Dec
1000	1,200	1,400	1,600	1,800	2,000	2,200	2,600

(d) Production quantities

May	June	July	Aug	Sept	Oct	Nov	Dec
1,200	1,400	1,600	2,000	2,400	2,600	2,400	2,200

(e) Cash sales at a discount of 5% are expected to average 100 units a months.

(f) Customers are expected to settle their accounts by the end of the second month following sale.

(g) Suppliers of material are paid two months after the material is used in production

(h) Wages are paid in the same month as they are incurred.

(i) 70% of the variable overheads is paid in the month of production, the remainder in the following month.

(j) Corporation tax of K18, 000 to be paid in October.

(k) A new delivery vehicle was bought in June. It cost K8, 000 and is to be paid for in August. The old vehicle was sold for K600, the buyer undertaking to pay in July.

(l) The company is expected to be K3,000 overdrawn at the bank at 30 June 2013

(m) No increases or decreases in raw materials, work in progress or finished goods are planned over the period.

(n) No price increases or cost increases are expected in the period.

Solution

CASH BUDGET FOR JULY 1 TO DECEMBER 31 2013

	July	Aug	Sept	Oct	Nov	Dec	Total
	K	K	K	K	K	K	K
Receipts							
Credit sales	40,000	48,000	56,000	64,000	72,000	80,000	360,000
Cash sales	3,800	3,800	3,800	3,800	3,800	3,800	22,800
Sale of vehicles	600						600
	44,400	51,800	59,800	67,800	75,800	83,800	383,400
Payments							
Materials	24,000	28,000	32,000	40,000	48,000	52,000	224,000
Labour	6,400	8,000	9,600	10,400	9,600	8,800	52,800
Variable overheard(W)	3,080	3,760	4,560	5,080	4,920	4,520	25,920
Fixed costs	6,000	6,000	6,000	6,000	6,000	6,000	36,000
Corporate tax				18,000			18,000
Purchase of vehicle		8,000					8,000
	39,480	53,760	52,160	79,480	68,520	71,320	364,720
Receipts less payments							
Balance b/f	4,920	(1,960)	7,640	(11,680)	7,280	12,480	18,680
Balance c/f	(3,000)	1,920	(40)	7,600	(4,080)	3,200	(3,000)
	1,920	(40)	7,600	(4,080)	3,200	15,680	15,680

Workings

Variable overheards

	June	July	Aug	Sept	Oct	Nov	Dec
	K	K	K	K	K	K	K
Production cost	2,800	4,000	4,800	5,200	4,200	4,800	4,400
70% paid in month		2,240	2,800	3,360	3,640	3,360	1,440
30% in following month		3,080	3,760	4,560	5,080	4,920	4,520

Comments

●There will be a small overdraft at the end of August but larger one at the end of October. It may be possible to delay payments to suppliers for longer than two months or to reduce purchases of materials or reduce the volume of production by running down existing stock levels.

●If neither of these courses is possible, the company may need to negotiate overdraft facilities with its bank.

●The cash deficit is only temporary and by the end of December there will be a comfortable surplus. The muse to which this cash will be put should ideally be planned in advance.

The master budget

When the sales, cash, production and related budgets have been prepared, the budgeted **profit and loss account and budgeted balance sheet** (**the master budget**) provide the overall picture of the planned performance for the budget period.

Example 3

CM Engineering Limited produces two products, bolts and nuts. The budget for the forthcoming year 31 March 2013 is to be prepared. Expectations for the forthcoming year include the following.

(a) CM ENGINEERING LTD
BALANCE SHEET AS AT 1 APRIL 2012

	K	K
Fixed asset		
Land and buildings		45,000
Plant and equipment at cost	187,000	
Less accumulated depreciation	75,000	
		112,000
Current assets		
Materials	7,650	
Raw materials	23,600	
Finished goods	19,500	
Debtors	4,300	
Cash	55,050	
Current liabilities		
Creditors	6,800	
		48,250
		205,250
Financed by		
Share capital		150,000
Retained profit		55,250

(b) Finished products

The sales director has estimated the following:

	Bolts	Nuts
(i) Demand for the company's products	4,500 units	4,000 units
(ii) Selling price per unit	K32	K44
(iii)Closing stock of finished products at 31 March 2013	4000 units	K1,2000 units
(iv) Opening stock of finished products at 1 April 2012	900 units	200 units
(v) Units cost of this opening stock	K20	K28
(vi) Amount of plant capacity required for each unit of product		
Machining	15 min	24 min
Assembling	12 min	18 min
(vii) Raw material content per unit of each product		
Material A	1.5 kilos	0.5 kilos
Material B	2.0 kilos	4.0 kilos
(viii) Direct labour hours required per unit of each product	6 hours	9 hours

Finished goods are valued on a FIFO basis at full production cost.

(c) Raw Materials material A material B

(i) Closing stock requirement in kilos at 31 March 2013	600	1,000
(ii) Opening stock at 1 April 2012 in kilos	1,100	6,000
(iii)Budgeting cost of raw materials per kilo	K1.50	K1.00

Actual costs per kilo of opening stocks are as budgeted cost for the coming year.

(d) Direct labour

The standard wage rate of direct labour is K1.60 per hour.

(e) Production overhead

Production overhead is absorbed on the basis of machining hours, with separate absorption rates for each department. The following overheads are anticipated in the production cost centre budgets.

	Machining department K	Assembling department K
Supervisors' salaries	10,000	9,150
Power	4,400	2,000
Maintenance and running costs	2,100	2,000
Consumables	3,400	500
General expenses	19,600	5,000
	39,500	18,650

Depreciation is taken at 5% straight line on plant and equipment. A machine costing the company K20,000 is due to be installed on 1 October 2012 in the machining department, which already has machinery installed to the value of K100,000 (at cost). Land worth K180, 000 is to be acquired in December 2012.

(f) Selling and administration expenses

	K
Sales commissions and salaries	14,300
Traveling and distribution	3,500
Office salaries	10,100
General administration expenses	2,500
	30,400

There is no opening or closing work in progress and inflation should be ignored. Budgeted cash flows are follows.

	Quarter 1	Quarter 2	Quarter 3	Quarter 4
Receipts from customers	70,000	100,000	100,000	40,000
Payments:				
Materials	7,000	9,000	10,000	5,000
Wages	33,000	20,000	11,000	15,000
Other costs and expenses	10,000	10,000	205,000	5,000

Required

Prepare the following for the year ended 31 March 2013 for CM Engineering Ltd.

(a) Sales budget
(b) Production budget (in quantities)
(c) Plant utilization budget
(d) Direct materials usage budget
(e) Direct labour budget
(f) Factory overhead budget
(g) Computation of the factory cost per unit for each product
(h) Direct materials purchases budget
(i) Cost of goods sold budget
(j) A cash budget
(k) Master budget consisting of a budgeted profit and loss account and balance sheet

Solution

(a) Sales budget

	Market demand	Selling price	Sales value
	Units	K	K
Bolts	4,500	32.00	144,000
Nuts	4,000	44.00	176,000
			320,000

(b) Production budget

	Bolts	Nuts
	Units	units
Sales requirement	4,500	4,000
(Decrease)/increase in finished goods stock	(500)	1,000
Production requirement	4,000	5,000

(c) Plant utilization budget

		Machining		Assembling	
	Units	Hours per unit	Total hours	Hours per unit	Total hours
Bolts	4,000	0.25	1,000	0.20	800
Nuts	5,000	0.40	2,000	0.30	1,500
			3,000		2,300

(d) Direct materials usage budget
Material A Machine B

		Kg	Kg
Required for production:			
Bolts:	4,000 X 1.5 kilos	6,000	-
	4,000 X 2.0 kilos	-	8,000
Nuts:	5,000 X 0.5 kilos	2,500	-
	5,000 X 4.0 kilos	-	20,000
Material usage		8,500	28,000
Unit cost		K1.50 per kilos	K1.00 per kilos
Cost of materials used		K12,750	K28,000

(e) Direct labour budget

Product	production	Hours required per unit		Rate per hour	Cost
	Units		Total hours	K	K
Bolts	4,000	6	24,000	1.60	38,400
Nuts	5,000	9	54,000	1.60	72,000
			Total direct wages		110,400

(f) Production overhead budget

	Machining dept K	Assembling dept K
Production overhead allocated and apportioned (excluding depreciation)	39,500	18,650
Depreciation costs		
(i) Existing plant		
(5% of K100, 000 in machining)	5,000	
(5% of K87, 000 in assembly)		4,350
(ii) Proposed plant		
(5% of $\underline{6}$ X K20, 000) 500		
12		
Total production overhead	45,000	4,350
Total machine hours (see (c))	3,000 hrs	2,300 hrs
Absorption rate per machine hour	K15	K10

(g) Cost of finished goods

		Bolts K		Nuts K
Direct material A	1.5 kg X K1.50	2.25	0.5 kg X K1.50	0.75
B	2.0 kg X K1.00	2.00	4.0 kg X K1.00	4.00
Production overhead				
Machining dept	15 mins at K15 per hr	3.75	24 min at K15 per hr	6.00
Assembling dept	12 mins at K110 per hr	2.00	18 mins at K10 per hr	3.00
Production cost per unit		19.60		28.15

(h) Direct material purchases budget

	A kg	B kg
Closing stock required	600	1,000
Production requirements	8,500	28,000
	9,100	29,000
Less opening stock	1,100	6,000
Purchase requirements	8,000	23,000
Cost per unit	K1.50	K1.00
Purchase costs	K12,000	K23,000

(i) Cost of goods sold budget (using FIFO)
    Niks Args

	Units		K	Units		K
Opening stocks	900	(X K20.00)	18,000	200	(X K28.00)	5,600
Cost of production	4,000	(X K19.60)	78,400	5,000	(X K28.15)	140,750
	4,900		96,400	5,200		146,350
Less closing stocks	400	(XK19.60)	7,840	1,200	(X28.15)	33,780
Cost of sales	4,500		88,560	4,000		112,570

Notes
(i) The cost of sales of Bolts = 90 units at K20 each plus 3,600 units at K19.60 each.
(ii) The cost of sales of Nuts = 200 units at K28 each plus 3,800 units at K28.15 each.

(j) Cash budget for the year to 31.3.13

	Quarter 1	Quarter 2	Quarter 3	Quarter 4	Total
	K	K	K	K	K
Receipts	70,000	100,000	100,000	40,000	310,000
Payments					
Materials	7,000	9,000	10,000	5,000	31,000
Labour	33,000	20,000	11,000	15,000	79,000
Other costs					
and expenses	10,000	100,000	205,000	5,000	230,000
	50,000	129,000	226,000	25,000	430,000
Receipts less					
payments	20,000	(29,000)	(126,000)	15,000	(120,000)
Opening cash					
balance b/f	4,300	24,300	(4,700)	(130,700)	4,300
Closing cash					
balance c/f	24,300	(4,700)	(130,700)	(115,700)	(115,700)

(k) Master Budget
Budgeted profit and loss account for year to 31.3.13

	Bolts	Nuts	Total
	K	K	K
Sales	144,000	176,000	320,000
Less cost of sales	88,560	112,570	201,130
Gross profit	55,440	63,430	118,870
Less selling and administration			30,400
Net profit			88,470

Note: There will be no under-/over-absorbed production overhead in the budgeted profit and loss account.

Budgeted balance sheet at 31.3.13

	K	K	K
Fixed assets			
Land and building (W1)			225,000
Plant and equipment at cost (W2)		207,000	
Less accumulated depreciation (W3)		84,850	
			122,150
			347,150

Current assets

Raw materials (W4)		1,900
Finished goods (W5)		41,620
Debtors (W6)		29,500
		73,020

Current liabilities

Creditors (W7)	10,750	
Bank overdraft (W8)	115,700	
		126,450
Net current liabilities		(53,430)
		293,720

Financed by
Share capital 150,000
Retained profit (W9) 143,720
293,720

Workings

1	K
Opening balance at 1.4.12	45,000
Addition	180,000
Cost at 31.3.13	225,000

2	K
Opening balance at 1.4.12	187,000
Addition	20,000
Cost at 31.3.13	207,000

3	K
Opening balance at 1.4.12	75,000
Addition in period	5,000
((f) (i) and (ii) of solution)	4,350
	500
Accumulated depreciation at 31.3.13	84,850

4	A	B	Total
Closing stock (kgs)	600	1,000	
Cost per kg	x K1.50	x K1.00	
Value of closing stock	K900	K100	K1, 900

5	Bolts	Nuts	Total
Closing stock (units)	400	1,200	
Cost per unit ((g) of solution)	xK19.60	x K28.15	
	K7,840	K33,780	K41,620

6

		K
Opening balance		19,500
Sales ((a) of solution)		320,000
Receipts (from cash budget)		(310,000)
Closing balance		29,500

7

	K	K
Opening balance at 1.4.12		6,800
Land	180,000	
Machine	20,000	
Labour	110,400	
Production overhead	39,500	
	18,650	
	58,150	
Materials	12,000	
	23,000	
Expenses	35,000	
	30,400	
Cash payments (from cash budget)		433,950
Closing balance at 31.3.13		440,750
		(430,000)

8   From cash budget K115, 750 overdrawn   10,750

9

	K
Retained profit b/f	55,250
Profit for year	88,470
Retained profit c/f	143,720

Example 4

A new company has gathered the following information for the six months from 1 January to 30 June 2007.

(a) Sales (in units) K40 per unit.

Jan.	Feb.	Mar.	Apr.	May.	June
200	300	200	400	300	400 units

(b) Production is 300 units per month for the whole 6 months.

(c) Fixed overheard costs will be K3000 per month, payable in the month after production.

(d) Variable overhead costs will be K15 per unit payable in the month of production.

(e) Direct wages will be K5 per unit payable in the month of production.

(f) Equipment costing K10 000 will be purchased in February and paid for in March. Once installed, it will allow production to increase to 500 units per month.

(g) Materials will cost K8 per unit and suppliers will be paid in the month following purchases.

(h) All sales of units are on credit. Debtors are expected to pay on 1 January is K10 000.

Required :

Prepare a schedule of payments and a cash budget for the six month period, January to June.

Solution

Schedule of payments

	Jan. K	Feb. K	Mar. K	Apr. K	May. K	June K
• Fixed overheard	-	3000	3000	3000	3000	3000
• Variable overheard (300 X K15)	4500	4500	4500	4500	4500	4500
• Direct wages (300 X K5)	1500	1500	1500	1500	1500	1500
• Equipment	-	-	10 000	-	-	-
• Materials (300 X K8)	-	2400	2400	2400	2400	2400
	6000	11400	21400	11400	11400	11400

Cash budget

	Jan K	Feb K	Mar K	Apr K	May K	June K
• Receipts (sales)	-	8000	12000	8000	16000	12000
• Payments	6000	11000	21000	11400	11400	11400
• Receipts less Payments	(6000)	(3400)	(9400)	(3400)	4600	600
• Bank balance b/f	10 000	4000	600	(8800)	(12200)	(7600)
• Bank balance c/f	4000	600	(8800)	(12200)	(7600)	(7000)

Note that receipts are calculated at K40 units' sales, allowing for one month credit.

Comment

The cash budget clearly highlights that the company does not have sufficient cash resources to finance the above plan. However, if it could lease the new equipment rather than buy it, or obtain more capital by March, the problem would be solved. If the company had not prepared a cash flow budget it would have had a deficit from March to June of a proportion it may not have planned.

By preparing a cash budget, the company can demonstrate it has some control in its financial affairs and is therefore more likely to accommodate the deficit period by negotiation with its creditors.

Example 5

The following information relates to a businessman, Francis Choonya, who has started business on1 January with K5000. He has made a forecast for the next six months concerning receipts and payments of cash:

(a) Production will involve the making of a freeze-it making machine. His plan is to produce 500 units per month in the first six months.

(b) Sales: each unit has a selling price of K12.50. the sales estimate for six months to 30 June was:

Jan	Feb	Mar	Apr	May	June
400	480	480	560	640	400 units

(c) Variable overheads (based on output) will be K1.50 per unit, payable in the month of production.

(d) Fixed costs will be K1000 per month payable in the month of production.

(e) Production wages (direct) will be K3 per unit payable in the month of production.

(f) Salaries will be K500 per month until April, but expected to arise by 10% in the following months.

(g) Equipment costing K8000 will be purchased in March. A 25% deposit will be paid in March, with the balance to be paid in the month after the purchase.

(h) All unit sales are on credit. Debtors are expected to pay in the month following their purchase.

(i) K500 was deposited in the business book account on 1 January.

Required:

(a) Prepare a cash budget covering the six month period from January to June
(b) Briefly analyze the cash budget
(c) Prepare an operating budget which will show to 30 June and a forecast balance sheet as on that date.

Cash budget

	Jan	Feb	Mar	Apr	May	June	Total
	K	K	K	K	K	K	K
Receipt:							
Sales	0	5000	6000	6000	7000	8000	32000
Payments:							
• Fixed costs	0	1000	1000	1000	1000	1000	5000
• Variable overheard) (500 X K1.50)	750	750	750	750	750	750	4500
• Production wages (500 X K3)	1500	1500	1500	1500	1500	1500	9000
• Salaries	500	500	500	550	550	550	3100
• Materials (500 K2)	0	1000	1000	1000	1000	1000	5000
• Equipment	0	0	2000	3000	3000	0	8000
Total payments	2750	4750	6750	7750	7800	4800	34600
Net cash flow	(2750)	250	(750)	(1750)	(800)	3200	(2600)
Opening balance	5000	2250	2500	1750	0	(800)	5000
Closing balance	2250	2500	1750	0	(800)	2400	2400

(a) Analysis of the cash budget

Note the different format of this cash budget including totals. Receipts are matched against payments so that an increase or decrease results. This is then added or subtracted to the opening bank balance to arrive at the bank balance carried forward (closing balance). In January, a decrease of K2 750 is deducted from the opening bank balance of K5000, providing a closing balance of K2 250.

From the forecast of cash flow, it appears that Francis may be a little short of liquidity in the months of April and May. This is not surprising because part of his expenditure is capital expenditure, purchasing equipment in March of K8000 and finishing the payment for it in May. He could ask the bank to tide him over during these months by arranging for an overdraft facility. He could, if he wanted, finance the asset purchase in other ways, probably by simply extending the period of
credit over 12 months or even more.

In June, however, the cash flow is back in surplus and certainly appears sound. Cash flow forecasts business liquidity. Can sales generate sufficient receipts of money to be able to finance labour, materials, overheard and capital expenditure?

Thus, budgets are an important management tool if they are taken seriously

(b) The operating budget refers to the forecast trading and profit and loss account and the balance sheet as on 30 June.

FRANCIS CHOONYA

BUDGETED TRADING FOR SIX MONTHS ENDING 30 JUNE

	K	K	K
Sales			37000
Less cost of sales			
• Stock (1/1)	0		
• Production cost	19500		
• Stock (30/6)	(260)		19240
Gross profit			17760
Expenses:			
• Fixed costs	5000		
• + Accrued (1 month)	1000	6000	
Salaries		3100	
Depreciating of equipment		800	9900
Net profit			7860

Workings:

1. Sales forecast is 2 9260 units X K12.50 per unit = K37000
2. The first six production months at 500 units per month would cost

	K
• Wages 3000 X K3	= 9000
• Variable overheard 3000 X K1.5	= 4500
• Materials 3000 X K2	= 6000
Total cost 1	9500 (production)

There was no opening stock because it was a new business and therefore there will be no closing stock carried forward from the previous period.

- If the closing stock was to be valued at production cost per unit then:

  Units produced: 3000 units
  Units sold   2960 units
                     ___
                      40 units in stock X production cost per unit

  Value of closing stock: 40 X K6.5 per unit = K260

- As far as any adjustments are concerned, Francis decided to depreciate the equipment by 20% per annum and a full 10% for the six months, even though it was to be purchased in March.

FRANCIS CHOONYA

BUDGETED BALANCE SHEET AS AT 30 JUNE

	Cost K	Dep K	NBV K
Non Current Assets:			
• Equipment	8000	800	7200
Current Assets			
• Inventory	260		
• Trade receivables(400 X K12.50)	5000		
• Bank	2400	7660	
Current Liabilities			
• Trade payables (500 X K2)	1000		
• Accruals (1 month fixed cost)	1000	2000	
• Working capital			5660
			12860
Financed by:			
• Capital (1 Jan.)	5000		
• + Net profit	7860		12860

Comment

Francis's prospects look very sound for a period covering the first six months' trading as far as the above data is concerned.

PROGRESS CLINIC 16

Question 1

1. I.G Agencies Limited has a cash balance of K800 000 on 31 December 2006. You are required to prepare a cash budget for January through March 2007 from the following details:

(a)

Month	Actual sales K'000		Forecast sales K'000
September 2006	2000	January	2800
October	2000	February	3200
November	2400	March	4000
December	2400	April	4000

(b) Debtors: 50% of total sales are for cash. The balance will be collected equally during the following two months. No debts are anticipated.

(c) Cost of goods manufactured equivalent to 70% of sales; 90% of this cost is paid during the month of purchase; the balance is paid in the subsequent month.

(d) Sales and administrative expenses: K400 000 per month plus 10% of sales. All these expenses are paid during the month of expenditure.

(e) interest payments: Semi-annual interest of K720 000 is paid in March. An annual K2000 000 sinking fund payment is also made at the same time.

(f) dividends: K400 000 dividend payment will be declared and made in March.

Capital expenditure: K16,000,000 will be spent in February

Taxes: The quarterly installment of K40 000 will be made in March.

Question 2

John Hake retired from government service in 2005 and received K10.0 million cheque retirement package. He started a 'Kantemba" business but became very unsuccessful, leaving him near-bankrupt. However, he still owns a house (residential property) in Kamwala.

"Look here, friend", he said. "I know where I went wrong and I will now get it right, so I want the security". John intends to revive his Kantemba business along the following lines:
(a) his current bank balance is K100 000
(b) the mark-up on his sales is 25%
(c) The first quarter sales shall be K1.5 million in the first month. Thereafter an increase of K500 000 per month.

The sales for the second and third quarters shall be K7.2 million and K8.4 million respectively to K9.0 million for the forth quarter. The monthly sales shall accrue evenly throughout the last three quarters.

    (a) There will be no stock at the end of each month.
    (b) Sales collection are:

        i)   50% same month
        ii) 30% first month after sale
        iii) 20% second month after sale

    (c) He will enjoy 60 days credit terms from suppliers

    (d) Wages bill of K250 000 will be paid at the end of each month

    (e) He intends to rent a store at Lumumba Market for which he will pay rent K50 000 per month, payable six months in advance, that is in month 1 and 7.

    (f) He will rent out his servant's quarter at K40 000 per month, receivable quarterly in advance at the beginning of each quarter.

    (g) He expects all expenses to be K150 000 per month, paid for in cash as they accrue.

    (h) In month 2 purchase a second-hand van for k6.0 million cash. It is to used for four years with no residue value. Straight-line method of depreciation is preferred.

Required: For the first year of trading

    (a) Cash budget
    (b) Budgeted profit and loss statement by quarter
    (c) Assessment of the project

Question 3

On January 1 2007 the summary balance sheet of PCBF was as follows:

	K'000		K'000
Share capital	400 000	Machinery at cost	800 000
15% loan stock	400 000	Less: Accrue Depreciation	(192 000)
Reserves	200 000	Stocks	242 000
Proposed dividends	10 000	Debtors	250 000
Bank overdraft	90 000		
	1,100,000		1,100,000

The following are expected during the next three months

Month	Sales K'000	Purchases K'000	Expenses K'000
January	1 500 000	1 000 000	200 000
February	2 000 000	1 500 000	250 000
March	3 000 000	2 800 000	300 000

All sales are on credit the collections have the next three months

- During the month of sale: 80% (a 4% discount is given for payment in this period)
- In the subsequent month: 20%.

Payment for purchases is made in the month of purchase in order to take advantage of a 10% profit settlement discount, Calculated on the gross purchase figures shown above.

Stock levels are expected to remain constant throughout the period.

Depreciation of machinery is calculated at 12% per annum on cost. The approximate portion for each month January to March is included in the expenses figures above. Expenses are paid for in the month they are incurred.

The proposed dividends will be paid in January. Loan interest for the three months will be paid in March.

Required:

(a) Prepare a cash budget for each of the three months January to March
(b) Prepare a forecast trading profit and loss account for the period
(c) Prepare a forecast balance sheet as at 31 March
(d) Briefly explain why the change in cash balance between 1 January and 31 March is not the same as profit (or) loss figure for the period.

BOOK TWO
Financial Management

BOOK TWO

Financial Management

CHAPTER 17

INTRODUCTION TO CORPORATE FINANCE

The study of corporate finance looks at the sources of finance and utilization of funds for limited liability companies. These are companies that are incorporated.

Corporate finance does not include sources of funding for unincorporated business such as sole traders and partnerships. Limited liability companies are special in that they operate as separate legal entities from their managers and owners. They are therefore called artificial persons for they can own resources, employ and fire workers and enter into any form of contract that a natural person can enter into. The fact that corporate entities have limited liability is very important because if a limited company fails to repay creditors, all that creditors would lay their hands on would be the assets of the company and nothing more.

The tenets of financial management

Financial management revolves around four different but related areas. These are:

1. **Financing decision**s – these are concerned with how the firm should sources finances. It looks at what are the available sources of finance for the company. It also considers what the appropriate capital structure is for the firm. i.e. a balance between equity and debt capital. Finally financing decisions also looks at the various costs of different sources of finance. The key object of financing decisions is to ensure that the company can raise the appropriate finance as and when required at the minimum possible cost.

2. **Investment decision** – once the firm has raised the needed funds, the next important question is how to utilize those funds. Thus, the investment decision will come up with a clear policy of the methods to be used in appraising projects and the decision criteria. The main objective of the investment decision also called capital budgeting is to ensure that the firm's resources that are scarce are only invested into those projects that will maximize future benefits of the firm. Therefore, the key topic under investment decisions is investment appraisal.

3. **Dividend decision** – this is concerned with the distribution of the company's profit to the shareholders. It is concerned with how much or what percentage of profit should be distributed to shareholders as dividends and how much should be retained for further expansion of the firm. The shareholders being the true owners of the firm will want to receive some returns from their investment. If these returns are not forthcoming, they might shift their investment to competitors. This will have a negative effect on the firm's performance of stock on the Stock Exchange.

4. **Financial analysis** – this is concerned with analyzing the financial position of the firm as shown in the balance sheet and the financial performance as shown in income

statement or the profit and loss account. The major tool used here is the ratio analysis. The calculation of ratios helps in determining the trends in the financial position and performance of the firm.

Corporate objectives

A firm is made up of two or more people who meet on a relatively continuous basis to achieve certain goals, which they cannot achieve as individuals. Form the above definition it can be seen that every firm is a social entity i.e. comprises of people and exist for a purpose. Though there are no generally acceptable conclusions regarding corporate objective, the following are the more important ones.

1. **Maximization of shareholder's wealth (profitability)**—this is assumed to be the primary objective of a private limited company. The company must be able to provide objective, the following can also be noted.

2. **Company growth** – most companies have the objective of growing as time passes by. Corporate growth is one issue, which symbolizes corporate success.

3. **Improved productivity** – every company would Endeavour to be as efficient as possible so as to gain competitive advantage

4. **Market leadership** – a company may pursue the objective of being the leader in the marketing of an identified product.

5. **Customer satisfaction** – every progressive company would want to satisfy its customers with its product or service.

6. **Employee satisfaction**—a company can only achieve customer satisfaction if the employees who deal with the customers are highly motivated and satisfied with their jobs.

7. **Innovation** – a company may pursue this objective by investing a lot of funds in research and development and also encouraging the culture of innovation.

8. **Survival** – companies that are facing financial difficulties such as threat of a takeover or liquidation will have as their main aim survival. All its activities will be directed at ensuring that it does not go under.

9. **Social responsibility** – a number of companies now are including social responsibility as one of the key objectives to be pursued.

From above, it could be seen that a firm may have a multiple of objectives to pursue. However, all these objectives can be summarized into four broad categories namely:

(a) Profitability i.e. the maximization of the wealth of shareholders

(b) Surrogate profitability objectives these include

    i.   Higher production
    ii. Customer satisfaction
    iii. Employee satisfaction

(c) Those objectives which reduce profits such as social responsibility

(d) Dysfunctional objectives which are contrary to profit objectives e.g. pursuance of market share at whatever cost.

Finally, all corporate objectives must meet the SMART criteria i.e. they should be specific, measurable, achievable, realistic and time bound.

Corporate social responsibility (CSR)

Corporate social responsibility is a new phenomenon in corporate governance. It arises from the recognition that a firm does not only exist for shareholders but for wider interest groups as well. It takes the stakeholders view of the organization as opposed to the shareholders view of the organization. The major stakeholders or interest group are:

    i.   Shareholders
    ii.   Employees
    iii. Customers
    iv. Suppliers
    v.   Lenders
    vi. Government and its agencies
    vii. Competitors
    viii. The general public

In its pursuit of the objectives of trying to satisfy the shareholders, it must take cognizance of the other stakeholders. It is much easier for the company to satisfy the needs of shareholders because they are required to do so by law. Companies are required to present the annual report to shareholders. But it is difficult to satisfy the objectives of all the other stakeholders. A good example of how a socially responsible company can satisfy the other stakeholders are:

(a) For customers – by ensuring that the firm supplies goods and services that are of high quality at affordable prices

(b) For lenders – by ensuring that the company pays the amount due as required

(c) For the government and government agencies – by ensuring that the company operates within the remits of the law by say paying tax due, avoiding pollution etc.

(d) For employees – by ensuring that the company provides job security, career development, safe and healthy working conditions.

(e) For competitors – by ensuring that the company does not win th4e customers by using anticompetitive means.

Examples of areas where banks have carried out CRS include:

Establishing community schools for the under privileged
  (a) Electing homes for the old aged
  (b) Providing some scholarships to under privileged students
  (c) Sponsoring sport and other related activities
  (d) Helping establish rural health centers

Whenever a company exercises CRS, this normally comes as a reduction to the company's profit and eventually the dividends that should be received by the shareholders. However, companies will always pursue CSR as it enhances the company's image in the eyes of the public.

The company will enjoy respect as a good neighbour. Some social responsibility activities also serve as a way of advertising the company and its products to the general public. This is public relations.

Value for money (VFM)

Value for money is an approach that recognizes the fact that not all organizations have profit maximization as the primary objective. Value for money simply refers to getting the best at an appropriate cost. It is mainly concerned with the quality of service provided at a given cost. It is very important for non-profit making organizations. For example, many NGOs are financed by well-wishers who do not wish to see profit at the end but all they need I that the service that has been provided is of high quality in relation to the expenditure.

Value for money as a concept has three main aspects. These are:

1. **Economy** – this means that the costs of input must be less than the benefits realized

2. **Efficiency** – this compares the relationships between inputs and outputs. If the efficiently ratio is falling, it is an indication of the improvement in overall efficiency.

3. **Effectiveness** – this refers to the response time and whether the service provided meets the set objectives.

The above three aspects are the main areas where performance for non-profit making organization can be measured. Finally, it should be noted value for money does not mean that

the product has to be produced at the lowest cost. Instead, it relates the cost to the quality of the service.

Agency-conflict

Managers are empowered by the owners of the firm – shareholders – to make decisions. However, managers may have personal goals that compete with shareholder wealth maximization and such potential conflicts of interest are dealt with under agency.

An agency relationship arises whenever one or more individual, called principals, (1) hires another individual or firm, called an agent, to some service and (2) then delegates decision-making authority to that agent. Within the financial management context, the primary agency relationships are those (1) between shareholders and managers and (2) between managers and debt holders.

Agency conflict: shareholders versus managers

A potential agency problem arises whenever the manager of a firm owns less than 100% of firm's ordinary shares. In most large corporations, potential agency conflicts are important because large firm's managers generally own only a small percentage of the shares. In this situation, shareholder wealth maximization could take a back seat to any number of conflicting manager's goals. For example, people have argued that some manager's primary aim seems to be to maximize the size of their firms.

By creating a larger rapidly growing firm, managers (1) increase their job security, because a hostile takeover is less likely (2) increase their own power, status and salaries (3) create more opportunities for their lower-and middle-level managers.

Furthermore, since the managers own only a small of percentage of the stock, it has been argued that they have a voracious appetite for salaries and perquisites, and that they generously contribute corporate funds to their favourite charities because they get the glory but outside shareholders bear the cost.

In particular, the following are the areas of conflict between shareholders and management:

a). **Time horizon.** One of the parties may be interested in short term objectives while the other in long term objectives. For example, managers may be interested in short term objectives so as to receive their benefits. This is because they are free to leave at any time in search of greener pastures.

b).**Renumeration**. Managers may award themselves excellent conditions of service which shareholders may not be happy with for example, driving very expensive personal-to-holders cars.

c).Merger and takeovers. Shareholders may welcome a takeover bid willingly while managers may try to repel it. This is because when a company is taken over management is always bound to be replaced.

d)Attitude to risk. Shareholders may be risk lovers while managers may be risk averse and vice versa. This means that this is another important area of agency conflict. For example, shareholder may wish manager to assume high risk projects with high returns while managers may be reluctant to do so. This is because high risk projects may make the company fail and they will have no jobs while shareholders may have investments elsewhere.

Measures to bring about Goal Congruence

Obviously, managers can be encouraged to act in the best interest of the shareholders through a set of incentives, constraints and punishments. |However, these tools are more effective if shareholders can observe all the actions taken by managers
A potential moral hazard problem, wherein agents take unobserved actions in their own behalf, arises, because it if not virtually important for shareholders to monitor all managerial actions.

In general, to reduce both agency conflicts and the moral hazard problem, shareholders must incur agency costs, which include costs borne by shareholders to encourage managers to maximize the firm 's stock price rather than act in their own self-interests.
There are three major categories of agency costs:

1. Expenditures to monitor managerial actions, such as audit costs

2. Expenditure to structure the organization in a way that will limit undesirable managerial behaviour, such as appointing outside investors to the board of directors.

3. opportunity costs which are incurred when shareholders – imposed restrictions, such as requirements for stockholder wealth votes on certain issues, limit the ability of the managers to take timely actions that would enhance shareholder wealth.

Agency conflicts 2: shareholders versus creditors

Creditors have a claim on part of firm's earnings stream for payment of interest and principal on the debt, and they have a claim on the firm's assets in the event of bankruptcy. However, shareholders have control (though the manager) of decision that affect the riskiness of the firm. Creditors lend funds at rates that are based on:

1. the riskiness of the firm's existing assets
2. Expectations concerning the riskiness of future asset additions
3. The firm's existing capital structure i.e. amount of debt finance used
4. Expectations concerning future capital structure decisions.

These are the primary determinants of the riskiness of a firm's cash flows, hence the safety of its debt issues.

Creditors attempt to protect themselves against shareholders by placing restrictive covenants in debt agreement. Moreover, if creditors perceive that a firm's managers are trying to take advantage of them, they will either refuse to deal further with it or else will charge a higher than normal interest rate to compensate for the risk of possible exploitation. Thus, firms which deal unfairly with creditors either lose access to the debt markets or are saddled with high interest rates and restrictive covenants, all of which are detrimental to shareholders.

Thus, in order to best serve their shareholders in the long run, managers must play fairly with creditors. Managers as agents of both shareholders and creditors must act in a manner that is fairly balanced between the two classes of security holders.

Financial institutions and markets

Most firms have an ongoing need for funds. They can obtain funds from external sources in 3 ways namely:

- **Financial Institution**: These institutions accept savings and transfer them to those that need funds.

- **Financial Markets**: These are organized forums in which the suppliers and users of various types of funds can make transactions.
- **Private Placement**: This involves the sale of a new security, typically bonds or preference shares, directly to an investor or group of investors such as insurance companies or pension funds. They have an unstructured nature.

Financial institutions

These serve as intermediaries by channeling the savings of individuals, businesses and governments into loans or investments. Many financial institutions directly or indirectly pay interest on deposited funds, others provide services for a fee (for example, current accounts institution accept customer's savings deposits and lend this money to other customers or to firms: Others invest customers' savings in earning assets such as real estate or shares and bonds.

Financial markets

These are forums in which supplier of funds and users of funds can transact business directly. Suppliers in the financial markets know where their funds are being lent or invested. Two key financial markets are the money market (i.e. short term debt instruments or marketable securities) and the capital market (i.e. long term securities-bonds and shares).

The relationship between institutions and markets

Financial institutions actively participate in the financial markets as both supplier and users of funds.

- **The Money Market**: This is created by a financial relationship between suppliers and users of short term funds (funds with maturities of one year or loss). The money market exists because some individuals, businesses, governments, and financial institutions have temporarily idle funds that they wish to put to some interest-earning use. Most money market transactions are made in marketable securities-short term debt instruments. By definition, the duration of transaction is up to one year.

- **The Capital Market**: The capital market is a market that enables suppliers and users of long-term funds to make long-term transactions. Included are securities issues of business and government. The backbone of capital market is formed by various securities exchanges that provide a forum for bond and share transactions.

CHAPTER 18

SOURCES OF FINANCE

A company may need additional finance for funding working capital or fixed assets. This finding can either come from the share holders of the firm or outsiders to the firm (lenders). The financial intermediaries play an important role in linking the borrowers with ultimate lenders.

Factors to consider when choosing the right source finance

The finance manager must consider the following factors when dealing on the appropriate source of finance for the company.

1. **Cost** – Generally debt finance is cheaper than equity financing. This is because the risk born holders. Further debt has tax allowances. That the right source of finance should be one which is cost effective.

2. **Duration** – In financial management the rule of the thumb states "working capital should be financed from short term sources while fixed asset should be financed from long-term sources".

3. **Gearing** – Gearing is the ratio of equity to debt capital. A firm that is highly geared will find it difficult to raise additional finding through borrowing, this is because lenders perceive it to be a high risk borrower especially if profit prospects are not very good.

4. **Security** – The finance manager must understand what type of collateral is required by the various lenders.

5. **Accessibility** – Not all sources of finance are available to all businesses for example, an unlisted company cannot raise funds through the stock exchange. This means that sources of finding is not available to such organization.

6. **Term structure of interest rates** – the term structure of interest rates show the relationship between the market interests and the maturity of the instruments generally lenders charge higher interests rates for long term borrowing than what is charged for short term borrowing to account for the increased risk. Thus it is important to monitor the charges in interest's rates

7. **Amount** – Note all sources of finance may provide the right amount, it is therefore important to determine which source will provide the amount with some kind of flexibility.

8. **Purpose** – The purpose for which the finding is require may dictate the right source of finance, for example one may not arrange for an overdraft to by fixed assets

Sources of finance

These may be classified as follows depending on time and source

Short term, medium and long tern sources of finance – time

Equity and debt capital – source

Short term sources – up to 12 months

These include:

1. Short term bank loan
2. Bank overdraft
3. Trade creditors
4. Accruals
5. Delayed payments
6. Factoring
7. Invoice discounting
8. Commercial paper
9. Bankers acceptances

Short Term Bank Loan

- it can be accessed by both account and non account holders
- it can be used for both working capital and fixed assets
- security is normally required for the facility
- there is an arrangement fee charged by the lenders
- interest rate charged is normally fixed
- interest is charged on the whole amount agreed upon whether used or not
- if any adjustment is made to increase the amount a fresh application is required.

Bank Overdraft

- this is available to current account holders only
- interest is charged on the outstanding balance that is on the actual amount overdrawn
- interest is normally floating or variable
- the overdraft is payable on demand
- generally no security is required for the facility
- it is highly flexible as long as the amount needed fall within the agreed overdraft limit, that is there is no need for fresh application when the overdraft limit is not exceeded

Trade Creditors

- This is a free spontaneous source of funding. It is spontaneous because if depends on the volume and value of credit, purchases, the higher the volume and value of credit purchases the higher the amount of funding from this source.
- It is free because there is no interest charged as it arises from the normal trading activities
- It is the major source of funding for super markets.

Accruals

Accruals represent the liabilities which have already been incurred and not yet paid for:

The common sources here include:

- Salaries delayed for a month and a tax liability to ZRA which are paid quarterly semiannually and sometimes annually, thus the company is able to borrow from the employees and ZRA at no cost.

Delayed Payments

Delayed payments as a source of finance involves the exceeding the specified period for settlement.

- delay payments must be at the concept of the other party. E.g. the supplier.

- it is a free source of fiancé and the company can have huge amounts available for other purposes, however delaying payment namely have negative effects to the company for example suppliers may no longer be interested in extending credit to the company and the company may also loose out it may receive bad publicity.

Factoring

This is financing from the debtors accounts; the factor will make an advance payment to the firm and change a certain percentage as commission. The factor will then undertake sales ledger administration monitoring of debtors accounts as well as actual collection from the debtors.

The factoring service may be with or without recourse.
The major advantage with company is that it is able to receive immediate cash from credit sales as well as some cash servings involved in sales ledger administration and collection cost.

The major drawback is that the debtors will perceive that the company is experiencing a financial crisis for it to hand the debtors to the factor.

Invoice Discounting

This is similar to factoring except that the company continues with its responsibilities with sales ledger administration and debt collection.

Commercial Paper

This is a short term unsecured source of funding involving large corporations, a large corporation can borrow immediate funds by issuing commercial paper which is sold to other corporations, the company issuing commercial paper must be of good credit standing.

Bankers' Acceptances

This is a source of funding involving discounting bills of exchange. Banks are able to accept the bill pay an amount less than the face value and recover the amount with commission when the bill matures.

Medium term sources of finance (intermediate) leasing

A lease is a contract between a leassor and the lessee for the hire of a particular asset.

The leaser retains ownership of the asset but conveys the right to the use of the asset to the leasee for an agreed period in return of payment for specialized rentals.

Leasing is now common for vehicles, office and production equipment etc.

Leasing is therefore a means of financing the use of capital equipment, the underline principle being that use is more important than ownership.

There are different types of lease arrangement; in particular lease purchases are the modern equivalent of Hire Purchase (HP). There are fundamentally two types of lease agreements namely:

1. **Capital or Finance Lease**

   This is one in which the leaser transfers substantially all the risks and rewards of ownership of an asset to the leasee.

2. **Operating Lease**

   This is defined as nay other lease apart from finance lease, the major difference between the two are summarised below:

Finance lease	Operating lease
● One lease exists for the whole useful life	● The lease period is less than the useful
● The leaser does not retain the risks or Rewards of ownership.	● The leaser is normally responsible for Repairs and maintenance.
● the lease agreement can't be cancelled	● The lease can sometimes be cancelled at short notice.
● the leaser does not usually deal directly In this type of asset.	● The leaser may very well carry on a trade in this type of assets.
● The substance of the transaction is the Purchase of the asset by leasee, financed By a loan from the leaser	● The substance of the transaction is the short term rental of an asset.

The popularity of leasing has grown over recent years as the medium term source of finance.

The reasons behind this popularity include the following:

- Easy of borrowing – In a lease transaction, the asset provides the needed security itself, there is not even the need even to cross examine the financial standing of the leasee.

- Flexibility – a lease transaction particularly on operating lease can be highly flexible in the sense that it can be cancelled at short notice to reflect changes in technology.

- Cash flow – lease transaction perceives and smoothens the cash flow of the business, this is because rental payments are structured throughout the life of the asset.

- Cost – lease transactions have some cost advantage for the leaser, allowing the leaser to charge very attractive rental payments than could be charged over the traditional loan

- This is possible of lower administration cost involved in a lease transaction.

Medium term bank loan

This is similar to a short term bank loan, the only term that it is for more than one year.

Long term sources of finance

Long term sources of finance may either be debt capital, that is debentures or equity capital that is ordinary shares and preference shares.

A debenture is a written acknowledgment of a debt by a company normally containing provisions as to the payment of interest and the terms and repayment of principle. It may also be referred to as a corporate bond or a loan stock.

Debentures are traded on the stock market, in much the same way as shares and may be secured or unsecured and redeemable or irredeemable. Debenture holders owe creditors of the company and they rank first in an event where the company is liquidated.

The term bond is now usually to mean any kind of long term marketable debt securities.

Equity capital is divided into ordinary shares and preference shares.

The major difference between ordinary and preference shares are the following.

Ordinary shares	preference shares
- they have voting rights at the company AGM	- they don't have the voting right at the company's AGM
- they receive variable dividends depending on the performance of the company and the declaration of the board of directors	- they receive fixed dividends regardless of the performance of the company. If the company has not performed well, areas are where they will rank before ordinary share holders receive
- They rank after preference shares in payment under a liquidation exercise	- They are paid before ordinary share holders receive anything
- Legally a company can be financed by wholly by ordinary shares alone.	- legally a company cant be financed from preference shares alone.

Because of the special characteristics of preference shares they are treated as part of debt capital in financial analysis. This is the reason why preference shares are included as part of prior charge capital in the calculation of the company's gearing.

Hybrid of debt and equity

The following sources of finance are said to be hybrid of debts and equity because they have the element of both equity and debt. They include the following:

Convertibles

These are issues of bond that gives the holder the right to convert to other securities normally ordinary shares at a predetermined price, rate and time.

The conventional rights on convertibles are either estimated in terms of a conversion ratio that is the number of ordinary shares to a given debt or in terms of conversion price, which is the right to convert in ordinary shares at a given specified price.

A conversion premium exists when the market value of convertibles exceeds the current market price of the sharers into which they are or will become convertibles.

Warrants

A warrant gives the holder the right to subscribe at fixed future date for a certain number of ordinary shares at a predetermined price.

The difference between warrants and convertibles is that with the warrant a loan stock itself is not converted into equity but bond holders make cash payment to acquire the shares and retain their loan stock.

This means that the loan stock will continue in existence until it is redeemed.

Attractions of convertibles and warrants as a source of finance

A warrant is merely an option not linked to an underlined security while a convertible combines an option with a debenture.

The following are the advantages

Advantages

1. Immediate finance at low cost

    Because of the conversion option, the loan can be received at below normal interest rates.
2. Self liquidating where the loans are converted into shares. The problem of repayment disappears.

3. Attractive share prices

    Where the company wishes to raise equity finance but share prices are currently depressed, convertibles offer a back door share issue method.

4. Exercises of warrants related to need for finance

Options would normally only be exercised where the share price has increased.

If the option involves the payment of extra cash to the company, this creates extra funds when they are needed for expansion.

The stock exchange

The stock exchange is an organization which provides a marked for companies' shares and debentures and certain other securities. It thus allows the transfer of these investments from one owner to another.

It does not itself contribute any funds to the process and is not therefore, directly the mechanism by which a business gains access to funds.

It thus fulfills the same kind of function for shares as is performed for property by an estate agent.

The Lusaka Stock Exchange (LuSE) is Zambian's only stock exchange market. LuSE functions both as a primary marked and secondary market.

A primary market is one in which organizations raise new funds by issuing shares or loan stock. The primary market is also called the new issue market.

A secondary market is one for dealing in existing securities.

Firms do not raise new funds in the secondary market. In additional to acting as primary and secondary market for shares and loan stock, the LuSE also functions as a market for dealings in Gilts (government securities).

Interims of operations the LuSE is divided into two categories as follows:

A. **The main market**

This is the market which are fully listed are dealt with.

B. **Second tier Market** – The second tier market which is commonly referred as the alternative investment market is designed to deal with small companies which cannot manage to obtain full listing.

Requirements for obtaining full listing

The listing rules are contained in the stock exchange yellow book and the yellow seeks to secure the confidence of investors in the conduct of the market.
This is done by

1. Ensuring that application for listing one of at least of the minimum size. The size rules relate to the market capitalization and annual profit figures.

2. Requiring the companies to have a successful track record of at least three years.

3. ensuring that companies requesting listing at least appears to be financially stable

4. Insisting that a sufficient number of shares of a tradable value made available to the general public to allow a free marked to exist in the companies shares.

5. Requiring directors of the company to make a company resolution to adopt the terms and conditions of the stock exchange listing agreement. This includes the provision of sufficient information e.g. interim results to form a reliable basis for market evaluation note that a firm is said to be listed if its shares are publicly held. The other term that relate to listing include public flotation, going public or getting a listing on the stock exchange.

Advantages and disadvantages of full listing

Form the companies' view of pond there are both advantages and disadvantages in obtaining a full listing.

Advantages

i. once listing is obtained a company will generally find borrowing funds easier as its credit rating will be enhanced
ii. Additional long term funding can be raised by a new issue of securities.
iii. Shares can be easily traded facilitating the expansion of capital base.
iv. Future acquisitions will generally be easier because the company will have the ability to issue equity as a consideration for a transaction
v. Shares options can be arranged potentially attracting the highest caliber of employees
vi. The profit of business and its management team can be raised considerably
vii. There are tax reduction advantages for listed companies
viii. Property transfer tax is not paid
ix. The company gains better prestige
x. There is better price formation of shares in the secondary market.

Disadvantages

i. publicity will not be always of advantage
ii. The costs of entry to stock exchange are high
iii. At least some control will be lost when shares are available to the general public
iv. The requirements of the stock exchange are owners and compliance is enforceable
v. The company can potentially be more exposed to a hostile takeover bid
vi. Costs of share issues.

Costs involved in stock issues include:

i. Fees of advisors and sponsors
ii. Underwriting costs
iii. The compulsory advertising in newspapers
iv. The printing and distribution costs of details and prospectors
v. Compliance with stock exchange rules is also a cost to be born by a company

Methods of Issuing Shares to Various Investors

The following are the most common methods that firms can use to raise equity finance

1. **Public offer (offer for sale)** – This method is used by a large corporations in need of raising huge sums of money. It is the most common method of issuing shares to new investors and also bringing a company to a market quotation. An institution, usually a merchant bank, called an issuing house, offers the shares to the general public through what is called an Initial Public Offer (IPO).

   It involves a company making an appeal to the general public to subscribe for its shares. The company is required to prepare and publish and distribute a prospectus which shows the company's performance in the past three years as well as its future prospects. This prospectus must be advertised in newspapers. This is done to ensure that potential investors receive sufficient relevant information to enable them to decide whether or not to buy the shares. Usually, the application for allotment form accompanies the prospectus. With this method the company can raise large sums of money required as long as the company' reputation is beyond reproach. However, this is the most expensive method of all.

2. **Private placing** – This is mainly used by private limited companies. It involves identifying potential investors who are approached to buy the shares. There is not general invitation to the public to purchase shares. Instead, the issuing house or sponsoring broker buys the shares and places them directly with its clients (normally institutional investors such as Pension Funds, Insurance companies and Unit trusts). To ensure a market for these shares the Stock Exchange insists that the issuing house make 25% of the shares being placed available to the Stock market through market makers so that they can reach the general public. The Stock Exchange does not like companies making new issues by this method because it tends to mean that the new shareholders gain at the expense of the existing shareholders and the market in shares is not sufficiently wide. It will therefore only allow such an issue when it involves a small amount of capital and where the offer for sale method is not available. Companies often prefer placing as they are cheaper and quicker to arrange than other methods of issuing shares. The method does not require the preparation of prospectus hence cheaper then public offer

3. **Rights issue** – This is the issue of new shares to existing share holders on a pro rata basis, that is, at price lower than the current market share price. It is an offer to existing shareholders which enables them to subscribe for additional shares in proportion to their existing holdings. This is because shareholders enjoy **Pre-emptive rights.** A rights issue cannot be used in conjunction with obtaining a listing on the a Stock Exchange but is used by companies which are already quoted and wishing to raise more capital. Rights issues are cheaper than an offer for sale since there is not a requirement to produce a prospectus and they are sometimes not underwritten. Since the company is rising funds from its own members, administrative costs are much

lower than any of the above two methods. There is also a greater chance of making a successful issue, first, because of the pricing structure and, second, because it is made to existing shareholders who presumably are satisfied with their investment.

However, if company needs large sums of money this method may not suffice as the existing share holders may not have that money or may not be willing to invest more funds in the company, for whatever reasons.

4. **Fixed price issue**. The majority of offers for sale are at affixed price. This is determined by the company in conjunction with the issuing house and with advice from a firm of stock-brokers. Setting an issue price can be difficult. If it is too low then a large number of applications will be received resulting in the issue being oversubscribed. This will either result in applications being scaled down or in a ballot to determine who receives shares. Investors who obtain shares stand to gain from the issue as the share price is likely to be rather higher than the issue price. It is the existing shareholders who lose out. If the issue price is set too high then few investors will subscribe for shares are the shares will be left with the underwriters. The issue would be regarded as a failure and could damage the company's reputation amongst institutions.

5. **Tender issue**. A tender issue is exactly the same as a normal offer for sale at a fixed price except that investors are invited to apply or tender for shares at whatever price they see fit, provided it is at or above an indicated fixed minimum price. The price at which shares are allotted is called the striking price. This will not usually be set at the highest price where the number of shares allotted would exactly match those available, but will be set somewhat lower to obtain a sufficient spread of holdings. Usually all investors pay the striking price irrespective of the amount they tendered at. However, in some issues the amount tendered equals the amount payable.

Methods/Terms used to Issue Shares

1.Bonus Issue. This is the issue of shares to existing share holder in proportion of their share holding. The share holders do not have to pay anything for the shares. The source of payment is normally from the use of company reserves. Thus the number of shares will increase without the company raising additional funds.

A bonus issue may be made for example on a one to one basis, which means that for every one share, one more is added to every share. The bonus issue is also called the script issue.

2.Stock Split. This involves dividing the higher value of shares into smaller denominations, for example, a K400 share may be split into four shares of K100 each. The number of shares will increase, but the company does not raise any funds.

3.Stock Dividend. This is where the company pays the share holders a dividend in the form of shares rather than cash.

The share holding of individuals will increase but the company will not raise additional funds to make the exercise attractive to share holders, stock dividends have a value above the market price of shares hence named enhanced stock dividends.

4.Employee Share Purchase Scheme. These are schemes which enable employees especially the directors of the company shares on favourable terms. This is designed to motivate employees and the employees are required to pay for their purchase using installments deducted from their salaries.

5.Stock Repurchases. This is where the company buys back part of its shares from share holders and cancels them. The initiative is undertaken when the company wants to reduce the number of shares in issue; the company wants to get rid of some dissident share holders etc. For the company to repurchase its own stock this must be allowed and provided for in its Articles of Association and the Memorandum of Association.The source of payment for the shares is by use of reserves.

Stock market or capital market efficiency

A stock market is said to be efficient if it can incorporate new information into the prices reasonably quickly.

The body of study which looks at how efficient the stock market is called the Efficient Market Hypothesis (EMH). According to the EMH, there are three levels or forms of market efficiency. These are.

1. Weak Form

This is where the current prices is a reflection of the past share prices and volumes. A weak form is not very useful for predicting future share price movements. It is basically in historical nature.

2. Semi Strong Form

This prostrate that the current share price is a reflection of the published information which is readily available to the general public. This information may relate to, the company's reported result for the financial year, its earnings announcements, its dividend policy, its projected future investment, its new product development etc.

Under semi strong efficiency, an investor who has privilege information can bit the market. That is he can take an unfair advantage over other investors who don't' have that percentage information.

For this reason stock exchanges do not allow what is called inside earnings as a lot of reports on the directors interest in the company made public regularly

3. Strong Form

This postulate states that the current share price is a reflection of both publicly and privately available information. Under such competition no one can bit the market. Thus, the other professional investors and a layman may achieve the same level of returns. The stock market is said to be efficient in the weak and same strong forms. Interim dividends is issued before the year end and final dividends is issued after the year end.

CHAPTER 19

COST OF CAPITAL

Introduction

It is essential for a company to know the cost of the various types of funds included in its capital structure in order to satisfy the terms of the providers of that capital – the investors. If the investors are not satisfied with their returns they may remove their money from the firm. The required rate of return to investors is how much the company has to pay to obtain its finance – i.e. the cost of capital to the firm.

In addition, it is important for companies to know their cost of capital in order to ensure that projects they invest in achieve the level of return required to satisfy those who provide funds which finance the project.

We will consider initially the costs of the different types of capital individually, before looking at the cost of the capital structure of the company as a whole.

It is important when you are revising this area to also consider the capital asset pricing model (CAPM) that we will discuss later in the course.

Investors and the cost of capital

It is important to remember that the cost of finance to the firm is the return required by investors in the firm.

The Required Rate of Return

The required return of investors will be determined by the opportunity cost foregone of the investors, and the risk they are required to bear. For example, if the return on a company's ordinary shares is 8% with no real prospect of capital growth in the short term, and a building society deposit will yield 10%, it is unlikely that the shares will be attractive to investors – the opportunity cost (the building society rate) is greater than the projected return, and the risk of investing in a company is generally considered to be higher than that of depositing the money in a building society account.

The Effect of Risk

Investing in companies involves risk – investors may lose some or all of their funds placed in the company. The risk comprises two elements:

- Business risk due to a lack of certainty about the firm's prospect and projects, and financial risk–the higher the level of gearing the higher the risk for bankruptcy.

The return investors require depends on the risk – the higher the risk the higher the expected return, because people expect to be compensated for bearing additional risk. This "risk premium" (made up of premiums for business and financial risks) will be required in addition to the risk-free rate is typically taken to be the return on government bonds.)

Thus the return required from investing in different companies will vary with the differing levels of risk involved in the firms.

1. Cost of equity

The requirements and expectations of shareholders must be considered when looking at the cost of equity. The effect that changes in earnings and dividends may have on the share price must also be considered.

Traditionally, there are three approaches used in calculating the cost of equity, namely:

a) **Dividend yield (or dividend valuation) method**

The main method of calculating the cost of equity is the dividend valuation or dividend yield model. The precise form of model used varies with the assumptions used. The simplest model to use assumes that dividends will remain at a constant level in the future.

$$Ke = \frac{De}{Se}$$

Where: Ke = cost of equity

De = current dividend payable

Se = current share price (ex div)

Example 1

Tigger plc's current dividend is 25 and the market value of each share is K2. What is the cost of Tigger's equity?

Using the above formula $Ke = \frac{De}{Se}$

$$Ke = \frac{25}{200} = 0.125 = 12.5\%$$

b) **Dividend Growth Model or Gordon model of Dividend growth**

However, shareholders prefer a constant growth in their dividends. In order to reflect this in the dividend valuation method, we have to predict future in dividends. Growth generally reflects will be sustained in future years. The most usual approach is to take several historic data and attempt to extrapolate forward.

Example 2

Assume CEC PLC's past dividends have been:

Dividend per share   K

Year 1   26

Year 2   27

Year 3   28

Year 4   32

We can now find the average rate of growth by using the following formula:

$$\text{Growth rate (g)} = \sqrt[n]{\frac{\text{Latest dividend}}{\text{Earliest dividend}}} - 1$$

Where: n = number of years growth

Applying this to the above figures, we get:

$$g = \sqrt[3]{\frac{32}{26}} - 1 = 0.0717 \text{ or approximately } 7\%$$

Note that here we are using the **cube root** because there are three years of growth. If we had been given five years' data (from which we could project four years' growth) the fourth root would have been used.

When the expected growth figure has been determined we can calculate the value of the company's shares using the **Dividend Growth Model or Gordon's Model of Dividend Growth**.

This model states:

$$P_0 = d_0 \frac{(1 + g)}{(r - g)} \text{ which is also written as } Se = \frac{De (1 + g)}{Ke - g)} \times 100$$

Where: P_0 or Se = the current ex dividend market price
$\quad\quad\quad d_0$ or De = the current dividend

g = the expected annual growth in dividends

$\bar{r}$ or Ke = the shareholder's expected return on the shares

and can be rewritten as:

$$Ke = \frac{De\,(1 + g)}{Se} + g \times 100$$

Note that growth rate, must be expressed as a percentage.

Example 3

Using the example of CEC PLC above, and assuming its share price is K680, then:

$$Ke = \frac{K32(1.07)}{K680} + 0.07 = 12\%$$

The dividend valuation and dividend growth model are based on the following assumptions:

- Taxation rates are assumed to be constant across all investors, and as such the existence of higher rates of tax are ignored. The dividends used are the gross dividends paid out from the company's point of view.

- The costs of any share issue are ignored.

- All investors receive the same, perfect level of information

- The cost of capital to the company remains unaltered by any new issue of shares

- All projects undertaken as a result of new share issues are of equal risk to that existing in the company

- The dividends paid must be from after-tax profits – there **must** be sufficient funds to pay the shareholders from profits after tax.

Share Issue Costs

Share issue costs can be incorporated in the formula, especially if they are considered to be high. The formula then becomes:

$$Ke = \frac{De}{(Se - 1)}$$

Where: Ke = cost of equity
   De = current dividend payable
   Se = current share price (ex div)
   I = cost of issue per share

Thus, for the example for CEC above, if issue costs divided by the number of shares is K5, then the cost of equity becomes:

$$Ke = \frac{25}{200 - 5}\ 0.128 = 12.8\%$$

If you are given issue costs you should, unless told otherwise, incorporate them in the formula as shown above.

 c) **Capital Asset Pricing Model (CAPM)**

This model is used when the beta factor, return on government securities and the market return are known. These are usually available at a fee from stock brokers.

The Capital Asset Pricing Model, which we shall discuss later in the course, can also be used to value the cost of equity. You should revise this topic when you have worked through the relevant chapter.

$$Ke = R_f + \beta(R_m - R_f)$$

Where R_f is the risk free rate of return or return on government securities
R_m is the return on the market
β is the beta factor

2. Cost of Preference Shares

The formula for calculating the cost of preference shares is:

$$Kp\ \frac{dp}{Sp}$$

Where: Kp = cost of preference shares
   dp = fixed dividend based on the nominal value of shares
   Sp = market price of preference shares

Example
Jack PLC has 7% preference shares which have a nominal value of K1 and a market price of 120n. What is the cost of preference shares?

Using the above formula, dividends are 7% of the nominal value of K1 and such are 7n. Therefore:

$$Kp = \frac{7n}{120n} \times 100 = 6\%$$

Retained Earnings

Retaining earnings will also have an effect because, when left in the business rather than being distributed, they should achieve higher returns in the future to offset the lack of current dividends. The shareholder's expectations of increasing future dividends rather than constant payments may, however, persuade them to accept initial lower dividends.

Estimating the Future Annual Growth Rate of Dividends

If you need to estimate an expected rate of growth in annual dividends, formula is:

$$g = rB$$

Where: g = future rate of growth in dividends
r = return on new investment
B = proportion of earnings kept in the business as retained earnings

Example

If a company retains 45% of its profits and earns a return of 8% on its investments; find the expected future annual growth rate in earnings and dividends

Solution

$$g = rB = 0.08 \times 0.45$$

$$= 0.036 \text{ or } 3.6\%$$

3. Cost of debt capital

We saw earlier that debentures can be either redeemable or irredeemable. It is important that you know the type of debenture a firm has in issue when calculating its cost of capital because, as you will see, the approach used varies with the form of debentures being considered.

a) **Irredeemable Debt**

The formula for calculating the cost of irredeemable debt is:

$$K_d = -\frac{I(1-t)}{Sd} \times 100$$

Where: Kd = cost of debt capital

I = annual interest payment

Sd = current market price of debt capital

t = the rate of corporation tax applicable

Taxation is considered because the interest can be offset against taxation, which will lower its nominal rate, and thus its cost. The higher the rate of corporation tax payable by the company, the lower will be the after-tax cost of debt capital. Thus the cost of debt capital is much lower than the cost of preference shares with the same coupon rate and market value as the debentures because of the availability of tax relief on the debt. Naturally this only applies if the business has taxable profits from which to deduct its interest payments. When the business has generated a taxable loss, the interest will increase that loss for carry forward (to be offset against future taxable profits in later years), and the immediate benefit of tax relief will be lost.

Example

Aisha PLC has K10, 000 of 8% irredeemable debentures in issue which have a current market price of K92 per K100 of nominal value. If the corporation tax rate is 33% what is the cost of the debt capital? The annual interest payment will be based on the nominal value, i.e. 8% of K10, 000 or K800, so using the above formula:

$$Kd = \frac{K800(1-0.33)}{K92/K100 \times 10,000} \times 100 = 0.0583 = 5.83\%$$

Or Kd = $\frac{K8(1-0.33)}{K92}$ X 100 = 5.83% using per unit values.

b) **Redeemable Capital**

In order to determine the cost of such capital to the date of redemption we must find the internal rate of return (IRR). IRR is discussed in greater detail later, but basically involves calculating all the necessary cash flows (generally the assumption will be made that all payments and receipts are made at the end of the year) and determining at what cost of capital the value of future cash flows are equal to zero. The IRR is calculated using discount factors for the appropriate cost of capital and the following formula. Wherever possible the ex-interest values should be used, so if the cum-interest value is quoted (i.e. if the interest is due to be paid soon and thus is reflected in the market price of the debt) we should deduct the interest payment from the market price. The longer the period to maturity the lower will be the overall cost of capital. This is to be expected because the real cost of redemption will be lower in the future because of the effects of the time value of money.

$$Kd = IRR = A\% + (\underline{a}\quad (B - A)\%$$
$$\qquad\qquad\qquad a\text{-}b$$

Wher A = Lower discount rate giving positive NPV
    B = Higher discount rate giving negative NPV
    a = Positive NPV
    b = Negative NPV

Cost of Floating Rate Debt

If a company has floating rate debt in its capital structure, then an estimated fixed rate of interest should be used to calculate its cost of debt in a way similar to the above. The "equivalent" rate will be that of a similar company for a similar maturity.

Cost of Fixed Rate Bank Loans

The cost of this major source of finance is given by:
Cost = interest rate = $(1 - t)$

Cost of Short-Term Funds and Overdrafts

The cost of short-term bank loans and overdrafts is the current interest rate being charged on the capital lent.

Weighted average cost of capital (WACC)

The Weighted Average Cost of Capital (WACC) is defined as the average of costs of different types of finance in a company's structure weighted by the proportion of different forms of capital employed within the business. The cost of capital that should be used in evaluating projects is the marginal cost of funds raised in order to finance the project, and WACC is considered to be the best estimate of marginal cost. Note that it is only the most reliable if the company is assumed to continue investment in projects of a normal level of business risk and funds are raised in similar proportions to its existing capital structure. Investments which offer a return in excess of the WACC will increase the market value of the company's equity, reflecting the increase in expected future earnings and dividends arising as a result of the project.

Assumptions when using WACC

To use WACC in capital investment appraisal the following assumptions have to be made:

- The cost of capital investment appraisal is the marginal cost of funds raised in order to finance the project
- Now investment must be financed from new sources of funds, including new share issues, new debentures or loans.
- The WACC must reflect the long term future capital structure of the company.

Arguments against using the WACC

There are arguments against using WACC for investment appraisal based mainly on the assumptions underlying WACC

- Business may have floating rate debt whose cost change is used to calculate this type of finance. Thus the company's cost of capital will not be accurate and will need frequent updating.
- The business risk of individual projects may be different to that of the company and will thus require a different premium included in the cost of capital.
- The finance used for the project may alter the company's gearing and thus its financial risk.

Calculating WACC: book values vs market values

There is no one accepted method of calculating a company's WACC – some use book values in the proportions that they appear in the company's accounts and others use market values. For unquoted companies book values may have to used because of the problems of estimating market value for their securities. Book values are generally easier to obtain than market values. However, many would argue that for quoted companies market values are more realistic and, indeed may be easier because only the cost of equity is required-it being impossible to split the value of equity between the shares and the retained earnings.

Whether book values or market values ear used, the WACC can be calculated using either of the following:

(a) Tabular format as follows:

Source	Amount	Proportion	Cost	Proportion x cost
Total			WACC =	

Note: proportion = Amount from each source
                   Total capital structure

- Cost is calculated using the methods previously described in this chapter.
- WACC is the sum of the figures in the last column

(b) $WACC = KeW + KpW + KdW$

Where Ke = Cost of equity
   Kp = Cost of preference shares
   Kd = Cost of debt
   W = weighted or proportion

The formula simply means that WACC is equal t o cost of equity x it weight + cost of preference shares x weight + cost of debt x weight.

(c) $WACC = \dfrac{KeVe + + KpVe + KdVd}{Ve + Vp + Vd}$

Where Ke = cost of equity
   Ve = value of equity
   Kp = Cost of preference shares
   Vp = value of shares
   Kd = Cost of debt
   Vd = Value of debt

- This formula helps avoid the need to calculate "proportions".

Please work through the following examples paying particular attention to methodology depending on the information provided in the question.

Example 1

Calculate the WACC from the following information using:

(a) Book values
(b) Market values
(c) Which one is more reasonable

Balance sheet extract from ABC PLC

Capital: value	Balance sheet	Market value
• Ordinary shares (20 000 – 50n each)	K10 000	K1.72 per share
• 8% preference shares (K1 nominal value)	K5 000	K0.98 per K1
• 10% debentures	K7 500	K1.04 per K1

The cost of equity has been calculated at 9.5%

Solution

(a) WACC using book value

Source	Amount	Proportion	Cost	Cost x proportion
Equity	K10000	0.73	9.5%	6.9%
Preference shares	K5000	0.10	8%	0.8%
Debentures	K7500	0.17	10%	1.7%
Total	K22500		WACC =	9.40%

(b) WACC using market values

Source	Amount	Proportion	Cost	Cost x proportion
Equity	K34400	0.73	9.5%	6.9%
Preference shares	K4900	0.10	8%	0.8%
Debentures	K7800	0.17	10%	1.7%
Total	K47100		WACC =	9.34%

(c) Market values are more reasonable since this is a PLC hence data is readily available.

Notes to above calculations:

Market values:

- Ordinary shares: 20 000 x K1.72 = K34 400
- Preference shares: 5000 x K0.98 = K4 900
- Debentures: 7500 x K1.40 = K7 800

Proportions:

- Equity = $\frac{K34\ 400}{K47\ 100}$ = 0.73

- Preference shares = $\frac{K4900}{K47\ 100}$ = 0.10

- Debentures = $\frac{K7800}{K47100}$ = 0.17

Example 2

XYZ PLC is financed as follows:

	K'000
● Ordinary K1 shares	5000
● Reserves	1000
● 8% preference shares	400
● 12% Debenture loan	800

The rate of ordinary dividend is expected for the foreseeable future to remain at 5n interim and 10n final.

Calculate WACC of XYZ PLC

Solution

Source	Amount K'000	Proportion	Cost	Proportion x cost
Equity	1500	0.56	5%	2.78%
Preference shares	400	0.15	8%	1.19%
Debenture loans	800	0.30	12%	3.56%
Total	2700		WACC =	7.53%

Notes:

The cost of equity is calculated using the following:

● $K_e = \dfrac{\text{Interim Dividend} + \text{Final Dividend}}{\text{Equity}} \times 100$

● $= \dfrac{500\ 000 \text{ shares} \times 0.15}{150\ 000} \times 100 = 5\%$

● Equity = Ordinary shares + Reserves

● Total dividend per share = Interim + Final

$$= K0.05 + K0.10 = K0.15$$

● Note that there is no other way of calculating the cost of equity with reference to given data.

Alternatively, we can use:

$$WACC = \frac{KeVe + KpVp + KdVd}{Ve + Vp + Vd}$$

$$= \frac{(0.05 \times 1500) + (0.08 \times 400) + (0.12 \times 800)}{1500 + 400 + 800} \times 100$$

$$= \frac{75 + 32 + 96}{2700} \times 100$$

$$= \frac{203}{2700} \times 100$$

WACC = 7.5% as calculated before.

Example 3

The management of Jumbe Plc is trying to decide on cost of capital to apply to the evaluation of investment projects. The company has an issued share capital of 500 000 ordinary shares of K1, with a current market value of K1.17 per share. It has also issued K200 000 of 10% debentures which are redeemable at par in two years K95.30 and K100 000 of 6% preference shares, currently priced at 40 ngwee per share. The preference dividend has just been paid and ordinary dividend and debenture interest are due to be paid in the near future.

The dividend will be K60 000 this year, and the directors have publicized their view that earnings and dividend will increase by 5% a year into the indefinite future. The fixed assets and working capital of the company are financed by the following:

- Ordinary shares of K1 each   500 000
- 6% preference shares   100 000
- Debentures   200 000
- Reserves   380 000
-     1180 000

Note: Ignore inflation and assume corporation fax of 30%

Required:

    (a) Calculate the cost of equity (%)
    (b) Calculate the cost of preference shares (%)
    (c) Calculate the cost of debentures (%)
    (d) Calculate WACC (%)
    (e) Advice management as to the appropriate rate for the project.

Solution

(a) $Ke = \dfrac{De\,(1+g)}{Se} + g = \dfrac{0.12\,(1+0.05)}{1.17} + 0.05 = 16\%$

(b) $KP = \dfrac{dp}{Sp} \times 100 = \dfrac{6}{40} \times 100 = 15\%$

(c) Since debt is redeemable we have to calculate the internal rate of return (IRR) by finding two discount rates which will give us one positive and the other negative Net Present Values (NPVs).

First we need to determine the net cash flows:

Year	Cost	Interest	Tax relief	Net cash flow
0	(95.30)	-	-	95.30
1	-	10	3.00	7.00
2	100.00	10	3.00	107.00

Next we calculate the NPVs, at say 10% and 8%

Year	Cash flow	DF at 10%	PV	DF at 8%	PV
0	(95.30)	1.000	(95.30)	1.000	(95.30)
1	7.00	0.909	6.36	0.926	6.48
2	107.00	0.826	88.38	0.857	91.70
		NPV	(0.56)	NPV	2.88

$$Ke = IRR = A\% + \left[\dfrac{a}{a-b}\,(B-A)\%\right] = 8\% + \left[\dfrac{2.88}{2.88-(-0.56)}\,(10-8)\right]\%$$

$$= 9.67\%$$

$$= 10\%$$

Note: Interest is 10% of K100 = K10
Tax is 30% of K10 = K3

(d) Now we can calculate WACC

Source	Market value	Cost	Proportion	Cost x proportion
Ordinary shares	525 000	16%	0.69	11.04%
Preference shares	40 000	15%	0.053	0.795%
Debentures	90 000	10%	0.12	1.2%
Total	755 600		WACC	13.04%

(e) The best rates the WACC of 13%

PROGRESS CLINIC 19

Question 1

Imagine you are the Financial Manager of Sola Limited. Your company has 2 million ordinary shares in issue and the current market price is K10 per share. The company also has 400 000 preference shares in issue and has a market price of K15. The dividend paid on preference shares is K3 per share and on ordinary shares is K0.30 per share with the expected growth at 20%. He company's outstanding debentures have ten years to maturity a face value of K5 million, that pays an interest rate of 10% p.a. and currently trading at a yield—to—maturity (YTM) of 12%.

REQUIRED

Calculate the WACC using market values as weights.

Question 2

The following is an extract from the balance sheet of Mapalo International Plc at 30 June 2006.

	K'000
Ordinary shares at 50n each	5,200
Reserves	4,850
9% Preference shares at K1 each	4,500
14% Debentures	5,000
Total long term funds	19,550

The ordinary shares are quoted at 80n. Assume that the market estimate of the next ordinary dividend is 4n, growing thereafter at 12% per annum indefinitely. The preference shares, which are irredeemable, are quoted at 72n and the debentures are quoted at par. Company tax is 35%.

a) You are required to use the relevant data above to estimate the company's weighted average cost of capital ("WACC"), i.e. the return required by the providers of the three types of capital, using respective market values as weighting factors.

b) You are required to explain how the capital asset pricing model would be used as an alternative method of estimating the cost of equity, indicating what information would be required and how it would be obtained.

c) Assume that the debentures have recently been issued specifically to fund the company's expansion programme under which a number of projects are being considered and it has been suggested at a project appraisal meeting that because those projects are to be financed by the debentures, the cut off rate for project acceptance should be the after tax rate on the debentures rather than WACC.

You are required to comment on this suggestion.

Question 3

The following is an extract from the Balance Sheet of Gatta Plc at 30 September 2006:

	K
Ordinary Shares of 25ngwee each	250,000
Reserves	350,000
7% preference shares of K1 each	250,000
15% unsecured loan stock	150,000
	1000,000

The ordinary shares are currently quoted at 125 ngwee each, the loan stock is trading at K85 per K100 nominal and the preference shares at 65 ngwee each. The ordinary dividends of 10 ngwee has just been paid and the expected growth rate in the dividend is 10 per cent. Corporation tax is at the ratio of 33 per cent.

Required:

From the above details, calculate the following variables for Gatta Plc:

(a) Market value of equity;
(b) Market value of preference shares
(c) Market value of loan stock
(d) Total market value of securities.
(e) Cost of equity
(f) Cost of preference shares
(g) Cost of loan stock
(h) Weighted Average Cost of Capital (WACC)

Question 4

The dividends and earnings of Hara Plc over the last five years have been as follows:

Year	Dividends	Earnings
	K	K
20x1	120 000	400 000
20x2	192 000	510 000
20x3	206 000	550 000
20x4	245 000	650 000
20x5	235 000	700 000

The company is financed entirely by equity and there are 1 000 000 shares in issue, each share with a market value of K1.35 ex div.

Required:

From the above details:

(a) Calculate the dividend growth rate over the last four years. (Note – use dividend growth model)
(b) Calculate the cost of equity (in percentage terms)

(c) What implications does dividend growth appear to have for earnings retentions?

Question 5

Abaleya Plc is a transport haulage company with the following summarized Balance Sheet as at 31 December 2008

	K'000	k'000
Fixed assets		15 350
Current assets	5 900	
Current liabilities	(2 600)	
Net current assets		3 300
9% Debentures		(8000)
		10 650
Ordinary share capital (25n each)		2 000
7% Preference shares (k1)		1 000
Share premium account		6 550
Profit and Loss account		1 100
		10 650

The current price of ordinary shares is 135ngwee ex-dividend. The dividend of 10n is payable during the next few days. The expected rate of growth of dividends is 9% per annum. The current price of preference shares is77n and the debenture has been recently trading at K80 per K100 nominal. Corporation tax is at a rate of 30%.

Required:

a) Calculate the gearing ratio for Abaleya using:
   i) Book values
   ii) Market values
b) Calculate the company's WACC using market values as weighting factors.

c) Assume that Abaleya Plc issued the debentures one year ago to finance a new investment. Discuss any four reasons why Abaleya Plc may have issued debentures rather than preference shares to raise the required finance?

CHAPTER 20

DIVIDEND POLICY

Dividends are distributions of earnings to shareholders. Therefore dividend policy is the counter-part of retained earnings policy. The decision to pay a given dividend reflects a simultaneous decision not to retain that amount of profits. Dividend policy is important for two basic reasons.

(1) Payment of dividends may influence the value of ordinary shares.

(2) Retention of earnings usually is the largest source of additional equity capital to finance growth. Management is responsible for maintaining adequate capital at a minimum cost and maximizing the value of ordinary shares in the long run. The optional dividend policy strikes a balance between current dividends and future growth so as to maximize the firm's stock price. Essentially, dividend policy involves three key issues namely:

(1) What fraction of earnings should be distributed on average over time?

(2) Should the firm maintain a steady dividend growth rate?

(3) Should the distribution be in form of cash dividends or stock repurchases.

To focus on dividend policy more formerly, we refer to the basic constant dividend growth valuation model given as:

$$P = \frac{di}{Ke - g}$$

Where p = market price per share of ordinary shares
di = dividend to be paid next year
Ke = the cost of ordinary
g = growth rate

Every term in this valuation model relates in someway to dividend policy. The dividend to bepaid next year is di. The growth influenced by retained earnings, reinvested to increase futureearnings and dividends. Ke, the cost of common stock equity is influenced by the proportionoflower cost earnings to higher cost of new issues of common stock. The resultant value of common stock P reflects all these factors. The dividend payout ratio is the dividends paid and after rate earnings available to ordinary shares or common stock during the period. Formerly, dividend payout ratio is total dividends divided by total earnings or dividend by earnings per share.

DIVIDEND THEORIES

The 3 major popular basic theories of dividend policy are:

(1) Residual theory
(2) Indifference theory
(3) Bird in the hand theory

Each conflicts with the other and non-by itself provides a completely satisfactory guide to determining dividend policy. Nonetheless it is important to understand these theories before dealing with the complexities of real word dividend policy determination.

A. Residual Theory

This states that dividends should be the residual of capital investment decision-making process. The cost of equity Ke may have two components. The cost of retained earnings Kr and the cost of new common stock Kc. Kr is an opportunity cost reflecting the rate of return available to shareholders if earnings were paid to them in dividends and invested in other assets of comparable risk. Kr is lower than Kc because the latter includes consideration or floatation costs. Because Kr is lower than Kc, the shareholders would appear to be better off if available earnings were retained. Otherwise if dividends were paid, then the form would have to issue additional shares at a higher cost if it needed more financing. The residual theory holds that dividend decisions should be made as follows:

(1) Determine the Kwacha amounts of capital investment to be made
(2) Determine the equity financing required
(3) Retain earnings to provide as much of this equity financing as possible
(4) If retained earnings are insufficient, issue additional shares
(5) If earnings exceed the required retention, pay the excess in dividends.

Thus dividend policy is a passive result or residue of the capital investment decision making process. Only the earnings that ate left after financing capital investment projects should be paid out in dividends.

Limitations

(1) Instability in dividends from year to year. Dividends will be very unstable and might range on years when nothing was left over to large amounts in years when earnings substantially exceed equity financing request.

(2) Under this theory, dividends are not directly related to earnings. Thus, the obvious shortcoming of practical employment of residual theory is the inconsistent of dividends.

B. INDIFFERENCE THEORY

This theory also called dividend irrelevant theory holds that investors are indifferent to the payments or lack of payment of dividends. According to this theory, dividend policy simply does not matter because it is irrelevant to the value of stock. Its proponents Miller and Modigliani (M and M) argue that only the income stream accruing to the shareholders if relevant. Whether or in what proportion, it is paid their wealth. In brief, their arguments are that if the firm paid no dividends, this will enhance the value of stock by the amount of retained earnings. The individual shareholder, if cash were preferred sell could some of the now more valuable stock to create home made dividends. This shareholder investors not very interested in dividends wealth can neither be created nor destroyed by dividend policy. The arguments supporting the indifference theory rest upon the following assumptions.

(1) There are no taxes either on dividend received or capital gains

(2) The firm incurs no floatation costs in issuing additional shares.

(3) The investor incurs no transaction costs such as brokerage fees. Given these assumptions, indifference theory is valid. But as those perfect market assumptions are lifted and the imperfections of the real would are recognized, these imperfections make dividend policy relevant after all. This is because we live in a world of taxes; most firms cannot sell shares without incurring floatation costs and investors cannot buy or sell shares without paying brokerage fees.

C. BIRD IN THE HAND THEORY

This theory claims that shareholders are not indifferent to dividend payment versus retention of earnings. Therefore dividend policy is relevant to the value of the firm's shares. The leading proponents of this theory Lintner and Gordon hold that shareholders value a kwacha received in dividends now since, it is more certain than a Kwacha of earnings retained which is uncertain.

D. TAX MAXIMIZING THEORY

This theory was popular before the Tax Reform Act of 1986 in USA. It argued that when long term capital gains were taxed at only a fraction of the rate applicable to ordinary income in the form of dividends, it was in the best interest of shareholders that the firm

pay minimal or no dividends. Instead, retention of earnings would lead to capital gains taxed at lower rates. The force of this argument was destroyed when the 1986 Tax Act equalized the tax on all capital gains and ordinary income.

REAL LIFE CONSIDERATIONS

We live in a world influenced by laws and contractual obligations, internal considerations relative to investment opportunities. Stability of earnings and cash generation, availability of funds and control considerations. Most shareholders are people who have their individual needs, pay taxes and exhibit different motivations for investing in ordinary shares. These real life considerations have a strong bearing on the dividend policy appropriate to each firm and its shareholders. How these real life factors may influence the firm dividends policy is considered below?

1 External consideration

The Company Law prohibits an insolvent company from paying dividends. While dividends can be paid from past and present earnings, they cannot be paid from any capita reserves. So if any funds have been transferred from the income statement or another revenue reserve, into a capital reserve such as a capital redemption reserve, then this reserve is not available for payment of cash dividends.

Further, there are some contractual constraints from senior securities like bonds. In there contracts restrictive provisions ma be included. Constraints on dividends help to protect creditors from losses due to the firm's insolvency.

2 Availability of Cash

Dividends are paid out in cash, this is dominant restriction.

a) Although profits may have been made, these may not be available in cash.

b) Cash flow may have been used to finance increased accounts receivable, inventions or fixed assets or it may have been required to pay maturing debt obligation

3 Capital Investment Opportunities

- Availability capital investment opportunities to the firm may greatly Influence its dividends.

- In a growing firm nearly all or perhaps more than the firm's earnings will be required to finance growth in assets. This suggests a low dividend payout or perhaps no dividend at all, to finance as much as possible of the required increase in equity through retained earnings.

- Mature or perhaps declining firms in low technology industries simply do not have many favorable capital investment opportunities.

- This suggests a high dividend payout.

4 Stability Of Earnings And Cash Generation

- There is a reasonable correlation between dividend payment and the earnings and cash generated by the firm.

- If management is to attempt to pay stable dividends, earnings and cash generation must be relatively stable through time

5 Availability And Cost Of Funds

- Ready access to money and capital markets allows a firm to establish a dividend policy that will in the long run, comply with the residual theory but still maintain relatively stable dividend policy.

- Flexible borrowing or occasional sales of additional stock may avoid the dividend instability that would result from strict adherence to the residual theory in the short run.

6 Control Considerations

- This is more important if the firm's shares are privately held. If the owners do not want to lose this tight control, they will rather pay low or no dividends at all so that there is little demand for its shares. This is because if it pays a high dividend payout ratio, more investors will be attracted to the firm.

- Thus, if the firm wants to remain in tight control it will pay a low dividend payout ratio.

7. Stockholder Satisfaction Considerations

The stockholders own the corporation and the most direct and meaningful communications they receive from its management are dividend cheques. Therefore, it is of great importance that a firm's dividend policy satisfies their economic needs.

a) **Types of Stockholders**

- The initial consideration is whether shareholders seek current income (suggesting a high dividend payout ratio) or capital gain (suggesting a low dividend payout ratio).

- Ordinary shareholders vary greatly in this respect

- For example, most of the shareholders of company X may be individuals of modest means who depend on income from their investments to meet their living expenses. The institutional investors, maybe income motivated charitable foundations, university endowment funds, pension funds and trust funds. Such shareholders would be satisfied only by relatively high and stable dividends.

- At the other extreme, most of the shareholders of company Y, maybe individuals with high current incomes. These shareholders usually do not want current dividends. They seek the capital gains that will result from re-investment of earnings.

b) **Propensity To Bear Risk**

- The risk aversion versus propensity to bear risk of the share shareholders also must considered in the context of Lintner and Gordon's argument supporting the bird-in-the hand theory.

- Most of company X's shareholders probably are highly risk averse because a dividend received now contain while the reinvestment of earnings is so company X's shareholders will tend to prefer a high dividends payout ratio.

- But the shareholders of company X, wealth and wit large incomes from sources are more likely to be risk bears, they do not discount expected future benefits from reinvestment of earnings at high rates, they prefer to bear this risk.

c) **Legal Limitations Of Some Shareholders**

- Still another shareholder consideration involves legal limitations on investment by some financial institutions.

- Some regions/countries require institutional investors invest only in stock of issues qualifying for there "legal list". A typical qualification is that dividends have been paid consecutively on the ordinary shares over a stated period of time, say 5 to 10 years.

8 Information Content Of Dividends

- Payment of dividends is perhaps the most direct and important way companies communicate information about their economic health to the market.

- Payment of a stable dividend is a sign that the firm remains well. Management frequently will not increase the dividend unless it is confident that the higher rate may be continued in the foreseeable future.

- Therefore, a dividend increase sends a signal to investors that management believes that the earnings and cash flow have permanently improved.

- The market will usually react by biding the price of shares

- Conversely, reducing or eliminating dividend payments, particularly when they have been relatively stable over a considerable period of time, signals that something maybe wrong with the company. If accompanied by reported lower earnings, a dividend reduction may be interpreted to mean that the firms earnings power has been permanently impaired market reaction probably will be a drop in share price.

- Thus, markets interpretation of the information content of dividends is extremely important to the overall objective of maximizing the management believes that a decline earnings is only temporary, it may signal this by maintaining dividend payments at the existing level of course it is imperative that management not send misleading signals. A lack of condor will be doubly y damaging if the future unfolds unfavourably.

9 The Clientele Effect

- Shareholders requesting a particular dividend policy naturally gravitate towards firms that adhere to that policy. Therefore, rather than seeking to establish a dividend policy that satisfies present shareholders' desires, management might consider establishing a policy dominated by internal consideration.

- Then the clientele of shareholders whose inventive objectives will be satisfied by that dividend policy held firm, this clientele effect will tend to happen.

- However, it should not be inferred that the clientele effect allows management to change dividend policy without repercussions. Shareholder with various investment objectives do not gravitate from one firm to another without friction that may involve considerable effect on share price and risk to management.

- For example, company Z, for many years as been engaged in a relatively stable industry requiring low capital investment.

Throughout these years, it paid high and stale dividends thus attracting a clientele of income motivated investors.

Recently, a firm has been evolving into a high-technology industry. Its earnings are becoming volatile, and its capital investments requirements are increasing substantially. Management therefore, is considering changing its dividend policy from high and stable dividends to relatively low and unstable ones, a policy more suitable to the firm's internal needs.

- This should lead to a change in its shareholders clientele to growth-motivated investors who are willing to assume high risks. But this change may not go smoothly.

- Drastic reductions of the dividend may be interpreted to mean "something is wrong with company Z" investors, believing that its earnings power might be permanently improved and recognizing that the lower dividend payments will not satisfy their needs for current income, may sell their shares in droves. Thus, for a few weeks or months the price of company Z shares may decline drastically.

- During this period management may run the services risk of takeover attempt. Someone could accumulate the stock at the low price and appeal for the votes of the remaining unhappy shareholders on the promise level to restore the dividend to its previous level if control is achieved and new management installed. Eventually, if no such takeover happens, growth-motivated risk-taking investors will be attracted to company Z shares as brokerage houses gradually shift company Z from a "sell" recommendation on their income stock list to "buy" recommendation on their growth stock lists. The market price of the stock ultimately should recover as the result of establishing this new shareholder clientele.

- In summary, there will be a risky period during which the graph of the market price of company Z shares will be forming a V. Management may be reluctant to bear this risk and suffer sleepless night as the bottom of that V is approached. The change in dividend policy may be successful or management may lose a takeover battle and find itself in the street.

ALTERNATIVE PRACTICAL DIVIDEND POLICIES

The firm's dividend policy represents a plan of action to be followed whenever the decision must be made. The dividend policy must be formulated with two basic objectives in mind:

- Maximizing the wealth of the shareholders
- Providing for sufficient financing

These two interrelated objectives must be fulfilled in light of a number of factors-legal, contractual, internal, growths, owner-related and market related-that limit the policy alternatives. Three of the more commonly used dividend policies are presented here. A particular firm's cash dividend policy may incorporate elements of each.

● Constant Payout Ratio

One type of dividend policy occasionally adopted by firms is the use of a constant payout ratio. The dividend payout ratio, calculated by dividing the firm's cash dividend per share by its earnings per share, indicates the percentage of each Kwacha earned that is distributed to the owners in the form of cash. With a constant payout that a certain percentage of earnings are paid to owner in each dividend period. The problem with this policy is that if the firm's earnings drop or if a loss occurs in a given period, the dividends may be low or non-existent. Because dividends are often considered an indicator of share price may thus be adversely affected by this type of action.

● Regular Dividend Policy

Another type of dividend policy, the regular dividend policy, is based on the payment of a fixed Kwacha dividend in each period. The regular dividend policy provides the owners with generally positive information, indicating that the firm is okay and thereby minimizing their uncertainty. Often, firms using this policy increase the regular dividend once a proven increase in earnings has occurred. Under this policy, dividends are almost never decreased. Often, a regular dividend policy is built around a target dividend payout ratio. The firm attempts to pay out a certain percentage of earnings, but rather let dividends fluctuate; it pays a stated Kwacha dividend and adjusts it towards the target payout as proven earnings increases occur.

● Low-Regular and Extra Dividend Policy

Some films establish a low regular and extra dividend policy, paying a low regular dividend, supplemented by an additional dividend, when earnings warrant it. When earnings are higher than normal in a given period, the firm may pay this additional dividend, which is designated an extra dividend. By calling the additional dividend extra dividend, the firm avoid=s giving shareholders false hopes. The use of the "extra" designation is especially common among companies that experience cyclical shifts in earnings.

By establishing a low regular dividend that is paid each period, the firm gives investors the stable income necessary to build confidence in the firm, and the dividend permits them to share in the earnings from an especially good period. Firms using this policy must raise the level of the regular dividend once proven increases in earnings have been achieved. The extra dividend should not be a regular event, or it becomes meaningless. The use of a target dividend-payout ratio in establishing the regular dividend level is achievable

DIVIDEND PAYMENTS PROCEDURES

Dividend may be declared on by the board of directors. The chief financial officer advise the board on dividend policy and often recommends the specific amounts of dividend to be declared. Dividends are usually paid twice a year namely **interim dividend** and **final** dividend.

TERMINOLOGY AND SEQUENCE

1. **Declaration** – at the end of the Directors meetings at which a dividend is declared, the financial press will be notified. A typical dividend declaration announcement will read. "On August 12, the Directors of XYZ Corporation declared the quart dividend of 75n per share payable to holders of record on August 31. The dividends will be paid September 15 at the time the dividend is declared; the firm becomes liable for its payment. If XYZ has 100,000 shares outstanding, the accounting entry is:

	Dr	Cr
Retained earnings	750,000	
Dividends payable		750,000

2. Ex-Dividend And Record Dates

This dividend will be paid to the shareholder on the stock record at the close of the business on August 31 Beginning four (4) days of business before the date of record, the stock trade ex-dividend. The four-day periods is required by the stock exchanges to provide time for completion transfers and recording ownerships of the shares. XYZ stock will begin trading ex-dividend when the stock exchange opens on August 27, thus a shareholder who purchases shares on or after August 27 will not receive the dividend. The dividend on that stock being equal, the market price of stock will drop by the amount for the dividend, 75n in this case when trading opens on the ex-dividend date. The reason for this decline in the market price is that the person who purchases the stock on and offer the ex-dividend date will not receive the declared dividend on going value of the stock.

3. Payments

- On September is dividend cheques will be mailed to the holders of record of August 31.

- The accounting entry at this time will be.

	Dr	Cr
Dividend payable	750,000	
Cash		750,000

The net effect of the dividend declaration and payment is to reduce both cash and retained earnings by the amount of the dividend—K750,000

Dividend reinvestment plans (DRPs)

In recent years many large, publicly held firms have instituted dividend reinvestment plans (DRPs) by which their shareholders may elect to have dividends withheld and used to purchase additional shares for them.

Thus even through more emphasis is given to the payment of cash dividend payments alternative means of paying dividends by way of stock are becoming fashionable.

Progress Clinic

CHAPTER 21

RISK AND RETURN

Different investors have different attitudes to risk – some are risk-seekers and others are risk-averse. Obviously an individual's attitude to risk will affect his/her choice of portfolio. However, risk aversion is extremely difficult to quantify in tangible terms with many factors affecting it including age, personal wealth, family circumstances, taxation, time restrictions on the availability of investment capital and the requirements of trust deeds.

Traditional economic theory upon which much of this course, and portfolio theory in particular, is based assumes that individuals are 'rational risk-avoiders'-i.e. they are risk averse.

Expected Return

An investor will expect his individual investments and portfolio as a whole to yield a certain return. The expected return of a portfolio is the weighted average of the expected returns of its constituent investments weighed by their proportion in the portfolio. This is best explained by an example.

Mr. Toplis holds the following shares in his portfolio which have these expected returns:

Share	Proportion %	Expected Return %
A	25 20	
B	15	10
C	30	15
D	30	25

What is the expected return on his portfolio? It is the weighted average of return.

Share	Proportion %	Expected Return %	Proportion X Expected Return
A	25	20	0.25 X 20 = 5
B	15	10 0.15 X 10 = 1.5	
C	30	15	0.30 X 15 = 4.5
D	30	25	0.30 X 25 = 7.5

Total expected return from portfolio = 5 + 1.5 + 4.5 + 7.5 = 18%

Measuring Risk in a Portfolio

The return the investor will expect to receive from his portfolio is dependent principally on the risk of the portfolio. In the portfolio the greatest risk is that the investments will fail to achieve the required return. The risk can be measured at the standard deviation of expected returns. These expected returns are calculated using probabilities.

Let's consider an example of an investment with the following expected returns.

Probability factor	(P) Return (r)	Expected value
0.3	10%	3%
0.4	15%	6%
0.3	20%	6%

Here the expected (the most likely) return (r) is 5%—it is the most estimate from the information available to use. However, it is only an average figure and there will be variations around this point. To calculate the likely variation we need to work out the variance and, from this, the standard deviation:

P	Return (r)	(r – r)	$P(r-r)_2$
0.3	10%	(5%)	7.5
0.4	15%	0%	0
0.3	20%	5%	7.5
		Variance:	15

The standard deviation is the square root of the variance (15), which is 3.87%. in other words, we have found that our likely return could fluctuate by up to 3.8% in either direction.

The higher the standard deviation, the higher risk. Since the standard deviation shows the range of expected returns (in the above example these are 15% + 3.87%), we can see that the higher the risk, the higher the expected returns or expected losses.

Coefficient of variation (CV)

Further, we can use the coefficient of Variation to measure the risk. If two assets are being compared, the one with the higher CV is riskier.

$$CV = \frac{standard\ Deviation}{Mean}$$

In general, the higher the risk of the investment the higher the expected return. Investors will avoid as much risk as possible whilst aiming for the highest return.

The Impact of Diversification

Investors and companies generally have more than one investment in order to minimise their exposure to risk. A good example is the unit trust, which comprises a large number of investments thereby spreading the risk incurred by the investor and generally reducing it.

Portfolio theory states that it is the relationship between the returns from the individual investments which is important, rather than the return on individual investments. The relationship between the return is known as **correlation**.

Correlation

This can take three forms:

●**Positive correlation** – this concerns the situation which may arise when two or more investments in the portfolio are in connected industries. It is assumed that, if one investment is successful and rises in value, and then the other in a related industry will also do well. Similarly, if the first does badly, then the second will follow. For example, if there is a slump in the share price of related firms, such as those supplying building materials?

●**Negative correlation** – this concerns the theory that, if one investment performs poorly, the other will do well. In the real world negative correlation is almost impossible to achieve. One example could be a steep rise in the price of oil. Initially this will usually benefit oil companies, whilst the of the market will be depressed. You may like to try to think of similar circumstances.

●**Nil correlation** – here, the performance of an investment is unrelated to that of another. This situation would typically arise when investments include an engineering firm and a clothing manufacturer. Barring a total market collapse, both investments will be expected to perform entirely independence of each other.

From the above, we can see that, to reduce the risk, the finance manager in his or her role of investor should choose investments which are perfectly negatively correlated, and where this cannot be achieved, he or she should seek nil correlation as the next best alternative.

Assessing Risk under Different Forms of Correlation

We shall consider this through an example.

Two investment opportunities have the following potential outcomes

Investment 1

	Probability (p)	Return (r)
Worst outcome	0.3	10%
Most likely outcome	0.4	15%
Best outcome	0.3	20%

Investment 2

Probability	(p)	Return (r)
Worst outcome	0.3	9%
Most likely outcome	0.4	16%
Best outcome	0.3	21%

Where the investments are perfectly correlated, we can assume that if investment 1 yields 20%, then investment 2 will yield 21%, and so on. If they are negatively correlated, then investment I will yield 20% whilst investment 2 will yield 9%, etc.

Having accepted the theory, we can move forward and calculate the return of a portfolio which is composed of exactly half of each type of the above securities under conditions of positive, negative and nil correlation.

(a) Positive Correlation

Where the two investments are positively correlated, the worst outcome will occur the same time for both.
Firstly, we work out the expected return of the portfolio by combining the expected returns of each investment. The expected return for investment 1 is 15% (from the example considered previously). For investment 12 it is:

Probability factor (p)	Return (r)	Expected value
0.3	9%	2.7%
0.4	16%	6.4%
0.3	21%	6.3%
	Expected Return (r)	15.4%

The expected return on the portfolio is therefore:

(50% X 15%) + (50% X 15.4%) = 15.2%

Having determined the expected return from the investment, we now go on to calculate the likely variation in it. From the example above, we know the standard deviation for investment 1 is 3.87%. The standard deviations for investment 2 is calculated as follows:

P	Return (r)	$(r - \bar{r})$	$P(r - \bar{r})_2$
0.3	9%	(6.4%)	12.29
0.4	16%	0.6%	0.14
0.3	21%	5.6%	9.41
		Variance	21.84

The standard deviation of investment $2 = \sqrt{21.84} = 4.6\%$

We can now consider the standard deviation of the portfolio under perfect correlation:

	Return On 1	Return On 2	Combined Return	Probability	Expected Value	$(r - \bar{r})$ (50%)	$p(r - \bar{r})_2$ (50%)
Worst Outcome	5%	4.5%	9.5%	0.3	2.85	(5.7)	9.75
Most Likely Outcome	7.5%	8%	15.5%	0.4	6.20	0.3	0.04
Best Outcome	10%	10.5%	20.5%	0.3	6.15	5.3	8.43
Variance:	18.22						$\bar{r} = 15.20$

Standard Deviation $= \sqrt{18.22} = 4.27\%$

(b) Negative Correlation

If the two investments in our portfolio are negatively correlated, then the worst outcome for investment 1 should coincide with the best outcome for investment 2 and vice versa. Our calculations will look like the following:

	Return On 1	Return On 2	Combined Return	Probability	Expected Value	$(r - \bar{r})$ (50%)	$P(r - \bar{r})2$ (50%)
Worst Outcome	5%	4.5%	9.5%	0.3	2.85	(5.7)	9.75
Most likely Outcome	7.5%	8%	15.5%	0.4	6.20	0.3	0.04
Best Outcome	10%	10.5%	20.5%	0.3	6.15	5.3	8.43
Variance:	18.22						$-\bar{r} = 15.20$

Standard deviation $= \sqrt{0.21} = 0.46\%$

The figure demonstrates the difference which occurs between perfect positive and perfect negative correlation. With positive correlation, the standard deviation (the risk) is 4.27% on our return of 15.2%, whereas with negative correlation it is only 0.46%.

There is also a formula which you may encounter that can also be used to calculate the standard deviation of a portfolio which contains two investments:

$$S = \sqrt{(x_1)^2 Q_1^2 + (x_2)^2 Q_2^2 + 2 (x_1) (x_2) (c) (Q_1) (Q_2)}$$

Where: S = the standard deviation of the portfolio
x_1 = the weighting applying to the first investment
x_2 = the weighting applying to the second investment
Q_1 = the standard deviation of the first investment
Q_2 = the standard deviation of the second investment
C = the correlation coefficient between the investment

Using the two investment considered in the above example, we can use formula to calculate the standard deviation, and hence the risk, of the portfolio.

In a situation of perfect positive correlation, the correlation is expressed as $+1$ and the formula become:

$$S = \sqrt{(0.5)_2\, 15 + (0.5)_2\, 21.84 + 2(0.5)\, (0.5)\, (1)\, (3.87)\, 4.67)}$$

$\qquad = 3.75 + 5.64 + 9.04$

$\qquad = 18.25$

$S = 0.41\%$

The answers, as you can see, approximate very closely to the answer we calculated previously. The negative calculation shows a slightly variation because of its relative size, i.e. a standard deviation of less than half a percent.

Note that is not correlation existed at all, the correlation coefficient would be 0 and the second half of the formula would, therefore, equal zero.

DR. CRYFORD MUMBA

$$S = \sqrt{3.75 + 5.46 + 0}$$

$$= \sqrt{9.21}$$

$$= 3.03\%$$

The Importance of Correlation

You may be wondering why the relationship between the returns from the individual investments is more important than the returns on individual investments.

When considering the risk from holding securities, we saw above that we look at the variations in returns from individual securities and the correlation between the returns. If we call the variance of an individual security V, and the correlation between returns from securities C, we can see the factors affecting risk as the number of securities in the portfolio is increased:

Variance and correlation in a portfolio

Number of securities	1	2	3	4	5	6	7	8	9	10
1	V	C	C	C	C	C	C	C	C	C
2	C	V	C	C	C	C	C	C	C	C
3	C	C	V	C	C	C	C	C	C	C
4	C	C	C	V	C	C	C	C	C	C
5	C	C	C	C	V	C	C	C	C	C
6	C	C	C	C	C	V	C	C	C	C
7	C	C	C	C	C	C	V	C	C	C
8	C	C	C	C	C	C	C	V	C	C
9	C	C	C	C	C	C	C	C	V	C
10	C	C	C	C	C	C	C	C	C	V

Thus, as the number of securities in the portfolio increases, the significance of individual variances becomes less important, and it is the correlation between returns that is important.

PORTFOLIO COMPOSITION

When choosing his portfolio the investor will wish to maximize expected returns and minimise risk. We can illustrate the relationship between the two using graphs and this can help us determine portfolio composition.

Investment Indifference Curves

The basis for this is the indifference curve. The indifference curve for an investor represents the mixtures of risk and return which will be acceptable in terms of an investment. Consider figure 7.2, at any point along the curve, the risk-return relationship is the same for the investor and he will be indifferent to whether the investment is at point A or point B.

(Indifference curves are curved because of the diminishing returns provided as the quantities of risk or return become disproportionate in the mixture towards the extremes of the curves).

Figure 7.2: An Investor's Indifference Curve

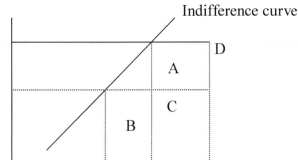

A will be preferable to D because it offers the same expected return for a lower risk and to C and D. Whether an investor will choose A or B depends on their attitude to risk – and remember that an investor may be risk averse or risk-seeking.

Traditional economic theory states that individuals will seek to maximize their utility. The Markowiz model of investment analysis seeks to measure the investor's utility function U as:

U = U (RQ)
Where r = the investor's expected return from the shares; and
     Q = the standard deviation or risk of the investment.

We can plot this as series of indifference curves for investors as

Figure: 7.3. An investor's indifference curves

Expected return (r)

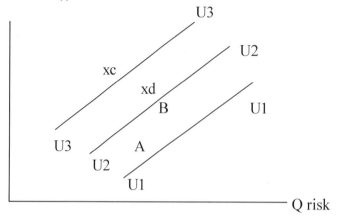

Thus shows the portfolio between which the investor will be indifferent. They all give equal utility – for example, A gives a lower return but has a lower risk than B.

The further the indifference curves go to the greater will be the value of utility of the investor, because these portfolios provide higher for the same level of risk, or lower risk for the same level or returns. Portfolios to the left to the curves are preferable because those below are mean variance inefficient and those on or above the utility curve are mean variance efficient. Mean variance efficient portfolios are those which give maximum return for a given level of risk, or have the minimum risk for a given level of return. Mean variance inefficient portfolios are those which are not efficient in the sense explained above.

Efficient Frontier

We can develop the above analysis into a model of expected risk and return for all possible investments.

If we plot the risk-return relationship for a number of investments, we get a scatter gram as shown in figure: 7.4. The resultant plot does not follow a linear course, but is regarded as having an "umbrella" shape.

Figure 7.4: The Efficient Frontier

Expected return

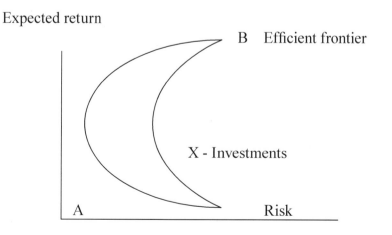

Those investments which maximize the expected return for a level of expected return can be seen to the line AB – this is known as the **efficient frontier**. A combination of investments falling on the line AB represent the most efficient portfolios. Before reading any further think why they give the most efficient portfolios.

The reason is that it is impossible to create a portfolio which gives a higher rate of return for a given level of risk, or a lower level of risk for a given level of return. Remember-the traditional economic theory on which it is based assumes that investors are risk averse.

We can combine the indifference curve for a particular investor with this concept of the efficiency frontier: consider figure 7.5. Utility curve/indifference curve

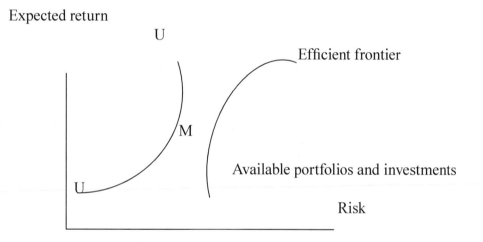

The optimum portfolio is the one where the efficiency frontier touches the individual's indifference curve at a tangent, shown as portfolio M. Indifference curves about the efficient frontier are not attainable there being no portfolios of securities offering both levels of expected return and risk.

The capital market line(CML)

The return on government stock is deemed to be risk-free (government can always print money to met their obligations). This is point on the y axis (return) of the risk-return graph where risk is zero and is shown in figure 7.6 as point Rf – **the risk-free rate of return**. If we draw a line tangential from Rf, to the efficient frontier we obtain the **capital market line (CML)**

The Capital Market Line

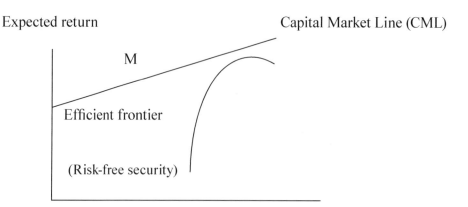

Any portfolio not on this line can be seen to be either mean variance inefficient (producing lower expected return or higher risk than those on the capital market line), or to be not obtainable (those above the line). Investors will be able to invest in a mixture of the market portfolio and the risk-free investments. They can either invest in the risk-free investment with or without investing in the market, or borrow at the risk-free rate and invest in the market portfolio, or invest solely in the market.

You may be wondering what portfolio M consists of since it is the only portfolio investors wish to hold. All shares quoted must be held and therefore M must consist of all shares on the stock market. In practice, no one shareholder will be able to hold every one, but a well diversified portfolio of 15 to 20 shares has been found to mirror M.

An efficient portfolio would be one that offers a better combination of risk and return than that offered by the CML (although as we say above it is unobtainable) and an inefficient one is one which offers a worse combination than that available on the CML.
Let examine this in more detail. Consider the CML shown below:

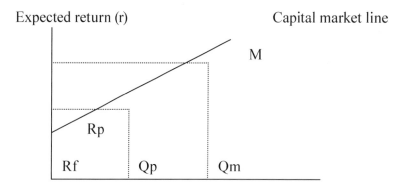

We see the higher the risk the higher the expected return (this is in line with all the theory we have discussed thus far). Using the equation for the gradient of a straight line ($y = mx + c$) we can give the gradient at any point on the CML.

Consider $y = \dfrac{Rm - Rf}{Qm}$

This shows the level of expected return required to compensate investors for the risk they are bearing (including both business and financial risk).

The expected return over and above the risk-free rate is known as the risk premium. If you look at the CML you can see that the statement "the greater the risk the greater the expected return" does indeed, hold, with riskier securities offering a higher level of risk premium.

We saw earlier that the expected rate of return comprises an element for the risk premium and return require on the risk-free securities. The return required on portfolio p (and the equation of the CML) is:

$Rp = Rf + \dfrac{(Rm - Rf)\, Qp}{Qm}$

The risk premium $\dfrac{(Rm - Rf)}{Qm}$ qp can be rewritten as qp $\dfrac{(Rm - Rf)}{Qm}$

The expression Qp is commonly known as the beta factor and thus, the equation can be written as:

$Rp = Rf\, B\, (Rm - Rf)$

Where Rp = the return on a portfolio by an investor
    B = the beta factor
    Rm = the return required for holding the market portfolio
    Rf = risk-free rate

The beta factor equation can also be used to determine the required on an individual investment or security. Thus, the required return on a portfolio is determined by the relationship of its risk in relation to that of the market. This is because the greater the difference in risk of the portfolio to that of the market (measured by their respective variances), the greater the difference in required returns

The beta factor can be used to measure the extent to which the return on a portfolio or security should exceed the risk free rate of return.

This point and the equation above is the basis of the capital asset pricing model which we shall discuss in the next study unit.

The capital asset pricing model can be used to calculate the market value of equity (see study unit 2) and the cost of equity (and thus the weighed average cost of capital) taking financial and business risk into consideration.

Efficient and Inefficient Portfolios

Consider the following information:

Expected return on market portfolio = 16%
Risk-free rate of return = 8%
Measure of risk on market portfolio = 4%

If we plot these figure on a graph it would give us the CML as shown in figure 7.8 plotting the CML simply involves locating the position on the graph which corresponds to the market portfolio (M) – here, where the expected return is 16% and the risk is 4%—and joining it to the point on the return axis corresponding to the risk-free rate (8

Expected return %

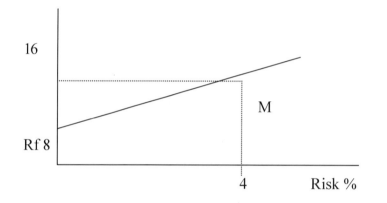

Now consider a number of portfolios with different risk-return relationships. If we plot these on the graph, we can establish whether they are efficient or inefficient.

Portfolio	Expected rate of return	Standard deviation (risk)
P	15%	5%
Q	15%	8%
R	17%	4%
S	23%	7.5%

These figures are shown plotted on figure 7.9

Expected return%

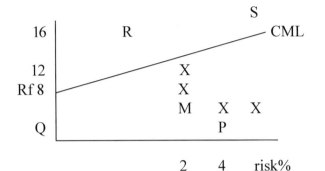

The efficient of each of the portfolio is given by their relationship to the CML:

- Portfolio P and Q are "inefficient" as they yield a lower risk/return combination than the market portfolio.

- Portfolio R is "super efficient" as it yield a higher risk/return combination.

- Portfolio S is "efficient" because it lies on the CML and therefore yields a risk/return combination equivalent to the market.

Securities Market Line(SML)

The securities market line (SML) is the same as the CIL, apart from the fact that beta co-efficient are substituted for levels of risk.

In the above example, therefore, a risk level of 4% (the market risk) is equivalent to a beta co-efficient (B) of 1.0. Similarly, a risk level of 2% would be equivalent to a beta co-efficient between two is that the CML measures total risk whilst the SML is related to market risk only.
The SML and beta co-efficient can be used in two ways

- If an investor knows the rate of return he or she requires, he or she can use a risk measurement service to identify the beta co-efficient of suitable shares, i.e. if he or she required a return of 12%, he or she would shares with a beta co-efficient of 0.5 (i.e. a risk level of 2%

- If the beta co-efficient of a share is known, it is possible to calculate the return it should provide, i.e. a beta co-efficient of 1.0 in the above example should yield 16%, and so on.

The application of portfolio theory

Portfolio theory is concerned with selecting and optimizing a set of investments by considering the returns on those investments and the variability of such returns. A "portfolio" is usually a collection of shares but it could also comprise other investment opportunities.

Planning Diversification

Portfolio theory demonstrates that risk can be diversified away with a carefully selected type and number of securities. However, if an investor such as a company is obliged to diversify (say by legislation or similar restrictions), portfolio theory can show that risk will actually increase. Such investment over larger than optimum numbers of securities is called naïve diversification.

We saw above that portfolio theory can be applied to investments other than stocks and shares, including is use by companies choosing a selection of projects and business ventures to invest in. Companies will be able to reduce risk and stabilize profits by investing in business with a negative or weak positive correlation between them – for example, a company which produces central heating systems would reduce its risk by a greater amount diversifying into paints than by diversifying into winter coats.

The advantages of diversification are:

- Reduced risk of corporate failure due to lower total company risk (and thus lower potential costs of redundancy.

- More stable internal cash flows, which should help increase debt capacity, thus reducing the cost of capital and, in turn, increasing shareholder wealth.

- Reduction in systematic risk may arise from investing in foreign markets generally protected by barriers to trade, thus increasing the risk/return combinations available to investors.

A company may, however, over-diversify and may experience the following problems

- Conglomerates often have indifferent returns leaving them vulnerable to takeover. The stock market often values the P/E ratios of individual companies within the group higher than that of the conglomerates, thus providing an incentive for the buyer of the group to "unbundled" and sell off parts of the group.

- There will be difficulties in becoming familiar with the all parts of the group and this lack of knowledge could lead to missed opportunities.

- Companies may lack the skills and expertise to manage all the elements of the group, and indeed may lack the skills to manage a diversified group.

- Empirical evidence has found that investors can diversify more efficiently than companies.

Companies considering diversification should assess the above (tailored to their particular industry). However, in general, some diversification does help to protect against short-term profit fluctuations, but too much can create severe problems for the group.

Elected Versus Random Portfolio

Recent years have seen a market growth in investment trust, unit trust, and pension and insurance funds – all of which are, in effect, investors seeking a portfolio of investments. How, then, do these portfolio operates fare? How do they perform in relation to say, a random-selected portfolio?

There have been numerous surveys along these lines. One survey concluded that, on average, unit trust performed no better than randomly –selected portfolios in the industries in which the trust had invested – i.e. the trust managers probably picked the right branch of industry to invest in, but not necessarily the right company in that industry.

There is no great condemnation of professional portfolio managers, however. They will naturally tend to err on the prudent side and go for minimum risk, even though most of their promotional advertising stresses performance. What is never likely to be clarified is the extent to which portfolio managers use (or are even aware of) the formal portfolio selection techniques. Certainly, these large investors tend to have an effect on the shares they purchase, for large-scale
investments inevitably affect the market prices. The main theme of the findings seems to be that, during times of rising markets, unit trusts do worse than random investments: in failing
markets they do better.

Practical Difficulties

When considering the application of portfolio theory, all sorts of practical difficulties come to mind:

- Can we really measure risk in statistical terms?
- Is the standard deviation of future expected returns the only dimension involved?
- How many investments shall we consider out of the thousands available on the world's stock exchanges if the sheer volume of computation is not to be prohibitive?
- What about the changing, dynamic nature of investment, taxation provisions and world events?
- What of transaction costs in amending the portfolio, the marginal value of money to an investor, inflation, and so on?

Clearly, a great deal of work remains to be done on this topic. Markowitz refined his original model to cut down the volume of computation. Other writers have built on his basic work, and this is undoubtedly one area in which future bodies of theory will emerge in a more refined state than at present.

Limitations of Portfolio Theory

Portfolio theory is:

(a) Concerned with a single time-period framework. It is not a dynamic model and therefore, can only be revised as the anticipated performance of securities alters or new ones become available. In this respect, it has no predictive qualities.

(b) Concerned with guesswork to estimate the probabilities of different outcomes which may be a particular problem when the model is being used to assess diversifications by the firm into now uncharted markets or products.

(c) Subject to investor attitudes which may be difficult to determine and reflect on when making decision, and investor perception or propensity for risk may well change over time.

(d) Not the most convenient method for considering physical investment in fixed assets or those generating irregular cash flows. A mix of "paper" and "physical" investment is best handled by other techniques centered on risk-reward probability theory.

(e) Based on simplifying assumptions:

i. that investors behave rationally and are risk-averse

ii. The agency problem is ignored – managers may be more risk-averse than shareholders as they may be concerned about job security

iii. Legal and administrative constraints are also ignored

iv. Taxation, in particular, can give rise to very complex models-for this reason its effects are often ignored

(f) Not able to cope with investment policies, such as, "selling short" and other leverage devices.

(g) Assuming constant returns to scale and divisible projects, both of which may not occur in practice.

(h) Ignoring various other aspects of risk, e.g. the risk of bankruptcy.

The volume and type of information required can also be a disadvantage, although this is now more widely available than use to be the case (at a cost). The quality of information, however, is still somewhat variable, and in any case, portfolios have to be updated and revised regularly. (The principle "garbage out" applies here, too)! Each revision will carry administrative, transaction and switching costs.

A full understanding of the model required detailed mathematical skills and is therefore in danger of being seen as too theoretical to be useful and so ignored if its principles are not put across to skeptical managers in a convincing way.

PROGRESS CLINIC 21

Question 1

Ace limited has a beta of 1.2 calculate the required return of an investment if the average market return is 26% and the risk free rate of 14%.

Question 2

Suppose PPC Limited and ACC Limited have experienced the following returns for the last four years.

Year	PPC Returns	ACC Returns
	K	K
2000	0.5	0.09
2001	-0.20	0.05
2002	0.30	-0.12
2003	0.10	0.20

Required: Calculate:

a) The average returns
b) The variance
c) The standard deviation
d) Which investment was more volatile

Question 3

Suppose you have the following investments

Share	Amount invested	Percentage	Expected return	Beta
V	K1000 000	10%	8%	0.80
X	K2000 000	20%	12%	0.95
Y	K3000 000	30%	15%	1.10
Z	K4000 000	40%	18%	1.40
Total	K10 0000 000	100%		

Required: Calculate

(a) The expected return on the portfolio
(b) The Beta of the portfolio
(c) Does the portfolio have more or less systematic risk than an average risk?

Question 4

Suppose ABC plc has a beta of 0.9. The risk free return is 10% and the return of the market is 16%. The company's last dividend was K40 per share, and the expected dividend growth is 15%. The shares currently sell for K600.

Required

Calculate the company's cost of equity capital using:

(a) Gordon Growth Model
(b) Capital Asset Pricing Model (CAPM)

Question 5

Your friend Pamela has saved K2000 000 and has decided to invest in shares. However, she wants to ensure that the risk of her portfolio is not high. In fact, she has decided that the weighted average beta of the portfolio should not be greater than 1.00. She has already chosen four companies and wishes to invest K40 000 in each of the companies K, L, M and Q.

Company	Beta
K	0.80
L	0.90
M	1.08
Q	1.30

She has asked you for assistance in determining the amount to invest in Company L to achieve the portfolio that she wants.

Required

a) Calculate the beta of the portfolio of companies K, M and Q if she invest K40 000 in each of these companies.

b)After making the investments as detailed in (a), calculate the amount that should be invested in L to give a weighted average beta of less than 1.00.

c)Discuss the four (4) main critics of the Capital Asset Pricing Model (CAMP).

CHAPTER 22

WORKING CAPITAL MANAGEMENT

Typically, current assets represent more than half the assets of companies and they tend to be of particular importance to small firms. Small business often fails as a result of failing to control working capital investment and business liquidity, and there is a direct link between sales growth and working capital management. Financial managers therefore spend a considerable amount of their time on working capital management.

The two fundamental questions to be answered in the area of working capital management are the following:

- How much should the firm invest in working capital?
- How should the investment in working capital be financed?
  How to manage working capital investment can be considered in either of two ways:
- At the individual current asset or liability level, or
- In terms of total working capital requirement.

TOTAL INVESTMENT IN WORKING CAPITAL

For now, the total investment in working capital will be considered. Management of individual current asset and liability element (i.e. stocks, debtors, cash and creditors) will be considered later.

Overall investment in working capital concerns trade-off. Here, the firm must consider the cost of investment in working capital (largely the financial cost) against the benefits it brings. With no investment in working capital there would be no stocks and no debtors, which would probably result in few sales and, therefore, little profits.

The decision regarding the level of overall investment in working capital is a cost/benefit trade-off – liquidity v profitability, or cash flow v profits.

Liquidity in the context of working capital management means having enough cash or ready access to cash to meet all payment obligations when these fall due. The main sources of liquidity are usually:

- Cash in the bank
- Short-term investments that can be cashed in easily and quickly
- Cash flows from normal trading operations (cash sales and payments debtors for credit sales)
- An overdraft facility or other ready source of extra borrowing.

CASH FLOW V PROFITS

Cash flow is the life hood of the thriving business. Effective and efficient management of the working capital investment is essential to maintaining control of business cash flow. Management must have full awareness of the profitability versus liquidity trade-off.

For example, healthy trading growth typically produces:

- Increased profitability; and
- The need to increase investment in
- Fixed assets, and
- Working capital

Here there is a trade-off under which trading growth and increased profitability squeeze cash. Ultimately, if not properly managed, increased trading can carry with it the specter of overtrading and inability to pay the business creditors.

It is worthwhile stressing the difference between cash flow and profits. Cash flow is as important as profit. Unprofitable companies can survive if they have liquidity. Profitable companies can fail if they run out to pay their liabilities (wages, amount due to suppliers, overdraft interest, etc).

Some examples of transactions that have this 'trade-off' effect on cash flows and on profits are as follows:

(a) Purchase of fixed assets for cash. The cash will be paid in full to the supplier when the fixed asset is delivered. However profits will be charged gradually over the life of the asset in the form of depreciation.

(b) Sale of goods on credit. Profits will be credited in full once the sale had been confirmed; however the cash may not be received for some considerable period afterwards.

(c) Some payments such as tax and dividend payments have no effect on profits but no constitute a cash outflow.

Clearly, cash balances and cash flows need to be monitored just as closely as trading profits. The need for adequate cash flow information is vital to enable management to fulfill this responsibility.

WORKING CAPITAL FINANCING POLICIES

Forecasted sales levels have a major impact on the required level of working capital. As sales increase, so too will purchases and inventory, creditors, cash and debtors. In a sales growth situation, an increasing portion of the firm's fixed assets. Seasonal needs, however, are those current levels that fluctuate throughout the year. The fir's working capital policy will be defined by the manner in which it finances its permanent and seasonal current asset requirements, through a mix of long-and-short term finance. There are 3 basic approaches in this regard, each with a different risk and return impact on the firm.

1. **The aggressive Approach**

Short term credit is used to finance all seasonal, and some permanent, current asset needs. Investment in current assets is generally high, with a resultant heavy reliance on trade creditors. This can lead to opportunity costs involved in high inventory levels, bad debts due to large debtor book, and penalties for late payment or the withdrawal of credit facilities, by creditors. Short-term debt interest rates are generally lower than long-term rates, short-term funding is often easier to negotiate, and repayment terms are more flexible. On the other hand, short-term funding is considered more risky as overdrafts are repayable on demand and interest rates can fluctuate widely.

2. **The Conservative Approach**

Long-term finance is generally used to finance both permanent and a proportion of seasonal current assets. Little use is made of short term finance such as trade creditors. There is a relatively low investment in current assets such as debtors and inventory, which can lead to stock outs and the loss of customers to firms who offer more attractive credit terms. Long term finance is also less easily raised, with more stringent repayment terms than short term finance.

3. **The Moderate Approach**

This is where the firm attempts to match the maturity of the funding with the lifespan of the asset being financed. Non current assets and permanent current assets will be financed by long term finance through short term funding. This minimizes the risk of not being able to meet maturity obligations. This makes sense as a firm can hardly be expected to pay off a machine with a useful life of 5 years after one year only.

Finally, the option policy lies somewhere in between the conservative and aggressive approaches. Management should attempt to reduce the level of current assets as long as the turns from this action are greater than the expected losses that could result from a low investment in current assets i.e. strike a balance between risk and return.

FINANCING AND WORKING CAPITAL

Current assets have to be financed, with either short-term sources of finance. (By definition, working capital, which is current assets minus current liabilities, is the amount of current assets financed by long-term capital). A firm's investment in working capital can be reduced by taking more short-term credit.

For example, suppose that a company has K200 000 of stocks and debtors. It can finance these assets in any of the following ways:

- With long-term funding of K200 000. The cost of doing this could be calculated by applying the firms' cost of capital to the K200 000 investment. However, this form of funding should help to ensure adequate liquidity.

- With short-term credit of K200 000. If the credit is provided by trade creditors, there is no cost. If it is provided by a bank overdraft, there is an interest cost on the overdraft balance. Excessive short-term funding creates a risk to cash flows and liquidity, because the stocks and debtors must continue to generate enough cash to meet the payment obligations to the short-term creditors.

- With a combination of long-term and short-term finance. This is what normally happens in practice, although the proportions of long-term and sort-term funding can obviously vary.

A risk for rapidly-growing companies, particularly when profit margins are low, is that as they grow, they need larger investments in current assets (and fixed assets). If the increase in assets is financed largely by short-term credit, the risks of liquidity shortages will grow. Financing asset growth with short-term credit is called overtrading. Overtrading is explained in more detail later.

WORKING CAPITAL RATIOS

The adequacy of working capital management policies in maintaining liquidity can only be determined by a detailed analysis of current resources and requirements including regular cash flow forecasts. However, a broad indication of liquidity may be obtained by calculating various ratios.

These will be illustrated by difference to the following set of accounts:

Summarized balance sheet at 30 June

	2007		2006	
	K'000	K'000	K'000	K'000
Fixed assets (net book value)				
Current assets:		130		139
Stock	42		37	
Debtors	29		23	
Bank	3		5	
	74		65	

Creditors: Amounts failing due
within one year:

Trade creditor	36		55	
Taxation	10		10	
	46		65	
Net current assets		28		-
Total assets less current liability			158	139

Creditors: Amount failing due
beyond one year 5%

secured loan stock	40	40	99	118
Ordinary share capital (50n shares)			35	35
8% Preference shares (K1 shares)			25	25
Share premium account			17	17
Revelation reserve			10	-
Profit and loss account			118	99

The quick ratio excludes stock on the basis that the time scale over which this can be realized as cash may be considered longer than the period within which trade creditors and other short-term creditors will require payment.

The current and quick ratios are measures of short-term liquidity which indicate the extent to which current assets cover current liabilities.

A higher ratio indicates better liquidity. However, a very high liquidity ratio could indicate excessive liquidity.

The current ratio

2007	2006
$\frac{74}{46} = 1.61$	$\frac{65}{65} = 10$

The quick (or acid test) ratio

2007	2006
$\frac{32}{46} = 0.7$	$\frac{28}{65v} = 0.43$

Both of these ratios show an improvement. The extent of the change between the two years seems surprising and would require further investigation. It would also be useful to know these ratios compare with those of a similar business, since typical liquidity ratios for supermarkets, say, are quite difference from those for heavy engineering firms. In 2007 current liabilities were well covered assets, liabilities payable in the near future (trade creditors), however, are only half covered by cash and debtors (a liquid asset, close to cash).

In general, high current and quick ratios are considered 'good' in that they mean that an organization has the resources to meet its commitments as they fall due. However, it may indicate that working capital is not being used efficiently, for example that there is too much idle cash that should be invested to earn a return.

Conventional wisdom has it that an ideal current ratio is 2 and an ideal quick ratio is 1. It is very tempting to draw definition conclusions from limited information or say that the current ratio should be 2, or that the quick should be 1.

However, this is not very meaningful without taking into account the type of ratio expected in a similar business or within a business sector. Any assessment of working capital ratios must take into account the nature of the business involved.

Cash operating cycle

The investment made in working capital is largely a function of sales and, therefore, it is useful to consider the problem in terms of a firm's working capital cycle, or cash operating cycle.

The cash operating cycle is the length of time which elapses between a business paying for its raw materials and the business's customers paying for the goods made from the raw materials.

The cash operating cycle

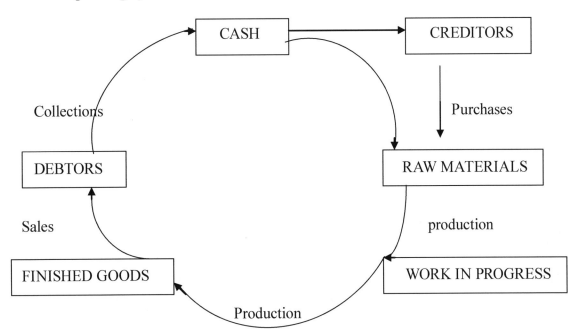

The cycle reflects a firms' investment in working as it moves through the production process towards sales. The investment in working capital gradually increase, firstly being only in raw materials, but then in labour and overheads as production progresses. This investment must be maintained through the production process, the holding period for finished goods and up to the final collection of cash from trade debtors. (Note: The net investment can be reduced by taking trade credit from suppliers).

The faster a firm can 'push' items around the cycle the lower its investment in working capital will be.

Calculating the cash operating cycle

With some fairly basic financial data it is possible to measure the length of the cash operating cycle for a given firm.

For a manufacturing business, such as that illustrated in the diagram above, the cash operating cycle will be measured by:

Cash operating cycle = raw materials holding period + WIP holding period + finished goods holding period + debtors' collection period – creditor's payment period.

For a wholesale or retail business, there will be no raw materials or WIP holding periods, and the cycle simplifies to:

Cash operating cycle = stock holding period + debtors' collection period – creditors' payment period.

SUMMARY

The cash operating cycle is measurable in days as:

Stock turnover days Plus debtor days Minus creditor days

A longer stock turnover period or allowing debtors longer to pay lengthens the operating cycle. It also increases the investment in stocks or debtors, tying up more cash in working capital.

A task for the financial manger is to maintain the length of the operating cycle at a level where the investment in working capital is not excessive, but at the same time liquidity is sufficient.

The periods relating to the individual current assets and liabilities are also useful ratios in their own rights; we shall first consider them individually for our illustrative accounts (assuming its stock companies only finished goods), and then combine them into the cash operating cycle.

Stock holding period (stock turnover period)

Stock holding period = $\dfrac{\text{average stock held}}{\text{Cost of sales}}$ x 365 days

Stock turnover = $\dfrac{\text{cost of sales}}{\text{Average stock held}}$

For example, the stock holding periods are as follows

2007	2006
$\frac{1}{2}$ (37 + 42) x 365 days = 92 days	$\frac{1}{2}$ (29 + 37) x 365 days = 80 days
157	151

These show that stock turnover has fallen. In 2006 average stock was sold 4.6 times per year. In 2007 it was sold 4.0 times per year.

If you are required to compare stock holding periods between two balance sheets, it is acceptable to base each stock holding period on balance sheet stock, rather than average stock, in order to see whether the stock holding has increased or decreased.

Debtors' collection period (debtor days)

Debtor' collection = $\dfrac{\text{closing trade debtors}}{\text{Average daily sales}}$

Businesses which sell on credit terms specify a credit period. Failure to send out invoices on time or to follow up late payers will have an adverse effect on the cash flow of the business. The debtor's collection period measures the average period of credit allowed to customers.

	2007	2006
Average daily sales	$\dfrac{\text{K209 000}}{365}$ = K573	$\dfrac{\text{K196 000}}{365}$ = 537
Closing trade debtors	K29 000	K23,000
Debtor days	$\dfrac{\text{K29 000}}{573}$ = 50.6 days	$\dfrac{\text{K23 000}}{537}$ = 42.8 days

Compared with 2006 the debtor's collection period has worsened in 2007. If the average credit allowed to customers was, say, thirty days, then something is clearly wrong. Further investigation might reveal delays in sending out invoices or failure to 'screen' new customers.

In general, the shorter the debtors' collection period the better because debtors are effectively 'borrowing' from the company. Remember, however, that the level of debtors reflects not only the ability of credit controllers but also the sales and marketing strategy adopted, and then the nature of the business. Any change in the level of debtors must therefore be assessed in the light of the level of sales.

Note: The quickest way to compute the debtor days is to use the following formula (we are assuming that all sales are on credit).

Closing trade debtors x 365
Credit sales for year

2007
$\underline{29\ 000}$ x 365 = 50.6 days
209 000

2006
$\underline{23\ 000}$ x 365 = 42.8 days
196 000

Note: Instead of using the current value of trade debtors to calculate debtor days, the average value of debtors could also be used.

Creditor's payments period (creditor days)

Creditor's payment period = closing trade creditors
                          Average daily purchases

This measures the average period of credit allowed by suppliers

	2007	2006
Average daily purchases	$\underline{K162\ 000}$ = K444 365	$\underline{K156\ 000}$ = K436 365
Closing trade creditors	K36 000	K55 000
Creditor's payment period	81.1 days	126.2 days

The creditor's payment period has reduced substantially last year. It is however, in absolute terms still a high figure. Often, suppliers request payment within thirty days. The company is taking nearly three months. Trade creditors are thus financing much of the working capital requirements of the business, which is beneficial to the company.

An increase in creditor days be good in that it means that all available credit is being taken, but there are potential disadvantages of taking extended credit.

* Future suppliers may be endangered
* Availability of cash discounts is lost
* Suppliers may quote a higher price for the goods knowing the company takes extended credit.

The calculations of creditor's payment period (creditor's days) is:

<u>Closing trade creditors</u> x 365
Credit purchases for year

2007	2006
<u>36 000</u> x 365 = 81.1 days	<u>55 000</u> x 365 = 126.3 days
162 000	159 000

Note: Instead of using the current value of trade creditors to calculate days, the average value of trade creditors could also be used.

The length of the cash operating cycle

We are now in a position to compute the length of the cash operating cycle for our example.

	2007 Days	2006 Days
Stock holding period	92	80
+		
Debtors' collection period	50.6	42.8
-		
Creditors; payment period	(81.1)	(126.2)
=		
Cash operating cycle	61.5 days	(3.4 days)

Our example shows that, in 2007, there is approximately a 62 day gap between paying cash to suppliers for goods, and receiving the cash back from customers. However, in 2006, there was the somewhat unusual situation where cash received from the customers, on an average, more than 3 days before the payment to suppliers was needed.

The length of the cycle depends on the efficiency of management and the nature of the industry. The optimum level is the amount that results in no idle cash or unused stock, but that does not put a strain on liquid resources. Trying to shorten the cash cycle may have detrimental effects elsewhere, with the organization lacking the cash to meet its commitments and losing sales since customers will generally prefer to buy from suppliers who are prepared to extend trade credit, and who have items held in stock when required.

Again, any assessment of the acceptability or otherwise of the length of the cycle must take into account the nature of the business involved.
A supermarket chain will tend to have a very low or negative cycle – they have very few, if any, credit customers, they have a high stock turnover and they can negotiate quite long credit period with their suppliers.

A construction company will have a long cycle –their projects tend to be long-term, often extending over more than a year, and whilst progress payments may be made by the customer (if there is one), the bulk of the cash will be received towards the end of the project.

It would be useful to have industry average figures with which to compare our results. Cash must be in place to meet obligations as they fall due. If insufficient cash available, the company will suffer from illiquidity. A lot of academic research work has been carried out in recent years to try to develop warning indicators that a company might be going to fail through illiquidity, particularly by professor Altman in developing Z-scores.

Profit earned will, to a certain extent, alleviate the effect of illiquidity, but the strain on operating cash flow will be accentuated by the need to provide for investment in fixed assets for the firm's future, dividends and interest for the providers of long-term capital, and taxation.

Management of cash flows therefore involves the interrelationship of the following items:

- Profits
- Working capital levels
- Capital expenditure
- Dividend policy
- Taxation

The emphasis in this section of the text is on the control of levels of working capital.

Short-term cash controls

Control of cash short periods is best achieved by preparing short-term cash forecasts for comparison with actual results. If the cash forecast shows an unacceptable cash balance or a cash deficit, then it will be necessary to review a number of items as follows:

- Profit levels, including changes in selling price or improvements in operating efficiency
- Working capital requirements, i.e. stock holding, credit periods given and taken, invoice processing procedures, etc.
- Fixed asset requirements, having regard to the timing and amounts of capital projects
- Dividend policy

Example

Assume the following financial information:

Item	Amount
Inventory	30 000
Receivables (debtors)	21 270
Payables (creditors)	14 850
Cost of sales	146 000
Credit sales	390 000
Credit purchases	175 000

Required: Calculate the operating cycle and cash cycle.

Solution

- Accounts receivable period = $\dfrac{\text{Receivables}}{\text{Credit sales}}$ x 365 days

$$= \frac{21270}{390000} \text{ x } 365 \text{ days} = 20 \text{ days}$$

- Payables period = $\dfrac{\text{Payables}}{\text{Credit purchases}}$ x 365 days

$$= \frac{14850}{175000} \text{ x } 365 \text{ days} = 31 \text{ days}$$

- Inventory period = $\dfrac{\text{Inventory}}{\text{Cost of sales}}$ x 365 days

$$= \frac{30000}{146000} \text{ x } 365 \text{ days} = 75 \text{ days}$$

Operating cycle = Inventory period + Receivable period

= 75 + 20 = 95 days

Cash cycle = operating cycle – payables period

= 95 – 31 = 64 days

Interpretation: on average, during the period in question, this firm's inventory stays on the premises for 75 days; the firm collects on sales in 20 days, and pays its bills after 31 days. 95 days lapse from the time that inventory is purchased until payment received from the customer. Firms differ with respect to "norms" for the particular market in which they operate. Most important is the trend in these figures over time given the nature of the business.

Most firms require a positive operating and cash cycle, as they are unlikely to purchase inventory, manufacture the end-product, pay for inventory, sell the product and receive cash for the product, all within a single day! Thus most firms require finance for their inventories and receivables. The longer the operating and cash cycles, the more financing is required, hence the importance of monitoring both these cycles. A lengthening in either cycle can indicate slow-moving stock or collection inefficiencies. Such problems could be hidden by an increased payables period, so the payables period requires close attention. Management's goal should be to shorten the operating cycle as far as possible without compromising efficiency. Examples of measures that can be taken to ensure a shorter cycle would be:

- Reducing manufacturing and selling period/without compromising product quality).
- Reducing the accounts receivable period (without antagonizing customers)
- Lengthening the accounts payable period (without losing suppliers and getting a poor credit rating).

Overcapitalization

A firm is overcapitalized if its working capital is excessive for its needs. Excessive stocks, debtors and cash will lead to a low return on investment, with long-term funds tied in non-earning short-term assets. Overcapitalization can normally be identified by poor accounting ratios (such as liquidity ratios being too high or stock turnover periods being too long).

Overtrading

A firm is overtrading if it is trying to carry on too large a volume of activities with its current levels of working capital. Overtrading in essence means undercapitalization.

Often a company may try to grow too fast, reporting increasing profits while its overdraft soars. Remember that more companies fail when the economy is recovering from a recession than when the economy is entering a recession.

Overtrading serious problems that shall but rapidly-expanding businesses can easily fall into.

Symptoms of overtrading

- A rapid increase in stock levels, matched by a large increase in trade creditors or bank overdraft
- Deteriorating current ratio (ratio of current assets to certain liabilities) and quick ratio (ratio of current assets excluding stocks to current liabilities).
- A significant slow-down in the average time for paying trade creditors

- Sometimes, a large increase in debtors, with debtors also taking longer to pay. (Rapidly-growing businesses might sell on easy credit terms to win new customers)
- Decrease in current and liquid ratios
- Stock increase without a relative increase in turnover
- The ratios sales/working capital and sales/capital employed increase significantly
- The company takes longer to pay off its creditors. Increase in the total creditors or creditors in relation to debtors and sales
- There is a growth in the rate of borrowing particularly short-term bank borrowing and interest expense increases
- Fixed asset investment is curtailed
- Not all accounting records are made available to the auditors
- The directors prevent a particular necessary audit procedure form being carried out e.g. where the evidence or ownership of material assets.

Causes

- Financial planning errors
- Volume of business exceeding available resources

Effects

- Over-reliance on external finance
- Unfavourable financial ratios: debt/equity, debt/assets, debtors/creditors, current and liquid ratios
- Constant change of suppliers
- Inability to meet obligations as they because due (wages, taxes, creditors), excessive credit taken from suppliers, loss of bargains (e.g. discount)
- Inability to offer credit to customers
- Major cause of business failure

Control of orders received

Overtrading can cause grave financial problems, so it may be vital to limit the amount of business that is accepted. In a manufacturing firm, for instance, each order must be analyzed to discover the following:

- Its effect on factory capacity
- The amount of working capital tied up in the order
- The length of time for which the company must provide finance
- The estimated profit or contribution of the order

Management will wish to select the most profitable orders and could perhaps formulate a selection factor relating the contribution to the total order value and the total financing period, e.g.

Selection factor = <u>contribution</u>
                    Order value x financing period

It might also be possible to limit the orders taken by a salesperson to a certain order value, with an overall ceiling any month. Beyond this, the salesperson must obtain approval from the sales manager. In that way, a profitable mix of orders could be selected which can be handled comfortably by the firm. Another aspect of orders is the relationship between quotations sent and orders received: if, say, 90% of quotations are accepted and firm orders received, the company may be under-pricing its products.

Control of purchase commitments

A firm's creditors can put the firm into liquidation if their demands for settlement are not satisfied. It is clearly important therefore to apply controls to the routines which create the liabilities, i.e. purchasing of material and plant, etc. The purchasing manager should verify that materials to be purchased will be resold or used in production within a reasonable time-say two months. In many cases this factor should carry greater weight than the savings that can be made by bulk-buying. The purchasing manager should, however, seek to negotiate with suppliers in an attempt to obtain bulk discounts by placing larger orders, but taking delivery over a long period-thereby reducing the total initial liability.

Management of stock

The objective of stock management is to ensure sufficient levels of stock to maintain an acceptable level of available on demand whilst minimizing the associated holding, administrative and stock out costs.

Costs of holding stock

Holding stock is an expensive business-it has been estimated that the costs of holding stock each year is one-third of its production or purchase cost.

Holding costs include:

- Interest on capital
- Storage space and equipment
- Administration and staff costs
- Lease

On the other hand, running out of stock (known as a stock) incurs a cost. If, for example, a shop is persistently out of stock on some lines, customers will start going elsewhere. Stock out costs are difficult to estimate, but they are an essential factor to consider in stock control.

Finally, order set-up costs are incurred each time a batch of stock is ordered. Administrative costs and, where production is internal, costs of setting up machinery will be affected in total by the frequency of orders. The two major quantitative problems of determining re-order levels and order quantitative are essentially problems of striking the optimum balance between holding costs, stock out costs and order set-up-costs.

Before looking at theoretical approaches to determining optimum re-order quantities and levels-in particular, the Economic Order Quantity (EOQ) model-we shall briefly consider the practical systems and issues involves in the control of stock levels.

Stock management systems

Two Bin Systems

This system utilizes two, e.g. A and B. Stock is taken from A until is empty. An order for a fixed quantity is placed and, in the meantime, stock is used from B. The standard stock for B is the expected demand in the lead-time (the time between the order being placed and the stock arriving), plus some 'buffer' stock.

When the new arrives, B is filled up to its standard stock and the rest is placed in A. Stock is then drawn as required from A, and the process is repeated.

Single Bin System

The same sort of approach is adopted by some firms for single bin with a red line within the bin indicating the re-order level.

Control levels

In bin systems, where order quantities are constant, it is important to identify alterations to the estimates on which that quantity was based. The stock controller should be notified when the stock level exceeds a maximum or falls below a minimum.

- Maximum stock level would represent the normal peak holding i.e. buffer stocks plus the re-order quantity. If the maximum is exceeded, a review of estimated demand in the lead-time is needed.

- Minimum stock level usually corresponds with buffer stock. If stock falls below that level, emergency action t replenish may be required.

The levels would also be modified according to the relative importance/cost of a particular stock item.

The costs of a continual review of bin levels, as implied by the two-bin or one-bin system, may be excessive, and it may be more economic to operate a period review system.

Periodic review system (or constant order cycle system)

Stock levels are reviewed at fixed intervals e.g. every four weeks. The stock in hand is then made up to a predetermined level, which takes account of likely demand before the next review and during the lead-time.

Thus a four-weekly review in a system where the lead-time was two weeks would demand that stock be made up to the likely maximum demand for the next six weeks.

Bin systems versus periodic review

Advantages of bin systems

- Stock can be kept at a lower level because of the ability to order whenever stocks fall.

- To a low lever, rather than having to wait for the next re-order date.

Advantage of periodic review system

- Order office load is more evenly spread and easier to plan. This reason the system is popular with suppliers.

Slow-moving stocks

Certain items may have a high individual value, but be subject to infrequent demand. In most organizations, about 20% of items stocked make up 0% of total usage (the 80/20 rule).

Slow-moving items may be ordered only when required, unless a minimum order quantity is imposed by the suppliers

A regular report of slow-moving items is useful in that management is made aware of changes in demand and of possible obsolescence. Arrangements may be made to reduce or eliminate stock levels or, on confirmation of obsolescence, for disposal.

Just In Time (JIT) System

JIT is a series of manufacturing and supply chain technique that aim to minimize stock levels and improve customer service by manufacturing not only at he exact time customers require, but also in the exact quantities they need and at competitive prices.

JIT extend much further than a concentration on stock levels. It centers around the elimination of waste. Waste is defined as any activity performed within a manufacturing company which does not add value to the product. Examples of waste are:

- Raw material stock
- Work-in-progress stock
- Finished goods stock
- Materials handling
- Quality problems (rejects and reworks etc)
- Queues and delays on the shop-floor
- Long raw materials lead-times
- Long customer lead-times
- Unnecessary clerical and accounting procedures

JIT attempts to eliminate waste at every stage of the manufacturing process, notably by the elimination of:

The combination of these concepts in JIT results in:

- A smooth flow of work through the manufacturing plant
- A flexible production process which is responsible to the customer's requirements
- Reduction in capital tied up in stocks

The impact of JIT

A JIT manufacture looks for a single suppliers who can provide high quality frequent and reliable deliveries, rather than the lowest price. In return, the supplier can expect more business under long-term purchase orders, thus providing greater certainty in forecasting activity levels.

Long-term contracts and single sourcing strengthen buyer-supplier relationships and tend to result in a higher quality product. Inventory problems are shifted back onto suppliers with deliveries being made as required.

The spread of JIT in the production process inevitably affects those in delivery and transportation. Smaller, more frequent loads are required at shorter notice. The haulier is regarded as almost a partner to the manufacture, but tight schedules are required of hauliers, with penalties for non-delivery.

Reduction is stock levels reduce the time taken to count stock and the clerical cost. For business that does not use JIT, there is an optimum order quantity for stock items, known as the economic order quantity or EOQ.

Buying stock items in this quantity minimize the combined costs of holding stock and ordering new stocks. With JIT, stockholding costs are close to zero, but ordering costs are high.

Economic order quantity (EOQ) model

We now turn to the theoretical side of stock control. Essentially, two problems need to be answered under either of two assumptions.

When to re-order
How much to re-order

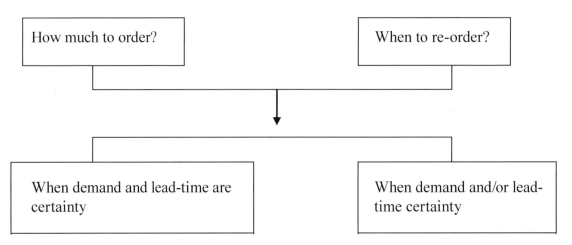

<u>Pattern of stock levels</u>

When new batches of an item in stock are purchased or made at periodic intervals the stock levels are assumed to exhibit the following pattern over time.

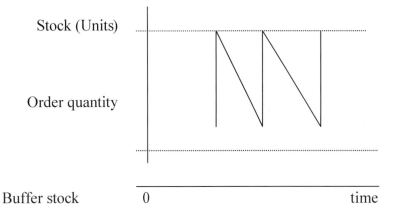

When should stock be re-ordered?

A gap (the lead-time) inevitably occurs between placing an order its delivery. Where both that gap and the rate of demand are known with certainty, an exact decision on when to re-order can be made.

In real world both will fluctuate randomly and so the order must be placed so as to leave some buffer stock if demand and lead-time follow the average pattern. The problem is again the balancing of increased holding costs if the buffer stock is high; again increase stock out costs if the buffer stock is low.

How much stock should be re-ordered?

Large order quantity (EOQ) is the quantity of stock ordered each time which minimizes annual costs (order set-up-holding costs). Note that EOQ is not affected by uncertainty of demand and lead-times, as long as demand is independent of stock levels.

Tutorial note: Often the 'holding cost' will reduce quantity discounts are taken because this cost often relates to the original cost of buying an item.

When to re-order stock

Having decided how much stock, the next problem is when to re-order, the needs to identify a level of stock which can be reached before an order needs to be place. The re-order level (ORL) is the quantity of stock on hand when an order is placed. When demand and lead-time are known with certainty the re-order level may be calculated exactly.

Re-ordered level with variable demand or variable lead-time

When lead time and demand are known with certainty, ROL = Demand during lead time. Where is uncertainty, an optimum level of buffer stock must be found.

If there were certainty, then the last unit of stock would be sold as the next delivery is made. In the real world, this ideal cannot be achieved. Demand will vary from period to period, and re-order levels must allow some buffer (or safety) stock, the size of which is a function of three factors:
- Variability of demand
- Cost of holding stocks
- Cost of stock outs

Management of debtors

Extending trade credit

A firm must establish a policy for credit terms given to its customers. Ideally the firm would want to obtain cash with each order delivered, but that is impossible unless substantial settlement (or cash) discounts are offered as an inducement. It must be recognized that credit terms are part of the firm's marketing policy. If the trade or industry has adopted a common practice, then it is probably wise to keep in step with it.

A lenient credit policy may well attract additional custom, but at a disproportionate increase in cost. The optimum level of trade credit extended represents a balance between two factors:

- Profit improvement from sales obtained by allowing credit

- The cost of credit allowed

Management will be anxious to do the following

- Establish a credit policy in relation to normal periods of credit and individual credit limits

- Develop a system which will control the implementation of credit policy

- Prescribe reporting procedures which will monitor the efficiency of the system.

Thus management of debtors requires a credit policy to be established, properly implemented and continually monitored.

Establishing credit policy

The period of credit extended will be set by reference to:

- Elasticity of demand for the company's products
- Credit terms offered by competitors
- Risk of bad debts resulting from extended credit periods
- Risk of bad debts resulting from extended credit periods
- Financing costs and availability of finance
- Costs of administering the credit system

Individual credit limits depends on assessing the creditworthiness of a particular customer: in the first instance, whether the customer would be allowed credit at all; and secondly, the maximum amount that should be allowed. Assessment involves analysis of the prospective customer's current business situation and credit history, derived from information obtained from any available sources.

Credit policy must be reasonably flexible to reflect changes in economic conditions, actions by competitors and marketing strategy (e.g. the desire to' kill off' a new competitor in the market).

A study of the debtors of XYZ Co. Ltd has shown that it is possible to classify all debtors into certain classes with the following characteristics:

Category	Average collection period (days)	Bad debts (%)
A	15	0.5
B	20	2.5
C	30	5.0
D	40	9.5

The average standard profit/cost schedule for the company's range of products is as follows:

	K	K
Selling price		2.50
Less: Materials	1.00	
Wages	0.95	
Variables costs	0.30	
Fixed costs	0.05	
		2.30
Profit		0.20

The company has the opportunity of extending its sales by K1, 000,000 per annum, split between categories C and D in the proportions 40:60. The company's short-term borrowing rate is 111/2% per annum on a simple interest basis.

Evaluate the effect of the proposed increase in sales by carrying out the steps below:

Step 1: Calculate the additional contribution from the extra sales, split between the different categories of debtor. Assume that the contribution per K of sales will be as shown on the standard cost card.

Step 2: For each category of debtor, work out the bad debts arising from the sales, using the given percentages. Deduct the bad debts from the additional contribution worked out in step 1.

Step 3: For each category of debtor work out the (absolute) interest cost of allowing credit over the relevant period.

The cost equals: Annual interest rate x additional debtors, where

Additional debtors = additional annual sales x average collection period (days) / 365

Deduct this cost from the net additional contribution derived in step 2.

Settlement Discounts

A company may offer settlement discounts to its customers, by allowing debtors to pay less than their full debit if they pay sooner than the end of their credit period. The company must ensure that offering the discount it financially sensible, with the benefit of receiving the cash early exceeding the cost of the discount.

The mathematics of offering settlement discounts is very similar to the decision as to whether discounts should be taken from suppliers; this decision is examined later in this chapter.

DR. CRYFORD MUMBA

Implementing Credit policy

Implementation of a credit policy involves assessing creditworthiness, controlling credit limits, involving promptly and establishing procedures for collection of overdue debts.

Assessing Creditworthiness

A new customer's creditworthiness should be carefully assessed before extended credit terms are offered. Sources of information are:

- **Trade references**. The potential customer is asked to give names of two existing suppliers who will testify to the firm's credit standing. Note that there is a danger that firms will nominate only suppliers that are paid on time.

- **Bank reference**. Permission is sought to approach the customer's bank to discuss his creditworthiness. Note that banks are often reluctant to give their customers bad references.

- **Credit agencies and credit associations**. These bodies will provide independent assessments of creditworthiness for a fee. Short reports may be obtained from regularly updated registers or special, more detailed, reports may be commissioned. Dun and Bradstreet is possibly the most well-known credit agency in this area, but there are others.

- **Reports from salesmen**. Salesmen are often the only representatives of the supplying firm who actually meet the potential customer's staff and see the premises. They are therefore in a unique position to provide information on customer creditworthiness.

- **Information from competitors**. In 'close-knit' industries competing suppliers often exchange credit information on potential customers.

- **Financial statement analysis**. Recent accounts may be analyzed to determine the customer's ability to pay.

- **Credit scoring.** This can be applied in all circumstances where credit is under consideration, but is more applicable where sales are direct to the public, and the use of the above evaluation are either not possible or are too expensive.

Example

A sample of a firm's past customer identifies the factors associated with bad debts. Age, sex, martial status, family size, occupation etc may be significant factors. The firm allocates a points score to potential customers as follows:

Factor	points score
Aged over 40	15
Married with fewer than three children	20
Home owner	20
At same address for over three years	15
At existing job for over two years	20
Car owner	10
Total	100

Past records show that there have been no records of payment difficulties with customers with a score of 80 or over, bad debts of 10% for scores between 35 and 80 and band debts of 25% where customers had a score of less than 35. A 'cut-off' point of 35 would probably be established, and credit refused to any potential customer with a score of less than 35.
The factors which are considered most likely to influence creditworthiness are, of course, a matter of judgment, as are the respective weights which should be attached to each factor.

Preventing credit limits from being exceeded

Control of credit limits should occur at the ordered processing stage, i.e. the customer's ledger account will be adapted to reflect orders in the pipeline as well as invoiced sales.

Invoicing promptly

The customer's period of credit will relate to a receipt of invoice, so it is essential to minimize the time-lag between dispatch and invoicing e.g. by streamlining authorization and administrative procedures.

PROGRESS CLINIC 22

Question 1

A business that specializes in the manufacture and sale of exclusive clothing has been operating successfully for 5 years. Its 2006 financial statements show the following:

	K
Sales	300,000
Cost of sales (all variable)	180,000
Expenses (all fixed)	100,000

Profit	20,000

The year end balance sheet shows that the stock is valued at K36,000, the debtors are K50,000 and the creditors are K15,000.

Premises have been identified in Kabulonga. The rental is K12,000 per annum but it is expected that the firm will double its sales. This is expected to have a dramatic effect on the profits. However, a friend of the owner mentions that "overtrading" could be a problem.

Requirements:

a) Explain the concept of overtrading and identify three mistakes that the management have made if a firm finds itself in this position.

b) Suggest ways in which this business could prevent overtrading.

Question 2

The following information was collected from the records of Pelekelo Ltd, a manufacturer of products for the construction industry for the years 20x6 and 20x7:

	20x7	20x6
	Km	Km
Turnover	2065.0	1788.7
Cost of sales	1478.6	1304.0
Gross profit	586.4	484.7
Current Assets		
Stocks	119.0	109.0
Debtors (Note 1)	400.9	347.4
Short term investments	4.2	18.8
Cash at bank & in hand	48.2	48.0
	572.3	523.2

Creditors due in one year

Loans and overdrafts	49.1	35.3
Corporation taxes	62.0	46.7
Dividend	19.2	14.3
Creditors (Note 2)	370.7	324.0
	501.0	**420.3**
Net current assets	**71.3**	**102.9**

Notes:

	20X7	20X6
	Km	Km
1. Trade debtors	329.8	285.4
2. Trade creditors	236.2	210.8

Required:

(a) From the above information for each of the years, calculate liquidity and working capital ratios which are:

(i) Current Ratio

(ii) Quick Ratio

(iii) Debtors' payment period

(iv) Stock turnover period (number of days)

(v) Creditor turnover period

(b) Comment on the comparative performance of the company over the period of two years, namely 20x6 and 20x7.

CHAPTER 23

THE ANALYSIS OF EXCHANGE RATES

The foreign exchange rate is defined as the domestic currency price of a foreign currency. i.e. how many kwacha do we need to exchange a unit of foreign currency. Thus when quoting exchange rates, we do so in terms of domestic currency equivalent (K|$). The exchange rate can either be:

1. Spot rate in which settlement is completed within two working business days.
2. Forward rate – this is a rate agreed today for delivery of the foreign 1,3, 6 months after the contract.
3. Bilateral rate – this is an exchange rate between two countries.
4. Multilateral rates – this is an exchange rate involving more than two countries.

Foreign exchange market

A foreign exchange market is a market for buying and selling of foreign currencies. They are organized markets which are electronically connected.

Functions of foreign exchange markets

1. They are used to transfer funds or purchasing power from one nation and currency to another.
2.
3. They have a credit function of discounting bills
4.
5. They provide facilities for hedging and speculations. A hedger is one who is risk avoider while a speculator is a risk lover who will accept risk in the foreign exchange market for a profit motive.

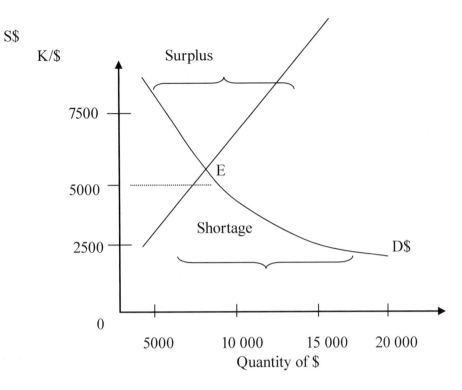

From the above graph, the following points can be noted:

1. Equilibrium is established at the exchange rate of K5000 to a US$ where 10000 US $ are supplied and demanded.

2. If demand exceeds supply, such as at an exchange rate of K2500 to a US$, there will be a shortage of the foreign exchange market. Only 5000 US $ will be supplied while 15000 US$ will be demanded. This creates an upward pressure in the exchange rate until the equilibrium rate is reached. Thus, when demand exceeds supply, the domestic currency will depreciate while the foreign currency will appreciate.

3. If supply exceeds demand, such as at an exchange rate of K10 000 per US$, the quantity of US$ supplied is approximately 15000 while only 5000 of the US$ is demanded. There is thus an exceed supply of US $ in the market.

4. This will create downward pressure on the exchange rate where the domestic currency will appreciate while the foreign currency depreciates.

Why do people demand foreign exchange

The sources of demand for foreign exchange are for following reasons:
1. In order to pay for imports
2. In order to pay for services e.g. Zambian tourist in Malawi.
3. For investment reasons abroad e.g. Zambian investors setting up operations in Malawi.

Sources of supply for foreign exchange

1. Exports are the major sources of foreign exchange.
2. Expenditure by tourists e.g. tourists from USA will supply us with the US dollar.
3. Investments by foreigners through the buying of domestic assets.
4. Grants given to the Zambian government from other countries.

Thus, the main players in the foreign exchange markets are individuals, firms and banks. Commercial banks operate in this case as clearing houses, facilitating these exchanges. Thus, the foreign exchange market can be analyzed in the same manner as the market for goods. The only difference is that in the foreign exchange market, the price refers to the exchange rate while quantity refers to the amount of the foreign currency. The foreign exchange market squarely follows the laws of demand and supply. The above scenario depicts the freely floating exchange regime.

Exchange rate management

Exchange rate systems or regimes may be broad categorized under the following headings:

1. A fixed exchange rate system
2. Free floating exchange rate system
3. Managed floating exchange rate system
4. A pegged exchange rate system

1. Fixed exchange rate

A fixed rate system is theoretically possible but not found in practices in modern economies. However, it provides a useful benchmark against which to compare other exchange rate arrangement including the advantages and disadvantages which are associated with them. A government may pursue a policy of keeping the exchange rate fixed by relying on 3 weapons:

a)Official reserves – these will be used not only to finance surpluses or deficits on the balance of payments but also to intervene the foreign exchange market to prevent the currency from either falling below or rising above a fixed value.

b)Interest rates – these can be raised to attract demand for the currency if it is falling below its agreed value or lowered to discover demand if it is becoming too strong.

c)Domestic policies to inflate / deflate the economy—deflationary policies are likely to be introduced (higher interest rates, higher taxation, lower government spending) if the currency is falling below the agreed value, these should result in a healthier balance of trade and increased investment by foreigners both of which will strengthen the currency. On the other hand, countries with strong currencies must inflate or reflate their economies. This should result in a worsening trade balance and reduced investment thus weakening their currency.

Advantages Of The Fixed Exchange Rate System

1. It remains uncertainty about exchange rates and therefore about the value of goods and services. It makes international trade easier because importers / exporters can agree prices without having to worry about potential loses through exchange rate movements. Similarly, sellers can give buyers credit without fear of adverse movement in the exchange rates during the credit period. In other words, fixed exchange rates remove the exchange risks from until trade as well as the need for forward exchange contracts which lost money.

2. A fixed exchange rate system also imposes a discipline on countries to pursue responsible economic policies which are consistent with the exchange rate for the currency. In other words, there must be broadly consistent policies about inflation and economic, if a country has a balance of payment deficit.

3. Different countries might have different economic and political objectives and so international co-operation in agreeing a broadly consistent policy for economic growth or price levels might simply be impossible to achieve.

4. A government might try to keep its exchange rate at its fixed level but if it can not control inflation, the real value of its currency would not remain fixed if one country's rate of inflation is higher than others, its export price would become uncompetitive in overseas markets and the country's trade deficit would grow. Devaluation of the currency would be necessary for the recovery.

5. If exchange rates are fixed, any changes in real interest rates in one country will create pressure for movement of capital into or out of the country. Capital movement would put pressure on the country's exchange rate to change. It follows that if exchange rates are fixed and capital is allowed to move freely between countries, that is there are no exchange controls all countries must have consistent policies on interest rates. Since consistent interest rates policies are required, there will be further requirement for consistent policies on growth of the money supplied deficit, the government will have pursue deflationary policies to dumper demand in the domestic economy, reduced the volume of importers restrict the rate of inflation and switch production capacity to export industries, where a country has a BOP surplus and ought to pursue inflationary policies to raise domestic prices and make imports more competitive and its export less competitive.

Disadvantages

1. In order to maintain their currencies at a fixed rate, the authorities must have very large quantities of foreign currency reserves and their own currency to intervene

2. in the exchange market to make an excess supply or demand for their currency. In practice, the official reserves of the government will be inadequate to guarantee a

fixed rate of exchange in the face of a serious controlling imbalance in current account trade or speculation.

3. If a country has a large deficit in its balance of payments then since its reserves are not limitless, there must be an adjustment process which can bring the balance of payments back into equilibrium. In theory, a disequilibrium in the balance of payments could be rectified by demand management that is a deflationary policy or an inflationary policy.

2. Floating exchange rates

These are at the opposite end of the spectrum to fixed rates. At this extreme, exchange rates are completely left to the free play of demand and supply market forces. And there is no official financing at all, the ruling exchange rate is therefore at equilibrium be

definition. In practice, there is no really a floating exchange rate, this is because government will want to have some control but when we refer to floating rate system are emphasis in an system where market forces are the major influence on the rates.

Advantages of freely floating rate system
1. Government is not required to undertake difficult and unpopular deflationary or inflationary policies at home to support the exchange rate. In other words the

2. Balance of payment ceases to be a constraint on government economic policy. Thus, the government is free to implement policies without concern as to whether the policies will maintain the exchange rate within specified boundaries.

3. Uncertainty about the future of a currency in a floating rate system can be reduced by the use of a forward exchange market in which contract can be trade to acquire or sale currency on a future date at a specified exchange rate.

4. There is no need to maintain huge reserves as there is an inbuilt self adjustment mechanism.

5. A freely floating exchange rate system encourages stability of the world economy.

- To smooth exchange rate movement so as to discourage wide fluctuations.
- It is a way of establishing implicit exchange rate boundaries
- It is also a way of dealing with temporary disturbances in the exchange rate movement.

Disadvantages

1. A freely floating exchange rate might disrupt the government domestic economic policies. For example, if the exchange rate depreciates import costs will rise and in a high importing country like Zambia inflation will also go up, in response to the importers of imported inflation, the country might get into a wages—prices spiral which is difficult to get out of.

2. The discussion of a government of one country might be acceptable to the government of another country. For example, if one country has subsidized exports, another country's domestic industry might be threatened by a flood of low price imports. The expansion of one country's exports might be harmful to another country's industries. Governments must show concern for the defense of their economy and export industries and managing the exchange rate is one way in which it can conduct policies.

3. In practice, government can not allow free floating even if they wanted to. Even if they do not intervene in the foreign exchange markets, their policies on interest rates, control of money supply of inflation, demand management exchange control import controls and employment will all have reparations on international trade, capital flows and exchange raw.

It is by no means certain that market forces will value the exchange rate of a currency at an appropriate level because speculation might undervalue or overvalue the currency.
Such an unrealistic exchange rate might affect the volume of business transactions in international trade. If a currency is overvalued, the volume of export contracts might be lower than it ought be, if a currency is undervalued, there might be too many export contracts. Resources would therefore be misallocated.

3. The pegged exchange rate system

This is a system in which the exchange rate of a domestic currency is tied to a few important foreign currencies. For example, the kwacha is pegged to the US $, pound and the euro. Any depreciation or appreciation of the kwacha is normally spoken of in line with these currencies and not all the currencies of the world.

4. Managed float exchange rates

In practice, governments seek to combine the advantages of exchange rate stability with flexibility and to avoid the disadvantages of both liquidly fixed exchange rates and free floating. Managed or dirty floating refers to a system whereby exchange rates are allowed to float but from time to time the authorities will intervene in the foreign exchange market.

To use their official reserves of foreign currencies to buy their domestic currency or

1. To sell their domestic currency to buy more foreign currency for the official reserves buying and selling in this way would be intended to influence the exchange rate of the domestic currency. Government do not have official reserves large enough to dictate exchange rates to the market and can only try to influence market rates with intervention.

Reasons for government intervention in the foreign exchange market

The reasons for government intervention in the foreign currency market include:

- To smoothen exchange rate movement so as to discourage wide fluctuations.
- It is a way of establishing implicit exchange rate boundaries
- It is also a way of dealing with temporary disturbances in the exchange rate movement.

Determination of exchange rates

International trading relationships in terms of either goods or services on the current account side of the balance of payments or in terms of capital flows on the external assets and liabilities side of the balance of payments result in demand for and supply of currencies in the market for foreign exchange. The exchange rate between two currencies is determined by the interaction of demand and supply condition.

On a general level are the following factors :

1. Relative inflation rates
2. Relative interest rates
3. Relative income levels
4. Government controls
5. Expectations
6. Balance of payment position

There are two main theories which seek to explain the determination of exchange rates:

The **purchasing power parity** (PPP) which relate to the current account of the balance of payment.

The **portfolio balance theory** which relates to the capital account (the flow of external assets and liabilities) of the balance of payments.

In essence, PPP theory emphases the differences between country's inflation rates as a determinant of exchange rate movements, while portfolio balance they emphasizes interest rate differentials.

Purchasing power parity theory

Under the original formulation of PPP theory developed in 1920's the equilibrium long run exchange rate between one currency and the other is the rate which equalizes the domestic purchasing power of the two currencies. Thus, under the PPP the exchange rate for the kwacha at any moment will be appropriate when it is possible to buy the same basket of goods and services in various countries for the same amount of money when that money is converted at the prevailing exchange rate. For example, if K1 buys a dozen of eggs in Zambia, then according to PPP theory, K1 converted into any other currency at

the currency exchange rate would buy a dozen of eggs in the country corresponding to each currency if the exchange rate is an equilibrium value. i.e. if K1 = 2 Zim dollar, then 2 Zim dollar should be the price of a dozen eggs in Zimbabwe. If this were not the case, there would be strong incentives to import goods from the cheaper country really in a deficit on the current account of the BOP for the expensive country. The foreign exchange markets would make down the value of the expensive country's currency and its exchange rate would fall. The incentives for importing the services from the cheaper country will only disappear when the prevailing exchange rate reflected equality of purchasing power in both countries.
(K1 = 2 Zim dollars in this case)

Purchasing power parity thus states that the exchange rate between the currencies of two countries A and B value according to relative price changes (inflation rates) so that:

New exchange rate = price level in country A x old rate
Price level in country B

Limitations of ppp theory

1. It does not allow capital inflows.
2. It does not allow until difference in patterns of consumption and level of income.
3. It ignores transportation and insurance costs and import duties whereas difference in these between countries will affect relative purchasing powers.
4. It depends on the extent to which the goods and services involved may enter into international trade but many goods and services can only be traded within the same country. E.g. houses which cannot physically internationally.

The portfolio balance theory

This theory stresses the importance of interest rate differentials between different countries and their impact on international investment and speculative capital flows as opposed to current account flows as a major determinant of exchange rates. For example, the higher interest rates on one country relative to other countries, will tend to attract inflows of capital from these lower interest rate economies for investment purpose unless they are other factors acting as disincentive to invest such as political and social environment or the belief for whatever reason the exchange rate is about to collapse. The capital inflows will push up the exchange rates of the recipient country because of the extra demand for the currency from overseas investors. It is assumed that large sophisticated investors are aware of interest rate differentials and move funds to take advantages of higher yield.

They also seek to reduce overall investment risk by diversifying their portfolio hence the term portfolio balance theory.

The link between interest rates and exchange rates is in fact one of the few ways in which a country can influence the demand for its own currency. However, overseas investors are mainly interested in real interest rate that is nominal rates minus rate of inflation as opposed to nominal interest rates. The discriminative of financial asset that the overseas investor is most likely to find attractive will be short term incase other opportunities arise elsewhere and carry a yield reflecting higher rates. Such things would include gilts, banks deposits, certificate of deposits and commercial bills. Of course if there were significant risks of capital loss as a result of investing overseas, even higher interest rates (real) would not necessarily create the demand for the currency in question.

Arbitrage

The relationship between capital flows and exchange rates as described in the portfolio balance theory of exchange rate determination is particularly significant in equalizing interest rate differentials between the major international financial centers. Interest arbitrage refers to the international flow of short—term liquid capital to earn higher returns abroad.

Alternatively, interest arbitrage can be said to be an act of simultaneously borrowing and lending with the hope of gaining from interest rate difference. Interest rate arbitrage could either be uncovered or covered. Uncovered interest arbitrage (UIA) involve transfer of funds abroad due to higher interest rate return which involves the conversion of initially the domestic currency into the foreign currency and the re-conversion of the funds (principal and interest) into domestic currency at maturity of investment. This transaction involves the foreign exchange risk as the foreign exchange can either go up or down during the period of the investment.

1. Kwacha converted to US $ for investment in New York
2. US $ (principal+ interest) converted back into kwacha

Covered Interest Rate Arbitrage (CIA) refers to covering the foreign exchange risks when investing funds abroad. The investor exchange the domestic currency for foreign currency and invests abroad but at the same time, sale the principal and interest back into domestic currency at a forward rate to be assured of the return on his investment. For example, the Zambian investor would convert the kwacha into US $ to buy US asset. And at the same time sale the principal and interest at forward rate into the kwacha.

$$F_t = S_t + \frac{(1+I)}{(1+I^*)}$$

where I = domestic interest rates.

I* = foreign interest rates

S_t = spot

F_t = forward.

The examples of arbitrage include:
- Locational – where there are three financial centres involved
- Locational which is basically dependent on the region
- Covered interest arbitrage.

Definition
Arbitrage – the process of buying security at a low price in one market and simultaneously selling in another market at a high price to make a profit.

Effects of arbitrage
As arbitrage foes on, the exchange rate will be pushed towards their appropriate levels because the arbitrage will buy an under priced currency in a foreign market and then sell in an over priced currency in the market. Thus arbitrage increases the demand for a currency in an under-priced market for supply of dame currency in the overpriced market. This process continues until the exchange rates in all the centers are equalized so that the arbitrages can no longer benefit.

Exchange rate quotations
A foreign exchange dealer will quote both buying (or bid) rate and a selling (or ask) rate for a currency. The difference represents the dealer's profit margin when buying and selling currencies. For example the American dollar (USD) may be quoted in Kwacha as:

Bid K4700   Ask K5100

If the dealer buys from an exporter and then sells to an importer, $1 million, the importer will receive from the dealer K4, 700,000,000 for his dollars and the importer will pay K5, 100, 000, 000 for her dollars. The dealer will therefore make a profit of K400, 000, 000.

Types of transactions

There are two basic types of trades in the foreign exchange market: Spot trades and forward trades.
- A **spot trade** is an agreement to exchange currency "on the spot" which actually means that the transaction will be completed or settled within two business days. The exchange rate on a spot trade is called the spot exchange rate. Implicitly, all the exchange rates and transactions discussed so far have referred to the spot market. So if you are quoted a spot rate for Euro of 6400 – 6900, you could buy at the first price and sell at the second.

- A **forward trade** is an agreement to exchange currency at some time in the future. The exchange rate that will be used is agreed upon today and called the forward exchange rate. A forward trade will normally be settled sometime in the next 12 months.

Thus, you can buy US dollar today at K4700 or you can agree to take delivery of a US dollar in 180 days and pay K5100 at that time. Notice that US dollar is more expensive in the forward market (K5100 versus K4700). Since the US dollar is more expensive in the future than it is today, it is said to be selling at a ***premium*** relative to the Kwacha. For the same reason the Kwacha is said to be at a ***discount*** relative to the US dollar. We calculate the 6-months forward premium as follows:

$$\frac{\text{Forward} - \text{spot}}{\text{Spot}} = \frac{5100 - 4700}{4700} = 0.085 = 8.5\%$$

It is worth nothing that the premium/discount depends, among other things, on the length of forward agreement.

Forward exchange contracts

Such contracts allow importers and exporters to arrange for dealers to sell to them or buy from a specified amount of foreign currency at a given future date at an agreed exchange rate-that is, the rate is decided upon now, not when the need to deal in the currency arrives. If the exchange rate for the dollar strengthens, firm is protected from this change. If it should happen to weaken, then the firm is unable to profit from this, but has swapped this possible profit for the certainty of knowing at what rate it will be able to obtain the necessary dollar. Naturally, a forward exchange contract will cost money to arrange.

So how are forward exchange rates determined by dealers? First, we need to know the spot price of the currency in question and to this is added or subtracted an interest differential for the period of the contract, which will obviously be calculated with reference to the way the exchange rate is expected to move (see The Purchasing Power Parity Theorem). It is not an estimate of what the spot rate will turn out to be. This means that the forward rate may be higher or lower than the present spot rate i.e. the currency will be cheaper or more expensive than the spot rate.

Example 1

If the US dollar is quoted to the British Pound as follows

- Spot rate 1.4378 – 1.4388

- Three months" forward rate 1.4580 – 1.4590

(a) How much will the company sell 3000 dollars?

(b) How much will the company buy 3000 dollars?

Solution

(a) Spot rate = $\dfrac{3000}{1.4388}$ = £2085

Forward rate = $\dfrac{3000}{1.4590}$ = £2056

(b) The company could buy 3000 dollars for:

Spot rate = $\dfrac{3000}{1.4378}$ = £2087

Forward rate = $\dfrac{3000}{1.4580}$ = £2058

The dollar is being quoted forward at a higher, cheaper rate compared with the spot, or "at discount". If the rate quoted were lower, the dollar would be more expensive forward in terms of the pound sterling, and is therefore, quoted "at a premium". It may seem strange to talk about a higher figure being at a discount, whereas a lower figure is at a premium, but if you examine the example carefully, you will see that this is true. In the above example, we gave an actual rate for the forward rate. However, it is often not expressed like this-we have to work it out! The spot rate is given, together with either the discount or the premium on this spot rate, which we then have to add or subtract accordingly. The other factor that influences the forward rate should be obvious – the longer period, the higher the discount or premium will be.

Spot, cross and forward rates

Spot Rates
A spot rate is a rate, which is available for delivery immediately. That is within two business marking days. It is the rate quoted in the banks, on the exchange rate chart. Transactions involving the spot rate are called spot transactions.

Forward Rates
A forward rate is a rate, which is agreed today for delivery of the foreign currency, 1, 3, 6, months after the transactions contract. The transactions involving the forward rates are called forward transactions. The forward rate can be coated at a premium on at a discount. A forward rate is said to be coated at a premium if the forward rate is greater than the spot rate (positive figure) a forward rate is at a discount when the forward rate is less than the spot rate. The forward rate is said to be flat if the forward rate is equal to the spot rate.

Calculating Forward Discount Or Premium

Premium or = <u>forward rate – spot rate</u> x <u>360</u> x 100
Discount   spot rate   90

$$P \text{ or } d = \frac{FR - SR}{NSR} \times 100$$

Where n = time period

Example
FR = 8000------------3 months
SR = 5000
Solution
P or d = <u>FR – SR</u> x 100
        NSR
= K <u>(8000 – 5000)</u> x 100
      3/12 x 5000
= K <u>(8000 – 5000)</u> x <u>12</u> x 100
      K 5000   3
= <u>3000</u> x <u>12</u> x 100
  5000   3
Premium = <u>k240</u>

Cross rate

The cross exchange rate is the exchange rate between currency A and currency B given the exchange rate of currency A and currency B in respect to currency C. It is an exchange rate directly between two currencies. Cross rates are usually calculated on the basis of various currencies relative to the US$ which is called a Vehicle currency. For
exchange rate the cross rate between British pounds and French, France is computed as follows:

Cross rate = <u>Dollars</u> x <u>Francs</u> = <u>Francs</u>
         Pounds   Dollar   Pound

Dollar being the common currency is used to determine the exchange between the France and the Pound.
K/ $ = K4000
K/ E = K8000
$/ E =?

$ / E = <u>1</u> X 8000
       4000$ / E = $2

Exposure management

Dealers in international trade expose themselves to foreign exchange risks. Foreign exchange risks are risks that result from changes in the exchange rate over time and are faced by anyone who expects to make or receive payment in foreign currency at a future date. The dealers are said to be in an open position. Importers will face risks of a depreciation of the domestic currency because they will be required to pay more. Exporters on the other hand, do not want the domestic currency to appreciate because they will end up receiving less and this will negatively impact on the competitiveness of their product in the international market.

Exchange rate risk is the natural consequence of international operations in a world where relative currency values move up and down. Managing exchange rate risk is an important part of international finance. There are three different types of exchange rate risk or exposure. These are:

1. Translation exposure

Translation exposure arises from differences in the currencies in which assets and liabilities are denominated. These effects are most obvious when consolidated group accounts are prepared and the values of assets and liabilities denominated in a foreign currency are translated into the home currency. For example, Shoprite Zambia's performance must be reported in Rands in South Africa!

The implications of translation exposure are:

- Effect on accounts – The exact effect translation exposure has on the accounts will depend on the methods of translation used. Legislation or accounting standards will prescribe which method to be used.

- Effect on cash – Translation exposure is essentially an accounting measure and does not involve actual cash flows.

- Investor's and payables' attitude – However, if markets are not strongly efficient investors and payables may interpret loses on translation as a reduction in the financial worth and credit worthiness of the company. This risk can be reduced if assets and liabilities denominated in particular currencies are held in balanced accounts.

Economic exposure

Economic exposure is the risk that the present value of the company's future cash flows might be reduced by unexpected adverse exchange rate movements. Economic exposure, to a large extent includes transaction exposure.

The implications of economic exposure include:

- Effect on international competitiveness – This can affect the companies through its purchases (where raw materials from abroad become more expensive because of the depreciation of the home currency) or its sales (where an appreciation in the home currency will mean that sales priced in foreign currencies will be worth less in home currency terms).

- Effect on remittances from abroad – If a subsidiary is set up in an overseas country, and that country's exchange rate depreciates against the home exchange rate, the remittances will be worth less in home currency terms each year.

- Effect on accounts – Investors will identify economic exposure as having an adverse effect on accounts if the markets are efficient.

- Effect on operations and financing – In order to hedge the adverse effects of economic exposure, companies will consider diversification of operations, so that the sales and purchases are made in a number of different currencies. The financing of operations can also be done in a large number of currencies.

3. Transaction exposure

Transaction risk is the risk of adverse exchange rate movements in the course of normal trading transactions. This would typically arise as a result of exchange rate fluctuations between the date when the price is agreed and the date when the cash is paid. For
example, a Zambian importer of Television sets from Japan may be committed to pay Y100 million at the end of 12 months if the value of the Yen appreciates rapidly over this period, it will cost more Kwachas than the firm anticipated. The opposite holds, if the Yen depreciates. The implications of transaction exposure include:

- Effect on accounts – This form of exposure can give rise to real cash flow gains or loses. It is necessary to set up a treasury management function whose role would be to assess and manage this risk through various hedging techniques.

- Effect on remittances abroad – If the Kwacha depreciates against a foreign currency; remittances will be quite costly in Kwacha terms. For example, at the exchange rate of K/£ = K7000, my Kwacha equivalent of £100 to ACCA would be K700 000. But if the Kwacha depreciates so that the new exchange rate is K/£ = K10 000, I need K1000 000 to remit the same £100!

- Effect on international competitiveness – Generally, when the local currency appreciates, imports become cheaper and when it depreciates exports become cheaper in local currency terms. Thus, depreciation favours local exporters while appreciation favours local importers.

Hedging foreign exchange risk

Foreign exchange risk exposure is driven by a mismatch of currency trade flows and the variability of the exchange rates. For capital flows the ultimate target must be to match currency assets and liabilities. Hedging is costly. The expenses associated with establishing a treasury function and developing the in-house expertise can be considerable. Hedging though derivative contracts can be avoided by the creation of internal hedging arrangements whereby finance is raised in the country of operations. This matches costs with the revenue streams.

Hedging FOREX risk using derivatives can be expensive especially when the exposure is uncertain. Where the exposure is certain, the use of futures or forward contracts can eliminate a large element of the risk at a much lower cost. The policy to hedge against FOREX will depend on:

- The magnitude of the risk exposure value at risk may be an appropriate method for measuring the likely financial exposure.
- The materiality of the exposure in terms of the magnitude of the sums involved.
- The extent to which the risk can be mitigated by matching agreements
- The extent to which the exposure has crystallized. If it is uncertain, FOREX options allow the hedging of the downside risk but at a high cost.

The following are the methods that can be used to manage adverse currency movements. They can broadly be divided into those involving financial derivatives (forward contracts, futures contracts, swaps and options) and other which do not make use of financial derivatives.

1. Forward contracts

The risk of the exchange rate moving in an adverse manner compared to the forecast can removed by taking out a forward contract. This fixes the rate today for delivery at a specified future rate. The relevant rate for the forward contracts is the forward rate. Forward contracts are traded in a forward market.

Advantages of Forward Contracts

- The trader will know in advance how much money will be received or paid.
- Payment is not required until the contract is settled.
- Contracts are available in a very wide range of currencies.

Disadvantages of Forward Contracts

- The user may not be able to negotiate good terms; and how the user is rated.
- Users have to bear the spread of the contract between the buying price and the selling price.
- Deals can only be reversed by going back to the original party and offsetting the original trade.

- The credit worthiness of the other party may be a problem.
- Long maturity contracts are rare, and some currencies do not have a forward marketing (only active in 3 to 6 months).
- Prices can vary according to the size of the deal and the customer
- Significant changes in flows would require separate forward contracts, thereby increasing costs and administration.

2. **Futures contracts**

A futures contract is similar to a forward contract, but with three key differences namely:

- Futures contracts are "marked to market" on a daily basis meaning that gains and losses are noted and money must be put to cover losses. This greatly reduce the risk of default that exists with the forward contract.

- With futures, physical delivery of the underlying asset is never virtually taken-the two

- Futures contracts are generally standardized instruments that are traded on exchange while forward contracts are generally tailored-made negotiable between two parties and are not traded after they have been signed.

Advantages of Futures Contracts

- There is a single specified price determined by the market, and not by negotiating strength of the customer.
- Transaction costs are generally lower than for forward contract
- Reversal can easily take place in the market
- Because of the process of 'marking to market there is no default risk.
- The exact date of receipt or payment of the currency does not have to be known, because the futures contract does not have to be closed out until the actual cash receipt or payment is made.

Disadvantages of Futures Contracts

- The fixing of quantity and delivery dates that is necessary for the future to be traded means that the customer's risk may not be fully covered.
- Futures contracts may not be a available in the currencies the customer requires
- Volatile trading conditions on the futures markets mean that the potential loss can be high
- Futures contracts are not very flexible. Contracts are only of a specified size and maturity
- An initial margin (deposit) is required, and further variation margin may be necessary.

3. **Currency Swaps**

These are arrangements between two parties to swap payments on each other's loans, those loans being in different currencies. For example, a company may arrange to make the payments on counterparty's US dollar loan, while the counterparty makes payments on the company's kwacha loan. The effect is to enable the company to switch its effective interest payments from kwacha to dollars. An equivalent effect would be achieved by terminating the company's kwacha loan and taking out a new loan in US dollars.

Advantages of swaps

- Companies may have a comparative advantage borrowing in their own currency. Doing this and agreeing a currency swap may produce cheaper interest rate than trying to borrow directly in a foreign currency.

- In some countries, it is difficult or impossible for foreign registered companies to borrow in the local currency. A currency swap gets round these restrictions.

- Termination costs for an existing loan may make it prohibitively expensive to change finance. A bank's service fee to arrange a swap may be lower than the termination charge. Also, if a company has long term borrowings in one currency but needs to switch to paying interest in another currency for a shorter period, a swap can enable this without having to terminate the original loan.

- Borrowing in a foreign currency is an effective method of hedging income in that currency, and currency swaps are one way of achieving this. The cost is often cheaper than using the market for long term forward contracts. Currency swaps have also been used as a method of avoiding exchange control restrictions.

Problems of swaps

- The counterparty to the swap arrangement may default if it gets into financial difficulties. In this case the company is till liable to pay the interest on the original loan. In general, banks make less risky counterparties than many corporate.

- If the swap is into a developing country's currency, there may be significant risk of adverse government restrictions being introduced.

- If the swap has been entered into to reduce currency risk as with any hedging instrument, the exchange rate may move in a direction that means it would have been better not to have undertaken the hedge.

- A swap between two floating rate loans may introduce basis risk if the interest rates are not referenced to the same base rate (Base is risk arises from the fact that the price of a futures contract may not move as expected in relation to the value of the instrument being hedged.

Currency Options

A currency option is an agreement for the opportunity to buy/sell an amount of a particular currency at a given rate of exchange at a stated time in the future. When this time arrives, there is no obligation to honour the option-it can be a abandoned. For this privilege, the option must be brought.

The reason for wishing to participate in such agreements is again to reduce/eliminate risk in exchange rate movements, and they are very useful for companies wishing to have price lists expressed in foreign currencies, or for those tendering for overseas contracts do not know is whether they will be receiving any foreign currency income-the will be receiving any foreign currency income-the sales have yet to be made, and the tenders to be awarded. Therefore, if they try to make forward exchange contracts, they will be taking more risks, so they could buy an option instead.

Option transactions involve specialized vocabulary some of which include the following:

- **Call option** – an option to buy currency

- **Put option** – an option to sell currency

- **American option** – any option that can be at any time during the period stated.
- **European option** – can only be used at the end of the period.

- **Over-the-counter option**-Tailor-made to the specific needs of a particular company.

- **Exchange traded option** – also called standard option can be obtained in some designated currencies from an option exchange. In the UK the London Stock Exchange and the London International Financial Futures Exchange (LIFFE) are used. Other exchanges are in US, Canada and Amsterdam but not yet in Zambia!

The price of an option could be:

- The same as the spot rate—**at the money**
- More favourable than the spot rate—**in the money**.
- Less favourable than the sport rate – **out of the money**.

Factors determining the value of the option

The value of the option depends on the following variables:

- The price of the security – A decrease in the price of the security will mean that a call option becomes less valuable. Exercising the option will mean purchasing a security that has a lower value.

- The exercise price of the option—A decrease in the exercise price will mean that a call option becomes more valuables: the profit that can be made from exercising the option will have increased.

- Risk free rate of return – A decrease in the risk free rate of return will mean that a call option becomes less valuable. The purchase of an option rather than the underlying security will mean that the option holder has spare cash available which can be invested at a risk free rate of return. A decrease in that rate will mean that it becomes less worthwhile to have spare cash available, and hence to have an option rather than having to buy the underlying security.

- Time to expiry of the option – A decrease in the time of expiry will mean that a call of the option becomes less valuable, as the time premium element of the option price has been decreased.

- Volatility of the security price – A decrease in volatility will mean that a call option becomes less valuable. A decrease in volatility will decrease the chance that the security price will be above the exercise price when the option expires.

Advantages of Options

- Currency options provide protection against losses in the event of unfavourable exchange rate movements, but allow the company to take advantage of exchange gains in the event of favourable movements. This is because an option does not have to be exercised unless it is to the investor's advantage.

Disadvantages of Options

- The major problem with this method of hedging is cost. A premium needs to be paid on the option irrespective of whether the option is exercised or not. The larger the amount to which the option relates or the greater the chance the option can be exercised profitably then the higher the premium.

- Over the-counter options, i.e. the ones that have been specifically arranged for individual companies cannot be negotiated successfully to other companies.

- The traded options are obviously negotiable, but are not available in all currencies.

5. **Leading and Lagging**

Companies not wishing to make forward exchange contracts, and preferring to be involved in the currency market directly, could make payments beyond their official date (lag) in order to benefit from exchange rate movements. This is speculating as to what the currency movements will be. If you are an importer and expects the future exchange rate to go up, you must lead but if you expects it to go down, you must lag. A lead payment costs the company the interest on the money used to make the payment. Similarly, consistently lagging payments will not make you popular with your suppliers. It also means that you could miss out on future discounts.

For example, suppose a Zambian importer owes K500 million, payable in 30 days to a French supplier. The company's financial director is certain that the exchange rate currently K500/€ when buying, will move adversely. This is because he has noted that the forward rate for 1-month buying is quoted at a premium. He therefore, advises paying the debt now at a cost of €100 000 (i.e. K500 000 000 ÷ 5000). This payment could have been delayed for 30 days, and so will cost €100 000 x the company's borrowing rate divided by 12. if he is right, and the rate does strengthen, it would need to strengthen sufficiently to offset this interest cost if his move is to be successful.

6. **Money Market Hedge**

Money market hedge which is also called borrowing and depositing is an alternative means of hedging an expected receipt in another currency. That is to borrow now in that other currency, convert the money received now into Kwacha at today's spot rate and place this Kwacha on deposit, then to use the expected receipt in the other currency to repay the borrowing on maturity.

An exporter can try to speculate against adverse currency movements by borrowing an amount in a foreign currency now, converting this into Kwacha at the present spot rate, and then repaying the loan with interest out of the foreign currency that will eventually be received. If, in the meantime, the currency rate moves against him, he will hope that it will be by a greater amount than the interest rate he will have to pay on the loan!

- An importer could buy currency now at spot rate, lend it until it was needed to pay the supplier, and use the interest received plus the amount originally invested to pay the supplier if the rate has moved against the importer.

The cost is having to find the sum to buy currency now. The key problem with borrowing is that, as with forward contract, it creates an exposure to foreign currency which will still be there if the expected receipts from the investment do not flow through.

7. Netting Off

Netting inter-company transfers is a common international cash management strategy to manage foreign currency risk. The basis of netting is that within a closed group or related companies, total payables will always equal total receivable. The advantages of netting are the reduction in foreign exchange conversion fees and funds transfer fees and a quicker settlement of obligations reducing the group's overall exposure. If only two companies in a group are involved it is called ***bilateral netting***. If more than two companies are involved it is called ***multilateral netting***. The arrangement can be coordinated either through the group's central treasury function or alternatively through the company's bankers. Given that a group treasury function already exists it would be sensible to use the in-house expertise to carryout the netting.

It is also necessary to determine the common currency in which netting needs to be effected as well as the method of establishing the exchange rates to be used for netting purposes. In order to agree the outstanding amounts in time, but with minimum risk of exchange rate fluctuations, it may involve using exchange rates applying a few days before the date at which payment is to be made.

Benefits of netting

The benefits of netting are:

- Reduced foreign exchange costs including commission and the spread between selling and buying rates as well as reduced money transmission rates.
- Less loss in interest from having money in transit

Note that it is necessary to check local laws and regulations for these foreign currencies to ensure multilateral/netting is permitted. It should be noted, however, that once netting has been accomplished then the foreign exchange exposure will need to be hedged in the normal way, i.e. through the use of forward contracts, currency options and matching of receipts and payments within the individual company.

8.Holding foreign currency account – companies that frequently make payments, say US$ open US$ accounts with their Zambian banks. This means that the movement in the exchange rate between the kwacha and the US $ would not be relevant to them in as for as they concerned.

9.Domestic currency quotation – quoting prices in domestic currency helps the exporters to completely eliminate foreign exchange risks. The risk is however shifted to the importer. However domestic currency quotations affect the competitiveness of the company's products for various reasons.

Exchange rate forecasts

How do banks forecast exchange rates? What models do they use? To forecast exchange rate banks use two of the following theories/models namely Interest Rate Parity (IRP) and the Purchasing Power Parity (PPP).comparisons of the results of interest rate parity and purchasing power parity illustrate why bank's forecasts may differ.

- Interest rate parity is based on the assumption that differences in interest rates will cause changes in capital between countries and hence increased demand currencies which will be reflected in changes in exchange rate. For currencies which will be reflected in changes in exchange rates.

The formula for interest rate parity can be expressed as:

Forward rate a/b = spot rate a/b x $\frac{(1 - \text{interest rate in country a})}{(1 - \text{Interest rate in country b})}$

- Purchasing power parity theory suggests that changes in exchange rates are caused by differences in the rate of inflation between countries, that is the exchange value of a foreign currency depends on its relative purchasing power.

The formula for purchasing power parity can be expressed as:

Forward rate a/b = spot rate x $\frac{(1 - \text{inflation rate in country a})}{(1 + \text{inflation rate in country b})}$

- In practice also forecasts made by banks will be the result of calculations using models that incorporate several factors, not just interest rates or inflation rates. This will inevitably result in different forecasts, as the weightings given to each factor will differ between models, and the assumptions made about each factor may also differ.

Mechanisms influencing exchange rate forecasts include:

- Market efficiency – A key determinant will be the degree of efficiency of the foreign exchange markets. If the markets are **strongly efficient**, exchange rates will change in random events occur which cannot be anticipated by the market. This includes political or natural events, but may also include movement in economic variables that cannot be predicted. If markets are not strongly efficient, exchange rates may be influenced by subjective market sentiments or possibly speculation.

- Market contagion – the degree of market contagion may also influence how exchange rates are affected, by determining when and by how much a country's exchange rate is affected by developments elsewhere in the world's financial system.

- Reserve currencies – if a currency is being held as a reserve currency, as part of the reserves of another country, then its exchange rate will depend on the actions not just of its own government but other countries that hold it in their reserves. Further, forecasting of exchange rates is influenced by the exchange rate regime.

- Floating rates – it is thus extremely difficult to forecast exchange rates especially if movements are dependent on unpredictable future events. In theory freely floating rates will be exposed to the full impact of random events.

- Managed rates – Exchange rates may be more predictable if their level is managed by governments buying and selling currency in the markets. The degree of predictability will depend on how well government criteria for intervention are understood. However, sometimes market pressures can overwhelm government attempts at intervention.

- Fixed rates – Fixed rates should be the easiest to predict, at least in the short term. However, in the longer term changes in economic variables will put pressure on the exchange rate levels that will eventually cause realignments. Knowledge of economic indicators can be used to predict the likely direction of any revaluation, but not necessarily its timing or depend on non-financial factors such as political pressures.

The international fisher effect

In the shorter term, the exchange rate is determined by reference to interest rate differential between the two currencies which in turn will depend on relative supply of and demand for those currencies. The longer term exchange rates are determined by purchasing power parity and the inflation differential between two currencies. The interest rates, inflation and the foreign exchange markets are linked by the international Fisher Effect.

Fisher states that the nominal rate of return (R), i.e. the interest rate changed is equal to the real rate of return (R) adjusted to compensate for the effect of inflation (i) as follows:

$$(1 + r) = (1 + R)(1 + i)$$

- The above relationship applies in all economies and can be extrapolated to mean that the interest rate differentials in the long run equate to inflation rate differentials over the same period. Taking this to its logical conclusion it is possible to state that the exchange rate differentials in the long term are driven by inflation rate differentials between the two economies concerned.

Example: mathematical application

At a luncheon meeting the Managing Director of ABC Plc has told two of his colleagues, who hold senior executive positions in different companies that he has recently obtained from his bank forecasts of exchange rates in the one year's time. His two colleagues also for companies that are heavily engaged in international trade and both the three again meet to lunch and compare forecasts made by their banks. These forecasts are shown below:

	$/€	£/€	Yen/$	$/£
Bank 1	0.76	0.56	120	1.36
Bank 2	0.84	0.64	140	1.31
Bank 3	1.00	0.65	140	1.54
Current spot rates	0.88	0.62	125	1.42

	USA	UK	Euro block	Japan
Annual inflation rates	3%	2%	3%	(1%)
Annual short term interest	3.25%	4.75%	4.18%	0.01%

The three senior executives are puzzled by this information.

Required:

Carryout calculations based upon inflation rates and interest rates, explaining why the banks' forecasts might differ.

Solution

- The formula for interest rate parity can be expressed as:

Forward rate a/b = spot rate a/b x $\dfrac{(1 + \text{interest rate in country a})}{(1 + \text{interest rate in country b})}$

- The formula for purchasing power parity can be expressed as:

Forward rate a/b = spot a/b x $\dfrac{(1 + \text{inflation rate in a country a})}{(1 + \text{inflation rate in country b})}$

Using the two formulae produces the following predictions for forward rates:

	Interest rate parity	Purchasing power parity
$/€	0.872	0.880
£/€	0.623	0.614
Y/$	121	120
$/£	1.400	1.434

Not only do the exchange rate movements differ whatever the formula, in some cases the movement has been in different directions. This is because for example American inflation rates were higher than UK inflation rates, but UK interest rates are higher than American rates. Further, differences will have been caused by banks using predicted exchange or interest rates rather than current rates.

An addendum—export quotation

Here we are concerned with the make up of the export price. There are two important aspects of quoting export prices.

a) The currency of the quotation
b) The terms

Foreign currency pricing

Above 95% of Zambian imports are paid for in foreign currency. However, about 95% of Zambian exports are invoiced in foreign currency. Since the kwacha has not been stable in recent years, there are advantages and disadvantages to Zambian importers and exporters.

In international trade, the exporter must invoice the buyer in a foreign currency (e.g. the currency of the buyers' country) or the buyer must pay in foreign currency (e.g. the currency of the exporter's country). It is also possible that the currency of payment will be the currency of a third country e.g. a Zambian firm might sell goods to a buyer in Brazil and ask for payment in US Dollars.
One problem for imports is therefore the need to obtain foreign currency to make a payment and for exporters there can be a problem of exchanging foreign currency received for currency of their own country. Banks provide the service to importers and exporters of buying and selling foreign currency.

The cost of imports to the buyers or the value of exports to the seller might be increased or reduced by movements in foreign exchange rates. For example, if a Zambian importer buys goods from a US supplier for $15000 when the exchange rate between the kwacha and the US dollar is K / $ = 4000, the import would expect to pay K60, 000,000 for the goods. However, if by the time the date of payment arrives, the exchange rate is K / $ = 3000 (i.e. kwacha has appreciated against the US dollar) the cost to the importer would be K45, 000,000 or K15, 000,000 less than originally anticipated.

The US exporter would receive $15,000 and would not be affected by the exchange rate movement. However, in the same example, if the invoice had been in kwacha (K60, 000,000 rather than $15,000) the Zambian importer would not have had any effect by this exchange rate movement. Instead the US exporter would have gained from the exchange rate movement from K4000 to K3000 receiving $20,000 (K60, 000,000) instead of the $15000 originally expected.

The firm paying in a foreign currency or earning revenue in a foreign currency therefore has potential exchange risk from adverse movement in foreign exchange rates.

There is also a chance of making a profit out of unfavorably movements in the exchange rates but although gains as well as loses are made movements of foreign exchange rates – which occur continually in the foreign exchange markets – introduce a serious element of risks (gambling or lottery on the way exchange rates move) which might defer firms from entering international trade agreements.

The foreign exchange risk does not arise from a business that makers payments and earns receipts in the same currency (foreign) because payments I the currency can be out of cash income in the same currency. For example, if a Zambian firm buys goods from suppliers X costing US$ 10,000 and a the same time the Zambian firm sell goods abroad to customer X for US$ 10,000 (in dollars) the firm can use the US$ 10,000 dollars it receives from customer Y to pay the US$ 10,000 dollars to supplier X. if matching receipts and payments is carried out in this way, the exchange rate between the foreign currency and firm's domestic currency would by irrelevant and exchange risk would be avoided.

Matching receipts and payments is made easier by the ability of the individuals or organizations in Zambia to hold a foreign currency account. For example, a company that earns receipts and makes payments in US dollars can choose to hold a US dollar accounts with its Zambian bank and to maintain as much as possible of its dollar receipts as it chooses in this account until the time comes to use the currency to make dollar payments

Matching currency receipts and payments is only feasible if the international trader has receipts and payments in the same currency to match. Many traders are not so luck and must either make a net payment in a foreign currency or earn net receipts = a foreign currency.

Foreign currency exposure refers to his situation and so any trader who has foreign exchange risk – i.e. a risk of losses from adverse movements in exchange rates. It is possible to set up heading arrangements to reduce the risk of losses.

Quotation in own currency—advantages

From the Zambian trader's point of view this offers the following advantages:

1) Price of the contract is known at the outset and accurate comparisons can be made.
2) Exchange risks are avoided as these are borne by the foreign customer.
3) It is administratively convenient as bookkeeping is straight-forward. This is an important factor for the same firm or the firm where export revenue is a small proportion of the total revenue.

Quotation in own currency – disadvantages

Business might be lost to competitors prepared to invoice in the foreign currency, for example, if I quote my exports to China in Zambian kwacha, the Chinese customer may find it difficult to obtain the kwacha or simply calculate how much it is that he has to pay. He will therefore decline my offer. This is the reason why many developing countries like Zambia should always quote the prices acceptable to both.

Quotation in foreign currency

Here the exporter accepts any exchange risk of fluctuating values. This risk can be covered in the forward exchange market. The exporter however can accept exchange risk (profit or losses) if he wishes but in this role exporters are acting as currency speculators, is this part of their mission? These risks become even greater the 'softer' a currency is i.e. the less easy to convert into other currencies. The exporter might be made vulnerable to a severe risk of loss.

Foreign currency quotation advantages

1) Where a forward marker exist (as it is being developed in Zambia) for a currency and where dealing is at a premium to kwacha receivable may be sold forward from the date of the contract to increase their kwacha revenue or lower the effective cost of kwacha export finance while at the same time minimizing the exchange risk.

2) Thanks to any forward premium the exporter could increase volume by offering a lower currency price than the spot rate of exchange would indicate i.e. foreign currency pricing can help secure contracts in the first pace

3) An exporter can gain a competitive edge by quoting in a foreign currency if the importer would prefer his own currency either to avoid exposure to currency fluctuations or because of exchange control regulations. Foreign currency pricing also makes it easy to relate to retail prices overseas. In addition, constant adjustment to a kwacha price list is avoided.

4) Foreign currency invoicing can sometimes help exporters to borrow at lower rates of interest than at home.

5) Currency received can be used to pay for goods and services in the buyer's country, thereby eliminating the need to convert the kwacha.

Foreign currency quotation – disadvantages

1) By agreeing to invoice in the foreign currency the Zambian trader incurs en exchange risk until the funds are converted to or from kwacha US exchange rates will fluctuate between the date that the price is agreed with the overseas trader and the date that settlement is made.

2) Because of the above reason, planed profits margins may be eroded.

3) Additional bookkeeping will be necessary to monitor the situation.

Quotation in third currency

In cases where trade is conducted with a country that has a currency regarded as 'exotic' i.e. currencies in which only a small market exist such as the Zambia kwacha, Kenya shillings etc, it is common to invoice in an international currency, for example, the US dollars. However, though this will improve competitiveness there is an exchange risk and planned profit margins may be eroded. Additional bookkeeping will be necessary to monitor the situation.

Resolving differences between exporter and importer

Despite the advantages of foreign currency pricing noted above, UK exporters like ACCA, CIMA. CIPS, CIM etc frequently prefer to quote prices in sterling. This is because it makes calculations of profits, cash flows and possibly costs easier and avoids exposure to exchange rate risks. This is the exact opposite to Zambian firms, which quote in foreign currency or third currency notably the US dollar. This is because foreign customers normally prefer to receive price quotations in their own currency since it places the risk of exchange rate fluctuation on the exporter and facilitates comparison of prices from a number of foreign sources. Resolution of this potential conflict depends to a large extent on:

-   The relative strength of the two parties
-   The importance of the contract to either party
-   Occasionally the economic situation in both countries (such as balance of payment position)

Whichever currency is needed there are a number of ways of minimizing the problem caused by foreign currencies.

-   The simplest way is to have an appropriate clause in the contract to adjust the price if it fluctuates within agreed limits or to renegotiate if these are exceeded.
-   To purchase (or sell) forward as appropriate whereby a fixed rate is agreed for a given sum at a specified date in the future by a bank. The net sum (after commission) received or paid at end of the period is at least guaranteed.
-   In a situation – where either or both currencies are unstable, a third currency can be quoted, e.g. the US dollars. A strengthening or weakening in one party's currency would be felt in relation to the dollar and the other party would not be affected. Each party to the transaction thus takes on the risk associated with its own currency. If the dollar changed volume, it would be likely to be relative to both currencies and the risk or benefits would be shared. The one disadvantage is that there is a double exchange transaction involved. However, this may be more acceptable than other alternatives.

CHAPTER 24

THE ANALYSIS OF INTEREST RATES

Zambian investors are on record to have complained of high costs of production. Among the most important cost here is the "cost of capital". Banks have also been reducing their lending rates called base rates. In this chapter, we analyze interest rates.

When you have studied this chapter you should be able to:
- Define interest rates
- Distinguish between nominal and real interest rates.
- Explain the pattern and term structure of interest rates.
- Describe the yield curve.
- Identify and explain factors affecting interest.
- Describe the effects of interest rates on personal sector, corporate sector and the commercial banks.

Interest rates

An interest rate is the cost of money i.e. it is the money paid by borrowers to the lenders. Alternatively, an interest rate is the return received by the lenders of money from the borrowers of money.

Nominal interest rates and real interest rates

The real rate of interest is the rate of interest that investors get from their investment, after taking account of inflation. The actual or 'nominal' interest rate on an investment can be said to consist of an amount of provide for the effect of inflation on the yield. In other words, nominal interest rates are the ones quoted by banks which do not take inflation into account.

Nominal interest rates must always be greater than the rate of inflation if investors are to receive "capital gain". This is the reason why the bank's base rate is always greater than the rate of inflation. If the bank's base rate is less than the rate of inflation the base would suffer a "capital loss".

Calculating real interest rate

The most common method of calculating a real interest rate in approximate terms is to subtract the current rate of inflation from the nominal rate of interest.
Thus, real interest rate = nominal interest rate −current inflation rate.
For example, if a bank offers 16% interest on deposits, and current rate of inflation is 12%, the real rate of interest could be calculated as (16-12)% = 4%.

The above real interest rate of 4% is only an approximation. The actual real interest rate can be calculated using the following formula:

Real interest rate = $\dfrac{(1 + \text{nominal interest rate})}{(1 + \text{inflation rate})} - 1$

In the above formula, both nominal interest rate and the inflation rate are expressed as proportions or decimals.

Thus, the real interest rate in the above example is:

$\dfrac{(1 + 0.16)}{1 + 0.12} - 1 = \dfrac{1.16}{1.12} - 1 = 0.036 = 3.6\%$

From above, an increase in real interest rates will occur either if nominal interest rates rise, or if inflation rate falls.

An increase in real interest rates would affect commercial banks in a variety of ways.
- A higher interest rate would be charged on advance.

- A higher interest rate would be paid to customers on interest – bearing deposits

- A large proportion of the deposits of retail banks in Zambia are non-interest-bearing current accounts and since banks profit by the excess margin of interest rates charged on advances over interest (if any) paid on deposits i.e. excess of interest income over interest expense (if any), higher interest rates will tend to increase the benefits of the endowment effect of the non-interest-bearing current accounts. There will be an increase in profits to the extent that advances are financed by non-interest—bearing deposits. At higher interest rates, the margin between interest rates on advances and deposit interest rates may also be higher, thus improving profitability.

- An increase in interest rates is likely to have some effect on the volume of demand from customers for loans. The extent of the reduction in demand would depend on its interest elasticity. Interest elasticity of demand refers to the effect on the demand for borrowing of a change in interest. When arise in interest rates result in only a small fall in demand for loans, demand would be interest inelastic, whereas if they would be a large fall in demand for loans, demand would be interest elastic. The interest elasticity of demand varies between the short term (relatively inelastic) and the longer term (relatively elastic).
- With higher interest rates, there may be a greater incidence of default on advances to customers. Banks might try to apply greater controls to retting request for new loans or overdraft facilities, and profitability may suffer from increase bad debts.

- When lending is at a fixed interest rate, an increase in interest rates will affect deposits and new loans, but not existing loans. Existing borrowers pay at the old, lower interest rate, and so bankers' profitability will suffer to some extent.

- Furthermore, an increase in interest rates would reduce the capital value of government securities held by the banks and banks' profits may suffer from capital losses on fixed interest government stocks. The extent to which banks might change their asset holdings would depend to some extent on the relative change in interest rates obtainable on different types of asset.

Note that real interest rates can be negative. This occurs when nominal interest rates are lower than inflation rate. Negative real interest rate implies that the purchasing power of the capital sum involved is declining.

The pattern of interest rates

The pattern of interest rates refers to the fact that at any given time there will be different interest rates. There are many financial assets and each of them has its own interest rate. The following are the common interest rates categories:

a) Base rate – this is the lending rates by the commercial banks. Banks can increase or reduce the base rate depending on the prevailing economic conditions.

b) Discount rate – this is the rate which the bank of Zambia changes to commercial banks that borrow from it. When the discount rate is changed, it is expected that commercial banks' base rate will be changed in same direction i.e. when the discount rate is reduced, base rates are also expected to be reduced, so here is an increase in credit creation.

c) Treasury bill rate – this is the rate paid to holders of treasury bills.

d) Gilts rate – this is the rate on government gilt-edged securities.

e) Certificate of deposit rate – this is a rate on the certificate of deposit.

Commercial bank's pattern of interest rates

A commercial bank operates with a widely varied pattern of interest rates for the following reasons:

i) Banks will lend money at a lower interest rate to lower risk customers. This is apparent in short term lending, where low interest rates are charged on lending in the inter-bank market to lending banks, whereas higher interest rates are charged on similar short-term lending to even large and well-established companies. Higher interest rates are also charged on personal loans to customers in a higher risk category.

ii) Interest rates also vary with the duration of the loan or deposit. Interest rates on deposit: saving schemes requiring some notice of withdrawal will attract a higher yield than an ordinary deposit account. With an ordinary current account where customers can with draw funds on demand, no interest at all is paid.

iii) The lower interest rate is charged to wholesale loans and the higher interest rate offered for wholesale deposits. Thus, the size of the loan or deposit affects the banks' interest rate.

iv) The need to make a profit on re-lending is clearly evident in the banks. For example, retail loans to customers will be at an interest rate higher than the banks' base rate, whereas low or nil interest rate is paid on deposit accounts, and the rate paid on deposit accounts is less than the bank's base rate. Thus, a bank whole base rate is 35% would offer ,say, 10% interest rate on deposit per annum.

v) A substantial proportion of a bank's business is conducted in foreign currencies. The interest rate in which a bank deals, in the Eurocurrency markets will vary according to the currency, and the general level of interest rates in that country.

The term structure of interest rates

The term structure of interest rates refers to the way in which interest rates vary according to the term of the financial instrument – for example, there will be a difference between short term and long—term interest rates. Thus, a 91 days treasury bill may offer 14%, 182 days 16.5%, 273 days 18% and 364 days 21%. The term structure of interest rates is shown by the yield curve

The yield curve

A yield curve is a curve that can be drawn showing the relationship between the yield on financial instrument and the term to maturity of that same financial instrument. It shows how the rate of interest varies with different maturities.

To construct a yield curve you need to gather information about interest rates on short—term stock, medium term stocks and long-term stocks. These rates can then be plotted on a diagram against the maturity dates of those same stocks.

Normally, interest rates are higher for longer term of lending. The normal yield curve is shown below.

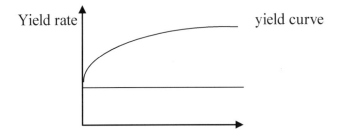

Term to maturity (days, weeks, years)

From above figure, the longer the time to maturity, the higher is the yield (interest rate). There are several reasons why a normal yield curve looks like this:

a) People need to get a reward for tying their money up. This is because they lose the use of this money whilst it is tied up. The longer the period that people lose liquidity in this way, the greater the reward they demand.

   The only way that borrowers are going to get people to part with the use of their money for long periods of time is to offer them more. The first reason for higher yields over longer periods then is to reward people for the loss of their liquidity.

b) The second reason why yields are generally higher for long terms is due to the increased uncertainty associated with longer time periods. If you tie money up for long periods of time, there are many extra uncertainties that you face compared with tying money up for short periods of time in short term assets. The major uncertainty is that inflation over longer—term is more difficult to predict than over a shorter—term. Investors are particularly anxious about the effect of inflation on their investments. A yield of 10% may look quite good now, but if you look into this rate for a long period of time there is considerable risk. In 10 years time inflation may be much higher and short—term interest rates may be 15%. If you are in any doubt that this might happen you would want to tie up your money up at 10% for a 10 year term. This is one main reason why rates for long periods are usually above rates for short-terms.

c) If we consider yield on assets other than government stock, there are other risks. The longer the term, the greater the risk that they borrower may not repay the loan. To cover this risk of default, rates are usually higher for longer term.

d) Another problem could be that the investor may wish to cash in his investment before maturity. There is a greater risk that this would involve closer to maturity trade close to their par value.

The shape of the yield curves

The shape of the yield curve depends very much on expectations about the future. Reward for loss of liquidity is likely to remain fairly constant. Reward for possible default is likely to remain constant also. Reward for the risk of having to cash in before maturity and suffering a loss are also likely to stay fairly constant. The only factor which will vary widely is expectations – in particular – expectations about future short term interest rates.

Expectations about the future level of short—term interest rates are the most important factor in determining the shape of the yield curve. Although the normal yield curve is upward sloping, expectations of rises in future interest rates can cause the yield curve to be steeper than the normal curve and expectations of falls in interest rates can cause, the yield to flatten, or if substantial falls are expected, to become downward – sloping as shown below:

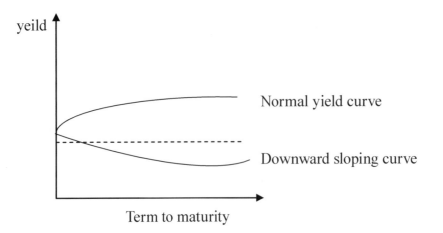

If interest rates are now expected to rise, investors will not wish to lock in to lower interest rates and will therefore sell short. Borrowers will wish to borrow at lower long term rates to avoid exposure to the higher rates expected in the future. These demand and supply factors will result in a shortage of long term funds, which will push up long term money market rates, and to an excess supply of short term funds, which will lead to a reduction in short term rates. The resulting yield curve will be more steeply upward-sloping than the normal curve.

If there are new expectations that interest rates will fall, investors will prefer to lock in at higher long rates, while borrowers will not wish to be committed to higher long term rates and will prefer to borrow short. There will be an excess supply of funds at long maturities. This will tend to lower the yield curve, possibly resulting in a flat curve or even a downward sloping curve.

Short-term interest rates are in turn determined partly by expectations of inflation rates in the near future. If high inflation is expected, investors will seek higher nominal rates of interest in order to achieve a real return. If people believe that inflations is falling, then they will not require such a high return

How true is the expectations theory

The validity of the expectations theory is hard to prove. Expectation about future short—term interest rate is affected by many factors. This makes it hand to predict the future short—term interest rates with reasonable accuracy. For example, future short—term interest rates are closely field to changes in inflation rates are affected by many factors as discussed in the last chapter. Occurrence such as draught, shortage of fuel, and so on have a direct inflation rate and ultimately interest rates.

Factors affecting general level of interest rates

The general level of interest rates is affected by several factors. These include:

1) **Inflation**—nominal rates of interest should be sufficient to cover expected rates of inflation over the term of the investment and to provide a real return. When investors are uncertain about what future nominal and real interest rates will be, they are likely to require higher interest yields to persuade them to take the risk of investing, especially in the longer term. The altitude of investors to this risk (i.e. the risk of the real returns being less than expected) will also to help to determine the general level of interest rates.

2) **Expectations** about future interest rate influences, for example, if it is expected that the government will move to raise interest rates in the future to curb inflation, this will be reflected in current rates which for various terms to maturity.

3) **Liquidity preference** and the demand for borrowing (Keynesian theory) or the supply and demand of loanable funds (loanable funds theory, supported by monetarist economists). It is generally accepted that investors will want to earn a 'real\ rate of return on their investment. When the demand to borrow increases, interest rates will go up. A high PSBR, for example, is likely to result in high interest rates whereas PSDR might depress long—term interest rates.

4) **The balance of payments and the exchange rate**. When a country has a continuing deficit on the current account of its balance of payments, and the authorities are unwilling to allow the exchange rate to depreciate by more than a certain amount, interest rates may have to be raised to attract capital into the country, so that the country can finance the deficit by borrowing from abroad.

5) **Monetary policy**. The government might be able to influence the general level of interest rates. In Zambia, the government can influence very short-term money market rates by means of open market operation, and so give notice to the financial community of its wish for interest rates to go up or down. Usually, but not always, longer term money market rates, and then banks' base rates, will respond to the government's wish for interest rate changes.

6) **Interest rates abroad.** An appropriate 'real' rate of interest in one country will be influenced by external factors, such as interest rates in other countries and expectations about the exchange rate.

In summary, the general level of interest rates depends on the real return required by investors, with nominal yields including an additional allowance for expected rates of inflation and compensation for investment risk. Other factors can influence interest rates e.g. government monetary policy.

(a) Short-term interest rates in the London Money Markets such as the key three-month London Inter-bank Offered Rate (LIBOR) are influenced by the general factors listed above, but more specific influences are as follows:

1) **Government monetary policy**. The government can use open market operations by the bank of England to influence very short-term interest rates in the discount market (i.e. discount rates on eligible bills that it buys or sells, usually in bands 1 and 2 of the four maturity bands). When the government wants interest rates to go up, it can increase the rate of discount at which it will buy eligible bills from the market. By raising interest rates, there will be a 'knock-on' effect through the money markets. The government can also influence interest rates downwards in these operations.

   Government influence on short—term money market rates can only be exercised with reasonable and realistic limits. When the markets consider that the interest rates that the government is trying to persuade them to adopt are untenable and unrealistic, they will not alter in the way that the government wants. If the market expects official action on interest rates, then market rates will move to reflect that expectation.

2) **The term of the loan**. Short-term money market loans may range from overnight loans to loans up to a year or so. Longer—term loans tend to have higher rates than shorter—term loans

3) **Competition**, and the pattern of interest rates in the discount market and parallel markets. The various money markets complete for funds, and so there are likely to be differentials in interest rates between the various markets. For example, inter-bank interest rates might be slightly higher than discount market rates, and finance house deposit rates be slightly higher than inter-bank rates. The base rates of the UK commercial banks are administered rates, set by administrative decision rather than directly by market factors. However, the main influence on base rates is the marginal cost of banks' funds. The banks use the inter-bank market and CD market to supplement their funds when necessary. The cost of borrowing in these markets is therefore the banks' marginal cost of borrowing, especially the 1-3 month LIBOR rates (since no bank will like to borrow large amounts for a term below one month, and most borrowing is in the 1-3 month range). An additional amount will be 'added' to compensate the banks for the cost of having to hold low yield liquid assets against its deposits, and so the base rate will be the marginal cost of banks' funds plus this additional amount.

The concept of long term interest rates applies to fixed-interest financial assets such as sterling certificates of deposit and, especially Government gilt-edged securities, we can state the main influences on long—term interest rates by considering the determinants of the yield on long—term gilts, which are as follows:

1) Supply and demand. The supply of gilts depends on the size of the PSBR and the need to issue gilts as a means of funding it. When the government wants to issue a large

quantity of gilts, it will probably have to increase the yield so as to attract enough investors into buying up the issue

2) Government borrowing. This is risk-free, and so the yield on long-term gilts will be less than the yield on riskier corporate borrowing.

3) The term structure of interest rates. When investors expect interest rates to rise, long-term yields on gilts will be higher than short term yields. Conversely, when a fall in interest rates is expected, long—term yields will be lower than short term yields.

4) Expectations of inflation. When prospects for inflation in the economy worsen, so that long—term inflation is expected to be higher than originally the thought, yields on all long—term investments, including gilts will need to rise.

In normal conditions, an investor should expect extra compensation for tying up his money in financial assets that have a longer period to maturity and so are more illiquid than shorter—term financial assets. To overcome this liquidity preference, it is generally considered that investors need to be compensated with higher yields on longer—term assets. (with financial assets that are traded on a stock market, investors have the option to sell their assets for cash before maturity, and so in this respect, even longer term assets are liquid, however, the sale of financial assets on a stock market, where market prices fluctuate according to current interest rates, there will be some risk of capital loss. The liquidity preference argument that yields need to be higher on longer term assets to compensate investors for tying up money without risk – i.e. until maturity – remain valid).

However, if there are expectations of a fall in interest rates, short—term interest rates may be higher than long—term interest rates. Borrowers will tend to borrow short term in the expectation that when the loans mature they can borrow at a lower rate. Thus the demand for short—term funds will be high relative to long—term funds. Lenders will prefer to lend at long term rates if falls in rates are expected, and so there will be greater supply of long-term funds relative to short—term funds. These tendencies in demand and supply will depress long-term interest rates lower relative to short—term rates.

Effects of changes in interest rates

It might be expected that higher interest rate on saving and bank / building society deposits should encourage households to save more out of their income. However, higher interest rates may be unlikely to encourage significantly greater personal savings unless there is an increase in total household income too. A further point to note is that it is believed that many individual carry out 'target saving' – saving for a particular item such as a new car or a holiday. Higher interest rates may simply enable such individuals to reach their 'target' sooner, reducing their need to save.

A fall in interest rates should have broadly the opposite effect.
a) Mortgage costs would fall. Interest costs on other borrowing would also fall.

b) Personal disposable income would rise.
c) Individuals may be encouraged to borrow more (and so increase their total spending, particularly on consumer durable such as cars and furniture).
d) Interest rates on saving would fall.

The commercial sector of the economy and changes in interest rates.

The commercial sector of the economy consists of firms.

An increase in interest rates will have several implications.

a) It will increase the cost of existing variable rate loans, such as bank overdrafts companies that are 'highly geared' – i.e. rely heavily on debt capital for their finance – may find that higher interest costs reduce their profits significantly.

b) Companies might try to reduce their interest costs by reducing their investment in assets i.e. cutting their investment in stocks and debtors and selling off some parts of their business.

c) New investment decisions might be postponed, or abandoned altogether. This possibility is considered further in paragraphs

d) Cash-rich companies, which have spare funds to invest, will earn more interest and so higher profits from their investments in interest securities.

e) The effect of higher interest rates on firms that export or import goods and services will be considered later.

Higher interest rate and corporate investment decisions

A company borrows money to invest in assets from which it expects to make a return over the life of the assets. Companies should not borrow unless they expect the return from their assets to exceed the cost of financing, to give them a profit on their investment.

If this is so, then in theory, if the rate of interest on borrowing goes up, some projects which are under consideration and which were marginally profitable before will now cease to be profitable at all, and they should be abandoned.

Higher interest rates could be seen as a change that will depress future demand in the economy. If there is a slow-down in the economy, there will be fewer profitable projects to invest in, and so companies will invest in fewer new projects for this reason too.

However, this might not be the case in practice as illustrated below.

a) In a recession, 5ay try to borrow money at whatever rate of interest is necessary to obtain enough funds to stay in business. Distress borrowing could even result in a higher demand for loans by some companies.

b) Many investment decisions have a long planning horizon. A decision to construct new premises, or purchase and install new equipment, might take several years to put into effect. The decision to invest might be a fixed commitment by the time a company needs to obtain the money to pay its supplier.

To the extent that the demand for company loans is interest-sensitive, there will probably be a time lag before a raising or lowering of interest rates has any effect on this demand. This is because a decision to reduce the amount of new investments will only take effect a time, when new investments which are already in the pipeline have been undertaken and financed.

Even so, allowing for a time lag before an interest rate change takes effect, it might still seem logical to suppose that an increase in interest rates will lower the demand by companies for loans, whereas a fall in rates will raise the demand. Empirical evidence to prove this point is scarce, however, and what evidence we have is far from conclusive.

If interest rates fell, the effects on the corporate sector would be broadly the opposite of those described above.

a) The cost of holding stocks and work in progress, if financed by borrowing, will fall, leading to improved company profitability.

b) Depending on the interest elasticity of demand for company loans, there might eventually, after a time lag, be an increase demand for loans to purchase plant and machinery, etc.

c) There will again be effect on firms that export or import, which will be discussed later.

Changes in interest rates and the banks

Higher interest rates will affect the banks in a variety of ways.

a) A large proportion of the deposits of retail banks are non-interest-bearing current accounts. These have a cost (i.e. the cost of maintaining a banking service through a branch network and the clearing system) and the cost of this service might currently be about 5-10% of the value of non-interest bearing deposits. The clearing banks are well aware of the need to control their operating costs for this reason. Even so, banks profit by the excess margin of interest rates on their advances over the cost of their deposits. A rise in level of interest rates, without any rise in the cost of non-interest bearing deposits, will increase the benefits of this 'endowment effect' for the banks.

b) The demand for loans might be reduced, and so banks might have more difficulty in putting their deposits to profitable use.

c) There might be an increase in defaults (bad debts) for the banks, with customers unable to make the higher loan repayments.

d) Higher interest rates usually cause a fall in the market value of stocks and shares. Since banks hold government stocks in their asset portfolio, the value of these assets will be reduced when interest rates go up.

e) Fixed interest loans will earn any extra income. To the extent that banks are financed by interest-bearing deposits (whose cost will have risen) the profitability of fixed interest loans will be reduced.

A fall in interest rates would affect commercial banks in the following ways.

a) A lower rate of interest will be paid on interest-bearing deposits

b) The rate of interest on advances would also fall.

c) The extent to which banks would be more or less profitable would demand on the interest elasticity of the demand for loans. If there is a relatively inelastic demand for loans (and the empirical evidence we have suggests that this might be so, especially in the short term) then the banks would charge lower interest without a compensating increase in the volume of advances.

On the other hand, if the demand for loans is interest-elastic, a fall in interest rates would crease a larger demand for loans. If banks responded by granting the extra loans, the benefits from a greater volume of lending to customers might outweigh the effect of a lower interest charge.

d) The benefits of the endowment effect will be reduced.

e) When interest rates fall on retail bank deposits, building societies may be slow to follow suit and so offer a higher relative rate to investors. This might case a transfer of retail deposits form banks to the building societies.

f) A fall in interest will tend to squeeze the profits of banks from re-lending and banks may wish to act to restore their profitability, such a restoration of profitability might be achieved: (1) by cutting operating costs (2) by raising the level of banks charges and commissions (3) By developing alternative services for customers which are not dependent on interest levels (e.g. stock market services, estate agent services) (4) by reducing the interest rate paid on deposit accounts by a greater amount than the reduction in interest rates charged on advances.

g) Banks hold fixed interest securities (e.g. government stocks) as a part of their asset portfolio. A fall in interest rates will provide them with a capital gain, which they might realize by selling off the assets.

h) Since the cost of borrowing to customers is lower, there is a possibility that there might be a fall in the number of bad debts incurred by the banks. When lending is at a fixed rate of interest, a reduction in interest rates will only affect the rate on new lending. Existing borrowers must pay at the old rate. This will provide added profitability to the banks because the interest paid on existing deposit accounts will fall, but the fixed rates charged on existing advances will stay at their previous level.

In the UK, much short and medium-term bank lending is at a variable rate of interest. (1) Bank overdraft rates vary with the general level of interest rates. (2) Medium-term lending is likely to be a variable interest rate, so that the interest charged will be adjusted at a periodic roll-over date (every 3,6,9 or 12 months) in line with recent movements in the LIBOR.

Interest rate and the balance of payments

The balance of payments is the subject of a later chapter in this text (chapter 9). A country's balance of trade consists of:

a) Exports and imports of goods and services. The difference in the value of exports and imports creates a surplus or a deficit on the 'current account' of the balance of payments.

b) Inflows and outflows of capital. The difference in the amount of capital inflows and capital outflows on the 'capital account' of the balance of payments will be either: a surplus of inflows over outflows equal to the deficit on the current account, with this net capital inflow 'financing' the current account deficit, or a net outflow of capital, which is equal to the current account surplus.

The level of interest rates, and changes in the level of interest rates, can have effects on both the capital and current accounts of the balance of payments.

An increase in domestic interest rates in Zambia, without any matching rise in interest rates in other countries, would have effects on:

- The capital account of Zambian balance of payments
- The exchange rate for Kwacha
- The current account of the Zambian balance of payments

The capital account. Higher interest rates on kwacha investments would make sterling more attractive to overseas investors (and to UK investors who currently have investments in non-sterling currencies).

There would be an increase in the demand to buy kwacha investments, and so there would be a flow of capital into the country.

Interest rate risk management

a) **Hedging** is a means of reducing risk. Hedging involves coming to an agreement with another partly who is prepared to take on the risk that you would otherwise bear. The other party may be willing to take on that risk because he would otherwise bear an opposing risk which may be 'matched' with your risk, alternatively, the other partly may be a speculator who is willing to bear the risk in return for the prospect of making a profit. In the case of interest rates, a company with a variable rate loan clearly faces the risk that the rate of interest will increase in the future as the result of changing market conditions which cannot now be predicted. Many financial instruments have been introduced in recent years to help corporate treasurers to hedge the risks of interest rate movements. These instruments include forward rate agreements, financial futures, interest rate swaps, options, and options on interest rate swaps.

b) An **interest rate swap** is an agreement by means of which the parities 'swap' their interest rate commitments. The two parties are usually brought together through a financial intermediary such as a bank. The parties to the agreement swap the interest payments made, but do not exchange the amounts of principal on which the transaction is based.

Interest rate swap can be used where one party wants a fixed rate loan but only has access to variable rate finance, while conversely the other party wants a variable rate loan but only has an access to fixed rate finance.

The party wanting variable rate finance may be expecting interest rates to fall, the party wanting fixed rate finance may be expecting interest rates to rise, or may want to avoid the risk of such a rise occurring. Thus, different perceptions of likely rate movements may be involved as well as a desire hedge risks.

It is possible to swap interest rate commitments in different currencies through 'currency swaps'. In this case, the parties to the agreement exchange the underlying nominal amounts of principal along with the interest payments.

c) c) A **forward rate agreement** (FRA) is a contract between two parties which agrees an interest rates on a nominal loan or deposit of a specified maturity at a specified future date and which the parties agrees to make payments to each other which are computed in accordance with changes in the rates of interest.

The point of an FRA is that it provides a means by which interest rates may be fixed in advance for specified period. If a company enters into an FRA with a bank at a specified rate of interest, the bank will pay to the company the excess interest it must pay if the interest rate above the specified level. Conversely, if the rate falls below the rate specified in the FRA, the company must pay the difference. The price of an FRA will in practice be a function of the current interest rates for the period of maturity which the FRA covers.

d) **Financial futures** are essentially agreements based on the future price of a financial variable. Interest rate futures contracts exist to enable hedging of companies exposure to interest rate risk: in entering into such a contract, a party may be seen as 'betting' that interest rates will move in a particular directions over some future period. In the case of a party wishing to hedge risk, the purpose of this 'bet' is really to match the risk of adverse rate movements. The most important features of financial futures are that they are contracts which are 'packed' in standard amounts, and are traded on futures exchanges. As well as the amount of each contract, the settlement date and the interest period are also standardized.

A company which has a variable rate loan may hedge against the risk of a rise in rates by taking out future contract to the size of the loan, so that if rates rise, the company receives payment to compensate under the futures contract, while if rates fall the company must pay out the difference. It is possible to take out future contracts purely as a speculative bet while having no underlying borrowing or lending commitments which you wish to hedge.

The standardized features of futures contracts make them relatively inflexible, and as a result they may be of limited use of most corporate treasures. However, futures contracts are used widely by banks and other financial institutions which do not seek an exact matching of underlying risk exposure for the purpose of hedging their own asset portfolios.

Chapter 25

SOME SELECTED PROGRESS CLINICS SOLUTIONS

PROGRESS CLINIC 1
SOLUTION 1

(a) Historical cost accounting has been criticized for a number of reasons, the main one are as follows:-

    i)   Fixed asset values are unrealistic—This is particularly marked when one looks at how property values increase from year to year.

    ii) Depreciation is inadequate to finance the replacement of fixed assets – Linked with this is that the Profit and Loss does not fully reflect the value of the asset consumed during the accounting period, thus leading to an over statement of profits.

    iii) Holding gains on stocks are included in profit – During a period of high inflation the monetary value of stocks held may increase significantly while they are being processed. The conventions of historical cost accounting result in the realized part of the holding gain being included in profit for the year.

    iv) Profits or Losses on Holdings of net monetary items are not shown—In a period of inflation the value of money its purchasing power, falls, hence losses arise on monetary assets, profits on monetary liabilities.

    v) The true effect of inflation on capital maintenance is not shown—Hence in effect by failing to take this into account before calculating profit available for distribution, dividends may effectively be paid out of capital.

    vi) Comparisons overtime are unrealistic – Company profits over a number of years give an unrealistic picture of growth, particularly in time of high inflation.

(12 marks)

(b) However, given the above criticisms and despite numerous attempts to more towards some method of counting for changes in price levels, historical cost accounting is still in general use:

    i)   It is easy to prepare the accounting information as specific and accurate figures can be obtained.

    ii) Users of financial information are able to understand and interpret the financial accounting information.

    iii) In times of low inflation, historical cost convention costs give a true and fair view of a company's position.

All of the 'inflation' accounts proposed have been difficult or time consuming to prepare and difficult for the user to understand.

SOLUTION 2

An immaterial item is one which is not significant enough to affect evaluations or decisions relating to the financial statements.

The judgment as to whether an item is material or immaterial is subjective. Materiality may be considered in the context of individual items within the financial statements. From a financial point of view an immaterial item is one which whether included or left out does not have significant effects on the accounts – that is it could be less than 5% in value terms.

SOLUTION 3

Users of financial statements

i) The Bank (and other long term long providers – will need to asses the quality of the assets upon which loans are secured and the company's ability to pay outstanding loans and overdrafts.

ii) Shareholders – will be interested in how well the directors have fulfilled their role as stewards of the company. Shareholders will look at the quality of earnings. Is the company providing long term growth and or profitability.

iii) Employees – will seek to assess how secure their futures are and whether the company can provide sustainable wages.

iv) Suppliers – will base the credit they supply to the company on the information provided in the financial statements.

v) Customers – may want to know that the company will be in existence when products need parts for servicing or replacing completely.

vi) Government and Tax authorities – the financial statements are used as the basis for tax computations.

vii) The public – the local community may wish to seek assurances that the local economy will remain stable and the continuing financial success of local companies is one indication of this.

viii) Environmental agencies – with the increased environmental reporting, agencies will use the information disclosed to assess how environmentally friendly the company is.

SOLUTION 4

(a) Accrual Concept – this concept says that net Profit is the difference between revenues and expenses.

(b) Dual Aspect Concept – This concept states that there are two aspects of accounting, one represented by the assets of a business and the other by the claims against them. Double entry is the name given to the method of recording the transactions for the dual aspect concept.

(c) Business Entity Concept – There is need for clear separation between the business entity and the owner of the business. In this case the items recorded in a firm's books are limited to the transactions that affect the firm as a business entity.

(d) Going Concern Concept – This is an assumption that a business entity will continue with its operations in a continuous manner into the unforeseeable future without ceasing operations.

(e) Money measurement Concept – It says that accounting is concerned only where facts can be measured in money terms.

1. MATCHING and PRUDENCE both suggest that anticipated future warranty expenditure be estimated as a liability. The benefit of the sale is then reduced by the (expected) cash paid for repairs, irrespective of the fact that it is not incurred in the same accounting period as the sale. The QUANTITATIVE boundary rule that only data capable of being easily quantified should be included is likely to be over-ruled by the PRUDENCE concept.

Solution 5

a) Despite the temptation to say that the matching concept implies that such training expenditure builds up a human asset that will enhance future profits, the prudence or conservatism convention rules against such optimism. The trained people may leave (putting employees in the accounts is difficult as they are not owned), or there may be no measurable and clear benefit from training. This also, then, would probably contravene the money measurement rule if we wished to match the cost against the benefit.

b) Again conservatism says that you should never include predicted profit. The K5 million per annum will have to wait until each year comes by. A sensible chief executive would make much of winning such a contract, but perhaps not too much of its profitability in case future deals are harder to secure with such good profits.

c) Again conservatism recommends that the cost be taken early. If the company knows the details, it can take the hit against this year's profits. If this year has been good and next year may not be, such forward planning just before a year end is quite tempting!

d) At K5 million per car the warranty is clearly material. The matching concept suggests that the warranty costs are part of the costs of sales, so when a sales is recorded K5 million needs to be deducted from profit and put aside (a provision) for claims when they arise. Clearly this is also prudent.

e) Again we must not include predicted profits. We need to recognize the cost of hiring now and then match the salary cost each year with the work that the chemist will do. This is prudent as the chemist might leave or for some reason, be less inventive than was hoped.

Solution 6

a) Understandability. This is the quality required for information to achieve decision usefulness. Users are assumed to have a reasonable knowledge of business and economic activities and accounting and a willingness to study the information with reasonable diligence. However, information about complex matters that should be included in the financial statements because of its relevance to the economic decision making needs of users should not be excluded merely on the grounds that it may be too difficult for certain users to understand. This characteristic gives rise to difficulties when we have the task of reporting on complex activities to non-expert users.

b) Relevance. Information has the quality of relevance when it influences the economic decision making of users helping them to evaluate past, present or future events or confirming or correcting their past evaluations. Thus relevant information is both predictive and confirmatory and these roles are interrelated. For information to be relevant it must therefore give the user what he or she wants and this presupposes that those preparing financial statements know; who the user is, what the user's purpose is, and what information he or she requires for that purpose. Clearly these change as time goes by.

c) Reliability. Information has the quality of reliability when it is free from material error and bias and can be depended upon by users to represent faithfully that which it purports to represent or could reasonably be expected to represent. Information may be relevant but also unreliable. For example, the amount of internally generated goodwill within the enterprise could be regarded as relevant information to users but it is usually difficult to identify or recognize that goodwill reliably and therefore it is generally not recognized.

d) Comparability. Users must be able to compare financial statements of an enterprise through time to identify trends and with different enterprises in order to evaluate their relative financial position, performance and changes in financial position. Consistency of treatment of transactions is therefore very important and leads to the need to disclose accounting policies and any change in those policies. Compliance with IASs helps to achieve comparability.

Solution 7

a) Washing machine. This is a non business asset and consequently falls under the entity concept. The entity concept draws an imaginary boundary around the business and anything that falls outside of the boundary is not included in financial statements. In this case the washing machine value should be treated as part of drawings and consequently taken out of the balance sheet and into the 'private' affairs of Mr. Mbewe.

b) Liquidity/ profitability. Cash is not the same thing as profit. The accruals concept acknowledges that costs incurred but not yet paid for should be included in the profit and loss account. Fixed assets purchased are represented in the balance sheet and do not directly impact the profit and loss account. Similarly, shareholder funds and loans are reflected in the balance sheet and not in the profit and loss account.

c) Gross profit margin. Gross profit is the proportion of gross profit to sales expressed as a percentage. If the gross profit margin is different from what is expected it may indicate errors in calculation or theft of stock or cash; or failure to deliver all goods by suppliers.

d) Freehold shop. Following the historical cost concept the freehold shop has been included in the balance sheet at its original cost. This is the most common method of accounting for fixed asset costs. This approach provides a high degree of objectivity and verifiability. The realization concept is of relevance here which links to prudence (extra amount represents unrealized profit). There is a danger, as identified by Mr. Mbewe that the historical cost value does not reflect the current market value.

e) Van. The van is a fixed asset and as such not for resale. Depreciation seeks to allocate cost over the estimated useful life of the van. Following the historical cost convention the value as shown in the balance sheet does not necessarily reflect the current market value.

Market value is not essential where the company is a going concern as depreciation reflects the allocation of the original cost to the profit and loss accounts of the years benefitting from its use.

Solution 8

Matching concept. The matching concept states that revenue and costs are accrued or matched with one another insofar as their relationship can be established or justifiably assumed, and are dealt with in the income statement for the period to which they relate. This concept is a consequence of the fact that a business periodically reports on its financial performance and financial position. It is thus necessary to organize all income and expenses into the relevant periods. In particular, it is necessary to ensure that all income earned for a period, whether received or not, and all expenses incurred in earning that income, whether paid for or not, are included in the determination of net income for that period.

Solution 9

Consistency concept. The convention of consistency is designed to provide a degree of uniformity concerning the application of accounting policies. We have seen that, in certain areas, there may be more than one method of accounting for an item, for example, stock valuation. The convention of consistency states that, having decided on a particular accounting policy, a business should continue to apply the policy in successive periods. Whilst this policy helps to ensure that users can make valid comparisons concerning business performance over time, it does not ensure that valid comparisons can be made between businesses . this is because different businesses may consistently apply different accounting policies.

PROGRESS CLINIC 3
SOLUTION SIX

a) DR Motor vehicle A/c
   CR Cash A/c
b) DR Office machinery A/c
   CR J Gwaba & Sons
c) DR Cash A/c
   CR Capital A/c
d) DR Bank A/c
   CR Mailesi Banda A/c
e) DR Aaron Muleya A/c
   CR Cash A/c

PROGRESS CLINIC 4
Solution 1

a). i). The straight line method is the most commonly used method of at all. The cost of the asset (less any residue value) is charged in equal installments to each accounting period over the useful life of the asset. In this way, the net book value of the fixed asset declines at a steady rate, or in a straight line over time.

ii). The reducing balance method of depreciation calculates the annual depreciation charge as a fixed percentage of the net book value of the asset, as at the end of the previous accounting period.

b). i). Depreciation using the straight line method $\underline{K17,000,000 - K2,000,000} = K3,000,000$ p.a.
$$5$$

ii). Using the reducing balance method, depreciation for each of the five years would be:

Year	Depreciation calculation	Depreciation Charge
1	35% of K17,000,000 K5,950,000	
2	35%of (17000000-5950000=11050,000)	K3,868,000
3	35% of (11,050,000 – 3,868,000 = 7,182,000)	K2,514,000
4	35% of(7,182,000 – 2,514,000 = 4,668,000)	K1,634,000
5	Balance to bring the book value to:	
	K2,000,000 = K4,668,000 – K1,634,000 – K2,000,000	K1,034,000

c). Reducing balance method.

1. a) Plant and machinery cost account

	K
31 May 2011	
Balance b/d	842,370
Additions	172,000
	1,014,370

Disposal	(148,000)
Balance c/d	866,370

Plant and machinery accumulated depreciation account

Balance b/d	247,350
Disposal	(68, 000)
	179,350
Balance c/d	261,087

Plant and machinery—disposals account

Proceeds 78,200 Depreciation 68,000 P/L account	1,800
	K
Proceeds of sale	78,200
Accumulated depreciation	68,000
Depreciation underprovided on disposal	1,800
	148,000
Replacement cost of new machine	254,000
Therefore shortfall	106,000

b) Reply to the director

Before dealing with your specific point I would like to explain the basis of the depreciation charge shown in your annual accounts. These accounts have been prepared on the historical cost convention. Under this convention, the depreciation charge attempts to allocate the original (historical) cost of the plant and machinery over its estimated useful life. Over this period, each year's profit and loss account is charged with depreciation. By reducing the net profit figure, funds which might otherwise have been distributed by way of dividends are retained within the business. At the end of the useful life of the asset, provided the replacement cost of a replacement asset is the same as the original cost of the old asset, sufficient funds should be available to finance the replacement. It is up to the management of the company to ensure that such funds are in a sufficiently liquid form when the moment for replacement arrives.

Problems occur when, for several possible reasons, the cost of replacement is far in excess of the original cost. The company may well have insufficient funds from within the business and be forced to borrow from outside.

For example, in the case of your company the position is as shown in the plant and machinery disposals account in (a) above.

This shortfall has arisen because the replacement cost exceeds original cost by K106,000 and the company has based its depreciation charge on historical cost.

One way around this problem in the future would be to base each year's depreciation charge on the then current replacement cost. This would involve setting up a replacement reserve. The main advantage of this would be that the profit and loss would be charged with a realistic depreciation charge, thus avoiding the dangers of over distribution of profit.

Solution 3

(a)

Computer Account

2005	K	2005	K
1.1 Balance b/d	**9,500,000**	1.1 Computer Disposal	**9,5000,000**

(b)

Provision of Depreciation Account

2002	K	2002	K
31.12 Balance c/d	**1,900,000**	1.12 P & L A/c	**1,900,000**
2003	K	2003	K
31.12 Balance c/d	3,800,000	1.1 Balance b/d	1,900,000
		21.12 P & L A/c	
1,900,000	————		
	3,800,000		**3,800,000**
2004	K	2004	K
31.12 Balance c/d	5,700,000	1.1 Balance b/d	3,800,000
	————	31.12 P & L A/c	1,900,000
	5,700,000		**5,700,000**
2005	K	2005	K
1.1 Disposals A/c	**5,700,000**	1.1 Balance b/d	**5,700,000**

(c)

Computer Disposals Account

2005	K	2005	K
1.1 Computer A/c	9,500,000	1.1 Depreciation	5,700,000
31.12 P & L A/c	450,000	1.1 Bank A/c	4,250,000
	9,950,000		**9,950,000**

(d)

Profit and Loss Account (extracts)

2002 prov for depreciation	1,900,000	2005	P& L A/c (profit on sale) 450,000
2003 prov for depreciation	1,900,000		
2004 prov for depreciation	1,900,000		

(e)

Balance Sheets (Extracts)

	2002	2003	2004
	K	K	K
Computer at cost	9,500,000	9,500,000	9,500,000
Less: Depreciation to date	1,900,000	3,800,000	5,700,000
Net Book Value	7,600,000	5,700,000	3,800,000

PROGRESS CLINIC 5

Solution 1
Revised cash book

	K'000
Original cash book figure	2,490
Less: Adjustment –ref charges	(50)
Less: Adjustment—ref dishonoured cheque	(140)
	2,300

SOLUTION 2

(a)

Revised Cash Book

	K000		K000
Balance b/f	1,831	Bank charges	22
J Wasa: C Transfer	54	Balance c/d	1,863
	1,885		**1,885**
Balance b/d	1,863		

(b)
Bank Reconciliation Statement as at 31 December 2012

		K000
Balance as per Cash book		1,863
Add: Unpresented cheque: G Saamu		115
		1,978
Less: Bankings: Uncredited cheques:		
K Wole	249	
M Bunda	178	
		427
Balance as per bank statement		**1,551**

OR

Bank Reconciliation Statement as at 31 December 2012

	K000	K000
Balance as per Bank Statement		1,551
Add: Cheques not yet credited:		
K Wole	249	
M Bunda	178	
		427
		1,978
Less: Unpresented cheque		
G Saamu		115
Balance as per Cash Book		**1,863**

SOLUTION 3

Three Column Cash Book

Date	Details	Dis	Cash	Bank	Date	Details	Disc	Cash	Bank
May		K000	K000	K000	May		K000	K000	K000
1	Balances b/f		29	654	8	R Lungu			95
2	B Kangwa	3		117	11	Cash C			100
11	Bank C		100		25	Wages		92	
16	N Choongo	7		273	29	U Banda	3		57
28	D Siwale	2	38		30		11		429
					31	Balances		75	362
	Balances	**12**	**167**	**1,044**			**19**	**167**	**1,044**
1									
June			75	363					

R Kangwa A/c

	K000		K000
1.5 Balance	120	2.5 Bank	117
		2.5 Discount	3
	120		**120**

N Choongo A/c

	K000		K000
		16.5 Bank	273
1.5 Balance	280	16.5 Discount	7
	280		**280**

D Siwale A/c

1.5 Balance	40 28.5	Cash	38
	—	28.5 Discount	2
	40		**40**

U Banda A/c

29.5 Bank	57	1.5 Balance	60
29.5 Discount	3		—
	60		**60**

R Lungu A/c

	K		K
8.5 Bank	95	1.5 Balance	100
8.5 Discount	5		—
	100		**100**

A Akimo A/c

30.5 Bank	429	1.5 Balance	440
30.5 Discount	11		—
	440		**440**

Wages Account

25.2 Cash	92

Discount Received A/c

29.5 U Banda	3	30.5 Creditors A/c	19
8.5 R Lungu	5		
30.5 A Akimo	11		—
	19		**19**

Discount Allowed A/c

30.5 Debtors	12	2.5 B Kangwa	3
		16.5 N Choongo	7
	—	28.5 D Siwale	2
	12		**12**

Solution 4

a) Outstanding lodgement are the amounts that have been paid into the bank but are not yet shown on the bank statement

Unpresented cheques are cheques that have been written but are not yet shown on the bank statement

446

b) Adjusted cash book balance for Kachepa at 31 May 2012

	K
Balance per cash book	2,908.53
Add: rent received not entered	500.00
	3,408.53
Less: Bank charges	(68.75)
Less: Cheque 100222understated	(27.00)
Adjusted cash book balance at 31/5/2007	3,312.78

c) Bank reconciliation for Kachepa at 31 May 2012

	K
Balance as per bank 31/5/07	3,395.88
Add: outstanding lodgement	840.85
	4,236.73
Less: Unpresented cheque 100225	(695.00)
100226	(22.95)
Balance as per adjusted cash book at 31/5/2012	3,312.78

d) There are a number of reasons why it is important for a business to prepare regular bank reconciliations:

• The bank statement is an independent accounting record and when used to confirm the accuracy of accounting records maintained by the business, will assist in deterring fraud because irregularities should be detected.

• By comparing entries on the bank statement with those in the cash book, accounting errors can be detected.

• The business will have an up to date cash book figure to enter into its trial balance.

• The bank reconciliation will identify any old and unpresented cheques.

Solution 5

	K'000
Balance brought forward	5,675 o/d
Less: Standing order	(125)
Add: Dishonoured Cheque (450x2)	900
Correct balance	6,450 o/d

Solution 6

	K'000
Cash book balance	10,500 o/d
Add: Bank charges 1	75
Add: (Transposition (75 - 57)	18
Adjusted cash balance	10,693
Less: Uncleared cheques	(1,050)
Balance as per bank statement	9,643 o/d

Solution 7

a) CASH ACCOUNT

	K'000		K'000
Balance B/f	4,500	Balle insurance	600
Interest received	720	Bank charges	90
Kello Ltd	780	Dishonoured cheque	210
Bank deposit	4,200	Balance c/d	9,300
	10,200		10,200

b) BANK RECONCILIATION

	K'000	K'000
Balance as per cash book		9,300
Add: Unpresented cheque - Yeta	750	
Chama	870	1,620
		10,920
Less: Uncredited cheque		(2,070)
Balance as per Bank Statement		8,850

Solution 8

a) REVISED CASH BOOK

	K'000
Cash balance brought forward	805
Add: Correction of undercast	90
Corrected cash book balance	895

b) BANK RECONCILIATION STATEMENT

	K'000
Balance as per bank statement	1,112
Add: Outstanding lodgements	208
	1,320
Less: Unpresented cheques	(425)
Balance as per cash book	895

Solution 9

Balance on bank statement is calculated as follows:

	K'000
Balance as per cash book	(1,240)
Add unpresented cheques	450
Less Uncleared deposit	(140)
Less bank charges	(75)
Balance as per bank statement	1,005

PROGRESS CLINIC 6

SOLUTION 1

CREDITORS CONTROL A/C

	K		K
Bank	271 845	Balance b/f	76 104
Discount received	5 698	Purchases	286 932
Contra: Debtors' ledger	866	Debtors' ledger	107
Balances written off	82		
Purchases returns (Balancing figure)	4 009		
Balance c/d	80 643		
	363 143		**363 143**
		Balance b/d	80 643

PROGRESS CLINIC 7

Solution 1

a) Capital expenditure
(b) Revenue
(c) Revenue
(d) Revenue
(e) Revenue
(f) Revenue
(g) Revenue
(h) Capital
(i) Revenue
(j) Revenue
(k) Revenue
(l) Revenue

Solution 2

a) It is important to make distinction between capital and revenue expenditure in order report the financial position and performance of the business truthfully i.e. to show a true fair view business.

b) Profits and non current assets are under-estimated b K2320.

Solution 3

T Muke
Trading and Profit and Loss Account for the year ended 31 December 2006

	K000	K000	K000
Sales			52,790
Less: Returns Inwards			490
			52,300
Cost of Goods Sold			

Opening stock		5,690
Purchases	31,000	
Add: Carriage Inwards	1,700	
	32,700	
Less: Returns Outwards	560	
		32,140
		37,830
Less: Closing stock		4,230
		33,600
Gross Profit		18,700
Less: Expenses		
Rent	1,460	
Salaries and wages	5,010	
Motor expenses	3,120	
Carriage outwards	790	
General expenses	420	
		10,800
Net Profit		**7,900**

SOLUTION EIGHT

Mr Yorumu
Trading and Profit and Loss Account for the year ended 31 May 2006

	K000	K000
Sales		138,078
Opening stock	11,927	
Purchases (W1)	84,561	
	96,488	
Less: Closing stock	13,551	
		82,937
Gross Profit		55,141
Less Expenses:		
Carriage Out (W2)	2,933	
Rent, rates and Insurance (W3)	5,952	
Postage and stationery	3,001	
Advertising	1,330	
Salaries and wages	26,420	
Bad debts	877	
Depreciation charge (W4)	8,700	
Increase in bad debts provision	40	

		49,253
Net profit		**5,888**

Mr Yoram
Balance Sheet as at 31 May 2006

	Cost	Dep	NBV
	K000	K000	K000
Fixed Assets			
Equipment	58,000	27,700	30,300
Current Assets			
Stock		13,551	
Debtors (12,120 – 170)		11,950	
Prepayment		880	
Cash		177	
Bank		1,002	
		27,560	
Current Liabilities			
Creditors	6,471		
Accruals	210	6,681	
			20,879
			51,179
Capital			
At 1 June 2005			53,091
Profit for the year			5,888
			58,979
Less: Drawings			(7,800)
			51,179

Workings

		K
1.	Purchases	82,350
	Add: Carriage Inwards	2,211
		84,561
2.	Carriage	5,144,000
	Less: Carriage Inwards	2,211,000
	Carriage Out	**2,933,000**
3.	Rent, Rates and Insurance	
	Rent, rates and insurance	6,622,000

DR. CRYFORD MUMBA

<u>Add:</u> Rent accrual	210,000	
<u>Less:</u> Rates prepaid	(880,000)	
Profit and Loss A/c	**5,952,000**	

4. Depreciation charge
   (15% x K58,000,000) = **8,700,000**

Question 5

a) The purpose of the Trading, Profit and Loss Account is to calculate the profit earned during a particular period and due to the owners of the business after all relevant expenses have been deducted.

The Balance Sheet shows what the business owns (assets), owes (liabilities) and capital(money invested in the business by the owners).

b) JUMA

TRADING,PROFIT AND LOSS ACCOUNT FOR THE YEAR ENDED 31 MARCH 2012

	K'000	K'000
Sales		221,850
Cost of sales:		
Stock at 31/3/2011	20,250	
Purchases	110,925	
131,175		
Less: Stock at 31/3/2012	(23,400)	(107,775)
Gross profit		114,,075
Less: Expenses:		
Telephone	2,645	
Heat and light	6,720	
Rent	12,000	
Advertising	3,475	
Administrative	4,424	
Plant—depreciation for the year	9,675	
Motor vehicles—depreciation for the year	7,690	(46,629)
Net Profit		67,446

JUMA
BALANCE SHEET AS AT 31 MARCH 2012

	K,000	K,000
		NBV
Fixed assets:		
Plant		64,500
Motor vehicles		30,750
		95,250
Current assets:		
Stock	23,400	
Debtors	36,975	

452

Bank	<u>4,782</u>	
	<u>65,157</u>	
Current liabilities:		
Creditors 24,650		
Bank loan 20,000		
VAT	<u>5,510</u>	
	<u>50, 160</u>	
Working capital		<u>14,997</u>
Capital employed		<u>110,247</u>
Represented by:		
Capital at 1 April 2011		57,801
Add; profit for the year		<u>67,446</u>
		125,247
Less: drawings		<u>(15,000)</u>
Capital at 31 March 2012		<u>110,247</u>

c) The Accounting equation is Assets = Liabilities + Capital
    Assets = K95,250,000 + K65,157,000 = K160,407,000
    Liabilities = K50,160,000
    Capital = K110,247,000
    Therefore K160,407,000 = K50,160,000 + K110,247,000.

PROGRESS CLINIC 8
Solution 1

(a) Lombe and Maale
     <u>Trading and Profit and Loss Account for the year ended 31 March 2006</u>

	K000	K000
Sales		90,370
Less: Cost of Goods sold:		
Opening stock	24,970	
Add: Purchases	<u>71,630</u>	
	96,600	
Less: Closing stock	<u>27,340</u>	
		<u>69,260</u>
Gross Profit		21,110
Less: Expenses		
Salaries	8,417	
Office expenses (1370 + 110)	1,480	
Discounts allowed	563	
Depreciation: Motor vehicles (20% x 9200)	1,840	
Depreciation: Office equipment (10% x 6500)	<u>650</u>	
		<u>12,950</u>
Net Profit		**<u>8,160</u>**

(b) Lombe and Maale
   Profit and Loss Appropriation Account for the year ended 31 March 2006

	K000	K000
Net Profit		8,160
Add: Interest on Drawings:		
Lombe	180	
Maale	210	
		(3,900)
Less: Salary: Maale		(500)
		4,150
Share of Profits:		
Lombe(3/5)		2,490
Maale (2/5)		1,660
		4,150

c) Lombe and Maale
   Balance Sheet as at 31 March 2006

	Cost K000	Dep K000	NBV K000
Fixed Assets			
Office equipment6,500 Accounting equation is As2,6003,900			
Motor vehicles	9,200	5,520	3,680
	15,700	**8,120**	**7,580**
Current Assets			
Stock		27,340	
Debtors		20,960	
Bank		615	
Cash		140	
		49,055	
Current Liabilities			
Creditors	16,275		
Expenses due	110		
		16,385	
			32,760
		40,250	
Capital			
Lombe			27,000
Maale			12,000
			39,000

Current Accounts

Lombe	889
Maale	361
	1,250
	40,250

Workings 1: Current Accounts

	Lombe	Maale		Lombe	Maale
	K000	K000		K000	K000
Drawings	5,550	4,000	Balances	1,379	1,211
Interest on drawings	180	210	Interest on capital	2,700	1,200
Balances c/d	889	361	Salary share of profits		
				2,490	1,660
	6,569	**4,571**		**6,569**	**4,571**

PROGRESS CLINIC 9

Solution 1

(a)   DENNIS LTD
       TRADING AND PROFIT AND LOSS AND APPROPROATION ACCOUNT
       FOR THE YEAR ENDED 31 DECEMBER 2012

	K	K
Sales		418 250
Less: Returns		4 025
		414 225
Cost of goods sold		
Opening stock	136 132	
Add: Purchases	232 225	
	368 357	
Less: Closing stock	122 000	
		246 357
		167 868
Gross profit		
Expenses		
Salaries and wages	46 260	
Rent, rates and insurance		
(18 095 + 2 000)	20 095	
Motor expenses	4 361	
General expenses	1 240	
Director's remuneration	18 750	
Debenture interest (1 000 + 1 000)	2 000	
Depreciation: Equipment		

(10% x 122 55)	12 250	
Depreciation: Vehicles		
(20% x 99 750)	19 950	
		124 906
Net profit		42 962
Add: Unappropriated profit b/f		13 874
		56 836
Less: Appropriations		
Transfer to general reserve	5 000	
Preference dividend (8% x 35 000)	2 800	
Ordinary share dividend		
(10% x 125 000)	12 500	
		20 300
Unappropriated profit c/f		**36 536**

Notes:

i) Directors' remuneration is shown as an expense in the Profit and Loss Account.

ii) Debenture interest is an expense to be shown in the profit and loss account.

iii) The final dividend of 10 percent is based on the issued ordinary share capital and not on the authorized ordinary share capital.

(b) DENNIS LTD
BALANCE SHEET AS AT 31 DECEMBER 2012

	COST	ACC DEP	NBV
Fixed Assets	K	K	K
Equipment	122 500	41 650	80 850
Motor vehicles	99 750	56 175	43 575
	222 250	**97 825**	**124 425**
Current Assets			
Stock	122 000		
Debtors	94 115		
Bank	12 751		
Cash	630		
		229 496	

Current Liabilities
Creditors (93 085 + 2 000)	95 085	
Dividends owing	15 300	
Debenture interest due	1 000	
	111 383	
		118 111
		242 536

Financed by
Preference shares	35 000
Ordinary shares	125,000
Reserves	
General reserve	26 000
Profit & Loss Account	36 536
Loan Capital	
10% Debentures	20 000
	242 536

Solution 2

Workings (all in K'000)

W1. Closing stock is K46,638

W2. Insurance expense (5,688-300) = K5,388 and prepayment is K300

W3. Wages expense (2,400 + 840)= K24,840 and accrual is K840

W3. Depreciation: Buildings 10% of 114,000 = K11,400 expense in Income statement and K11,400 + 18,000 = K29,400 in the balance sheet.

Fixtures and fittings 20%of (66,000—30,000) = K7,200 as expense in the income statement and KK7,200 + K30,000 =K37,200 in the balance sheet

W4. Doubtful debts 5% of K37,920 = K1,896 which is subtracted from debtors figure in the balance sheet. In the income statement, change in doubtful debts is K2,448 – K1,896 = K552. Therefore bad debts is K2,028 – k552 = K1,476

W5. Debenture interest is 5% of K48,000 = K2,400 as expense in the income statement. Since K1,200 is already paid the accrued amount is K1,200.

W6. Dividends: Ordinary is 5% of K60,000 = K3,000

Total preference dividend is 6% of K60,000 = k3,600. Of this K1,800 is already paid hence due is K1,800. Only the dividend due appears in the balance sheet.

W7. Transfer to General Reserve K24,000 in the income statement and K24,000 + K30,000 = k54,000 in the balance sheet.

W8. Accrual in the balance sheet K840 + K1,200 = K 2,040 in respect of wages and debenture interest.

W9. Bank balance is credit which means that the account is overdrawn hence the overdraft which is a current liability is K18,000

NYAMA LIMITED
INCOME STATEMENT FOR THE YEAR ENDED 30 SEPTEMBER 2012

	K'000	K'000
Sales	240,000	
Less: Returns inwards	1,116	238,884
Csot of Sales:		
Opening stock	42,744	
Add: purchases	131,568	
	174,312	
Less: closing stock	(46,638)	127,674
Gross profit		111,210
Add: discount received		5,292
		116,502
Less: Expenses:		
Insurance (5688 – 300)	5,388	
Wages and salaries (24000 + 840)	24,840	
Debenture interest (1200 + 1200)	2,400	
Bad Debts (W5)	1,476	
Rates	6,372	
Depreciation: Buildings (W4)	11,400	
Fixtures and fittings	7,200	
General expenses	1,308	60,384
Profit before tax		56,118
Taxation		(20,000)
Profit after tax		36,118
Add: unappropriated profit		6,000
Profit for the year		42,118
Less: Appropriations:		
Transfer to general reserve	24,000	
Ordinary dividends	3,000	
Preference dividends	3,600	30,600

Unappropriated profit c/f 11,518

NYAMA LIMITED
BALANCE SHEET AS AT 30 SEPTEMBER 2012

	Cost Acc.	Dep.	NBV
	K'000	K'000	K'000
Land	54,000	-	54,000
Goodwill	49,200	-	49,200
Buildings	114,000	29,400	84,600
Fixtures and fittings	66,000	37,200	28,800
	283,200	66,600	216,600
Current Assets:			
Stock	46,638		
Debtors (37920 – 1896)	36,024		

Prepayment	300	
Cash	<u>696</u>	<u>83,658</u>
Current Liabilities:		
Overdraft	18, 000	
Creditors	18, 900	
Accruals	2, 040	
Dividends: Ordinary	3, 000	
Dividends: Preference	1, 800	
Corporation tax	<u>20, 000</u>	<u>63, 740</u>
Net current assets		19, 919
Capital employed		236, 518
Long term- Liabilities:		
5% Debentures		<u>(48, 000)</u>
Net assets		188, 518
Financed by:		
Ordinary share capital		60,000
Preference shares		60,000
Share premium		3,000
General reserves (30000 + 24000)		54,000
Profit and Loss Account		<u>11,518</u>
		<u>188,518</u>

Solution 3

ASOZA LIMITED
INCOME STATEMENT FOR THE YEAR ENDED 31 DECEMBER 2012

	K,000	K'000
Sales		80,000
Cost of sales:		
Opening stock	10,000	
Purchases	49,000	
Add: carriage inwards	<u>1,000</u>	
	60,000	
Less: closing stock	<u>(15,000)</u>	<u>(45,000)</u>
Gross profit		35,000
Add: discount received		<u>200</u>
		35,200
Less expenses:		
Discount allowed	400	
Carriage outwards	800	
Administration expenses	4,000	
Staff salaries	4,000	
Directors' salaries	5,000	

Audit fee	1,000	
Depreciation	4,600	
Debenture interest	5,000	(24,800)
Profit before tax		10,400
Corporation tax		(5,000)
Net profit after tax		5,400
Less Appropriations:		
Transfer to reserves	,000	
Preference dividend paid(5%)	1,000	
Ordinary dividend proposed(5%)	3,000	5,000
Retained profit		400
Add: P & L B/f		8,000
P & L C/f		8,400

ASOZA LIMITED
BALANCE SHEET AS AT 31 DECEMBER 2012

	K'000	K'000	K'000
Non-current assets:			
Land and buildings	230,000	104,600	125,400
Current Assets:			
Stock	15,000		
Debtors	10,000		
Cash	5,000	30,000	
Current Liabilities:			
Creditors	2,000		
Current taxation	5,000		
Dividend proposed	3,000		
Accruals (5,000+ 1,000)	6,000	(16,000)	
Net current assets			14,000
Capital employed			139,400
Long term Liabilities:			
10% Debenture			(50,000)
Net assets			89,400
Capital and Reserves:			
Ordinary shares of K0.50 each			10,000
5% Preference shares of K1 each			20,000
Plant Replacement reserve			1,000
Profit and Loss Account			8,400
			89,400

Note:
Number of ordinary shares is 12,000 that is, K60,000/K0.50. Thus, total ordinary dividend is K0.025 x 120,000 = K3,000. Preference dividends is 5% of K20,000 = K1,000.

PROGRESS CLINIC 10
Solution 1

Net cash outflow means the cash paid for new additions minus the cash received from disposals.

	K
Carrying amount of assets	
Disposed of	15 000
Loss of disposal	6 000
Cash from disposals	9 000
Cash paid for new additions	(102 000)
Net Cash out flow	**93 000**

Solution 2
KANYELELE
CASH FLOW STATEMENT FOR THE YEAR ENDED 31 MARCH 2012

	K	K
Cash Flows from Operating Activities:		
Net Cash Inflow from operating Activities		746 000
Interest paid (6% x 1 200 000)		(72 000)
Dividends paid (W10		(150 000)
		524 000
Cash Flows From Investing Activities		
Payment to acquire Fixed Assets (W2)	(1 400 000)	
Receipt from sale of Fixed Assets	280 000	
		(1 120 000)
Cash Flows From Financing Activities		
Issue of ordinary Share capital (W3)	200 000	
Issue of Loan (1 200 000 – 800 00)	400 000	600 000
		4 000
Opening Cash & Cash equivalents		14 000
Closing Cash and cash equivalents		**18 000**

Workings

W1: The profit for the year was K260 000 and the increase in retained profit was K110 000 (590 000 – (480 000), therefore dividends paid were K150 000.

W2

Fixed assets – Cost

	K		K
Opening balance	2 140 000	Transfer (disposal)	480 000
Purchases (balance)	1 400 000	Closing balance	3 060 000
	3 540 000		**3 540 000**

W3

Share capital and share premium at end of year = K1 100 000 + 900 000 = 2 000 000.

Share capital and share premium at start of year = 1 000 000 + 800 000 = 1 800 000.

So cash raised by issuing new shares = 2 000 000 – 1 800 000 = 200 000.

Solution 3

PCBF'S CASH FLOW STATEMENT FOR THE YEAR ENDED 31 DECEMBER 2012

	K'000	K'000
Cash flows from operating activities:		
Operating profit	146	
Add :Depreciation charge	81	
Less: Increase in stock	(38)	
Add: Decrease in debtors	78	
Add: increase in creditors	74	
Cash flow before financing costs	341	
Less: costs of financing:		
Interest received	22	
Interest paid	(106)	
Dividend paid	(47)	
Less: Taxation paid	(189)	
Net cash flow from operating activities		21
Cash flows from investing activities:		
Less: Purchase of fixed assets	(264)	
Add: Sale of fixed assets	64	
Net cash flows from investing activities		(201)
Cash flows from financing activities:		
Loan issue	142	
Share issue	30	
Net cash flow from financing activities		172
Decrease in cash		(8)

b) •Shows where the cash has been spent and raised
  •Help analysts in making decisions on the amount and timing of cash flows
  •Provides information about liquidity and financial viability of the business.

Solution 4

KAMUZATUTILES LTD

CASH FLOW STATEMENT FOR THE YEAR ENDED 31 MARCH 2006

	K'000	K'000
Cash flows from operating activities:		
Profit before tax	14,033	
Adjustments for:		
Depreciation	6,991	
Profit on sale of tangible non-current assets	(1,436)	
Interest income	(111)	
Interest expense	1,556	
Operating profit before working capital changes	21,033	
Increase in inventories	(1,389)	
Decrease in trade receivables	3,337	
Increase in trade payables	96	
Cash generated from operations	23,077	
Tax paid (W1)	(3,515)	
Net cash flow from operating activities		19,562
Cash flows from investing activities:		
Interest received	111	
Purchase of property, plant and equipment (W2)	(33,561)	
Proceeds from the sale of property, plant and equipment	4,900	
Net cash flow from investing activities		(28,550)
Cash flows from financing activities:		
Interest paid	(1,556)	
Dividends paid (W3)	(4,131)	
Proceeds from issuance of share capital	4,318	
Proceeds from long-term borrowings	5,269	
Net cash flow from financing activities		3,900
Net decrease in cash and cash equivalents		(5,088)
Cash and cash equivalents at beginning of period(note)		1,492
Cash and cash equivalents at end of period (note)		(3,596)

Note: cash and cash equivalents	At 31/3/2006	31/3/2005
	K'000	K'000
Cash on hand and balances with banks	2,548	1,569
Bank overdrafts	(6,144)	(77)
Cash and cash equivalents	(3,596)	1,492

DR. CRYFORD MUMBA

Workings:

W1 Tax payable

					W2 Dividends payable		
Cash paid	3,515	B/f	2,826	Cash paid	3,131	B/f	2,840
C/f	3,082	P&L charge	3,771	C/f	3,310	P&L	4,601
	5976,		6,597		7,441		7,441

W2 Property, plant and equipment at NBV

B/f	81,814	Disposal	3,464
Reval'n	10,991	Dep'n	6,991
Cash paid	33,561	C/f	115,911
	126,366		126,366

Note: the entries in italics in these T-accounts are the balancing figures that have been deduced. These working are in T-account form, but other presentations are acceptable.

b) The purpose of the cash flow statement is to show what cash has been generated and where the cash has gone. The value of the statement derives from the nature of cash flow information and provides deeper insight into the performance of the company over and above the balance sheet and the income statement. The balance sheet and income statement are based on the accruals concept while the cash flow statement shows either the actual cash flows or derived cash figures. This gives rise to the difference between profit and cash. Accruals accounting incorporates debtors, creditors and stock, these are not included in cash. The balance sheet includes movements in assets and liabilities and where these are on credit terms will not be included in cash.

Solution 5
CHOOMBE
SIMPLE CASH FLOW STATEMENT

	K'000	K'000
Cash flow from operating activities:		
Profit for the year	18,750	
Add depreciation	1,250	
Less increase in debtors	(1,000)	
Add decrease in stock	1,800	
Add increase in creditors	350	
Net cash flow from operating activities		21,150
Cash flows from investing activities:		
Purchase of fixed assets		(8,000)
Increase in cash		13,150

Solution 6

<u>JONAH COMPANY LTD</u>
<u>CASH FLOW STATEMENT FOR THE YEAR ENDED 31 DECEMBER 2012</u>

	K000	K000
<u>Cash flows from operating activities</u>		
Profit before taxation		30
Depreciation		100
Loss on sale of property, plant and equipment		20
Loss on sale of investments		10
Interest expense		15
Inventory		(30)
Receivables		(70)
Payables		<u>10</u>
Net Cash inflow from operating activities		<u>85</u>
Cash generated from operations		85
Net interest paid		(15)
Net cash from operating activities		70
<u>Cash flows from Investing Activities</u>		
Purchase of property, plant and equipment	(450)	
Proceeds from sale of property, plant and equipment	60	
Proceeds from sale of Investments	<u>40</u>	
Net Cash used in Investing Activities		(350)
Cash flows from financing Activities		
Equity dividends paid	(30)	
Share issue	180	
Loan note issue	<u>50</u>	
Net Cash from financing activities		200
Net decrease in cash and cash equipment		(80)
Cash and cash equivalents at start		(20)
Cash and cash equivalents at end of period		**(100)**

Workings

1.	<u>Profit before taxation</u>	K000
	Retained loss for the year (200 – 190)	(10)
	Final dividend	<u>40</u>
		<u>**30**</u>

2.   Property, plant and equipment

Opening balance	(730)
Disposal	80
Depreciation for the year	100
Closing balance	1,100
Revaluation in the year	(100)
Property, plant and equipment purchased	**450**

PROGRESS CLINIC 11
SOLUTION 1

K		Pvt Co.	J Pvt Co.
(a)	Gross Profit Ratio		
	$\dfrac{GP}{Sales} \times \dfrac{100}{1}$	$\dfrac{20\ 000}{80\ 000} \times \dfrac{100}{1}$	$\dfrac{24\ 000}{120\ 000} \times \dfrac{100}{1}$
		= **25%**	= **20%**
(b)	Net Profit Ratio		
	$\dfrac{NP}{Sales} \times \dfrac{100}{1}$	$\dfrac{10\ 000}{80\ 000} \times \dfrac{100}{1}$	$\dfrac{15\ 000}{120\ 000} \times \dfrac{100}{1}$
		= **12.5%**	= **12.5%**
(c)	Expenses Ratio		
	$\dfrac{Expenses}{Sales} \times \dfrac{100}{1}$	$\dfrac{10\ 000}{80\ 000} \times \dfrac{100}{1}$	$\dfrac{9\ 000}{120\ 000} \times \dfrac{100}{1}$
		= **12.5%**	= **7.5%**
(d)	Stock turnover Ratio		
	$\dfrac{CGS}{Av.\ Stk}$	$\dfrac{60\ 000}{20\ 000}$	$\dfrac{96\ 000}{20\ 000}$
		= **3 times**	= **4.8 times**
(e)	ROCE		
	$\dfrac{PBIT}{Capital\ employed}$	$\dfrac{10\ 000}{(38\ 000+42\ 000)\ /2} \times \dfrac{100}{1}$	$\dfrac{15\ 000}{(36\ 000+44000)\ /2} \times \dfrac{100}{1}$
		= **25%**	= **37.5%**

(f)   Current Ratio

	Current Assets	45 000	40 000
	Current Liabilities	5 000	10 000

$$= \quad \textbf{9:1} \qquad\qquad = \quad \textbf{4:1}$$

(g)   Quick Ratio

	CA – Stock	45 000 – 15 000	40 000 – 17 500
	C/ Liabilities	5 000	10 000

$$= \quad \textbf{6:1} \qquad\qquad = \quad \textbf{2.25:1}$$

(h)   Debtor Period

	Debtors x 12	25 000 x 12	20 000 x 12
	Sales 1	80 000 1	120 000 1

$$= \quad \textbf{3.75 months} \qquad = \quad \textbf{2 months}$$

(i)   Creditor Period

	Creditors x 12	5 000 x 12	10 000 x 12
	Purchases	50 000 1	91 000 1

$$= \quad \textbf{1.2 months} \qquad = \quad \textbf{1.3 months}$$

Comments on the two firms

i)   Possibly K Pvt managed to sell far more goods because of lower prices i.e. it took only 20% margin as compared to J Pvts's 25% margin.

ii)   May be K Pvt made more efficient use of mechanized means in business. Note that it has more equipment and perhaps as consequence it kept other expenses down to K 6000 as compared to J Pvt's K 9000.

iii)   K Pvt did not have as much stock lying idle. K Pvt turned over stock 4.8 times in a year, as compared to 3 times of J Pvt.

iv)   J's current ration of 9.1 was far greater than normally need. K Pvt kept its ration down to 4.1. J Pvt therefore had too much money lying idle.

v)   The Acid Test ratio for J Pvt was higher than necessary and followed a similar trend to that shown by the current ratio.

vi)   One reason for the better current and acid test ratio for K Pvt was that debts were collected on a 2 months average.

vii)   J Pvt also paid creditors more quickly than K Pvt but only slightly fast. K Pvt more efficient than K Pvt.

Solution 2

(a) Ratio   2011   2012

    (i) Gross Profit Ratio = $\frac{GP}{Sales} \times \frac{100}{1}$

       GP Ratio   = $\frac{2,600}{14,400} \times \frac{100}{1}$ $\frac{4,400}{17,000} \times \frac{100}{1}$

                                       18%   **26%**

    (ii) Net Profit Ratio = $\frac{NP}{Sales} \times \frac{100}{1}$

                  = $\frac{1,400}{14,400} \times \frac{100}{1}$ $\frac{2,400}{17,000} \times \frac{100}{1}$

                                         10%   **14%**

    (iii) ROCE   = $\frac{N\ Profit}{Capital\ Employed} \times \frac{100}{1}$

                  = $\frac{1,400}{6,700} \times \frac{100}{1}$ $\frac{2,400}{5,720} \times \frac{100}{1}$

                                         21%   **42%**

    (iv) Current Ratio = $\frac{CA}{CL}$

                                  $\frac{5,700}{1,500}$ $\frac{4,420}{2,700}$

                                       3.8:1   **1.6:1**

    (v) Quick Ratio = $\frac{CA - Stock}{CL}$

                                $\frac{5,700 - 1,300}{1,500}$ $\frac{4,420 - 2,000}{2,700}$

                                       2.9:1   **0.9:1**

(b) The performance of the year 2012 is much better than that of 2011. One reason is that of loan interest in the year 2011.

    There was a fall in bank balances in the year 2012.

Unfortunately, the payables increased in the year 2012 and this affected negatively the current ration and also the quick ratio. The receivables also fell in the same period.

Solution 3

a) Profitability ratios look at the relationship between profit and sales. This can be either gross profit or net profit

Liquidity ratios measure the financial stability of the business. They consider whether the business can meet its current liabilities with its current assets.

Resource utilization or efficiency ratios examine how effectively management are using the working capital of the business.

b) Ratios for ABC Ltd for the year ended 30 November 2012

 i) Gross profit percentage = 72,000/288,000 x 100 = 25.0%

  For every K1 of sales the business makes 25n of profit.

 ii) Net profit percentage = 28,600/288,000 x 100 = 9.9%

  The business makes 10n profit for every K1 of sales after all expenses have been accounted for.

 iii) Debtor days 24,000/288,000 x 365 = 30.4 days

  This is the average number of days the company has to wait before receiving payment from debtors.

 iv) Creditors days 16,800/212,500 x 365 = 28.9 days

  This is the number of days the company takes to pay its creditors.

 v) Current ratio 41,300/18,150 = 2.3:1

  This is the number of times that current liabilities are covered by current assets.

 vi) Acid test ratio 26,300/18,150 1.5:1

  This is the number of times that current liabilities are covered by current assets without including stock.

Solution 4

a) The fact that a business operates on a low profit margin indicates that a small percentage of profit is being made for each K1 of sales generated. However, this does not mean necessarily that the ROCE will be lower as a result. If the business is able to generate a large amount of sales during a period, the total profit may be very high even though the net profit per K1 of sales is low. If the net profit generated is high, this can lead, in turn, to a high ROCE, since it is the total net profit that is used as a numerator (top part of the fraction) in this ratio. Many businesses, including supermarkets pursue a strategy of 'low margin, high turnover'.

b) The balance sheet is drawn up at a single point in time – the end of the financial period. As a result, the figures shown on the balance sheet represent the position at that single point in time and may not be representative of the position during the period. Whenever possible, average figures (perhaps based on monthly figures) should be used. However, an external user may only have access to the opening and closing balance sheets for the year and so simple average based o these figures may be all that it is possible to calculate. Where a business is seasonal in nature, or is subject to cyclical changes, this simple averaging may not be sufficient.

c) Three possible reasons for high stock turnover period are:

    i) Poor stock controls, leading to excessive investments in stock

    ii) Stock hoarding in anticipation of price rises or shortages

    iii) Stock building in anticipation of increased future sales

    A low stock turnover period may be due to:

    i) Tight stock controls, thereby reducing excessive investment I stocks and/or the amount of obsolete and slow moving stocks

    ii) An inability to finance the required amount of stock to meet sales demand

    iii) A difference in the mix of stocks carried by similar businesses (for example, grater investment in perishable goods which are held for a short period only)

d) The P/E ratio may vary between businesses with the same industry for the following reasons:

    i) Accounting conventions. Differences in the methods used to compute profit (for example, stock valuation and depreciation) can lead to different profit figures and therefore, different P/E ratios

    ii) Different prospects. One business may be regarded as having a much brighter future due to factors such as the quality of management, quality of its products, location and so on. This will affect the market price investors are prepared to pay for the shares and hence, the P/E ratio

    iii) Different asset structure. The business's underlying asset base may be much higher and this may affect the market price of the shares.

PROGRESS CLINIC 12

Solution 1

(a) IAS 38 recognizes three categories of research and development expenditure and these are:

    (i) <u>Pure of Basic Research</u> – which is directed primarily towards the advancement of knowledge.

    (ii) <u>Applied Research</u> – this one is directed towards exploiting pure research, for a specified aim or objective, other than work defined as development.

    (iii)<u>Development Research</u> – this is directed towards the introduction of specific products or processes.

(b) Only development research expenditure may be capitalized and then only if it satisfies all of the following conditions.

There is a clearly defined project;

    (i) The relevant expenditure is clearly and separately identifiable;

    (ii) The project is considered to be technically environmentally and commercially feasible;

(iii) The expenditure is expected to be more than recoverable from the future revenues that will flow from the project.;

(iv) Adequate physical and human resources exist to complete the project;

(v) Management has made a decision to allocate the necessary resources to the project.

Solution 2

IAS 20: Treatment of Government Grants requires that government grant should be matched with the expenditure to which they relate. In the case of revenue expenditure, therefore the grant should be credited to the profit and loss account in the year in which the revenue expenditure takes place.

Each year, however, in accordance with prudence concept, the company should consider whether it is likely that the grant will have to be repaid. If it is probable, provision should be made. If repayment is possible, the fact should be disclosed in a note to the accounts.

Solution 3

a) Non-adjusting events are those which are indicative of conditions that arose after the balance sheet date and for which the entity does not adjust the amount recognized in its financial statements.

b) Examples of non-adjusting events are post year-end:
  i) Mergers and acquisitions
  ii) Issues of shares and debentures
  iii) Purchases and sales of non-current assets
  iv) Physical damage to non-current assets as a result of a fire or flood
  v) Decline in the value of non-current assets or inventories, if it can be demonstrated that the decline occurred after the year-end
  vi) Dividends declared after the balance sheet date
  vii) Decline in the market value of investments between the balance sheet date and the date when the financial statements are authorized for issue.

PROGRESS CLINIC 13

Solution 1

Let's start with standard workings discussed in the text book:

W1: Group structure =12,000/200,000 x 100 = 60%, hence minority interest is 40%.

W2: Net assets of Mau Ltd at Acquisition date at reporting date

	K'million	K'million
Share capital	20	20
Share premium	15	250
Revenue Reserves	140	250
	175	285

W3: Goodwill	K'million
Cost	153
Less: Group share (60% of K175)	(105)
Goodwill	48

Goodwill p.a. = K48/8 =K6 million per annum for 5 years.

W4: Reserves:

	K'million	K'million
Jose's share		194
Mau's share	250	
Less: Mau's reserves at acq'n	(140)	
Add:Mau's post acq'n (250 – 140)	110	
Less: amount of goodwill	30	66
Group reserves		230

W5: NCI = 40% of 285 = K114 million.

Now we can answer the questions quickly as follows:

a) Ownership interest = 60%
b) Goodwill = K48 million
c) Cost of goodwill 48
   Less:5 years amortization of K6 p.a.   (30)
   NBV of goodwill   18
   Note K18 million will be recognized as an intangible non-current asset while K30 million will be deducted from group reserves.
d) Minority interest Is K114 million
e) Group reserves is K230 million
f) Consolidated Balance Sheet as at 31 December 2012

	K'million
Tangible fixed Assets(45 + 106)	151
Goodwill at NBV	18
Net current assets(71 + 179)	250
Net assets	419
Ordinary share capital(Peter's only)	50
Share premium	25
Revenue reserves	230
Group shareholder's funds	305
Minority interest	114
	419

Solution 2
PETER GROUP CONSOLIDATED BALANCE SHEET

	K'000
Goodwill (3 – 1)	2
Stock (12 +5 – 1)	16
Other net assets (85 + 95)	178
	196
Financed by:	
Called up share capital	50
Profit and Loss Account	126.2
	176.2
Minority interest	19.8
	196

Workings

W1: Group structure = 32,000/40,000 x 100 =80%, hence NCI = 20%

W2: Seta's net assets At acquisition date At reporting Date

	K'000	K'000
Share capital	40	40
Profit and Loss Account	50	60
	90	100

W3:Goodwill :

Cost	75
Less: Group share(80% of K90)	(72)
Total goodwill	3

Goodwill per annum= K3/3 =K1

W4: Reserves:

	K'000
Peter's Share(100%)	120
Seta's (80% of(60 – 1) – 50)	7.2
Less: Goodwill written off	(1.0)
Group reserves	126.2

W5: NCI

	K'000
Share capital	40
Profit and loss Account(60 – 1)	59
	99
NCI's share 20% of 99	19.8

Note: K 1000 is called unrealized profit as a company is not allowed to make profit by trading to itself. Unrealized profit is K5,000 x 25/100 = K1,000

Solution 3
HARA GROUP CONSOLIDATED BALANCE SHEET AS AT 30 JUNE 2010

	K'million	K'million
Non-Current Assets:		
Property, Plant and Equipment (120 + 100)		220
Current Assets:		
Inventory (56 + 60)	116	
Debtors (40 + 30)	70	
Cash (4 + 6)	10	196
		416
Equity:		
Ordinary shares 100		
Retained earnings (95 + 28)	123	223
Non-current Assets:		
10% Loan stock	75	
12% Loan	30	105
Current liabilities:		
Creditors (47 + 16)	63	
Taxation (15 + 10)	25	88
		416

Note: 40% of K50,000 = k20,000 and K50,000 – K20,000 = K30,000.
K20,000 is cancelled leaving only K30,000 which is recorded as a liability of the group.
Thus, the uncancelled loan stock of Saka Ltd becomes a liability of the group.

Solution 4
CONSOLIDATED BALANCE SHEET OF H LTD

	K'000
Assets:	
Non-current assets	
Goodwill	16,000
Property, plant and Equipment(50,000 + 20,000)	70,000
	86,000
Current Assets:	
Inventories(25,000 + 20,000)	45,000
Trade receivables (20,000 + 15,000)	35,000
Bank (5,000 + 15,000)	20,000
	100,000
Total Assets	186,000
Equity and Liabilities:	
Ordinary Share Capital	80,000
Retained earnings	44,500
	124,500
Minority Interest	16,500

Current Liabilities:

Trade payables (30,000 + 15,000)   45,000

Total equity and Liabilities   186,000

Workings:

W1: Group structure H Ltd 70%, S Ltd 30%

W2: S's Net Assets   At acquisition date   At reporting date

    Ordinary Shares   30,000   30,000

    Reserves   10,000   25,000

                             40,000   55,000

W3: Goodwill

    Cost   60,000

    Less; Group share(70% of K40,000)   (28,000)

    Goodwill (total)   32,000

Amortization is 50% of 32,000 = K16,000

W4: Reserves

H's Share   50,000

70% of (25,000 – 10,000)   10,500

Less; goodwill written off (50% of 32,000)   (16,000)

                                                     44,5000

W5: Minority interest 30% of K55,000 = K16,500

Or Using T Accounts

W1:   Cost of control

    Cost   60,000   Shares   21,000

                                  Reserves   7,000

                                  Goodwill   32,000

W2: Consolidated Reserves

    Goodwill   16,000   B/f   50,000

    Group Reserves 44,500   Post acq'n reserves   10,500

Solution 5

CONSOLIDATED BALANCE SHEET FOR HERO GROUP AS AT 30 SEPTEMBER 2007

                                      K'000

Assets

Non-current Assets:

Land and Property (11000 + 6000 +1000)   18,000

Plant and equipment (10225 + 5110 +2000 – 400 depreciation)   16,935

Intangible assets (1240 goodwill – 400 impairment)   840

                                                     35,775

Current assets

Inventory (4925 + 3295 – 40 unrealized profit)   8,180

Trade receivables (5710 + 1915)   7,625

Cash   495

                                                     16,300

Total assets   52,075

Equity and Liabilities
Equity:

Ordinary share capital	5,000
Retained earnings (295920 +(8290—4200 pre acq'n – 400 dep – 40 urp)	
80%—400 impairment)	28,440
Minority interest (20% (10790 – 400 – 40 + 3000 revaluation)	2,670
Total equity	36,110
Non-current liabilities:	
10% loans (6000 + 2000)	8,000
Current Liabilities:	
Trade payables (3200 + 2255)	5,455
Bank overdraft	285
Tax (1235 + 990)	2,225
	7,965
Total equity and liabilities	52,075

Note: Calculation of goodwill

Paid 2million x K4.50	9,000
Bought	
2 million K1 shares	2,000
80% revaluation of assets K3 million	2,400
80% retained earnings at acquisition dateK4.2 million	3,360
	7,760
Goodwill	1,240

Solution 6
HIGH LIMITED
CONSOLIDATED BALANCE SHEET AS AT 30 SEPTEMBER 2012

	K'000
Fixed Assets:	
Goodwill	13,500
Property plant and Equipment (37,000 + 25,000)	62,000
	75,500
Current Assets:	
Inventories (40,000 + 23,000)	63,000
Debtors (25,000 + 8,000)	33,000
Bank (15,000 + 4,000)	19,000
	115,000
Total Assets	190,500
Equity and Liabilities:	
Capital and Reserves:	
Ordinary Share capital	100,000
Retained earnings	63,500
	163,500

Current Liabilities:

Trade creditors (17,000 + 10,000)		27,000
Total equity and liabilities		190,500

Workings:

W1 Structure 100% ownership.

W2: Small's net Assets	at acq'n date	at reporting date
Ordinary shares	30,000	30,000
Reserves	15,000	20,000
	45,000	50,000

W3: Goodwill

Cost	63,000
Less: group's	(45,000)
	18,000
Less : impairment	(4,500)
	13,500

W4: Group reserves

High's	63,000
Add: Post acq'n(20000 – 15000)	5,000
Less : impairment	(4,500)
	63,500

W5 : Minority interest = 0% of K50,000 = K0.

PROGRESS CLINIC 14

SOLUTION 1

(a)   BEP (Kwacha)

$$BEP = \frac{FC}{CS\ Ratio}$$

$$C = S - VC$$

$$= K150 - 60$$

$$= \textbf{K90}$$

$$CS\ Ratio = \frac{C}{S} \times \frac{100}{1}$$

$$= \frac{90}{150} \times \frac{100}{1}$$

$$= \textbf{60\%}$$

$$\text{BEP} = \frac{FC}{CS \text{ Ratio}}$$

$$= \frac{K80\ 000}{0.6}$$

$$= \textbf{K133 333}$$

(b) $$\text{BEP (units)} = \frac{FC}{Contribution}$$

$$= \frac{K80\ 000}{K90\ 000}$$

$$= \textbf{889 units}$$

(c) CS Ratio = 60% (already calculated above).

(a) MS(units) = 1600 – 889 = 711

MS(Revenue) = 711 x k150 = K106 650

MS(%) $$\frac{711}{1600} \times 100 = 44\%$$

(b) Total Contribution = K90x 1600 = K144 000
Less FC   =K 80 000
                          K 64 000

(c) Required Sales Volume = $$\frac{FC + Target\ Profit}{CPU}$$
$$\frac{K80\ 000 + K1000\ 000}{K90}$$

= 12 000 Units.

It is not possible since the plant capacity is only 1600.

PROGRESS CLINIC 15

SOLUTION 1
Workings:
(75,000 units x (K3 – 2.50) = K37 500 a year
Additional costs = K7 500 a year
Net Cash savings will be

K

    Savings 37 500
    Less: Additional costs   <u>7 500</u>
                                30 000 a year

It is assumed that the machine will be sold for K10 000 at the end of year 4.
    DCF (Net Present Value)_____

Year	Cash Flow K	Pv Factor 12%	Pv Cashflow K_
0	(90 000)	1.00	(90 000)
1	30 000	0.893	26 790
2	30 000	0.797	23 910
3	30 000	0.712	21 360
4	40 000	0.636	<u>25 440</u>
			+ 7 500

Decision:
The NPV is positive and so the project is expected to earn more than 12% a year and is therefore acceptable.

PROGRESS CLINIC 16
Solution 1
CASH BUDGET FOR JANUARY – MARCH 2007

CASH Receipt:	Jan K'000	Feb K'000	March K'000	Total K'000
. Cash Sales (50%)	1400	1600	2000	5000
. Credit Sales (25% 1 month)	600	700	800	2100
. Credit (25% 2 months)	600	600	700	1900
Total Cash Receipt	2600	2900	3500	9000
Cash Payments:				
Purchases (70% of sales	1960	2240	2800	7000
.Current Month (90%)	1764	2016	2520	6300
. Arrears (10%)	168	196	224	636
.Administrative expenses	400	400	400	1200
. Sales expenses (10% of sales)	280	320	400	1000
.Interest (semi – annual)	-	-	720	720

. Interest (sinking fund)	-	-	2000	2000
. Dividends	-	-	400	400
. Capital expenditure	-	1600	-	1600
.Taxes	-	-	40	40
Total Cash Payments	2612	4532	6704	13848
Receipt less Payments	(12)	(1632)	(3204)	(4848)
Opening Cash balance	800	788	(844)	800
Closing Cash balance	788	(844)	(4048)	(4048)

b) Comment: There is going to be a cash deficit in February and March which may require an overdraft or short term loan. However, those should not be used to finance capital expenditure hence not appropriate. Similarly, the sinking fund is not proportional to the trading activities and cannot therefore be financed out of working capital. There is a mismatch on the type of expenditure and finance.

SOLUTION 2

A) CASH BUDGET FOR JOHN HAKE

Month	1	2	3	4	5	6	7	8	9	10	11	12	Total
Receipt:	K'000	K'000	K000	K'000	K'000	K'000	K000	K'000	K'000	K'000	K'00	K'000	K'000
.Sales(W1)	750	1450	2150	2350	2420	2400	2600	2720	2800	2900	2960	3000	28500
. Rent	120	-	-	120	-	-	120	-	-	120	-	-	480
Total rec	870	1450	2150	2470	2420	2400	2720	2720	2800	3020	2960	3000	28980
Payments:													
.creditors	-	-	1200	1600	2000	1920	1920	1920	2240	2240	2240	2400	19680
.wages	250	250	250	250	250	250	250	250	250	250	250	250	3000
.Rent	300	-	-	-	-	-	300	-	-	-	-	-	600
.Other exp.	150	150	150	150	150	150	150	150	150	150	150	150	1800
.Motor van	-	6000	-	-	-	-	-	-	-	-	-	-	6000
Total payments	700	6400	1600	2000	2400	2320	2620	2320	2640	2640	2640	2800	31080
Net cashflow	170	(4950)	550	470	20	80	100	400	160	380	320	200	(2100)
Opening bal.	100	270	(4680)	(4130)	(3660)	(3640)	(3560)	(3460)	(3060)	(2900)	(2520)	(2200)	(100)
Closing bal.	270	(4680)	(4130)	(3660)	(3640)	(3560)	(3460)	(3060)	(2900)	(2520)	(2200)	(2000)	(2000)

b) PROJECTED INCOME STATEMENT

	QTR 1	QTR2	QTR 3	QTR 4	TOTAL
	K'000	K'000	K'000	K'000	K'000
Sales	6000	7200	8400	9000	30600
Less cost of sales	4800	5760	6720	7200	24480
Grossprofit	1200	1440	1680	1800	6120
Expenses:					
.wages	750	750	750	750	3000
.Rent	150	150	150	150	6000
.Depreciation	250	375	375	375	1375
.other expenses	450	450	450	450	1800

Total expenses	1600	1725	1725	1725	6775
Net profit (loss)	(400)	(285)	(45)	75	(655)

c) Assessment of the project

. it is difficult to make assessment due to lack of comparative data—historical and industrial.

. The margin is too low thus adversely affecting cash flow and profitability of the proseit.

. The project is non—bankable)

    i   Financing capital expenditure through short term borrowing (overdraft).

    ii   Credit terms are excessive: normally 15—30 days.

    iii Unable to carry stock – in –trade.

    iv Inability to repay back overdraft within current 12 months period.

    v   Bank borrowing will be increased by interest charge (not incorporated in the cash budget).

. Breakeven point = fixed cost/% margin = K6775/20% = K33875

There is therefore need to generate additional sales in order to breakeven.

Workings:

W1.s Sales receipt

Month	1	2	3	4	5	6	7	8	9	10	11	12	Total
Sales	1500	2000	2500	2400	2400	2400	2800	2800	2800	3000	3000	3000	30600
Collections:													
50%:	750	1000	1250	1200	1200	1200	1400	1400	1400	1500	1500	1500	15300
30%:	-	450	600	750	720	720	720	840	840	840	900	900	8280
20%:	-	-	300	400	500	480	480	480	560	560	560	600	4920
Total	750	1450	2150	2350	2420	2400	2600	2720	2800	2900	2960	3000	28500

W2. Gross proifit

- Mark-up = 25% = ¼
- Margin = ¼+1 = 1/5 = 20%
- Gross profit = 20% of sales = 20% x 30,600 = 6120
- Cost of sales = sales-gross profit = 30,600 – 6,120 = 24,480

SOLUTION 3

a) CASH BUDGET FOR PCBF LTD FOR JANUARY – MARCH

	January	February	March	Total
Cash Receipts	K'000	K'000	K'000	K'000
. Sales receipt (wl)	1,402,000	1,836,000	2,704,000	5,942,000
Cash Payments:				
. Purchases(90% of monthly purchases)	900,000	1350 000	2520 000	4770 000
. Expenses	192 000	242 000	292 000	726 000
. Interest (400 000 x 15 x 3/12)	-	-	15 000	15000

. Dividends	10 000	-	-	10 000
Total cash payments	1 102 000	1 592 000	2 827 000	5 521 000
Receipt less payments	300 000	244 000	(123 000)	421 000
Opening cash balance	(90 000)	210 000	454 000	(90 000)
Closing cash balance	210 000	454 000	331 000	331 000

b) FORECAST INCOME STATEMENT – JAN – MARCH 2007

	K'000	K'000
Sales		6 500 000
Less: cost of sales		5 300 000
Gross profit		1 200 000
Discounts received		530 000
Total income		1 730 000
Discounts allowed (4% x80% x 6 500 000)	208 000	
Expenses	750 000	
Loan interest	15 000	(973 000)
Net profit		757,000

C) FORECAST BALANCE SHEET AS AT 31 MARCH 2007

	K'000	K'000
Fixed assets:		
Machinery at cost		800,000
Less: Accumulated (192,000+(800x 3)		216,000
		584,000
Current assets:		
Stock	242,000	
Debtors(20% of March sales)	600,000	
Cash (from (a) above)	331,000	1,173,000
Total assets		1,757,000
Long term liabilities:		
15% loan stock		400,000
Financed by:		
Share capital	400,000	
Reserves	200,000	
Net profit	757,000	1,357,000
Total liabilities and capital		1,757,000

d)This is because there is a big difference between cash flow and profit . Some of the expense items like deprecation which is included as an expense in the income statement does not appear in the cash budget as it is a non-cash item.

PROGRESS CLINIC 19
Solution 1

Market Values of securities:
Ordinary shares 2000 000 x K10 = K20 000 000

Preference shares 400 000 x K15 = K6 000 000

I = Interest rate x principal

I = 10% x K5 000 000 = K5 00 000.

P_o = I(Annuity Factor) + A(Discount Factor)
  = 500 000(5.6502) + 5 000 000(0.3220)
  = 2 825 100 + 1 610 000
  = K4 435 100

Total Market value = k20 000 000+6 000 000+4 435 100 = **K30 435 100**

$K_e = \dfrac{d_o(1+g)}{S_e} + g = \dfrac{0.30(1.20)}{10} + 0.20 =$ **23.6%**

$K_p = d/S_p = 3/15 \times 100 =$ **20%**

$K_d = YTM(1-t) = 12\%(1-0.30) =$ **8.4%**

Source	Amount	Proportion	cost	cost x proportion
Equity	20 000 000	0.66	23.6%	15.58%
Preference	6 000 000	0.20	20%	4.00%
Debenture	4 435 000	0.14	8.4%	1.18%
Total	**30 435 000**		**WACC**	**20.76%**

Solution 2

MAPALO INTERNATIONAL PLC

A) Market value of securities

	K' million
Equity (K_e) 10.4 million X 80n	8.32
Preference (V_p) 4.5 million X 72n	3.24
Debentures (V_d) 5.0 million X 100n	5.00

	16.56
	====

Cost of Equity (K_e)

$$K_e = \frac{d_o(1+g)}{Se} + g$$

$$= (4/80) + 0.12$$
$$= 17\%$$

Cost of Preference Shares ($K_{p)}$

$$K_{pf} = d/Sp$$
$$= 9/72$$
$$= 12.5\%$$

Cost of loan stock (K_d)

$$K_d = \frac{i(1-t)}{Sd}$$

$$= \frac{14(1-0.35)}{100} = 9.1\%$$

$$WACC = \frac{K_e V_e + K_p V_p + K_d V_d}{V_e + V_p + V_d}$$

$$= \frac{(0.17 \times 8{,}320{,}000) + (0.125 \times 3{,}240{,}000) + (0.091 \times 5{,}000{,}000)}{16{,}560{,}000}$$

$$= \frac{1{,}414{,}000 + 405{,}000 + 455{,}000}{16{,}560{,}000}$$

$= 13.73\%$

b) The above calculations were based on explicit forecasts of dividends. In practice these are not available and outsiders looking in have to resort to other approaches. The capital asset pricing model *("CAPM")* is one such approach and involves the following steps:

i) The identification of the so called market risk premium, i.e. the excess of equity yields over bond yields for a particular period of time; and then the beta of the share price over the same period, i.e. its volatility relative to the market. There are consultants who will provide this information for a fee.

ii) Presumption that, if investors had foreseen the particular volatility of the share, they would have expected a return which amounted to the bond rate plus the risk premium factored by the beta.

iii) Presumption that this will be replicated in future

iv) Calculation, therefore, of the cost of equity capital as the cost of debt, plus a premium based on the equity market average factored by the beta.

c) The linking of particular branches of funds with particular parts of the business is frequently debated. The capital structure determines how the overall risk is shared between investors. The evaluation of an individual project should concentrate on its projected cash flows and the perceived margin of error therein. Others point to particularly large projects, where it is only natural to consider the financing at the same time. So, it depends to an extent on the business. It also depends on how the margin of error in cash flow forecasts is dealt with. If it is allowed for depressing the forecast cash flows, then the cost debentures is going to approximate the pure cost of capital. It should be borne in mind, however, that the cost of capital appropriate to decision making is the opportunity cost: were interest rates to rise, for instance, the historical cost of the debentures would be too low a figure.

Solution 3

(a) The dividend growth model will be used.

Dividends have risen from K120 000 in 20x1 to K235 000 in 20x5. The increase represents fours years' growth. (Check that you are aware that there are four years of growth, and not five of growth).

The average growth rate of may be calculated as follows:

Dividend in 2001 x $(1+g)^4$ = $\underline{\text{Dividend in 2005}}$

$$(1+g)^4 = \text{Dividend in 2005}$$
$$\text{Dividend in 2001}$$

$$= \frac{\text{K235 000}}{\text{K120 000}}$$

$$= 1.985333333$$

$$1+g = \sqrt[4]{1.985333333}$$

$$g = 0.18$$

$$= \underline{\textbf{18\%}}$$

(b) The growth rate over the last four years is assumed to be expected by shareholders into the indefinite future, so the cost of equity will be:

$$Ke \ = \ \frac{do(1+g)}{Se} + g$$

$$= \ \frac{0.235\,(1.18)}{1.35} + 0.18$$

$$= \ 0.9$$

$$g \ = \ \mathbf{\underline{39\%}}$$

Where:

do = The current dividend

g = The Expected annual growth in dividend payment (proportion)

Se = The current market price (ex div)

(c) Retained profits will earn a certain rate of return and so growth will come from the yield on the retained funds. It might be assumed that g = br where r is the yield on new investments and b is the proportion of profits retained for reinvestment.

If this concept is applied, the future annual growth rate would be 18% if br continued to be 18%. If the rate of return on new investments averages 39% (which is the cost of (equity) and the proportion or earnings retained is 62.5% (which is has been, approximately, in the period 2001 – 2005 then

g = br = 62.5% x .39 = **24%**

Solution 4

Market Value of Securities

		K
(a) Equity (Ve)		
	(1,000,000 x 125n)	1,250,000
(b) Preference shares (Vp)		
	(250,000 x 65n)	162,500
(c) Loan Stock (Vd)		
	(150,000 x 85%)q	<u>127,500</u>
		<u>1,540,000</u>

(d) Cost of Equity (Ke)

$$Ke = \frac{do\,(1+g)}{Se} + g$$

$$= \frac{10\ (1.10) + 0.10}{125}$$

$$= 0.088 + 0.10$$

$$= \underline{\textbf{18.8\%}}$$

(e) Cost of preference shares (Kp)

$$Kp = \frac{d_p}{Se} \times 100\%$$

$$= \frac{7}{65}$$

$$= \underline{\textbf{10.8\%}}$$

(f) Cost of Loan Stock (Kd)

$$Kd = \frac{i(1-t)}{Sd}$$

$$= \frac{15(1 - 0.30)}{85}$$

$$= \underline{\textbf{12.4\%}}$$

Weighted Average Cost of Capital (WACC)

$$WACC = \frac{KeVe + KpVp + KdVd}{Ve + Vp + Vd}$$

$$WACC = \frac{(0.188 \times 1{,}250{,}000) + (0.108 \times 162{,}500) + (0.124 \times 127{,}500)}{1{,}540{,}000}$$

$$WACC = \frac{235{,}000{,}000 + 17{,}550 + 15{,}810}{1{,}540{,}000}$$

$$WACC = 0.174$$

$$= \textbf{17.4 \% WACC}$$

Solution 5

$$Gearing = \frac{Prior\ Charge\ Capital}{Prior\ Charge\ Capital + Equity} \times 100$$

$$\frac{8\ 000\ 000 + 10\ 000\ 000}{9\ 000\ 000 + 9\ 650\ 000} = \textbf{48.3\%}$$

Or Gearing = $\frac{\text{PCC}}{\text{Equity}}$ x 100

$$\frac{9\ 000\ 000}{10\ 650\ 000} = \textbf{84.5\%}$$

Market Values for securities:

. Equity (Ve): 8 000 000 x 135n   = K10 800 000
. Preference (Vp): 1 000 000 x 77n   =   K770 000
.Debentures(Vd): 8 000 000 x 80/100   =   k6 400 000
Total   **k17 970 000**

Gearing = $\frac{6\ 400\ 000}{17\ 970\ 000}$ = **39.9%**

Or Gearing = $\frac{7\ 170\ 000}{10\ 800\ 000}$ = **66.4%**

. $K_e = \frac{10(1.09)}{135} + 0.09 = \textbf{17.1\%}$

. $K_p = 7/77 = \textbf{9.1\%}$

.$K_d = \frac{9(1-0.30)}{80} = \textbf{7.9\%}$

.WACC $= \frac{(0.171 \times 10\ 800\ 000) + (0.091 \times 770\ 000) + (0.079 \times 6\ 400\ 000)}{17\ 970\ 000}$

$= \frac{1\ 846\ 800 + 70\ 070 + 505\ 600}{17\ 970\ 000} = \textbf{13.5\%}$

- Debentures are a cheaper source of finance than preference shares
- Interest is a tax deductible expense whereas the preference dividends are appropriations from post tax profits.
- Both are treated as prior charge capital in the gearing calculation but debenture-holders will always rank before preference shareholders in a liquidation exercise.
- Debentures will normally be secured on the company's assets which make them more attractive to investors than preference shares.
- Debentures allow control of the firm not to be sacrificed as debenture holders have no direct control whatsoever of the company.

PROGRESS CLINIC 22

Solution 1

Ace limited

$Re = Rf + B (Rm - Rf)$
$= 14\% + 1.2 (26\%—14\%)$
$= 14\% + 14.4\%$
$= 28.4\%$

The returns of Ace Limited are expected to be more volatile than the average share on the market. It has a beta in excess of 1. Because of this risk, an investor who considers holding this share within a portfolio requires the return, which is higher than the market average.

(a) To calculate the average returns, we add up the returns and divide by four i.e.

- PPC average return $= \dfrac{0.50 + 0.50 + (0.20) + 0.30 + 0.10}{4} = \dfrac{0.70}{4} = 0.175$

- ACC average return $= \dfrac{0.09 + 0.05 + (0.12) + 0.20}{4} = \dfrac{0.22}{4} = 0.055$

(b) Variance for PPC

Year	Actual return	Average returns	Deviation	Squared deviation
2000	0.50	0.175	0.325	0.10565
2001	‑0.20	0.175	‑0.375	0.140625
2002	0.30	0.175	0.125	0.015625
2003	0.10	0.175	‑0.075	0.005625
Total	0.70		0.000	0.267500

The variance can now be calculated by dividing the squared deviations, by the number of returns less one. Thus, var $(R) = \dfrac{0.2675}{4 - 1} = 0.892$

(c) Variance for ACC

Year	Actual return	Average return	Deviation	Squared deviations
2000	0.20	0.055	0.145	0.021025
2001	0.05	0.055	ˉ0.005	0.000025
2002	0.09	0.055	0.035	0.001225
2003	ˉ0.12	0.055	0.175	0.030625
Total	0.22		0.000	0.0529

$$\text{Var (R)} = \frac{0.0529}{3} = 0.0176$$

(d) Standard Deviation (σ)

PCC: $\sigma = \sqrt{0.0892} = 0.2987 = 29.87\%$

ACC: $\sigma = \sqrt{0.0176} = 0.1327 = 13.27\%$

(e) The standard deviation for PPC is much higher than ACC. Thus PPC company is a more volatile investment.

SOLUTION

a) Expected Return (ER) = 0.10 (8%) + 0.20 (12%) + 0.30 (15%) + 0.40 (18%)

$$= 0.8 + 2.4 + 4.5 + 7.2$$

$$= 14.9\%$$

b) The portfolio beta (Bp)

Bp = 0.10 (0.8) + 0.20 (0.95) + 0.0 (1.10) + 0.40 (1.40)

$$= 0.08 + 0.19 + 0.33 + 0.56$$

$$= 1.16$$

c) Since the beta is higher than 1.0, this portfolio has a greater systematic risk than an average asset.

PROGRESS CLINIC 23

Solution 1

(a) The company expects to double its sales. This will mean that the stock, debtors and creditors can also be expected to double. From the information that is provided within the question, funds of about K17,000 will be needed to expand the business into new premises. Although this amount will not be required from the beginning, it is important that financial arrangements are made to prevent 'overtrading.' 'Overtrading' results from a lack of capital invested when the business commences operations. It is often difficult for the owner to raise sufficient funding as it is well known that high proportion of business fail after a relatively short of time. As they are unknown and untested, investors will be reluctant to invest or lend money to business at start up.

Early success can also result in funding problems. The expansion suggested in the question requires the company to find about K1,000 per month (or even more if the landlord requires the rent to be paid six months in advance) and about K71,000 additional working capital. Last year, the total profit before interest and tax was only K20,000. This means that it will be difficult to obtain the additional funds that are required to double the sales.

Poor management of working capital is another possible cause of overtrading as if the stocks and debtors are allowed to increase disproportionately; it will create a shortage of funds.

(b) Overtrading can result in the failure of the business through liquidity problems. A possible solution is to reduce the level of sales. This will mean either turning profitable business away, or increasing selling prices which should decrease demand and increase profits.

Alternatively, tight control could be introduced to ensure that the stock levels are reduced and outstanding debtors collected to improve the liquidity position of the firm.

Another possibility is to increase the capital by introducing more capital through increased investment by owners or stakeholders. Long term loans could also be a solution to the problem.

DR. CRYFORD MUMBA

Solution 2

			20x7	20x6

(a) Current Ratio

$$\frac{CA}{CL} = \frac{572.3}{501.0} \quad \frac{523.2}{420.3}$$

$$= \quad \textbf{1.14:1} \quad \textbf{1.24:1}$$

Quick Ratio

$$\frac{CA - Stock}{CL} \quad \frac{453.3}{501.0} \quad \frac{414.2}{420.3}$$

$$= \quad \textbf{0.9:1} \quad \textbf{0.99.1}$$

Debtors' Payment period

$$\frac{Trade\ debtors}{Turnover} \times \frac{365}{1} = \frac{329.8}{2065} \times \frac{365}{1} \quad \frac{285.4}{1788.7} \times \frac{365}{1}$$

$$= \quad \textbf{58 days} \quad \textbf{58 days}$$

Stock Turnover Ratio

$$\frac{Stock}{Cost\ of\ sales} \times \frac{365}{1} = \frac{119.0}{1478.6} \times \frac{365}{1} \quad \frac{109}{1304} \times \frac{365}{1}$$

$$= \quad \textbf{29 days} \quad \textbf{31 days}$$

Creditors' turnover period

$$\frac{Trade\ Creditors}{Cost\ of\ sales} \times \frac{365}{1} = \frac{236.2}{1478.6} \times \frac{365}{1} \quad \frac{210.8}{1304} \times \frac{365}{1}$$

$$= \quad \textbf{58 days} \quad \textbf{59 days}$$

(b) As a manufacturing company in construction industry, the company would be expected to have a comparatively lengthy debtors' turnover period because of the relatively poor cash flow in the construction industry.

It is clear that the company compensates for this by ensuring that they do not pay for raw materials and other costs before they have sold their stocks of finished goods (hence the similarity of debtors and creditors' turnover period). The company's current ratio is a little lower than average but its quick ratio is better than average and very little less than the current ratio. This suggests that stock levels are strictly controlled which is reinforced by the low stock turnover period. It would seem that working capital is tightly managed to avoid the poor liquidity which could be caused by a higher debtors' turnover period and comparatively high creditors.

Creditors' turnover is calculated by:

Average creditor x 365
    Purchases   1

However, it is rare to find purchases disclosed in published accounts and so cost of sales serves as an approximation. The creditors' turnover ration often helps to assess a company's liquidity; an increase in creditor days is often a sign of lack of long term finance or poor management of current assets, resulting in the use of extended credit from suppliers, increased and overdraft and so on.